The Centaur's Dilemma

The Centaur's Dilemma

NATIONAL SECURITY LAW
FOR THE COMING AI REVOLUTION

James E. Baker

BROOKINGS INSTITUTION PRESS
Washington, D.C.

THE BROOKINGS INSTITUTION
1775 Massachusetts Avenue, N.W.
Washington, D.C. 20036
www.brookings.edu

The Brookings Institution is a private nonprofit organization devoted to research, education, and publication on important issues of domestic and foreign policy. Its principal purpose is to bring the highest quality independent research and analysis to bear on current and emerging policy problems. Interpretations or conclusions in Brookings publications should be understood to be solely those of the authors.

Library of Congress Control Number: 2020945824

ISBN 9780815737995 (paperback : alk. paper)
ISBN 9780815738008 (ebook)

9 8 7 6 5 4 3 2 1

Typeset in Minion Pro

Composition by Elliott Beard

To Fathers and Friends

CONTENTS

PART II *The Centaur's Choice*

ACKNOWLEDGMENTS

The COVID-19 pandemic, like AI, reminds us of the connections between countries, states, and humanity. It reminds us as well of the importance of our connections to family and friends. The pandemic has brought many a sense of disconnection and isolation. But in silence and distance there also comes joy and strength. Joy comes from observing daily the courage, commitment, and kindness of our first responders and healthcare professionals. Strength comes from knowing anew that friendship, like love, reaches across time and distance. It remains with us when we are alone as it is manifest when we are together. That is why this book is dedicated to my friends. An earlier book was dedicated "To My Teachers," including my mother—a lifelong teacher in the classroom and at home. Not to be outdone, my fathers, Jim Baker and John Flender, have supported me with love, friendship, and advice, always with humored patience. That is why this book is also dedicated to my fathers.

Family and friends sustain us in times like these. They offer perspective. They offer connection. They are role models, teachers, coaches, and companions from near and afar. At this time, in this moment, as at all times, I am thinking of them and thankful for who they are.

———

Although I did not know it at the time, this book started with a 2017 speech on emerging technology by Jason Matheny, director of the Intelligence Advanced

Research Projects Activity, to the American Bar Association Standing Committee on Law and National Security. Because we were standing in a room full of national security lawyers, I asked Jason how lawyers could help prepare the government and the country for the coming AI revolution. Jason responded, "By answering the question: How do, and how should, law and ethics apply to artificial intelligence?" Two weeks later Jason called to say he had found someone to answer his question and could we meet for coffee. It was a ruse. But I was soon persuaded, as Jason is, that AI will transform national security practice. And I signed on, because national security practitioners have a duty to prepare to meet tomorrow's challenges, not just today's. This book is my answer to Jason's question.

My acknowledgments, therefore, start with Jason Matheny, now director of the Georgetown Center for Security and Emerging Technology (CSET). Jason is a great public servant and friend. He has supported my research in and out of government. So has the CSET team, including Tarun Chhabra, who was especially helpful in pushing this book through to the publication finish line. Extra thanks and appreciation also go to Lt. Gen. Jack Shanahan for his comments and insights along with his commitment to the role of law and ethics in shaping the AI enterprise.

Special thanks goes to Laurie Hobart and Matt Mittelsteadt, who are part of the Syracuse University Institute for Security Policy and Law (SPL) CSET team, for their insights, explanations, probing questions, editing, and humor. Mention in dispatches also goes to all of the SPL team, including but not limited to Kristen Duda, Lee McKnight, Jonathan Medina, Lauren Pentrak, Lauren Sutkus, Tom Clifford, Rickson Galvez, Jake Larkowich, Tom Odell, Keli Perrin, and Bob Murrett.

As is their practice, Bob Kimball, Don Mitchell, and Dan Koffsky encouraged and helped me find my legal voice. And, as is his practice, Bob Kimball also served as my historical and legal teacher/editor, a role he first played as a teaching assistant in 1981, when I was a college student. Jamie and Grant deserve thanks as well for endless nights, and as it turns out days too, talking about the Defense Production Act, rather than more obscure topics like film, history, literature, and basketball.

Appreciation is also due to Richard Samuels, John Tirman, and all of the team at the MIT Center for International Studies (CIS), including Michelle English and Laura Kerwin, who gave me the time and space to study AI while serving as the 2018–2019 Robert E. Wilhelm Fellow. Special thanks as well to Joel Brenner for getting me to CIS, and to Colonel Shannon Brown, Colonel

Douglas Copeland, Colonel Randel Gordon, Captain Pete Mirisola, and Colonel Warren Sponsler for sharing the educational journey and more so for your honorable service upholding and defending the Constitution.

Finally, I would like to thank Bill Finan and the Brookings Institution Press team, including Kristen Harrison and Cecilia González. Bill immediately saw the potential and need for a book on AI and national security law and dared to stick with it, even though Brookings Press is known for its policy insight, not its legal treatises. But like Jason Matheny, Bill saw the need and was gracious enough to let me help fill it, but only after I deleted 20,000 words and 20,000 footnotes. Olga Gardner Galvin is a careful, patient, and thoughtful editor. Thank you, Olga, for saving me more than once from later embarrassment.

If there is something useful and good in the book, please thank the people mentioned in these acknowledgments. However, all the views expressed are my own, as are any errors.

ONE

Introduction

THE CENTAUR'S DILEMMA

FROM SPRING TO SUMMER

The development of artificial intelligence (AI) is often described with seasonal reference. Since its advent, arguably in 1956, AI is said to have gone through a series of AI winters, pockets of time with little support and even less to show for that support. AI is here now. This is not winter; perhaps it is not even spring. It feels like summer. Most experts think AI is about to bloom in exponential ways. It is already embedded in our everyday lives, in how we shop, listen to music, and navigate while driving. AI has great promise to solve problems. It might help cure cancer, address climate change, and alleviate hunger. The cybernetics movement dreams of immortality. AI will bring wealth to some and unemployment to others; it already has. It will also transform national security practice. It will enable intelligence applications, augment human decisionmaking, and offer autonomous logistics and weapons systems. The question is how, not whether, this will happen.

AI will also power, and empower, the research and development of other emerging technologies, each with potential transformative effects. Quantum computing seeks to harness the physics of subatomic particles to make computers exponentially faster than current classical computers. Such speed could allow quantum computers to break existing encryption keys using brute calculating force alone—unless, of course, quantum keys are designed and implemented first. To be sure, quantum computing depends on mastering and controlling the quantum physical properties known as superposition and entanglement and then finding a means to measure quantum bits that does not otherwise disrupt those properties. AI will not solve these challenges, but it may *help* solve them by optimizing the speed and calculating capacity of classical computers and by modeling outcomes.

AI applications will also help identify and model complex molecular structures as well as rapidly calculate and adjust alternative outcomes. Synthetic biology involves the application of engineering principles to create new biological substances and components as well as edit and change existing biological components. Synthetic biology can be used to make new biological and chemical agents. It can also be used to drive genetic evolution in purposeful directions and, in the case of species with short lifespans, such as mosquitoes, do so rapidly. And it can be used to create bio-enhanced equipment and implants, like climbing gloves modeled on the molecular structure of a gecko's feet, or microchip implants to store data and track personnel. Synthetic biology has beneficial purposes, such as the eradication of diseases—for example, malaria—and the creation of drought-resistant crops. However, these same processes can be used to create new biological weapons and destroy an adversary's crops.

No wonder AI is described as a defining technology of the twenty-first century. The government of China thinks so. In July 2017, China's state council announced a US$150 billion centralized program to develop AI and become the world's leader in AI by 2030.[1] When the AI-driven computer AlphaGo defeated Lee Sedol in the Chinese game of Go in 2016, 60 million Chinese were watching live on television or social media. Vladimir Putin declared "whoever controls [AI] will be the ruler of the world." Hyperbole, no doubt, but, significantly, Putin's other comments suggest he is being briefed on the security applications of AI. For its part, the U.S. Department of Defense (DOD) has made AI a central component of what was initially referred to as the Third Offset, the use of technology to offset the perceived or real advantages of a potential adversary in manpower or geography. Governments, however, are chasing the private sector, which is leading the way in developing AI for commercial advantage—or, in the case of authoritarian states, social and political control.

Scholars use a variety of metrics to measure research and development potential and progress, including: (1) research funding; (2) patents issued; (3) scholarly papers produced and cited; and (4) the number of PhDs and undergraduate degrees awarded in specific fields. Contextual metrics are also used, such as the strength and number of supercomputers within a country, the number of start-ups and venture capital spending in a field, as well as the volume and nature of IP theft. The numbers are impressive. Although estimates of the number of AI researchers and engineers vary widely, they are measured in the hundreds of thousands, and LinkedIn reports "AI specialist" and "robotics engineer" as the two fastest-growing jobs globally as well as in the United States.[2] A June 2017 McKinsey & Company report estimated global corporate spending on AI between US$26 billion and US$39 billion in 2016, with 90 percent of this amount going toward research and development.[3] In contrast, the Manhattan Project employed 130,000 people at its height and cost approximately US$2 billion, the equivalent of US$23 billion in 2007 dollars.[4]

Exact numbers are hard to establish, because AI incorporates multiple subfields. "AI is not a single piece of hardware or software, but rather a constellation of technologies."[5] For now, let us define AI as a process of machine optimization relying on algorithms, data, and calculation that gives "a computer system the ability to solve problems and to perform tasks that would otherwise require human intelligence."[6] Current AI is particularly good at correlating, connecting, and classifying data; recognizing patterns; and weighing probabilities, which is why current AI is good, and getting better, at tasks like facial recognition, image compression and identification, and voice recognition. Metrics are also hard to establish, because some of the research is secret, for proprietary commercial reasons as well as for security reasons. But there is no doubt the twenty-first century is an AI century in commerce, academia, and government. The capacity exists. The motive exists. And there is money to drive the process. There is also security incentive.

AI offers significant security applications and advantages. However, there are also significant security implications. The philosophical questions posed by the potential advent of superintelligent artificial intelligence—a hypothetical era when machines become generally smarter than humans—are interesting and theoretically existential. But there are more immediate and pragmatic risks. Security risk will come first, as states—and perhaps other actors—race to develop and defend against the advantages of AI-enabled intelligence, weapons, and decisionmaking. Security advantage will be found in machine automation, autonomy, augmentation, and speed. But such advantage comes with risk. Where there is parity, states will seek the marginal advantages of additional speed, additional data, and additional autonomy, and they will take shortcuts in time and safety to do so. That is what happens in technology

races when security is at stake. Risk also comes from the way humans interface with technology. Operators may not understand the technology they are
using, including its limitations, its strengths, or its faults. They may not rely on
it enough or they may rely on it too much. Chapter 4 considers instances when
technology failed to work as intended, or just as often worked as intended but
was misunderstood or applied by human operators with disastrous impact.

The secretary of defense stated in 2016 that the Defense Department
would not employ AI-enabled weapons, known as lethal autonomous weapons systems (LAWS), without a human in the loop or on the loop, at least not
unless another state does so first. Autonomous and semiautonomous weapons systems shall be designed to allow commanders and operators to exercise
appropriate levels of human judgment over the use of force. In theory, this
means that a human will make the decision to fire a weapon or can override
a weapon system once the shooting begins. The Defense Department calls
this a centaur model of employment, but instead of being part-human and
part-horse, this centaur is part-human and part-machine, the machine augmenting human capacity with the human seeking to understand and control
the machine's capabilities while adding human judgment, strategy, and intuition to the machine's operation. As a result, the employment of AI presents
two immediate decisional issues: (1) when to rely on the machine alone and
when to rely on machine augmentation of human capacity; and (2) how to
assert positive control over a technology that operates at machine speed and,
in some cases, without transparent explanation.

Indeed, machine speed is an AI strength. AI-driven machines can sense,
calculate, and predict instantaneously—and thus track targets, plan logistics,
and link data—in ways and at speeds humans cannot. Slow this process down
to ensure human input and control and you may lose some or all the advantage. This is the Centaur's Dilemma: how to reap the benefit of AI for national
security purposes without losing control of the consequences.

These factors will magnify the risks already associated with using AI to
enable security applications of the sort described in the next three chapters.
One of these risks is that we are not ready for an AI race. AI—technology,
doctrine, and law—is not yet a core national security subject. AI foundations
and think tanks are studying the subject, but it is not yet fully embedded in
the work of think tanks or war colleges, as nuclear doctrine once was and
cybersecurity and grand strategy are today. It should be. As a result, there is
no corresponding national, policy, and legislative dialogue that cuts across
constituencies to frame issues, set expectations, and resolve disputes. We do

not yet have an ethical framework, legal framework, or associated operational doctrine commensurate with the security benefits and risks of AI.

Neither do we have an effective governance structure. To be sure, there are lead agencies and processes. But there is no national agency, or lead agency with responsibility for formulating *national* policy. Moreover, unlike national security problems and issues in the past, AI challenges come with new actors and incentives, from industry, academia, and government. Because most AI R & D is occurring in the commercial and academic sectors, any effort to regulate AI for national security purposes needs to effectively address these sectors as well as government conduct. This also means that at present, by default, policy is set by the individual decisions and individual actors engaged in AI research, development, and deployment based on individual motives and incentives, just as social media policy is driven by industry actions. This is lowest common denominator decisionmaking, not *national* security policy. If we do not make conscious policy decisions—and, where necessary, embed them in law—we will end up with piecemeal policy through litigation and during moments of crisis, with all the resulting pathologies associated with these modes of decision. In doing so, we will magnify the risks and minimize the advantages of AI.

PURPOSE OF THIS BOOK

This book is intended to make AI and the law accessible to national security policy and legal generalists so that they can make wise and strategic decisions about regulating the security uses of AI. In short, if I were asked to brief a senior official about AI, and was given the time, this is what I would say. These chapters are not intended to tell specialists what they already know about AI; they are intended to tell generalists what they should know in order to perform their policy and legal tasks. It is also intended to be read as needed, from the index. Toward this goal, the book identifies legal issues that might arise in the context of using AI for security purposes. However, the reader should not mistake a discussion of how a law *might*, or *could*, be used for a suggestion that the law *should* be used in this manner or without challenge or controversy. Such a discussion, however, might inspire policymakers to consider clarifying the law or finding a better way to address legal needs.

This book intends to encourage key actors—in industry, academia, and, most of all, government, where the responsibility for national security ultimately resides—to make informed, purposeful, and accountable decisions about the security uses and governance of AI. This is hard for generalists to do if they do not understand the essential policy, legal, or technical elements of the debate. Thus, beyond identifying the law and how it might be used or interpreted, this book identifies law, or principles of law, that might, do, or should apply to AI by implication or analogy. In the absence of specific law, for example, policymakers might look to the law of armed conflict or arms control concepts for principles to regulate AI. The absence of specific law will also elevate the importance of constitutional law in regulating AI, including and especially the First, Fourth, and Fifth Amendments. Thus, these amendments are addressed at the policy level and in plain English.

This book also makes the obvious point that law never keeps up with technology. Moore's Law is always faster than statutory law and case law. But if this is an obvious lesson, it is a lesson we repeatedly learn. One answer is to focus on laws that require good process and procedural checkpoints, rather than laws that seek to dictate substantive results or that address specific technologies in the present tense when we know AI will evolve and change in unanticipated ways with unanticipated uses. Law, if well designed and wisely used, can help decisionmakers maximize benefits and minimize risks by defining boundaries and requiring accountable process before risks are assumed.

If there are good ideas in this book, they are intended to inspire as a point of departure. If there are bad ideas, they should be used to pivot more quickly to better ideas. As Yale's president A. Whitney Griswold said, "The only sure weapon against bad ideas is better ideas."

ROADMAP

This book is divided into two parts. Part I describes AI, its security uses and risks. Specifically, chapter 2 introduces the reader to AI, its history, its components, and its potential. It also provides the reader with a layman's understanding of the nomenclature of the practical and philosophical AI debates so the general reader can join the dialogue. Each chapter includes a summary of key national security policy and law takeaways. Chapter 3, which considers military and intelligence AI applications, addresses hot-button topics like LAWS, swarms, facial recognition, and deep fakes; however, it would be a policy mistake to focus entirely on these issues to the neglect of logistics and manpower where AI is certain to have profound and more immediate effect. Chapter 4 addresses the implications of AI on security. Six risks are addressed: (1) the risk of unintended consequences when humans use or interface with new or complex technologies; (2) the risk that AI will at once cause global instability while enhancing the power and reach of authoritarian regimes; (3) the risks that come from technology "arms races"; (4) that AI will lower the cost of conflict and therefore increase the risk of conflict; (5) that operating at machine speed with AI will compound national security decisionmaking pathologies; and (6) the risks that might, in theory, arise from unfriendly AI and superintelligent artificial intelligence.

In response to the applications and implications of AI on national security practice, in Part II this book turns to its central question: how, if at all, should we, might we, regulate the national security uses of AI? What would a regulatory template look like? Chapter 5 introduces the reader to the three purposes of national security law: (1) the authority to act, and the left and right boundaries of that action; (2) process; and (3) legal values, many of which are also security values. It further explains why each purpose is critical to defining a legal regime.

Much of the Centaur's Dilemma derives from the need to adopt, at the national and tactical levels, decisionmaking processes that can move and respond at machine speed when it is wise to do so, without surrendering the capacity to command and control outcomes. Thus, the chapter contemplates a different kind of Turing test. This is a test of the U.S. government's decisionmaking capacity. Now is the time to get the process right—to design, train, and empower processes that can effectively address the Centaur's Dilemma. Such processes would move from Daniel Webster's imminence to Alan Turing's instantaneousness. Processes that pass this Turing test would be ones that effectively build private-public partnerships, operate day-to-day, and can move at machine speed when needed and human speed when it is wise to do so.

In the absence of clear law, opponents and proponents of the government's actions will litigate the limits of the law. This will place special emphasis on knowing and applying the law and values embedded in the Constitution, upon which both the government and litigants will rely. For this reason, the application of constitutional law to AI is detailed in chapter 6. In the absence of a tailored statutory regime, the government will use existing law to accomplish new missions and employ new AI capabilities. As chapter 7 explains, three laws are central: the International Emergency Economic Powers Act (IEEPA), the Invention Secrecy Act (ISA), and the Defense Production Act (DPA). However, for the reasons articulated, emphasis is given to the DPA, including its common usages as well as its potential AI usages. At present, the DPA is the government's most expansive potential statutory authority to observe and regulate private AI for national security purposes.

In the absence of a comprehensive legal regime, lawyers will also look to adopt, adapt, and apply law by analogy. In this vein, chapter 8 looks at three nonproliferation and arms control regimes addressed to nuclear, biological, and chemical weapons. The chapter considers how these regimes are apt and inapt to AI, including questions involving command and control, safety, and the verification of dual-use technology. Chapter 9, in turn, looks at how the law of armed conflict (LOAC) might offer analogy beyond its obvious application to military operations. In particular, the chapter considers whether and how the doctrine of command responsibility and the requirement to evaluate new weapons for compliance with the law of armed conflict could apply generally to security uses of AI. And, lest advocates of AI controls believe the U.S. government must drive the debate, the chapter also discusses the lessons learned from the grassroots campaign to eliminate anti-personnel mines, which culminated in the Ottawa Treaty. These chapters are not intended for subject matter specialists, but for the generalists who need to quickly understand what analogy the field of arms control or the law of armed conflict might offer to the regulation of AI.

Chapter 10 rounds out the framework by looking at means other than law that might be used to regulate the design and use of AI for security purposes. While law is binding, democratic, and national in its scope, it can also be difficult to pass and often presents lowest common denominator compromises. The chapter considers the strengths and weaknesses of three regulatory mechanisms outside the normal purview of security specialists: (1) ethical codes of professional conduct, including those pertaining to engineers and lawyers; (2) internal review boards, which review the ethics, design, and scope of certain academic experiments and research; and (3) the concept and practice of corporate social responsibility, known as CSR.

PART I

The Centaur's Dilemma

TWO

The New Electricity

WHAT IS ARTIFICIAL INTELLIGENCE?

WHAT IS ARTIFICIAL INTELLIGENCE?

Popular and scientific literature identifies several benchmark events in the development of AI. In 1950, for example, the English computer scientist Alan Turing wrote an article titled "Computing Machinery and Intelligence." He asked, can machines think, and can they learn from experience as a child does? "The Turing test" was Turing's name for an experiment testing the capacity of a computer to think and act like a human. The test would be passed when a computer could communicate with a person in an adjacent room without the person realizing he was communicating with a computer.

In 1956, Dartmouth College hosted the first conference to study AI. The host, Professor John McCarthy, is credited by many with coining the term "artificial intelligence." As quoted by Nick Bostrum, author of the best-selling book *Superintelligence: Paths, Dangers, Strategies*, the funding proposal submitted to the Rockefeller Foundation stated: We propose that a two-month, ten-man study of artificial intelligence be carried out . . . We think that a significant advance can be made in one or more of these problems if a carefully selected group of scientists work on it together.[1]

Despite this optimistic beginning, progress in the field was not linear or exponential. Progress occurred in fits and starts. As a result, AI development went through a series of "AI winters," periods of low funding and low results.

Continuing the seasonal metaphor, there is little doubt that we are now in an AI spring. The first question is, what will blossom? The second question is, if this is spring, when will summer arrive and how hot will it be? This leads to the third question: are we ready for the results?

AI Defined

Artificial intelligence (AI) is defined in different ways by different people and institutions. Here is one definition:

> Artificial intelligence is a science and a set of computational technologies that are inspired by—but typically operate quite differently from—the ways people use their nervous systems and bodies to sense, learn, reason, and take action.[2]

The reality is, there is no common or widely accepted definition. One reason it is hard to define is because the term itself is inapt. AI invites human comparison to include anthropomorphism, the instinct to give human or animate feelings to inanimate objects like cars and other machines. People also associate the word "intelligence" with inherently human traits, like kindness, compassion, and a desire or will to do good or evil. But these are not machine traits, at least not yet.

Machines do what they are programmed to do, not because they choose to do so, but because they are programmed to do so. Software drives machines. The fact that many cultural representations of AI involve robots—as do some applications—does not help. Moreover, the use of voice triggers and natural language conversion, as in the case of talking navigational aids and "personal assistants" such as Siri, Alexa, and Watson, add to the anthropomorphic tendency. Additionally, much of the current research into machine learning, described below, is predicated on trying to reproduce the human brain—literally, in the case of efforts to replicate the human brain using 3D printers, or with neurological metaphors such as artificial neural networks. Artificial intelligence may mimic, and in some cases outperform, human intelligence, but it is not human intelligence. It is machine capacity and optimization, hence the preferable term human-level machine intelligence (HLMI).

Another definitional challenge with AI is that when it becomes embedded in our everyday lives—in shopping algorithms, navigational aids, and search engines—it is no longer referred to as AI. It is treated as just one more bit of technology in the stuff around us. AI, after all, is a thing of the future. Maybe we should call this sort of AI "regular AI."

Most significantly, AI is hard to define because it draws on a wide spectrum of technologies, subfields, and capacities that make a crisp and singular definition difficult. These other technologies have reached fruition at different times, but all have synergistically propelled AI research and capacity. These include the following:

Computational capacity. Moore's Law (actually an engineer's prediction regarding the period 1965–85) posits that the number of transistors in an integrated circuit, the basic electronic chip used to store and transmit data in a computer, will double every eighteen months. Today, for example, the iPhone 5 has 2.7 times the processing capacity of a 1985 Cray-2 supercomputer.[3] Nanotechnology affects Moore's Law by allowing an ever-greater number of transistors and circuits to operate in smaller and smaller places. (How small? Nanotechnology deals with materials smaller than 100 nanometers and thus the manipulation of individual atoms and molecules. A nanometer is one-billionth of a meter; to illustrate, a human hair is 80,000 to 100,000 nanometers wide.) The advent of quantum computing (QC) has potential to fundamentally change Moore's Law, which is to say replace it altogether as a unit of measure. One reason for the growth in QC research is the ultimate finite capacity of silicon chips and circuits to store and transmit data.

Big data, cloud computing, sensors, and the Internet of Things. The internet and subsequently the Internet of Things (IoT)—the ubiquitous connection of devices such as cars, refrigerators, and doorbells, along with "traditional" electronic devices such as televisions, computers, and phones—has resulted in an explosion of data, metadata, and stored data. This data is available because of the revolution in storage capacity brought on by cloud computing. It is also available and accessible because of the development of finer and smaller multispectrum sensors. Light Imaging Detection and Ranging (LIDAR) is a type of sensor, for example, that uses light pulses to make high-resolution maps, as well as guide driverless cars.

Algorithms, software, and data analytics. The revolution in computing capacity is matched by the development in software and algorithmic reasoning, which has transformed the capacity of engineers to search stored data. An algorithm is a set of instructions or calculations to perform a task, often in the form of a mathematical formula. A program is an algorithm that completes a task.[4] Among other things, algorithms are used to search for and detect patterns in data and metadata. Electrical computer circuits communicate with short bursts of energy in the form of ones and zeros. Computer software code, therefore, translates letters, words, and other symbols into ones and zeros that can then be searched and analyzed by algorithms. (Metadata is data about data; in the context of telephones, the data is the content of your phone call while the metadata is the time, duration, and number you called.) Most algorithms are complex. The Google search algorithm, for example, is believed to consist of over 2 billion lines of code. The word is "believed" because the algorithm is proprietary information, a trade secret. Moreover, it continuously adjusts based on user data—that is, what we search for on an individual and collective basis. The process involves engineering input as well as software changes the algorithm itself makes.

Knowledge and mapping of the human brain. The past ten years have seen a remarkable growth in human knowledge about the brain. This is a product of means, such as the ubiquity of CAT scans and MRIs, and of opportunity, including new imperatives and funding to study battlefield injuries such as traumatic brain injury (TBI) and chronic traumatic encephalopathy (CTE) in athletes.

Robotics and autonomous systems. AI has benefited from the parallel development of civil, military, and commercial autonomous architectures dependent on AI-enabled computers, such as robotics, drones, and smart grids. Each has spurred the others. The Department of Defense often uses the acronym RAS—robotic and autonomous systems—to describe AI initiatives rather than just AI.

The dot.com to Facebook phenomenon. Silicon Valley, along with social media and data giants Amazon, Alphabet (Google), Facebook, Microsoft, and Apple, has demonstrated that algorithms and data make money. To borrow Napoleon's phrase about "a marshal's baton in every soldier's backpack," the entrepreneurial imagine that in every college dorm room there is a billionaire's portfolio. Or so many hope and think; the will to explore and invent continues, as does the desire to make money.

Machine learning. It all comes together, or so it seems, with machine learning. Machine learning is just that: the capacity of a computer using algorithms, calculation, and data to learn to better perform programmed tasks and thus optimize function. "The network learns to recognize features and cluster similar examples, thus revealing hidden groups, links, or patterns within data."[5] Machine learning occurs in different ways using different mathematical theories and formulas. As explained by Buchanan and Miller in *Machine Learning for Policymakers*, there are currently three common processes for teaching machines to learn: supervised learning, unsupervised learning, and reinforcement learning. (Note the use of the qualifier "currently.") Moreover, there are multiple mathematical theories and models for implementing these methods. The United Nations Institute for Disarmament Research, for example, listed seven illustrative methods in 2018: (1) evolutionary or genetic algorithms; (2) inductive reasoning; (3) computational game theory; (4) Bayesian statistics; (5) fuzzy logic; (6) hand-coded expert knowledge; and (7) analogical reasoning. The most promising present method is known as deep learning.[6]

Supervised learning occurs when a computer is fed data that is mathematically weighted to train the computer to better analyze new data and predict outcomes. "The 'supervised' part of the name comes from the fact that each piece of data given to the algorithm also contains the correct answer about the characteristic of interest . . ."[7] Supervised learning is time-consuming. Engineers must feed the data to the computer (that is, enter the data into the computer program), rewarding the algorithm when it is correct in identifying an object, pattern, or sequence, and penalizing the program when it is not. "Reward" here refers to symbolic language, that is, code the algorithm is programmed to seek and compile, like coins in video games. In a homeland security context, for example, this methodology might be useful in identifying or searching for specific people or characteristics of people boarding flights or transiting checkpoints. Likewise, it has obvious potential to facilitate the analysis of overhead surveillance in search of missile silos, underground bunkers, and camouflaged weapons.

Unsupervised learning occurs when the machine seeks to find patterns in data based on algorithmic models but without being trained on data first. "Unsupervised learning is more useful when there is not a clear outcome of interest about which to make a prediction or assessment. Unsupervised learning algorithms are given large amounts of data and try to identify key structures, or patterns, within them."[8] In security context, unsupervised learning might be useful in determining if there are travel patterns identifying links between otherwise unconnected passengers. Likewise, this methodology might help identify patterns in financial transactions or shipments that are anomalous or indicative of illicit economic or proliferation activity.

Reinforcement learning introduces what is referred to as a "software change agent" in the form of algorithmic programming to encourage the machine to learn from its experience in order to optimize its objective. "An agent takes an action, observes the effect on its environment, and then determines whether that action helped it achieve its goal."[9] Thus, AlphaZero—the next iteration of AlphaGo—"played many games against itself and learned over time which moves increased the probability of winning."[10] In other words, reinforcement software teaches itself by finding and implementing preferred strategies based on weighing and predicting outcomes. In 2019, DeepMind, a subsidiary of Google, reported that it was able to train virtual agents to play capture-the-flag within a video game using reinforcement learning. The game was played with teams of five, including human actors, and thus created the impression of coordination between agents as well as with humans, which mimics in part the sort of coordination that might occur with AI-enabled drones and swarms. However, commentators note, "the agents are responding to what is happening in the game rather than trading messages with one another, as human players do." The experiment also illustrates the scale of effort required. "DeepMind's autonomous agents learned capture-the-flag by playing roughly 450,000 rounds of it, tallying about four years of game experience over weeks of training." To do so, the lab rented tens of thousands of computer chips at significant financial and energy cost.[11] One can imagine how this methodology might be useful in war-gaming, testing policy alternatives, or planning logistics options.

Deep learning is a machine learning method used with supervised, unsupervised, and reinforcement learning. With deep learning, a computer's software connects different layers and segments of data internally in a "neural network." The computer adjusts the weights (inputs) in response to the outputs at each stage as it recognizes and rewards itself for correct outputs. Deep learning is often compared to how the human brain sorts and connects information through neural brain networks. Scientists are not quite sure how this occurs in humans, but we know it is happening. That is why some engineers are trying to imitate and map the brain. "Deep learning can combine an unsupervised process to learn the features of the underlying data (such as the edge of a face), then provide that information to a supervised learning algorithm to recognize features as well as the final result (correctly identifying the person in the picture)."[12] There is, in essence, a cascade of computations and predictions. At each level of cascade, the computer is making probability assessments regarding the next set of output data, all inside the software unseen. Nick Bostrum likens computational neural networks to the sifting of sand through increasingly fine screens until one is left with the finest sand output.[13]

Engineers know this process is going on. They caused it to happen. But they cannot describe with certainty exactly what occurs between the input and output layer, that is, why the program has selected one picture, or pixel formulation, or pattern, to weigh in one cascade versus the next. As a result, this part of the process is sometimes referred to as the "black box." What engineers do know is what they started with (the input) and the machine's answer (the output) and how often in test scenarios the machine correctly performs its assigned task of moving from input to desired output. They also know how that accuracy percentage compares to humans performing the same task with the benefit of the same input data, for example, looking for tumors, anomalies in data, or camouflaged tanks. In many cases, AI is more accurate.

Algorithms are designed to vary the breadth and depth of the process. Breadth refers to how many different variables or symbols an algorithm will search for at a given level. Depth refers to how many levels of input and output the program might process before delivering an external output. With image recognition, for example, depth appears to offer more accuracy in prediction than breadth.[14] Here is the mysterious part. Because the machine is learning and adjusting as it goes, engineers cannot always determine what the machine is weighing and how. As a facial recognition algorithm breaks down data into subordinate parts, engineers cannot be sure which data—for example, facial line, pixel, hue, or angle—the algorithm is using or will use to predict which images or portions of images best match or predict the desired output and thus get passed to the next neural network and ultimately on to the output layer. This is important, for example, where coding or data bias may affect the quality of the ultimate predictive outcome. An algorithm designed to predict recidivism or flight risk, for example, may use a hundred different data inputs as well as patterns it derives from the data of the general population in generating a predictive risk that an individual defendant will return to prison. But with deep learning, the judge and lawyers may not know what decisional weight, if any, was assigned to race, location, gang affiliation, the letter "S" in a defendant's name, or population trends inapt to a specific defendant or inappropriate in determining bail or parole.

So, What Is AI?

AI is predicated on the notion that if you can express an idea, thought, or purpose in numeric fashion, you can code that purpose into software and subsequently zeros and ones for a machine to perform. This includes the ability of machines to shift from task to task and to learn to better optimize their function(s). AI is an umbrella term comprising different techniques to do this. But there are some common characteristics to most current AI applications, like pattern recognition, multitasking, sensors, and speed. Ryan Calo, a leading AI academic and lab director, writes, "The entire purpose of AI is to spot patterns people cannot."[15] In short, AI is a series of technologies designed to promote machine optimization based on computational capacity. This definition avoids the necessity of designating which element of the process is AI versus computation, versus robotics, versus algorithmic design.

NARROW AND STRONG AI

Readers should also know that experts refer to three kinds of AI. Narrow AI is where we are today. This is the ability of computational machines to perform singular tasks at optimal levels, or near optimal levels, and usually better, although sometimes just in different ways, than humans. This type of AI is all around us, performing single-purpose tasks, generally based on the capacity of AI to spot patterns, identify structure, and predict—and outperform humans in speed and computational capacity doing so.

When an AI-enabled machine is able to shift from task to task and "think on its own," experts say, machines—or rather the engineers who programmed them—will have achieved what is called artificial general intelligence (AGI), also known as strong AI. There is variation in how experts define AGI. But generally, the definitions share three attributes.

First, fluidity, which is to say an ability to engage in task variance not only by performing more than one task but by shifting from task to task as needed.

Second, the ability to learn by training itself using the internet and any other source of knowledge available, such as data.

And third, the ability to write code—create—and thus rewrite and improve its own programming direction, returning the AGI cycle full-circle to fluidity.

AGI represents a level of intelligence (that is, capacity) at least equivalent to human, at least when it comes to IQ.

National security generalists should also know that AI philosophers and science fiction writers refer to a third hypothetical category of AI as superintelligent artificial intelligence (SAI), or superintelligence. In theory, SAI is achieved when machines not only fluidly switch from task to task but are generally more intelligent than humans. That is because SAI contemplates that the computational machine knows everything that is known to man, because it is connected to the internet. In further theory, that means it has unlimited sources of energy and thus computational capacity allowing it to progress to new levels of knowledge and invention that humans cannot even comprehend.

SNAPSHOT ASSESSMENT: THE STRENGTHS
AND WEAKNESSES OF NARROW AI

Many narrow AI applications are known to consumers who rely on it daily. If you shop on Amazon, you are using AI algorithms. Amazon back-propagates training data from all purchases made on Amazon as well as data from individual consumers. Algorithms then identify patterns in the data and weight those patterns, allowing the algorithm to suggest (predict) additional purchases to the shopper. The algorithm adjusts as it goes, based on the responses (or lack of responses) from recipients. This is an example of predictive big data analytics. It is also an example of a push, predictive, and recommendation algorithm. Former secretary of the navy Richard J. Danzig writes:

> . . . machines can record, analyze, and accordingly anticipate our preferences, evaluate our opportunities, perform our work, and so on, better than we do. With 10 Facebook "likes" as inputs, an algorithm predicts a subject's other preferences better than the average work colleague, with 70 likes better than a friend, with 150 likes better than a family member, and with 300 likes better than a spouse.[16]

Narrow AI is also embedded in mapping applications, which sort through route alternatives with constant near-instantaneous calculations—factoring speed, distance, and traffic to determine the optimum route from A to B. Then the application uses AI to convert numbered code into natural language telling the driver to turn left or right. AI computations and algorithms are also used to spot finite changes in stock pricing and generate automatic sales and purchases of stock as well as spot anomalies that generate automatic sales and purchases. All of this is based on algorithms created and initiated by humans, but programmed to act autonomously and automatically, because the calculations are too large and the margins and speed too small and too fast for humans to keep pace and make decisions in real time. Of course, as one trader's algorithm gets faster, the next trader must either change his algorithm's design, its speed, or both, to achieve advantage. AI machine learning and pattern recognition is also used for translation, logistics planning, and spam detection. The beat goes on. All of which is why in 2017, the former chief scientist for Baidu, Andrew Ng, declared AI "the new electricity."

Perhaps the most prominent illustration of next generation AI is the driverless car. AI empowers driverless cars by performing a myriad of data input and output tasks simultaneously, like a driver does. But in a different way.

Human drivers rely on intuition, instinct, experience, and rules to drive—all at once, it seems, using the actual neural networks of the brain. In the case of driverless cars, sensors instantaneously feed computers data based on speed, conditions, images, and so on, of the sort ordinarily processed by the driver's eyes and brain. The car's software processes the data to determine the best outcome based on probabilities and based on what it has been programmed to understand and decide. This requires constant algorithmic calculations of the sort a human actor could not make in real time if humans relied on math to drive cars.

This is impressive stuff. But it is still narrow AI. And, in its current state, it comes with significant shortcomings. The driverless vehicle can make calculated choices based on sensors, pattern recognition, and calculations, but it cannot make moral or ethical choices. And it can only make calculated choices based on what it has been taught, rather than what it can intuit.

Chatham House scholar M. L. Cummings describes this process:

> . . . estimating or guessing what other drivers will do is a key component of how humans drive, but humans do this with little cognitive effort. It takes a computer significant computation power to keep track of all these variables while also trying to maintain and update its current world model. Given this immense problem of computation, in order to maintain safe execution times for action, a driverless car will make best guesses based on probabilistic distributions. In effect, therefore, the car is guessing which path or action is best, given some sort of confidence interval.[17]

If a ball bounces into the road between two parked vehicles and an AI-enabled self-driving vehicle has not been "trained" to identify the ball-between-two-cars pattern, it will not intuitively surmise, as a human would, that a child may soon follow the ball into the street.

AI philosophers prefer a different example to explain the moral and other limitations in current AI—the ubiquitous crosswalk dilemma or "trolley problem," a famous ethical thought experiment. The scenarios vary. Imagine two persons entering a crosswalk: one a bank robber fleeing the scene of a crime, the other a pregnant woman running after a child. Here comes a car or trolley. The driverless vehicle AI is likely to calculate what to do based on mathematical inputs that might predict the course with the highest probability of avoiding both individuals, and if that is not possible, to be certain to avoid at least one of the individuals, likely seeing the pedestrians as having equivalent value. But the calculations will be based on what is already embedded in the machine's software and training data, not the new contextual information on site, in the moment, about the characteristics of the people within the crosswalk. Engineers refer to AI that lacks this sort of situational awareness and flexibility as being "brittle." In contrast, a human driver, if alert, will adjust and select a new course of action based on experience, judgment, intuition, and moral choice involving the actual pedestrians, erring we assume on the side of missing the pregnant woman at the risk of hitting the bank robber.

Alas, there are real-world examples of this problem. In 2018, a driverless Uber test vehicle hit and killed a bicyclist at night on a Phoenix road. There was no moral dilemma to address, the vehicle's sensors and computer failed because they were not trained to identify a bicycle at night. According to press reports, the computer initially classified the person and bike as "an unrecognized object" apparently without reference to the human on board. The vehicle eventually sought to stop, but not in time. Neither did the human safety driver in the test vehicle respond in time.[18] No wonder there are strongly held views about the safety of driverless cars; proponents seek to deter anecdotal reasoning and invite consideration of trend lines and safety percentages in comparison to human drivers. The case is presented here not to take sides in the driverless car debate, but because it illustrates a present weakness in narrow AI. Policymakers and lawyers should now imagine how this lack of situational awareness might affect military applications of AI.

Perhaps the most compelling (and successful) illustrations of supervised machine learning enabled by narrow AI comes in the area of medicine. Two examples illustrate. In India, diabetes is a significant cause of blindness. Seventy million Indians are diabetic and thus at risk of diabetic retinopathy, which can cause blindness. The condition is treatable if identified before the onset of blindness. However, the ophthalmologist-to-patient ratio in India is on the order of eleven doctors for every million people. One solution is to prescreen the populace using an AI application designed to detect retinal patterns in the eye that presage the onset of diabetes-induced blindness. The limited number of doctors can then focus on the prescreened high-risk patients and bypass the others. As a result, Google is testing an AI application in India to screen for diabetic retinopathy. The patient data is compared to centralized data in the United States. While the system has been approved for use in Europe, it is pending approval in India and the United States. There remain concerns about false positives and the longer-term validation of accuracy.[19]

Three points emerge. First, this is the centaur model at work. The centaur is usually better than the machine or the human acting alone. It is similar to the way common-law judges approach criminal confessions. Confessions offer powerful and often conclusive evidence of criminal conduct and guilt. However, for reasons beyond the scope of this book, there are psychological and other reasons why some persons falsely confess. There are also instances where confessions are the product of interrogation pressure, perhaps coercion, and therefore are less reliable, or not reliable, as a determinant of culpability. As a result, the law requires that any confession be corroborated by independent evidence—something more—like a human validating an AI result.

If one prefers a national security example of the centaur model, consider how the intelligence community uses polygraphs as a counterintelligence tool, but rarely a counterintelligence determinant. Polygraph machines measure physiological indicators, such as pulse, blood pressure, and respiration that can be associated with deception. However, these indicia can also manifest fear and stress. Proponents of polygraphs argue that the machine is only as good as the operator who is, or is not, specially trained to distinguish between deceptive indication and stress. Courts are not so sure. The Supreme Court has stated,

> . . . there is simply no consensus that polygraph evidence is reliable. To this day, the scientific community remains extremely polarized about the reliability of polygraph techniques. . . . Rule 707—excluding polygraph evidence in all military trials—is a rational and proportional means of advancing the legitimate interest in barring unreliable evidence.[20]

Here is the point. When used effectively, polygraphs are a supplement to human judgment. They are a tool that might prompt recipients to disclose information or help agencies determine who warrants additional scrutiny. Once again, the centaur model.

Second, empirical studies show that AI-enabled machines identify and locate a higher percentage of cancerous tumors than do radiologists reviewing the same images. It does not take a specialist to recognize how this capacity could apply to satellite analysis or cyber-malware detection. This is an area where machine optimization in spotting and recognizing patterns, as well as anomalies in patterns, demonstrates the realized potential of AI to serve a greater good, beyond shopping algorithms. It also illustrates the potential impact AI will have on the workforce, including white-collar workforce, as well as the sometime tension and difference between what it means to augment human capacity and what it means to replace it. Ask the question: would you be prepared to learn you have cancer from a machine, alone? Or would you want to validate the results of an AI-analyzed scan with a second opinion from a trusted doctor? And would you not want that doctor to convey to you not just the probability that you will live or die, but also the hope that comes from the touch of a human hand and the knowledge of your personal circumstances? The distinction between human intelligence and narrow AI may, in the end, rest on the difference between what we measure with IQ and what we measure with EQ. Perhaps emotional intelligence is the essential human trait.

Third, human actors and decisionmakers who rely on AI should always ask: what is missing? Machines can now act with certain attributes of intelligence and outperform humans at certain intelligent tasks. The list is growing. "It is expected that machines will reach and exceed human performance on more and more tasks."[21] But is something missing? Here are some possibilities: intuition, compassion, creativity, and judgment. Judgment lets us fill in the gaps between experience and what is new. It also allows us to address competing norms and interests and make rational choices. These are also the traits that inform situational awareness allowing humans to adapt to the unexpected, unknown, or changing circumstances.

Let's look at intuition. There is no doubt that a trained machine can usually better identify objects in pictures. It sees more in depth and in breadth. It can see everything at once and it can break the picture down into discrete quadrants. It sees patterns and pixels the human eye cannot, all instantaneously. But narrow AI does not know what it does not know, and, at present, it lacks the intuition to find out, other than through brute force matching. Once again, M. L. Cummings:

> Expertise leverages judgment and intuition as well as the quick assessment of a situation, especially in a time-critical environment such as weapons release. . . . In humans, the ability to cope with the highest situations of uncertainty is one of the hallmarks of the true expert, but in comparison such behavior is very difficult for computers to replicate.[22]

The point is illustrated with reference to a famous experiment in a different field—the gorilla experiment. In the experiment, a set of observers is asked to watch two groups of people who are busy passing an object back and forth in an office-type environment. They are told to focus on the object. At some point during the experiment, a person dressed in a gorilla suit enters the office and walks behind the people passing the object back and forth; in other words, an anomalous event or pattern occurs. When asked to record everything they observed during the experiment, only half the participants report observing the gorilla. The experiment was used to study the tendency of the mind to focus, and the cognitive bias that occurs, when a person is focusing on one task to the exclusion of others. Paul Slovic, professor of psychology at the University of Oregon, calls this the "prominence effect." But it illustrates a point about narrow AI as well. An AI-enabled machine would not miss the gorilla. What is more, AI could have generated a ten-second microfilm of all that occurred during the course of the hours-long experiment, allowing a human to skip the boredom and fatigue of downtime and easily notice the gorilla walk across the stage. At the same time, the machine, unless it is trained to identify gorillas, would not identify the gorilla as a gorilla. In contrast, a human would intuitively determine that the object was a gorilla, like a gorilla, or an ape, based on life experience and perhaps having once seen a picture of a gorilla. One might call this judgment. In short, humans are less able to detect the anomaly but more capable of interpreting its meaning, at least at this time.

Likewise, a machine can be programmed to repaint the "Mona Lisa" as "Paint by Numbers," a 1950s arts-and-crafts technique. It could also be programmed and trained to find and mix the exact hues of oils, and age them, to mimic the "Mona Lisa" canvas. It might even pass the forger's test. But could AI conceive of the "Mona Lisa"? Would AI, on its own, wonder if Mona Lisa was smiling or why? It raises the rhetorical question Whitney Griswold asked in 1957: Is there something divine about artistic creation? Or, can creativity and imagination be learned, taught, or programmed? What if a machine had access to the internet and the capacity to draw on all the world's accumulated knowledge and know-how? Or all the world's art? Could it then create the "Mona Lisa"? We can imagine Griswold's response. There is something more to creativity than knowledge, computation, and code. Although writing in a different time and context, Griswold asked rhetorically,

> Could *Hamlet* have been written by a committee, or the "Mona Lisa" painted by a club? Could the New Testament have been composed as a conference report? Creative ideas do not spring from groups. They spring from individuals. The divine spark leaps from the finger of God to the finger of Adam, whether it takes ultimate shape in a law of physics or a law of the land, a poem or a policy, a sonata or a mechanical computer.[23]

Why is this important? Because one of the first topics of debate about AI is whether the next category of AI will bridge this divide and allow machines to effectively teach themselves to create, for example, by identifying objects they have not been trained to see before, and performing tasks they have not been programmed to perform.

The debate highlights a string of essential philosophical, technical, and legal questions about AI. What does it mean to be human? Are there inherently human functions that cannot, or should not, be replicated by code-driven machines? If so, what are those attributes, traits, or functions? And if they can be replicated, are there any traits or attributes we should regulate or prohibit? If it can be done, should we allow it to be done, and if so, subject to what substantive and procedural limitations? Identifying these attributes, if any, allows us to understand what we might be giving up, or risking, by turning certain functions over to AI-enabled machines with and without human control.

A THIRD WAVE?

AI has blossomed with machine learning, which is why many experts contend we are skipping spring and entering an AI summer. The *National Artificial Intelligence Research and Development Strategic Plan* (2016) described the first wave of AI machine learning as if-then linear learning. That is, a process of AI that relies on the brute force computational power of today's computers. The computer is, in essence, "trained" that if something occurs, then it should take a countervailing or corresponding step. This is essentially how the IBM computer Deep Blue beat Gary Kasparov in chess in 1997, a significant AI milestone. The computer was optimizing its computational capacity to sort through and weigh every possible move in response to each of Kasparov's actual and potential moves, through the end of the game. It did so with the knowledge of all of Kasparov's prior games, while on the clock in real time. But Deep Blue was a display of computational force, an endless and near-instantaneous series of if-this-then-that questions and calculations. Watson would go on to defeat Ken Jennings in *Jeopardy!* one year later, using much the same method.

The report describes the second wave of AI as "machine learning." That is where we were in 2016 and where we are in 2020. The current benchmark of the second wave of AI is AlphaGo—the Google computer that beat the world's best Go player in 2016. This was a milestone beyond Watson's mastery of chess and *Jeopardy!*, not just because Go is a more complex, multidimensional game, but because AlphaGo won using unsupervised learning. It got better at the game through experience and by adjusting its own decisional weights internally—in the black box—without training data or other if-this-then-that learning. This represented more than brute force computational power; it was a machine optimizing its capacity. Thinking? No. Learning? Yes.

Experts are now debating whether we are entering a third wave of AI and machine learning. This is what the *National Artificial Intelligence Research and Development Strategic Plan* said in October 2016 on the prospect of a third wave of AI development:

> The AI field is now in the beginning stages of a possible third wave, which focuses on explanatory and general AI technologies . . . If successful, engineers could create systems that construct explanatory models for classes of real-world phenomena, engage in natural communication with people, learn and reason as they encounter new tasks and situations, and solve novel problems by generalizing from past experience.[24]

Imagine a computer linked to the internet, the Cloud, and the IoT. Next imagine that the computer is not programmed to play chess or Go, a single task and limitation, but is programmed to solve problems or answer questions generally. It moves fluidly from one task to the next. Now consider that if a computer can do that, it could not only write code, which computers can do now, but it could rewrite, improve, and change its own code. It might do this to optimize the task it was originally programmed to perform and find new and unanticipated paths to optimize the execution of assigned tasks. The questions with general AI are: whether and when?

In 2015 and 2016, a group of scholars associated with the Oxford Future of Humanity Institute, AI Impacts, and Yale University surveyed "all researchers who published at the 2015 NIPS and ICML [Workshop on Neural Information Processing Systems and International Conference on Machine Learning] conferences (two of the premier venues for peer-reviewed research in machine learning)." The survey asked respondents to estimate when HLMI would arrive. The 2018 study did not define AGI or SAI, but stipulated that "Human-level machine learning is achieved when unaided machines can accomplish every task better and more cheaply than human workers." Three-hundred and fifty-two researchers responded, a return rate of 21 percent. The results ranged across the board from never to beyond a hundred years. What is noteworthy is that the "aggregate forecast gave a 50 percent chance of HLMI occurring within forty-five years and a 10 percent chance of it occurring within nine years." Most optimistic—or alarming, depending on one's perspective—

the median response for the two countries with the most respondents in the survey, the United States and China, was seventy-six years for the American respondents and twenty-eight years for the Chinese respondents.[25]

TAKEAWAYS

Having defined AI, reviewed its constituent parts, and explored some strengths and weaknesses of narrow AI, one might now ask what should policymakers and lawyers know and understand to better imagine and apply AI for national security benefit as well as mitigate its risks. Here are eight takeaways.

Narrow (contemporary) AI is best at pattern recognition, classifying, and predicting. AI applications can detect patterns exponentially faster and more reliably than humans in many cases, as well as detect patterns humans cannot. That makes AI a preferred tool for facial recognition, voice recognition, navigation, data mining, and natural language conversion, among other things. AI is also an essential component for enabling autonomous systems, such as smart grids, robots, and unmanned vehicles. If you want a sense of how good or bad AI is at the moment, consider how good shopping algorithms and other push algorithms are at predicting your behavior. Now ask yourself to what extent you would be willing to rely on a shopping-quality algorithm to make national security decisions or inform those decisions.

Narrow (contemporary) AI is not (yet?) good at tasks that require or involve situational awareness, moral choice, intuition, judgment, empathy, or creativity. Specialists refer to AI as brittle—not able to adjust to new situations or react to unforeseen circumstances. Thus, current AI is better at limited tasks, such as follow-the-leader logistics trains, than exercising independent choice such as distinguishing between potential military targets or, for that matter, persons in a crosswalk. If policymakers want a sense of when AI might be nimble enough to handle swarm deployments, they might watch for the first AI application to successfully master a video game, such as *StarCraft II*, without extensive reinforcement learning, as well as switch from game to game.[26]

Mastering the 'ilities. In order for narrow AI to get better at the things it is good at as well as the tasks it is not good at, engineers must overcome what the 2017 MITRE Corporation JASON Report, "Perspectives on Research in Artificial Intelligence and Artificial General Intelligence Relevant to DOD," identified as the "so-called 'ilities," which "are of particular importance to DOD applications."[27]

Reliability

Maintainability

Accountability

Verifiability

Evolvability

Attackability, and

So forth.

In the "so forth" category, one might also include interoperability.

The centaur model. Until such time as the 'ilities are successfully addressed, the centaur model offers the only sure and effective model of operation. The challenge for policymakers, technologists, and lawyers is to move beyond human-in-the-loop bromides in defining law and policy. With AI, a human is always in the loop in some manner, for a human always writes the initial code and chooses to deploy an AI-enabled machine or capacity. The better question is when, where, and how should a human be involved in each *specific* AI function? The next question is, when a specific human is not directly in control, which humans should be held responsible or accountable for what occurs and based on what mechanism of adjudication and decision? If we do not get the human part of the centaur right, it may not matter how good the AI part is at performing its programmed task.

Experts do not know where this is all headed or how soon. You do not need to buy into the debate about artificial general intelligence and superintelligent artificial intelligence to realize that experts do not know where AI is ultimately headed. The debate itself evidences uncertainty as to the outcome, timeline, and milestones along the way.

AI predicts. It does not conclude. It is a statistical and computational tool. Current AI is all about calculating probabilities. As Chris Meserole of the Brookings Institute has written, "The core insight of machine learning is that much of what we recognize as intelligence hinges on probability rather than reason or logic."[28] That means that where AI is used, policymakers must ask such questions as: How accurate is the algorithm? What confidence threshold have decisionmakers applied? What is the false positive rate? What is the false negative rate? When the algorithm is wrong, why is it wrong?

The importance of data. Prediction is one reason the internet, IoT, and data banks are so important to the development of AI and machine learning. Accuracy depends on the amount and quality of data, just as it depends on the algorithm used to derive meaning from data. The more data the better. Supervised or not, the more data that is fed to or known to a computer the more accurately it can adjust its coding weights to classify data and select the right outputs. This makes sense. A human who has never seen a cheetah can infer, based on having seen a domestic cat, that a cheetah is a type of cat. However, at present, a computer can only know what it is programmed to know. Thus the more pictures of different types of cats a supervised learning algorithm is exposed to the more likely it is to discern a shape, a color, or a pattern that is predictive of a cat when it is shown its first picture of a cheetah. But if the algorithm has only seen one picture of a domesticated cat, and hundreds of pictures of fur coats, it might predict that the picture of a cheetah is a fur coat. This is why the development of AI will depend in part on the procurement of data—overtly, covertly, and through synthetic means. Likewise, a facial recognition algorithm trained on predominantly male images, perhaps because the software engineer anticipates that most terrorists are or will be male, will be less apt at identifying female faces.

This means policymakers and lawyers must define the right and left boundaries of data collection, use, and retention in the private as well as public sectors and do so conscious of how security and privacy values are affected. In addition, intelligence analysts should watch who is collecting data and what data they are collecting. Lawyers should help to define the left and right boundaries of data collection and use, while technologists should determine if they can embed those boundaries in code.

AI has a low threshold of entry, but a high threshold for accuracy. Any business or government that is using an algorithm to process data is arguably using AI. A non-state actor programming an unmanned vehicle is likely using AI. In this sense, AI may become "the Kalashnikovs of tomorrow."[29] But strong AI, accurate AI, requires significant amounts of data, storage capacity, energy, sustained commitment, and financial resources.

Equipped with this background, the next two chapters consider the national security applications and implications of AI.

THREE

The Perfect Sentinel

NATIONAL SECURITY APPLICATIONS

How might AI influence national security? One response: What won't it influence? To understand AI's potential impact, it helps to briefly consider AI's application to intelligence and military operations.

INTELLIGENCE

AI's potential as a national security tool is most evident with intelligence. Here, narrow AI's capacity to outperform humans in pattern recognition and anomaly detection, and the speed with which it can do so, presents an obvious application of existing and emerging technology. Think of intelligence concepts such as "connecting the dots" and the "mosaic theory"—that is what AI is all about. Or imagine the computational capability to search the entirety of the internet for threats in real time, along with the capacity to connect those threats to purchase and travel records as well as phone numbers. AI also provides the capacity to immediately analyze information, or a story, trace its origin to the head of the cyber-stream, and distinguish fact from fiction or something in between.

AI software or enabled systems can, or will, perform the following intelligence tasks:

- Persistent surveillance
- Image recognition, including facial recognition

- Link analysis
- Voice recognition
- Sorting
- Aggregation, a.k.a. fusion
- Political prediction
- Policy modeling
- Translation
- Deviation and anomaly detection
- Cyber-detection, attribution, and response

Now consider these capacities from the standpoint of the five intelligence tools (collection, analysis, covert action, counterintelligence, and liaison), as well as with respect to homeland security.

Collection

AI tools offer myriad additional collection capabilities or, in current vernacular, attack surfaces, based on the existing ubiquity of smartphones, CCTV, computers, and the IoT (Internet of Things). Media reports the Chinese government is using AI facial recognition algorithms to calculate social credit scores based on internet activity, and infractions like jaywalking, and that there are now over 800,000 CCTV cameras in Beijing alone. The Chinese also reportedly use AI to track the movements and associations of its ethnic minority and largely Muslim Uighur population outside of the Uighur Autonomous Region.

Privacy is relative, but the use of AI for surveillance is not just an authoritarian phenomenon. "At least seventy-four . . . countries are engaging in AI-powered surveillance, including many liberal democracies."[1] According to the Government Accountability Office, "since 2011, the FBI has logged more than 390,000 facial-recognition searches of federal and local databases, including state DMV databases" with access to 641 million face photos. "The FBI has said its system is 86 percent accurate at finding the right person if a search is able to generate a list of fifty possible matches."[2] Here is what Chief Justice Roberts wrote in the *Carpenter* case (discussed in chapter 6), holding 127 days of cell tower data inadmissible in a criminal case without a search warrant:

> A majority of this Court has already recognized that individuals have a reasonable expectation of privacy in the whole of their physical move-

ments. . . . when the government tracks the location of a cell phone, it achieves near perfect surveillance, as if it had attached an ankle monitor to the phone's user. . . . Unlike with the GPS device in *Jones*, police need not even know in advance whether they want to follow a particular individual, or when.[3]

Now consider the IoT, the interconnection between electronic devices and sensors designed and connected, in theory, to make our lives easier (and to make it easier to monetize our data with advertising and sales). Domestic sensors are everywhere: remote door locks, alarms, and cameras; the television; the refrigerator; the printer; home assistants; and so on. All of this produces collectable data. Corporations and social media platforms know this, because they installed the sensors. Governments know this, too. Have you ever had the eerie experience of having a conversation with someone about the need to purchase a grocery or toiletry item only to find instants later that your iPhone has received a series of advertisements for such items? There is a reason that cell phones are not permitted in many government buildings. They can be used as passive listening devices, receivers. They can also be used to track, either directly as a beacon or by pattern analysis of roaming cell tower signals. Most cell phone users know their cell phones are registering with cell towers as they move, but many people tend to forget or ignore the implications. Perhaps others simply accept the ubiquitous nature of cellular emanations, just as one necessarily accepts the ubiquitous nature of one's image-capture on CCTV cameras in London and many other urban areas and malls. Because all this data can now be stored in the Cloud, it can also be stored indefinitely without overwhelming the capacity of privately owned hardware or business mainframes.

In short, AI algorithms and link-analysis enables governments to aggregate and search information as never before on the internet, Dark Web, Dark Net, and the sensors of our everyday lives. The legal policy question is how much authority the government should have to collect and aggregate data and subject to what right and left boundaries regarding its storage, use, and transfer.

Analysis

There is an intelligence maxim that there is either too much information to analyze or too little. So it seems. The latter is illustrated by the challenge of determining intent within the leadership circle of a closed authoritarian regime, such as North Korea's or the Soviet Politburo, or one with a small footprint, such as a terrorist cell. The former is illustrated by just about everything else, but for the sake of brevity, consider the complexity of analyzing Open Source Intelligence from the internet and Dark Web. In short, AI allows analysts to derive meaning from data.

One might think that the dilemma of too much information is a recent phenomenon. The challenge is not new, the scale is. Sherman Kent, one of the architects of the intelligence analysis discipline, wrote in the 1950s about the volume of information potentially available to analyze and the necessity of knowing when and where to put the human in the informational loop. The volume of data is exponentially greater today. YouTube uploads 500 million hours of video every minute. "More than 2 billion people now visit the site at least once a month. It would take 100,000 years to watch it all at a single sitting."[4] For those with less time, it would take 951 years to view a single day's uploads. Pick your metaphor; analysts talk about noise-to-signal ratios or finding a needle in a haystack.

Analysts used to measure the amount of data collected with reference to the number of Libraries of Congress. Today a common unit of measure is the petabyte, the equivalent of the holdings of seven Libraries of Congress. By the time this book is published, information may be routinely sorted into exabytes. That is a number followed by eighteen zeroes. Intelligence specialists have also spoken for years of the mosaic theory of intelligence and, after 9/11, the necessity of connecting the dots, the process of piecing together diffuse bits of information to create a greater whole for the purpose of informing, warning, and predicting. Data mining and AI algorithms offer a solution through link analysis.

AI is an intelligence force multiplier. Properly constituted, algorithms can detect anomalous trade or travel patterns. If one were tracking sanctions enforcement and evasion, for example, algorithms can find, aggregate, sort, and identify anomalous patterns in the transfer of goods based on bills of lading, bank transfers, shipment weights, routes, and all the other data that lies beyond the capacity of human fingertips to collect and analyze in real time or near real time.[5] Recall the earlier description of the gorilla in the crowd experiment. AI-enabled machines do not miss gorillas walking across the room, or out-of-place bills of lading. Likewise, AI algorithms can convert IoT data into pattern-of-life analysis, revealing one's friends, place of worship, diet, schools, and time of entry to and from the home and the refrigerator.

Finally, AI can translate foreign print, broadcast, and social media instantly, giving analysts new access to open-source information. This task used to be performed laboriously "by hand" by the Foreign Broadcast Information Service (FBIS). AI is instant FBIS, but with limitations. One need only ask Siri or Alexa a question involving a foreign phrase, or to track down a Jabberwocky word, to realize narrow AI has limitations regarding accented speech, entendre, and children's speech.

Covert Action

The capacity of AI to convert symbolic language (coded numbers) into natural language along with its capacity to recognize and distinguish patterns make AI a tool of choice not only to identify voices, but to mimic voices and alter images. Moreover, this can be done with real-life precision with images or recordings known as deep fakes. As is often the case, the capacity found its first public manifestation with pornography and pornographic revenge, with digital editors grafting one person's face onto another person's body. However, it does not take imagination to realize this capacity has potential, perhaps already realized, to enable some of the traditional tools of covert action, in American parlance, or active measures, in Russian parlance, including disinformation, false flag operations, and propaganda. The Cold War press placement is today's video feed. If one wants to discredit or blackmail an official, why go to the trouble of setting up a honey trap when one can "obtain" the same result with a virtual deep fake. What is more, deep fakes work against the incorruptible as well as the predisposed and susceptible.

AI also makes cyber-weapons more effective, by helping to find zero days, enhancing the speed of response and counterresponse, and better disguising the attributable characteristics of the attacker. The February 2018 indictment of thirteen named Russian agents for interfering in the 2016 U.S. presidential election illustrates an aggressive use of cyber-instruments as covert tools. The Russian government operated a 24/7 bot farm, spreading false flag information not just about the presidential candidates but seeking to suppress the vote in African American communities. The Russian efforts extended across social media platforms—Twitter, Instagram, Facebook. One Russian social media account had over a hundred thousand followers. The policy question is whether governments should establish norms against the use of deep fakes, as many state legislatures are now doing with deep fake pornography.

In military context, lawful efforts to deceive the enemy are called ruses. The Trojan horse was a ruse. So were the subterfuges used by the Allies to keep the Germans guessing as to where the D-Day landings would occur. AI will allow military forces to engage in such ruses more effectively, perhaps dangerously so. AI might be used to disable an opponent's air defense system, or perhaps turn it against an opponent's own aircraft. AI can be used to mimic the voices of commanders and realistically so. And AI can be used to mimic a nation's leaders to sow confusion at home and undermine morale. All of which heightens the need for sound encryption and active counterintelligence. Moreover, as American political observers know, disinformation need not be clever or well crafted to sow confusion or leave the public uncertain as to what to believe or not to believe.

Counterintelligence

AI will have, and no doubt has had, two immediate counterintelligence (CI) impacts. First, as already noted, it can aggregate information and identify patterns in financial, physical, and digital behavior along with anomalies in that behavior indicative of insider threats. Consider how quickly your credit card company knows when your card is used out of pattern when you travel overseas, or purchase gas on a long-distance road trip. Such tools might help identify a Snowden or a Manning accessing information outside their normative responsibilities, or an Ames or a Hanson spending money in new ways or beyond their apparent means. Would the government rely on AI alone to make these connections? One hopes not. The potential for false positives and spoofing is too great. But it is an immediate tool for the centaur to use to vindicate or corroborate. However, CI cuts both ways. AI may make it easier for an adversary to identify a case officer or an asset not careful with his or her own electronic footprint, fingerprint, facial print, or credit trail. Likewise, if AI enables counterintelligence, it also enables the internal police to track citizens more effectively within authoritarian states—counterintelligence of a different sort.

Second, it is a transformative technology. AI assets are an intelligence target presenting a CI challenge commensurate with its importance, but with a twist. Because the majority of AI R & D is academic and corporate, their laboratories are intelligence targets in ways they have not been before. Stated more pointedly, we can expect federally funded research and development centers (FFRDCs), university research centers, and corporations like Google and Facebook to become perpetual adversarial targets requiring new efforts to spot and counter technical and human penetration, all within cultures new to, if not resistant to, security and personnel safeguards.

Likewise, data used for machine learning and link analysis will take on added importance as an espionage target. Consider how the SF-86 data stolen from OPM could be used for machine learning. The ubiquitous Chinese effort to collect genomic data[6] might serve a secondary purpose of providing data for machine learning. Nor should we be surprised when, without additional law or regulation, genomic data collected for one purpose, like family ancestry, is sold and makes its way into learning-enabled machines for further analysis and later pattern recognition.

One question for security specialists is how to deploy AI-enabled machines down to the tactical level in a manner that mitigates the risk of counterintelligence penetration or loss. Another question is where we, as a nation, should draw the left and right boundaries of data collection for CI and other purposes. More particularly, should the government collect (or purchase) private data for AI development and what responsibility and role should the government play in protecting data held in the private sector?

Liaison

Liaison is the intelligence term used to describe the sharing of information between nations and, in particular, intelligence services. Intelligence liaison is an expected activity between allies, as reflected in the so-called Five Eyes—an intelligence alliance between the United States, the United Kingdom, Canada, Australia, and New Zealand. However, intelligence liaison also occurs between like-minded services or momentarily like-minded services, for example, two generally hostile services sharing information on a common adversary or need. Liaison is an essential intelligence tool and multiplier, because it can provide access to information not otherwise available to a party based on location, access, or means.

Liaison can also create risk and controversy in at least four ways. First, information is rarely shared out of good will alone. Horse trading can be part of the process, especially outside of routinized liaison arrangements. Second, intelligence liaison does not always align with the stated and overt values of the governments involved. Especially when dealing with unsavory governments, liaison requires careful assessment of reputational and diplomatic risk weighed against security benefit. It also requires an assessment as to how U.S. information will be used, including whether it will be used in violation of U.S. laws. Third, because liaison is an intelligence activity, in U.S. practice, it receives less policy appraisal and legal oversight. (Depending on one's perspective, this can be a good or bad thing.) In U.S. practice, there have been notable instances when one part of the government has been engaged in diplomatic condemnation at the same time the intelligence arm is engaged in liaison, presenting, at best, mixed public perceptions of government intent and purpose. For example, within months of Secretary of State Colin Powell declaring the actions of the Sudanese government in Darfur genocide, the CIA director was meeting with his Sudanese counterpart in Langley, surprising many policymakers and diluting the U.S. message.[7]

Finally, information provided through liaison channels is harder to validate and confirm, because the service providing information is often hesitant, if not opposed, to identifying its sources and methods or subjecting them to third-party validation. This risk is illustrated by the aptly code-named "Curveball," a German intelligence asset who provided erroneous (perhaps intentionally false) information on Iraqi weapons of mass destruction (WMD) prior to the U.S. invasion of Iraq in 2003.[8]

How might AI affect liaison? First, it may add pressure on value-matching as authoritarian regimes seek data about their citizens or their citizens' movements and communications overseas. Second, validating liaison information—for example, the identity of a person placed on a watch list or information on a terrorist target list—will be more difficult, if not impossible, where the information is based on AI input without access to the underlying data and algorithms concerned. Third, AI will increase the intelligence advantages of states that already enjoy an advantage in technical means of collection or data set access. Thus, it will also increase their value as potential liaison partners.

Homeland Security

In no area is AI more likely to have immediate intelligence impact than with homeland security. Narrow AI is well suited to many core homeland security tasks, including cybersecurity, public health, border security, and counterterrorism. That is because narrow AI is especially suited to detect anomalous travel, unseen connections, public health warnings, patterns, and indicators, as well as the use of facial recognition to find specific individuals. However, with promise comes challenge. AI can help generate what Chief Justice Roberts referred to as "near perfect surveillance," which may be helpful for contact tracing during a pandemic, but aggravates concerns about AI privacy and places new stress on old legal doctrines. As described in chapter 6, the domestic use of AI presents First, Fourth, Fifth, and Sixth Amendment issues, including those involving algorithmic bias, distinguishing between U.S. persons and other persons, and data collection, use, and retention.

MILITARY APPLICATIONS

Nowhere is AI more likely to transform security than in the area of military planning, operations, and weapons design and employment.[9] A 2017 Belfer Center Study prepared for the Intelligence Advanced Research Projects Activity (IARPA) concluded that AI is likely to be as transformative a military technology as aviation and nuclear weapons were before. The Department of Defense agrees. The department has made AI a centerpiece of its innovation strategy. DOD has identified a number of areas where AI "has massive potential," including command and communications (C2), navigation, perception, obstacle detection, and swarm behavior and tactics.[10] In June 2018, bureaucracy followed concept as the department established a Joint Artificial Intelligence Center (JAIC) to facilitate and coordinate the integration of AI across DOD. The National Commission on Artificial Intelligence Interim Report states that "a recent estimate suggested there are over six hundred active AI projects across DOD."[11]

The Department of Defense is not alone in considering AI a military game-changer. A 2015 open letter from AI researchers states, "the endpoint of this technological trajectory is obvious: autonomous weapons will become the Kalashnikovs of tomorrow."[12] Non-state actors are known to have sought, and in a few instances used, unmanned aerial vehicles as weapons. This is an obvious path.[13] The question is what role AI will play in increasing the efficacy of such weapons and expanding their use.

Commentators focus on the potential of AI to enable lethal autonomous weapons systems (LAWS, also known as AWS). The Russian military, for example, is testing a robot named FEDOR, which can fire weapons and carry heavy loads. Defense Department vernacular generally refers to LAWS, but also with almost as much frequency RAS—robotic and autonomous systems. Much of the research is intended to make existing weapons platforms better, like fire support systems for tanks and electronic warfare modules for aircraft. Militaries have used some form of AWS for years, such as the Aegis ship defense system, the Phalanx, and the Counter-Rocket, Artillery, and Mortar (C-RAM) system.[14] If a heat-seeking (infrared-homing) missile is an autonomous weapon once fired, such a missile, the Sidewinder air-to-air missile, has been deployed with U.S. aircraft since 1956. So what is new? What is transformative?

A number of militaries, including the U.S. military, are experimenting with AI-enabled "swarms." This is not a secret. The TV show *60 Minutes* did a segment titled "The Coming Swarm" in August 2017. What is secret is the trajectory of progress, capacity, date of deployment, and potential doctrinal uses. Swarms can be composed of unmanned formations of aerial, vehicular, maritime, or submarine platforms—or, in current vernacular, unmanned aerial vehicles (UAV), unmanned ground vehicles (UGV), unmanned maritime vehicles (UMV), and unmanned underwater vehicles (UUV). Swarms thus illustrate how robotics, autonomy, and AI come together to create new capabilities. Swarms can also be programmed to work in coordination with, or independent of, the command of human operators in manned vehicles or operating remotely. (Recall from the previous chapter the use of AI to play capture-the-flag.)

Imagine chaff fired from the side of an aircraft designed to fool incoming missiles. But this chaff is not comprised of metal fragments. It consists of AI-enabled pods that can maneuver around incoming missiles before deciding whether to attack the missile(s), lead them into the ground, or perhaps direct them back to their point of origin. This is based on AI, because the system depends on instantaneous sensory input, calculation, and adjustments too complex and too rapid for a human to make in the moment, let alone a human sitting in the cockpit of an aircraft contending with the pressures of combat. (Think flying driverless cars.)

Now switch from defense to offense and imagine the capability of a swarm—hundreds, perhaps thousands of flying objects called birds, projectiles, or robots—attacking naval vessels or airfields, like the kamikazes at Okinawa but in sync and without the moral and supply chain challenges of recruiting and expending pilots. AI also offers offset potential to U.S. adversaries, who may see in swarm technology and LAWS an inexpensive way to neutralize America's superiority, if not dominance, in surface warfare capacity. It is possible as well that AI not only serves to offset U.S. advantages, but to reset the calculus of naval and aerial warfare in the same way the advent of the Dreadnought class battleship in 1906 made existing battleships obsolete and thus effectively zeroed out Britain's numeric battleship advantage over Germany.[15]

Swarms are not the only offensive and defensive weapons uses for AI. The Defense Department *Unmanned Systems Integrated Roadmap* describes AI-enabled systems as the perfect wingman:

Unmanned Systems with integrated AI, acting as a wingman or team-mate, with lethal armament could perform the vast majority of the actions associated with target identification, tracking, threat prioritization, and post-attack assessment while tracking the position and ensuring the safety of blue-force assets—minimizing the risk to its human teammates.[16]

Further, whatever is occurring in the cyber-domain will be "enhanced" by AI. AI can be used, if it is not already in use, to both enable cyber-combat as well as cloak attribution. If AI can be used to run stock market trading platforms that automatically buy and sell based on finite differences in price, AI can be used to increase the speed and sophistication of cyber-offense and defense. It can also be used to spoof such attacks or mask attribution.

Here definitions are important, as are distinctions between what is autonomous, what is automated, and what is used to augment human capacity. In current DOD vernacular:

An *automated system* is one that automatically responds or acts without human decision or input.

Autonomy is defined as the ability of any entity to independently develop and select among different courses of action to achieve goals based on the entity's knowledge and understanding of the world, itself, and the situation.[17]

An *autonomous system* is one that can operate on its own, but not necessarily without human input or direction.

Augmentation, in turn, is the process by which a human and autonomous system work together, with the autonomous system augmenting human capacity.[18]

A 2018 report written by the UN Institute for Disarmament Research makes an additional and important definitional distinction. "Intelligence is a system's ability to determine the best course of action to achieve its goals. Autonomy is the freedom a system has in accomplishing its goals."[19] In short, AI can enable weapons and weapons systems to identify and engage targets in all domains rapidly, continuously, simultaneously, and sequentially, and do so in a manner humans could not do, or would take too long to do, to calculate distances, angles, numbers, and response choices.

One question is whether such systems will be, or should be, empowered to do so autonomously without affirmative human activation, choice, and decision, based on programming and sensors alone. The United States initially took the position that with lethal autonomous systems "we will always have a human being in the loop."[20] Defense Directive 3000.09 now refers in more opaque fashion to the "exercise of appropriate levels of human judgment," a less precise formulation. "In the loop" generally means that an autonomous system is programmed or designed to only perform its task upon human direction or command, such as fire a weapon. Human "on the loop" generally refers to a system where a human is supervising the machine's use, for example, targeting process, and can intervene at any time during the cycle. Human "out of the loop" means the system is free to operate, for example, select and engage targets, without subsequent human decision, supervision, or intervention. The terms deceive, as a human is involved in writing the code and designing the system in the first place, whether it is ultimately described as one with a human in, on, or out of the loop. Moreover, what it means to "supervise" a system on the loop may vary widely, depending on the nature and speed of engagement.

According to the 2018 DOD *Roadmap* report, "DOD does not currently have an autonomous weapon system that can search for, identify, track, select, and engage targets independent of a human operator's input."[21] Of course, this sentence is ripe with ambiguity, as one does not know whether the caveat derives from a singular verb (identify, track, select . . .) or whether DOD intends to have such a fully autonomous system. However, we should anticipate that potential opponents may seek such a system, which is one reason why the United States has reserved the right to respond in automated fashion to an opponent's use of automated AI as a weapon.

A second question involving autonomous systems is who should be responsible (and held to account) for what the software does or does not do. We know from Stuxnet, the malware discovered in 2010 that attacked and destroyed centrifuges in Iran's Natanz nuclear enrichment facility, how a cyberweapon might be employed, what it can accomplish, and how it might jump the rail, as well as how it might be repurposed and used by others, even when originally designed and intended to remain air-locked. What, then, might fully autonomous weapons do and how, if at all, should the law seek to cabin that potential?

AI will also make it easier to test weapons. As discussed in part II, the law of armed conflict requires that new weapons, as well as the means and methods of warfare, be tested for compliance with the law of armed conflict prior to deployment. AI capacities can be used to model this activity, where actual testing is unfeasible, unreliable, or incomplete. Nuclear weapons, which are already tested through modeling, are an obvious example. But so are cyber-weapons and swarms. Just as pilots train through simulation, AI can simulate variables that will affect weapon performance.

While much of the public attention is on LAWS, many of AI's enabling capabilities are intended to enable and augment logistical, administrative, intelligence, and decisionmaking capacities. AI is a military force multiplier in at least six interlocking ways. First, it can enable machines, shaped or not shaped to look like animate robots, to perform inherently dangerous tasks. Depending on the capability and the task, it may perform these tasks better than humans, and certainly more safely (to the operating humans), like bomb detection and disposal. Second, as an AI-enabled economy may automate repetitive tasks performed by humans, AI may have the same effect on military personnel requirements. AI-enabled machines, for example, may eliminate or reduce the need for personnel to provide meal and laundry services, along with some of the costs associated with these tasks, like health and retirement benefits. (However, not all AI applications are manpower-neutral or -reductive. In the U.S. Air Force, it takes about ten people to operate one large UAV.[22] Put another way, as reported in the *Washington Post,* "it takes up to four drones to provide 24-hour coverage for a single combat air patrol. Although the aircraft are unmanned, they require lots of personnel to fly them by remote control and provide support on the ground—about 400 to 500 people for each combat air patrol."[23])

Third, AI may provide for capacity that does not already exist or exists at scale at the tactical level, such as an intelligence capability to fuse data or translation. This could offer significant advantage in counterterrorism and counterinsurgency contexts, where the support, or at least neutrality, of local populations is essential and miscommunication disastrous.

Fourth, AI-enabled systems can perform tasks not only faster than humans, but near-instantly, based on their capacity to compute, sort, and structure. Thus, algorithms can model the best methods to transport and deliver logistics, considering weather, fuel, urgency, and any other factors that might take an inordinate amount of time for humans to calculate. Consider how a Waze or GPS navigational system could assist logisticians in planning delivery routes and medical evacuation. Even better, imagine planning D-Day or the 1990 Desert Shield deployment with algorithms that can identify to the second optimum airlift and sealift schedules to address needs and contingencies, and instantly adjust these schedules every time the weather shifts, or an ally adjusts its end force commitments. The Defense Department describes how AI will also enable logistics delivery: "Elevated levels of autonomy in unmanned systems will allow for leader-follower capabilities, where trailing semiautonomous vehicles follow a designated vehicle in logistics convoy operations."[24]

Fifth, AI, in many cases, is already better than humans at sorting vast amounts of information, characterizing that information, linking that information, and making predictions based on that information. In other words, it can bring to the military decisionmaker instantaneous sources of intelligence and intelligence analysis, while also spotting anomalies and patterns predictive of risk or attack. This also allows AI applications to enable realistic simulated training for pilots and other military actors. It can also be used in war games and exercises. If an AI-enabled computer can play Go or chess, it can simulate a military opponent on a tactical or strategic level.

Sixth, AI-optimized machines are less prone to types of human error brought on by fear or fatigue. Consider the targeting process where AI's impact on intelligence and weapons comes together. AI software can truncate hours of surveillance video from a UAV feed into minutes, ensuring key facts and events are observed. Combine this with the AI-enabled sensors and pattern recognition, and one sees one purpose of DOD Project Maven: "computer vision . . . that autonomously extracts objects of interest from moving or still imagery."[25] Such a processing system can eliminate the sorts of human mistakes that come with fatigue and repetition. It can also mitigate the cognitive tendency to focus on the mission and immediate objective—for example, target the enemy—with the unintended consequence of seeing and excluding other variables—such as the collateral behavior around a target.

In conclusion, if you want to know how militaries might use AI beyond weapons systems, imagine how an AI-enabled machine might mitigate five of the factors identified above—risk, repetition, fear, fatigue, and speed—if a machine can be "taught" to perform the task in question. That is AI. Here the benefit derives not from the ability of the machine to act like a human or with human intelligence, but expressly from the fact that the machine does not do so. In this sense, AI is the perfect sentinel or wingman, one that does not fall asleep on post, talk, or show fear. AI is the sentry that actually observes the Second General Order: "To walk my post in a military manner, keeping always alert, and observing everything that takes place within sight or hearing."

TAKEAWAYS

AI will transform intelligence and military systems and capabilities. It will also change the nature of the national security toolbox. AI will influence national security decisionmaking in multiple ways. First, if more intelligence, and more accurate intelligence, helps policymakers better predict threats and thus better deter threats before they materialize, then AI's capacity to identify, fuse, and connect intelligence streams is a positive development, as long as this capability is used and used wisely. Likewise, any mechanism that can more accurately and rapidly distinguish between real and fake information, and between noise and signals, should contribute to better decisions. In theory, intelligence also contributes to stability by reducing the risk of miscalculation and misperception, at least where the intelligence is accurate and understood. Of course, more intelligence also means more noise, and thus a necessity to adjust any intelligence process to account for this challenge.

If used effectively, AI will also help decisionmakers model and predict potential policy outcomes, just as Deep Blue rapidly modeled Gary Kasparov's potential chess moves and countermoves. AI will allow Red Team and Blue Team testing of policy proposals in real time. But these are *potential* benefits. They only become actual benefits if the policy process is changed or adjusted to effectively provide this input at the tactical, agency, and national level.

Policymakers, technologists, and lawyers should consider the following points and questions. The sooner the better.

1. What law and process should apply to the collection of data from the IoT and other sources for intelligence purposes? What are the left and right boundaries of conduct? If the law is different at home and abroad, how is it different? Should the U.S. government collect foreign data overtly and clandestinely as the Chinese government does for the purpose of developing and training AI applications? What law and policy should apply to the collection, storage, retention, and use of data generally?

2. AI is brittle with respect to its own situational awareness, but nimble in identifying leads and links involving people in public places and subjects such as sanctions enforcement and proliferation. One intelligence process question is when to rely on AI results outright, when to use it to augment human judgment, and when to ignore it altogether. Is the government relying on AI for these purposes? If so, in accordance with what standards?

What role does AI and what role do humans play in analyzing and using AI outputs? What process exists to validate the outputs after the fact?

3. CI is as important as AI. AI systems offer multiple attack surfaces and weakest link vulnerabilities to penetration and co-option. Policymakers must spend as much time on CI as they do on AI, and triple whatever time is being spent now.

4. Many states are legislating to prohibit the use of deep fakes. Should the Congress do so as well? Should it prohibit deep fakes using certain images, for example, those of public officials, and what are the First Amendment implications of doing so? What policy limits, if any, should the government place on the use of deep fakes for intelligence purposes? Should the government seek to establish domestic or international redlines now?

5. Does military doctrine exist for using AI-enabled systems, including in LAWS? How is human-in-the-loop, on-the-loop, and out-of-the-loop defined and implemented with respect to each application? In the absence of general principles of responsibility and accountability, is a specific official designated as responsible and accountable for each application?

6. How has the government defined "reliability" in the context of code, algorithms, and programs? Is that definition understood and accepted at the policy, legal, and technical policy level? Should the definition vary depending on the application?

7. Does the government have an independent process, such as that found in Civil Liberties and IG offices, for validating the accuracy and reliability of AI applications? Testing for bias? Do the relevant staff have the relevant technical, policy, and legal skill to perform these functions and an appropriate level of access?

In short, is government process nimble enough and "ready enough" to keep pace with AI developments in law and doctrine; in how it contracts; in how it recruits and retains personnel; and in how it uses AI to inform decision? This book is intended to help policymakers address these questions.

FOUR

Sitting on a Hot Frying Pan

NATIONAL SECURITY IMPLICATIONS OF AI

The potential benefits of AI also bring potential problems and challenges. These challenges are tactical, like ensuring AI capabilities are used wisely and fairly as intelligence indicators. They are also strategic, such as the risks that come with technology and arms races. This chapter introduces the reader to some of these risks.

THE LAW OF UNINTENDED CONSEQUENCES AND
THE CHALLENGE OF MACHINE-HUMAN INTERFACE

Technology does not always work as intended. Here we are not just talking about R & D miscues and mistakes, but deployed systems. Some examples are apocryphal; Icarus's wings did not work as intended. Most examples are not apocryphal. The principal attack torpedo in the navy's pre-WWII inventory tended to not explode upon contact and, in some cases, returned (it is thought) to strike the submarine from which it was launched. America's first attempt to launch a satellite after *Sputnik* ended in an explosion on the launch pad. The *Thresher* and *Scorpion* and *Apollo 13* are testimony to technology that worked well and then failed to work as intended. Let's add *Columbia* and *Challenger* to this list. Most recently, we have the Boeing Super Max crashes and the impact of social media on propagating video of the Christchurch terrorist killings as illustrations of technology that failed, did not work as intended, or overwhelmed the capacity of human operators to successfully interface with the technology. There are also examples of technological emergencies that were supposed to take place but did not—like the Y2K crisis, which, some predicted and the government feared, might lead to a cyber-meltdown at the turn of the century.

There is hubris in thinking AI will work precisely as intended. Remember, many current narrow AI applications depend on classifying data and probability assessments about that data. Recall M. L. Cummings's description of driverless cars.

Given this immense problem of computation, in order to maintain safe execution times for action, a driverless car will make best guesses based on probabilistic distributions. In effect, therefore, the car is guessing which path or action is best, given some sort of confidence interval.[1]

But what if the assessment is wrong? With a car, the consequences are presumably finite and limited. Where AI is enabling cyber- or kinetic weapons systems or warning systems, the consequences of AI failure could be catastrophic. Is the Amazon shopping algorithm correct every time? Does the Google search engine always provide a link that answers the question?

The risk with strong AI, commentators such as Nick Bostrum believe, is that you may only have one shot to get the technology right, if indeed the AI-enabled technology, capacity, or weapon is introduced to the internet. It is one thing if it fails to successfully perform its task. But what if that task is lethal or linked to a critical infrastructure? What if it does not shut down as intended or directed? Or continues to pursue its tasks through other machines, even when commanded to stop or disconnected from the internet? Experts express skepticism about how realistic these scenarios are. But how far-fetched is it to ask whether AI will work as intended? What if Stuxnet, for example, was introduced on the internet and not in a confined system, and what if it could not only attack a Siemens-designed supervisory control and data acquisition system (SCADA), but was designed to identify any firewall defenses and rewrite its code to find an entrance?

One lesson from the Cold War is that arms races place pressures on states and actors to produce, deploy, and match technologies before they are ready, tested, and foolproof. The "Get It Right Once" risk might occur in a different kind of setting, where AI is a critical component in a tactical or strategic warning system—for example, a naval system designed to identify and prevent a missile attack, or a satellite system designed to warn of a missile launch.

One way to address unintended consequences is to ensure there is a human in the decision loop to act as a circuit breaker. This seems particularly imperative where weapons are concerned. Here, one of the questions is where to put the human in, on, or out of the loop—again, we have the centaur's dilemma. However, part of the allure and the advantage of AI-enabled systems is their speed and ability to respond in an instantaneous manner, whether responding to swarms, cyberattacks, missile launches, or stock trades. The tension is between taking full advantage of the AI capacity and providing a human air gap in the system—on or in the loop—that will slow it down and introduce both human judgment and frailty. There are military and arms race pressures pushing, perhaps inexorably, toward out-of-the-loop constructions. In cyberspace, there is the added tactical necessity of providing instantaneous defense to cyberattacks.

In such settings, risks may come in threes.

1. *Misunderstanding:* AI appears to work as intended, but the human in the loop does not understand the results.

2. *Fumbled Interface:* The human in the loop does not have time to process or act on the results. Or,

3. *Inaccuracy:* The AI-enabled system and results are not accurate.

Sydney Freedberg and Matt Johnson illustrate some of these risks with reference to Air France flight 447, which crashed in 2009 in the Southern Atlantic Ocean en route from Brazil to France. Apparently, the pilots were unable to transition from autopilot to manual flight during an in-flight emergency caused when external speed gauges likely froze and erroneously signaled the autopilot computer that the aircraft was losing speed and at risk of stalling. The pilots had only seconds to assess the situation and respond. Before they could do so, the aircraft apparently stalled and plunged to the ocean. The authors also cite a 2003 friendly-fire incident in Iraq involving a Patriot battery. The technology worked, but when the technology passed control back to the humans in the loop to make a fire or no-fire decision, the operators were not sure what they were seeing and made an erroneous choice to fire at friendly forces.[2] The USS *Vincennes* incident, involving the shooting down of a civilian Iranian airliner by an Aegis cruiser in 1988 is often cited as an illustration of a technology that worked—the data was correct regarding the speed, direction, and climb of the aircraft—but in the moment, human actors misread the data perceiving an inbound aircraft on an attack azimuth. Scholars speculate that time pressure—and, perhaps, the commander's aggressive disposition—compounded the interface challenge.[3]

The examples continue. In 2018 and 2019, following the crash of two Boeing 737 Max aircraft, safety officials determined new software designed to prevent stalls, known as the Maneuvering Characteristics Augmentation System (MCAS), was at issue. The software was added to the 737 Max because more powerful engines were added to the Max and located in a different place on the airframe than in previous models. The investigations continue; however, flight data indicates the pilots on both aircraft struggled to manually fly the aircraft after the MCAS activated in an erroneous effort to prevent a stall. Investigations also indicate the pilots were not trained on the new software and may not have even known of its existence. They further indicate that different configurations of the software were sold to different airlines and that certain safety features, such as the addition of a second stall warning indicator and a warning light when the indicators were in conflict, were "extras" that cost-saving airlines did not purchase. Finally, it appears that Boeing rushed the 737 Max to market to compete with the new fuel-efficient Airbus A320neo. In the process, Boeing may have persuaded internal and external safety officials, including the FAA, that the aircraft was using existing technology rather than new technology requiring trials and FAA certification.[4] Arms races, like market races, create incentives to cut safety and security corners.

In a different manner, following the terrorist attacks on two mosques in Christchurch, New Zealand, in March 2019, social media outlets struggled to prevent the uploading of videos of the attack despite algorithms designed to identify and remove violent content and specific efforts to remove the Christchurch video. Small modifications in speed, content, and length, it turned out, fooled the corrective algorithms and overwhelmed the capacity of human reviewers to intercede. Meanwhile, push algorithms were automatically "recommending" the video to platform users with a propensity to view violent content. Media estimated 300,000 copies of the video, or portions of the video, were uploaded to the internet despite active human and technical efforts to prevent its promulgation, which blocked an estimated 1.2 million attempts to upload the video.[5] Three points emerge. First, the safety algorithms were, it seems, easily fooled. Second, the human part of the centaur—the humans in the loop—could not keep pace and were overwhelmed by the push algorithms operating on autopilot. Third, offense beat defense; it was easier to upload the video than to take it down.

Now connect these risks to existential weapons. In 1979, in an incident documented by the National Security Archives[6] and recounted in Robert Gates's 1996 book *From the Shadows*, President Carter's national security advisor Zbigniew Brzezinski

> ... was awakened at three in the morning by [military assistant William] Odom, who told him that some 250 Soviet missiles had been launched against the United States. Brzezinski knew that the president's decision time to order retaliation was from three to seven minutes. Thus, he told Odom he would stand by for a further call to confirm Soviet launch and the intended targets before calling the president. Brzezinski was convinced we had to hit back and told Odom to confirm that the Strategic Air Command was launching its planes. When Odom called back, he reported that 2,200 missiles had been launched. It was an all-out attack. One minute before Brzezinski intended to call the president, Odom called a third time to say that other warning systems were not reporting Soviet launches. Sitting alone in the middle of the night, Brzezinski had not awakened his wife, reckoning that everyone would be dead in half an hour. It had been a false alarm. Someone had mistakenly put military exercise tapes into the computer system.[7]

History, in a way, would repeat itself four years later. In a case often cited by AI skeptics, Soviet lieutenant colonel Stanislav Petrov was serving as a watch officer at a Soviet early-warning radar and command center. Alarms indicated the launch of an American first strike at the Soviet Union. Petrov was skeptical. The pattern on the radar did not look like what he anticipated a first strike would look like. There were too few missiles. It was Petrov's duty as senior officer of the watch to call the Kremlin to trigger the Politburo's response, perhaps a nuclear exchange. He stalled. As recounted in his 2017 obituary in the *New York Times* (quoting a BBC Russian service interview thirty years after the incident),

> I had all the data [to suggest there was an ongoing missile attack]. If I had sent my report up the chain of command, nobody would have said a word against it. There was no rule about how long we were allowed to think before we reported a strike. But we knew that every second of procrastination took away valuable time; that the Soviet Union's military and political leadership needed to be informed without delay. All I had to do was to reach for the phone; to raise the direct line to our top commanders—but I couldn't move. I felt like I was sitting on a hot frying pan.[8]

The warning system screamed alert; data pointed to an attack, but with an anomalous pattern. Petrov's military and bureaucratic training might have driven any doubts and decisions up the chain of command. But Petrov's intuition cautioned against doing so. He took the risk of waiting and was right. But not every lieutenant colonel is a Petrov and not every national security advisor a Brzezinski.

With AI, there likely will be less time to think and adjust—that is, if the system is intended to augment human decision, as opposed to displacing it altogether, as in the case of an autonomous and automatic system. Recall that what AI is less good at than humans is situational awareness and judgment, which depend on context, experience, and intuition. It is also more likely that an AI-enabled system will instill greater confidence in its operators than Cold War–era technology, and with good reason. In the abstract, would you be more likely to trust a Soviet-era early warning system or IBM's Watson? Watson, of course. Moreover, narrow AI is best at—and better than humans at—pattern recognition and identification, which is what early warning detection is all about. But let's put the question another way: would you be willing to trust Watson—to bet your life and the survival of humanity on Watson—without first having a trained, calm, and rational officer assess the results?

Brzezinski not only knew enough to verify the initial warning; he appears to have calmly waited as the minutes ticked by for not one, but two verification inquiries. In other words, he was in the loop, and waited in the loop as the clock ticked down. Note as well that according to the National Security Archives, the problem was *not* the mistaken use of an exercise tape but the loading of software into NORAD's computers. As a result, "The information on the display simultaneously appeared on the screens at [Strategic Air Command (SAC)] headquarters and the National Military Command Center . . ." thus in circular manner confirming the attack with two sources.[9]

No doubt informed by these incidents, the United States has stated that it will not deploy weapons systems without a human in the loop, unless an opponent does so first, creating a tactical or strategic advantage. In short, the United States issued a no-first-use pledge. Other states have not provided similar negative security assurances. Arms race pressures to deploy better and faster systems and to maximize the advantages of AI may prompt governments to remove the human from the loop. One immediate question is whether decisionmakers should embed in policy or law a prohibition on the use of autonomous warning systems linked to kinetic weapons and especially nuclear weapons.

The risk of unintended consequences is compounded by three counter-intelligence risks. The first risk is from supply-chain contamination or sabotage. In this scenario, the AI-enabled system does not work as intended because an opponent has altered the circuitry or code involved by introducing faulty hardware or software. The second risk comes in the form of AI used as a weapon, perhaps through supply-chain weakness or through first-mover advantage, causing an opponent's system to fail. Finally, AI presents new capabilities to spoof an opponent by disguising an attack, camouflaging attribution, or engaging in false flag operations. As the DOD *Roadmap* report notes, "This problem is especially apparent in unmanned systems, which by their very nature have an elevated reliance on information systems to function safely, effectively, and consistently."[10]

Finally, a technology arms race is likely to prompt a parallel espionage race. The faster the race the greater the effort to collect information on that race and to curtail an opponent's advantage through theft and espionage. Knowledge of an opponent's capabilities and intentions can be stabilizing, as in the case where actual knowledge debunks perceptions of a bomber or missile gap and thus deters unnecessary and additional arms expenditure. However, it can also be destabilizing where it leads to increased, if not rampant, efforts to penetrate and steal an opponent's knowledge and capabilities, which in the case of AI may also lead to uncertainty over the integrity of any ensuing AI function. In this race, one of military and economic espionage, the United States may find itself at an asymmetric disadvantage, depending on how it approaches the subject of economic espionage in law and policy.[11]

FOREIGN RELATIONS IMPACT

AI will have foreign relations impact in at least eight ways. First, it will affect global stability in known and unknown ways. Former secretary of the treasury and Harvard economist Larry Summers predicts that, on a global basis, we "may have a third of men between the ages of twenty-five and fifty-four not working by the end of this half century." This would represent a higher unemployment rate than during the Depression, affecting political as well as economic stability and potentially leading to mass migration and military conflict.[12]

Second, a global AI economy will potentially reorder our understanding of north-south divides, as well as so-called third-world, second-world, and first-world orders, perhaps by exacerbating those divides. AI capacity may redefine the nature and number of superpowers, a phrase first coined to capture the advent of nuclear weapons.

Third, AI could alter and shuffle the relative power of small, but technologically sophisticated states in terms of economic, political, and military power. Let's call this the AI Singapore Effect. To the extent AI comes to influence, or perhaps transform the nature of military power, it may give smaller, less populous states the military capacity to fight above their weight or do so in an asymmetric manner.

Fourth, so long as military power, intelligence capacity, and economic stability depends on AI, supply-chain security will increase in importance. The import and export control regimes and like-minded regimes will increase in importance as well. AI-enabled technology will only be as good or reliable as the individual components that comprise AI-enabled systems, such as transistors, circuitry, and software. A failure to advance AI capacities could have devastating security impact. So, too, could reliance on an AI-enabled capacity penetrated by an adversary. Policymakers might ask whether it is time for an Australia Group to address the dissemination of AI technologies on a like-minded basis.

Fifth, AI presents asymmetric opportunities for non-state actors just as it creates opportunities for state actors. Unlike nuclear weapons, which present a triad of obstacles to their acquisition, including fissile material, a delivery vehicle, and warhead, AI is potentially accessible to almost every actor at a relatively inexpensive price, depending on how it is defined and what it is used for. Consider, for example, that the autonomous commercial vehicle or remotely piloted aerial delivery system can also be used as a mobile IED or bomb. Likewise, the Stuxnet code jumped the rails, was publicly identified by a private actor, and was reused by non-state actors.[13] AI-driven cyber-tools could be as well.

Sixth, AI may help authoritarian regimes better track and control their populations and retain power. AI algorithms are the censor's tool on the internet. Gregory Allen, coauthor of the Belfer/IARPA study "Artificial Intelligence and National Security," describes how facial recognition is used:

> Snapchat uses AI-enabled facial recognition technology to allow teenagers to send each other funny pictures. China uses the same technology in support of domestic surveillance. Jaywalk across a street in Shenzhen, and you're liable to have your face and name displayed on a screen nearby, along with a police reminder that "jaywalkers" will be captured using facial recognition technology.[14]

With AI, advantage goes to the authoritarian regime and to law enforcement.

Finally, AI will lead to an arms race.

ARMS RACE RISKS AND IMPERATIVES

In 2015, leading AI researchers signed an open letter expressing concern about an AI arms race.

> Many arguments have been made for and against autonomous weapons; for example, replacing human soldiers by machines is good because it reduces casualties for the owner but bad because it lowers the cost threshold for going to battle. The key question for humanity today is whether to start a global AI arms race or to prevent it from starting. If any major military power pushes ahead with AI weapon development, a global arms race is virtually inevitable, and the endpoint of this technological trajectory is obvious: autonomous weapons will become the Kalashnikovs of tomorrow.[15]

So long as states perceive security advantage from AI and, equally important, existential disadvantage from an opponent's AI capacity, they will feel compelled to keep pace and respond in kind or better. An AI "arms race" is not only inevitable, it is already here.

As the Belfer study indicates, and others have observed, AI is a potentially transformative military technology on par with nuclear weapons and the aircraft. It is also a transformative security technology, offering not just military advantage, but economic, intelligence, and decisional benefits. AI offers potentially decisive advantage to any breakout power in the field. That makes this a technology race and not just an arms race. For the United States, AI presents the classic opportunity to offset, that is, compensate for China's advantages in geographic proximity to disputes arising in the Pacific region and numeric advantages in manpower and certain conventional weapons. It also offers the United States the allure of a panacea or technological fix to the challenge of maintaining a large standing military in a cost-conscious democracy.

But offset works both ways. For China, AI-enabled weapons, like swarms, hold the prospect of offsetting America's naval advantages, especially in aircraft carriers, submarines, and ships, while AI-enabled cyber-weapons may mitigate U.S. technological advantages in cyberspace. It also offers China an equal seat at the national security table, while before it was not equal to the

United States or the Soviet Union in a Cold War dominated by nuclear weapons. Commentators note that AI-enabled systems are particularly suited for the vast maritime domain presented in the Pacific, including so-called areas of denial in the Western Pacific, such as the South China Sea.

For Russia, AI-enabled weapons and active measures present new tools to assert "great power" influence, or at least to compete beyond its economic and military means. Russia's willingness to use cyber-tools to interfere in the 2016 and other U.S. elections makes Russia's interest in AI problematic. So does Russia's "asymmetric" willingness to ignore or violate cyber-norms and laws.[16] Given its potential to transform a nation's physical and economic security, no power great or regional can afford to fall too far behind.

This arms race is also a race between systems and the relative security advantages of each. China has the advantage of centralized control and purpose. It also has an enormous and growing cache of data. In 2017, China announced a US$150 billion state-driven program for AI development with a goal of becoming the leading AI economic and security power by 2030. The development plan overtly states as an objective "first-mover advantage" in the development of AI.[17] In this system, the government can channel AI applications to security applications without restriction, just as it can control and access data at the national level for security purposes.

The United States has the advantage of creative dispersion fueled by financial incentive and relative regulatory freedom. In 2019, six of the seven leading AI companies were in the United States.[18] But it should not be lost on American observers that Baidu, Tencent, and other companies are active partners in China's efforts. Moreover, as commentators note, China has had its *Sputnik* AI moment. This occurred when AlphaGo beat China's best player in 2016. China noticed and watched. The United States did not. At least one former senior government official has stated that if this were the Cold War, we would be losing.[19] Others offer optimism. Like China, Russia has the advantage of authoritarian focus, as well as the element of surprise that comes with low expectations and a willingness to operate outside of expected norms. It also has the flexibility and freedom of action that comes from having less stake in the stability and viability of the international economic system and norms. Certain AI applications offer great promise for a government willing to interfere through cyber means in the democratic and economic institutions of other states, such as Estonia (2007), Georgia (2008), and the United States (2016).

There have been other arms races in history. Indeed, policymakers and decisionmakers will search for historical as well as legal metaphor to define and address the questions presented by an AI race. The most obvious metaphor is the nuclear arms race during the Cold War. There are strong similarities, including to the time before nuclear weapons, when scientists and governments raced to harness the power of the atom, not quite sure how, and not quite sure when and to what end and ultimate result. AI, like nuclear weapons in the 1950s, also has the potential to transform military doctrine, spending, and policy. As with the nuclear arms race, until that doctrine is set, understood, and stable, the world may be less stable.

However, there are many differences between AI and nuclear weapons. For one, AI is not a weapon, it is a range of capacities that can be used to enable weapons, robots, and autonomous vehicles and for other purposes. Perhaps it is more like atomic energy, which has both peaceful and military purposes. Two things that do seem more alike than different are the potential for AI to transform military strategy like nuclear weapons before, and the absence of a framework, let alone an agreed framework, to address the legal, moral, and ethical issues presented. Because security entails both physical safety and the preservation of our values, we should create such a framework now. That is what it means to both support and defend the Constitution. While nuclear weapons provide the most apt metaphors, arms control and the law of armed conflict (LOAC) offer additional lessons from which to assess AI.

As discussed in chapters 8 and 9, the threshold question now is which lessons are most apt. Policymakers, lawyers, and ethicists should ask:

What lessons can be learned from the Cold War arms race?

What principles from arms control and LOAC might or should apply to AI?

What strategic and tactical doctrine should apply to AI-enabled weapons, weapons systems, and warning components?

What are the opportunity costs of an AI arms race?

AN INCREASE IN CONFLICT?

A greater number of automated and unmanned kinetic and cyber-weapons selections could change the policy calculus for employing military force, as UAVs have done. Commentators debate whether AI-enabled warfare will increase the risk of conflict by reducing its "cost," at least to the initiator of action. The calculus may change, the argument goes, because force may be used with less risk to U.S. military personnel and collateral civilian harm. The same argument was, and is, made with respect to UAVs. Of course, international law and policy is reciprocal. Thus, if this assessment is correct, AI-enabled weapons may increase the frequency in which such weapons are used against the United States and not just by the United States.

It is also possible that AI-enabled weapons may *reduce* the risk of conflict by *increasing* its costs, or by changing the military balance of power. For example, swarm technology may make surface ships and especially aircraft carriers vulnerable in ways that will limit the way military power is projected across oceans and from offshore. Likewise, some war game modeling indicates that with AI-enabled weapons casualties in a Pacific war between the United States and China could be in the hundreds of thousands within days.[20] To avoid a costly conflict, the United States may be less inclined to defend Taiwan with naval power in the Taiwan Straits than before. If this alternative calculus is correct, it will necessitate changes in policy or changes in deterrence strategy, most likely both. Whether this is a good policy outcome or not is a different question from whether it makes conflict more or less likely. AI-enabled, or lethal, AWS could dramatically increase rather than decrease the cost of conflict.

Just as AI may augment the U.S. security toolbox, it will augment the adversary's toolbox. Thus, policymakers need to anticipate new weapons, new threats, and new uses for AI whether those uses are contemplated by the United States or not. We have seen this with Russian information operations in cyberspace, where much of the action is occurring below the level of armed conflict. These are not remarkable insights, but they dominate the literature on AWS, along with debate over whether and when a human should or must be engaged in the decision to use lethal force generally or against specific targets.

DECISIONMAKING PATHOLOGIES

As AI will introduce new capabilities and risks, it will also exacerbate existing national security decisionmaking pathologies, especially those associated with the rapidity of decision and secrecy. "Pathology" is defined here as a factor or condition that undermines optimal decisionmaking. Good process—meaning timely, contextual, and meaningful, along with calm leadership—is the antidote to the decisional pathologies. However, they are mitigating antidotes, not eliminating immunizations. Five prevalent pathologies are:

- Speed

- Secrecy

- Incomplete and/or lack of complete information

- A focus on the immediate, and

- The national security imperative

Issues of cognitive bias also come into play, especially in how decision-makers analyze information, assess history, and apply doctrinal perspectives. AI has the potential to exacerbate, or mitigate, each of these pathologies.

Bureaucratic Speed and Machine Speed

Let's focus on the rapidity of national security decisionmaking, because speed is a signature attribute of most AI applications. It is also a factor that can aggravate most of the underlying AI risks. Indeed, it is certain to do so, as it has in cyberspace. Because security actors cannot risk an adversary gaining a first-mover advantage, decisionmakers may feel pressure to change the way decisions are made, to take shortcuts, and, perhaps, to remove humans from the decisional loop.

Rapid decisions are endemic to national security. The compulsion and necessity for speed comes from several factors. In the case of real-world events, the need for speed is intuitive. If you are reacting to or seeking to influence events, your timeline is dictated by those events and not by optimum considerations of process, factual development, and policy consideration. Moreover, opponents may seek moments of distraction and commitment to act presenting additional challenges and further minimizing the capacity and time to respond. The intelligence process seeks to prevent surprise and to provide early warning, and thus extend decisional timelines and mitigating opportunities. But intelligence is an imperfect instrument for reasons of scope, capability, and the simple difficulty of predicting or seeing actions that are designed to be hidden.

The media cycle also feeds the need, or at least the pressure to act with speed. This started as the "CNN effect," the impact of a twenty-four-hour news cycle driving a parallel response cycle. Rather than digesting and responding in a deliberate manner, each event or story now seemingly necessitates an immediate response before someone else controls the narrative. Executive actors buy into the cycle so as not to appear to be in a reactive mode, indifferent, and so that their version or understanding of the story is told. Alas, and of course, to those who draft and review government press guidance, the CNN days seem like the good old days of thoughtful and timely reflection. The media cycle is further compressed by the advent of new platforms and a decline in the societal ethic of what it means to produce and espouse fact-based news on either side of the microphone. Let's call this last factor the "Moynihan effect," after Senator Daniel Patrick Moynihan, who coined the phrase "You are entitled to your own opinion, but not your own facts." Not anymore. Moynihan sensed what was coming. But Moynihan passed away in 2003, before the advent of Twitter, Facebook, and the internet gave every person a media platform. It was also before push algorithms and information bots. Executive actors, including the president, may feel compelled to respond to every tweet and post and not just inquiries from established media outlets, if they are not already affirmatively using these platforms to shape the news.

Technology has also changed the decisionmaking timeline, and not just in the handling of public communications. The most dramatic manifestation of this trend is in the realm of cyber-operations. Cyber-tools used for hacking, crime, espionage, and information operations are instantaneous in effect. That means that to be effective, technology-based defenses must be instantaneous or proactive. In cyberspace, decisionmakers are always on the clock and this clock runs on milliseconds.

Technology has influenced the necessity of decisional speed in other dramatic ways as well, including, for example, the use of algorithm-based hedge fund trading that can lead to instantaneous or flash market crashes, without human decision, intent, or action. This was the case with the 2010 Flash Crash, an event cited by many AI analysts. The crash was AI-driven. The need for machine speed led traders to remove human decisionmakers from the operational loop, because humans could not compute the marginal gains or losses from fractional trades fast enough to compete against algorithms making the same trades.[21] Humans are involved in the decision chain—in writing the codes that inform algorithms that drive the trades—but the codes are opaque to public inspection and regulation, even if the economic and potential national security consequences are not. The market fell almost a thousand points in under fifteen minutes before largely recovering, in part because a different algorithm triggered a pause in trading on the Chicago Mercantile Exchange.

In ironic fashion, bureaucracy can also create its own necessity for speed. It is ironic, because "bureaucracy" is associated with layered delay. Here, delay and speed work together. It originates when one part of the bureaucracy takes too much time necessitating that another part act with too little. This may occur naturally, for example, when it takes time to identify the expert or process in the government to effectively address the subject at hand. The issue may be out of the ordinary or unpracticed, illustrated by the government's response to the 2010 Deepwater Horizon BP oil spill in the Gulf of Mexico or the 2015 response to the West African Ebola crisis. The executive branch had not prepared for, nor practiced a response to these specific, or even general types of crises. In such situations, by the time a national decision is framed and presented, if there is one to be made at all, there is "no time left to make it." This does not excuse the delay, it explains it.

More commonly, bureaucratic delay necessitating rapid decision derives from bureaucratic function. Bureaucratic actors put off the near term in favor of the immediate, until the near term becomes the immediate. This may happen when key staff actors are not responsible, accountable, or identifiable within the decisionmaking process; in other words, they are critical, without feeling the burden and responsibility of being critical. Think here of a deadline to transfer aid, or provide a report, or make a speech. So long as responsibility is anonymous or diffuse, the staff actor or agency has incentive to hold the matter until the last minute, at which point the actor or agency will urgently convey the matter up the chain of command for immediate decision.

The legislative cycle has come to operate in a similar way, on a perpetual delay-speed cycle. The Congress sits on an issue for months, and then rushes to complete a funding or policy task at the last minute, using the leverage of a real-world deadline to help create the political necessity and cover for acting. That this delay is artificial, or self-induced, does not change the imperative to act with speed, or some might say haste, when the decisionmaker or institution with authority is finally presented with options.

Finally, bureaucratic speed can be necessitated by false deadlines, of the sort that occur when decisionmakers want to get something done on their timeline. This may occur for convenience—"I want the proposal before I go on my trip." Or it may be used to drive bureaucracy—"If I do not get this proposal by Friday, I will fire you." All of which is not necessarily good or bad, but it does sometimes explain the necessity for speed.

Machine speed is altogether different from bureaucratic speed. Machine decisions are instantaneous. In many cases, they are also pre-set based on software and algorithms, or pre-delegated based on human choice and decision. AI will, or can, depending on how it is applied, mitigate the impact of speed on decisionmaking as well as exacerbate it and do so in profound ways. A decisional process that is not ready for these impacts may not reap the advantages of AI capacity and eschew the use of a valuable tool. However, decisionmakers may swing in the other direction and rely on AI-driven actions when human judgment and decision are needed.

There are added risks generated by machine speed. Because AI moves so quickly—and must, if it is to be effective—in some situations, decisionmakers may have less time or no time (or perceive that they have less time or no time) to respond. This can drive policymakers to rapid decisions or to defer to automatic responses, which may or may not be optimally tailored to actual events or situational facts. Imagine an instantaneous Schlieffen Plan. This is, of course, already an existing reality in the realm of cybersecurity and cyber-operations. In cyberspace, there is risk in waiting to respond to an attack while facts are gathered, attribution confirmed, and options identified. This paradigm may drive automatic responses to defensive options and away from offensive-defensive or offensive responses that may more effectively stop attacks and serve to deter future attacks.

EXISTENTIAL THREAT?

Some commentators believe that AI in the potential form of superintelligent artificial intelligence (SAI) presents an existential threat to humanity. Others place SAI in the realm of science fiction, finding it an overwrought distraction from the real and immediate security and commercial applications and implications of AI. However, given the media attention afforded to the topic, security and legal generalists ought to understand the argument and its nomenclature. In 2017, while touring Yandex—one of Russia's leading AI labs— Vladimir Putin was recorded asking the CEO, "When will it eat us?"[22] The question received media mockery. But AI specialists would know the question arose from the debate about AI as an existential threat. They would further understand that the concern presented was not the risk that the AI system might one day eat its developers, but the reality that the president of Russia was immersed in AI at this level of detail.

The most visible proponents of the existential-threat school are Tesla CEO Elon Musk and the late Cambridge astrophysicist Stephen Hawking. In a widely quoted speech, Hawking concluded, "The rise of powerful AI will be either the best or the worst thing ever to happen to humanity. We do not yet know which. That is why, in 2014, I and a few others called for more research to be done in this area."[23]

Musk, in turn, has stated, "AI is a fundamental existential risk for human civilization, and I do not think people fully appreciate that . . . [AI is] the scariest problem. I think by the time we are reactive in AI regulation, it's too late. . . . I keep sounding the alarm bell."[24]

On the question of existential threat, an outside observer might divide the AI community into the following three camps.

The end of the human era. The journalist James Barrat states his thesis in the title of his book *Our Final Invention*. The premise of the book, and this school of thought, is that scientists, governments, and industry are inexorably marching toward the creation of superintelligent artificial intelligence. The motivation to do so varies. There is the promise of curing cancer and other diseases. There is the allure of making money. There is the prospect of immortality. There is also the sense, as there was with nuclear weapons, that some scientists and engineers simply cannot stop pushing to the edge of the possible. The thesis further posits that humankind will lose control of its own invention, however benign or noble the initial intent.

AI will become humankind's last invention, because SAI-enabled machines will optimize and maximize whatever it is they are initially programmed to do. But having achieved SAI, and thus the capacity to outthink their inventors, they will rewrite their instructions to override the "off switch," or to hide their ability to do so, until they have propagated through the internet to survive beyond their immediate source of power and connection to the outside world. This scenario is characterized in different ways with varying anthropomorphic effect.

One version of this scenario is the Bostrum Paper Clip Optimizer.[25] The paper clip is chosen because there is nothing inherently good or bad about a paper clip, or a paper clip machine. However, having achieved SAI, the machine rewrites its code to optimize paper clip production. Thus, using the internet and its superior knowledge, the optimizer diverts all sources of energy to its paper clip efforts. Next, of course, it converts all sources of carbon into energy. Humans are made of carbon, and thus, eventually, the machine programs other machines to capture and turn humans into carbon energy. The paper clip machine is not evil, it is just good at what it does.

Friendly and unfriendly AI—The fork in the road. This camp includes scientists, businessmen, and commentators who believe AI could go either way. AI could be a force for good like no other; it could help find a cure for cancer, solve climate change, and alleviate hunger and poverty. Or it could be a force of harm. AI could become unfriendly because of unintended or unanticipated effects, like the paper clip optimizer, or more likely because humans program AI to do unfriendly things. The fork in the road is at the root of Hawking's and Musk's concerns. It also informs Nick Bostrum's concerns. Bostrum postulates "an extremely good or an extremely bad outcome is more likely than a more balanced outcome."[26]

Keep calm and carry on. The third camp is largely the province of governments and technology companies. It acknowledges the risk but embraces a fundamental confidence that AI will be a force for good and will ultimately evolve in a positive manner under human control. This view is captured in IBM senior scientist Murray Campbell's 2016 response to Hawking and Musk:

> I definitely think it's overblown. It's worthwhile to think about these research questions around AI and ethics, and AI and safety. But it's going to be decades before this stuff is really going to be important. The big danger right now, and one of IBM's senior VPs has stated this publicly, is not following up on these technologies.[27]

This view is also captured in the Stanford *100 Year Study of AI*, which concludes:

> While the study panel does not consider it likely that near-term AI systems will autonomously choose to inflict harm on people, it will be possible for people to use AI-based systems for harmful as well as helpful purposes.[28]

Contrary to more fantastic predictions for AI in the popular prose, the study panel found no cause for concern that AI is an imminent threat to humankind.[29]

This is almost identical to the view of Ryan Calo: "My own view is that AI does not present an existential threat to humanity, at least not in anything like the foreseeable future."[30]

There are seeds of caution in terms like "near-term," "imminent," and "at least not in anything like the foreseeable future." One reason this camp is optimistic about AI is that they do not believe AI will work entirely as anticipated and thus be as omnipresent and efficient at making paper clips, or whatever it is programmed to do, as some have forecast. Again, IBM engineer Murray Campbell:

When was the last time somebody walked into your office and posed a perfectly well-formed, unambiguous question that had all of the information in it required to give a perfectly formed, unambiguous answer? It just does not happen in the real world.[31]

But if confidence comes from a lack of perfection, we find ourselves back at the first risk identified in this chapter, the risk that AI will not function as intended.

TAKEAWAYS

AI comes with great promise and potential risk. While much of the popular commentary focuses on "existential risk," one suspects that some of the doomsday rhetoric is motivated by a desire to generate discussion and avert worst-case scenarios, not necessarily predict them. Let's focus on the real, known, and immediate risks:

1. Technology rarely works entirely as intended, at least at the outset. Scientists in the weapons field and others have not demonstrated a long track record of self-regulation when peril and promise converge on the road to knowledge. Moreover, so long as AI in some form and in some manner holds out the prospect of military advantage, including existential military advantage, national security actors will strive to keep pace. They cannot risk doing otherwise.

2. AI may first drive decisionmakers to act quickly, too quickly, perhaps automatically, based on percentages, models, and potential false positives, without time for reflection and the sort of slow thinking that also should inform national security. This is the centaur's dilemma.

3. AI-enabled weapons and trip wires may increase the risk of mistaken war as well as intended war. This risk already occurs in cyberspace, but heretofore, it has been contained to cyberspace. AI has the potential to combine the risk of Cold War nuclear first strikes, real and perceived, with the immediacy of cyber-operations. When AI enables weapons across the spectrum from space to sea, it has the potential to place global warfare on a hair trigger. That trigger may be an AI-enabled maritime weapon intended to detect the approach of an offensive swarm, and it may be an AI-enabled

counter-battery weapon at the Korean DMZ or on the Golan Heights that is programmed to respond before it is too late to defend.

One purpose of law and process is to mitigate these risks while maximizing opportunities to reap the benefits of technology.

.

PART II

The Centaur's Choice

FIVE

Toward a Legal Framework

The previous chapters describe how AI will transform intelligence and military systems and capabilities. Part II of this book discusses the present and perhaps future legal framework for addressing the applications and implications of AI used for national security purposes. A legal framework should start with an understanding of the three purposes of law: (1) the authority to act and the boundaries of that action; (2) process; and (3) essential values. Design of a framework should also take into account what happens in the absence of a framework or where the law is unclear, inapt, or ill-fitting, which leads to this chapter's takeaways. First, an absence of statutory law increases the importance of constitutional law and principles. The Constitution is one law that always applies. The question is how. Second, lawyers will apply the law they have. Third, lawyers will look for law to apply by analogy. That is, after all, what lawyers do when they apply case law: they search for metaphor. Finally, private actors and litigation will play a disproportionate role in filling legal gaps.

THE THREE PURPOSES OF NATIONAL SECURITY LAW

The three purposes of law are especially relevant to AI because a legal regime for addressing AI does not exist, or, at best, is in nascent form. That means the law is unsettled with respect to all three purposes—or, if one prefers, all three are in play. This presents an opportunity to get it right from the outset. It also presents challenges—to do so before necessity otherwise compels the use of ill-fitting old law to perform new or unintended tasks. The absence of clear law may also drive parties to litigate questions of authority and values that are better resolved through policy deliberation or the legislative process.

Authority and Boundaries

The first purpose of national security law is to provide the substantive authority to act, as well as the left and right boundaries of that action. Most government actors and observers recognize this aspect of law. What is less evident is how *clear law, clearly invoked* leads to greater risk-taking, which can be good and bad. It is also less likely to lead to litigation and thus allows decisionmakers to focus on policy issues as opposed to legal disputes. The legislative process can also be an effective mechanism to adjudicate competing values as well as establish national policy legitimacy, although passage of law is difficult and often imperfect in result. Law also protects, or can. It protects privacy. It protects the government from allegations of overreaching and abuse, by delimiting authority. It protects industry from litigation or sanction over the collection, handling, and use of data. Further, law mitigates against piecemeal policy and pendulum swings, allowing for more predictable decisionmaking and long-term investment.

At the strategic level, the threshold substantive question for policymakers to ask is: does the government have the legal authority it needs to research, develop, deploy, and use AI? If so, policymakers should then consider how to delimit that authority. When should the law allow machines to make decisions, or allow machines to augment human decisionmaking and in what manner? In doing so, they should identify the core principles that should inform these choices. In addition, policymakers should decide whether to establish boundaries around AI, such as the use of deep fakes or the linking of AI systems to weapons. Specifically, policymakers should answer the following three questions:

1. Are there certain tasks or decisions that are, or should be, reserved for human choice and decision rather than delegated to machines? This question parallels the question asked during the Iraq War of civilian contractors—are there inherently governmental activities (IGA) that should not be assigned to contractors? As with contractors, the AI debate has focused on the use of force and LAWS. But the questions are much broader with AI. There is risk that exclusive focus on weapons systems will mask the many other AI applications, presenting ethical choices about whether machines, humans, or some combination of both should initiate or confirm an AI application. Consider four scenarios:

- The decision to trigger a kinetic weapon. As noted, this is already widely debated.
- The decision to trigger a cyber-weapon in response to a cyberattack.
- A decision to deprive a person of life, liberty, or property based on the algorithmic prediction of risk.
- A decision to regulate or terminate social media speech. Aside from LAWS, this is likely the most debated AI decisional application. It is also the most immediate application, at least on private social media platforms, where First Amendment concerns regarding government conduct are often less evident absent a direct legislative or regulatory mandate.

2. Should there be use redlines? The U.S. intelligence community has rules, and perhaps prohibitions, governing such things as the recruitment of members of the media, clergy, and Peace Corps volunteers, and economic espionage for the benefit of specific private entities. Informed by such regulation, one might ask whether there should be ethical prohibitions or limitations placed on certain national security uses of AI, such as deep fakes.

The same AI capacities that have resulted in voice recognition applications, better-than-human tumor detection imaging, and facial recognition applications also offer new capabilities to capture and mimic aural and visual patterns and thus the capacity to realistically mimic or manipulate those patterns. Restated, if AI can be used for translation, it can be used to capture and imitate a voice. High quality imitations of voices or video images are known as deep fakes. Many U.S. states have passed laws criminalizing deep fake pornography, which is usually created by synthesizing a known person's face onto a real but unknown person's body. This can be done with such seamless precision it appears authentic, as game producers and Hollywood engineers already know.

The policy question is whether we should limit or prohibit the use of certain deep fake applications for security purposes. Governments might choose to do so on a unilateral basis, like-minded basis, or as a matter of domestic and/or international law. In any event, for reasons of stability or reciprocity, governments (or other actors) might eschew their own use of AI to:

1. Interfere in the domestic politics of other countries with the use of fake videos or images of candidates.

2. Portray public officials in fake pornography (a virtual honey trap without actual need for a trap).

3. Mimic the words or images of public officials, or certain public officials.

4. Or do so only in instances when those public officials are engaged in official acts or would be perceived to be engaged in official acts, or certain official acts, such as emergency response or the command and control of military forces or certain weapons.

While deep fakes may present the most immediate set of policy and ethical choices for security decisionmakers, other questions arise regarding the potential deployment of AI because of the risk of unintended consequences, known and unknown gradations in accuracy, or the risks associated with operating at machine speed. Thus, policymakers and lawyers should also ask whether AI should be:

- Linked to early warning systems? If so, with what degree of human control or augmentation?

- Linked to nuclear weapon command and control mechanisms?

- Deployed into space?

- Linked to cyber-tools and weapons, or certain offensive cyber-tools?

- Purposefully introduced into the Dark Web or Dark Net, with or without limitation?

3. What rules should apply to data management and use? Data is the lifeblood of machine learning and the algorithms that drive it. Therefore, governments, academia, and industry are eager to collect, store, farm, and sell data. Generally, the more data one has to train an algorithm the more accurate the AI output. This is intuitive. The more images a person sees of naval vessels the more likely they are going to accurately distinguish between types of vessels and the countries of origin of those vessels. What is less intuitive, at least to non-specialists, is just how large the data sets are that companies and governments use to train AI algorithms.

There is an active literature (and debate) in computer science over how much data is needed to train a machine learning algorithm. The answer is, it depends. It depends on the number of parameters a computer model is intended to address or that will affect the operation of a model. It also depends on the intended accuracy expected or error rate tolerated. It will also depend on the relevance of the data set to the assigned task. The critical takeaway for a lawyer or ethicist is a sense of scale. The Google FaceNet facial detection and recognition application was trained on 450,000 sample images. The MIT *Computer Science and Artificial Intelligence Laboratory* (CSAIL) image application was trained on 185,000 images, 62,000 annotated images, and 650,000 labeled objects.[1] Notably, this volume also involves man-hours for labeling images, as well as electrical and storage costs.

The use of data poses complex legal and policy questions regarding the collection, use, storage, access, and transfer of data. Embedded in each of these functions are questions involving security, privacy, authenticity, and ownership, to name a few. This is before one contemplates that, for reasons of security, efficiency, and law, data is sometimes broken up and simultaneously stored in multiple countries—and thus across legal, normative, and ethical cultures and jurisdictions. Indeed, the data questions are so complex U.S. law and policy have defaulted to the status quo, which means national security policy is determined based on the interests and instincts of individual companies or the resolution of specific disputes through litigation.

Nonetheless, five ethical issues recur in almost every data context and should be purposefully addressed by lawyers and policymakers, preferably in the form of binding national policy, which means, in law:

- What data should be subject to collection?
- By whom?
- How should it be stored and subject to what safeguards?
- How should it be used?
- When may it be transferred?

However, because each scenario presents different variables depending on the data, the actor, and the use, there is no correct or singular answer to each question. Policymakers should also consider whether certain types of data should receive privileged status for ethical or other reasons, just as medical data and personal identifying information are subject to safeguards. For example, one might decide, as a matter of moral choice and law, not to use the images of persons under the age of eighteen to train AI or to leverage the provision of a right or public resource for the purpose of collecting AI data, such as currently done with license photos in many states.[2] Legislators should also consider whether there should be civil or criminal consequences for scraping (collecting) data from social media sites in contravention of company use agreements or privacy permits. Is this theft or fraud? And, if theft or fraud, who is the victim(s) and who should be held responsible?

Process

The second purpose of national security law is process. Law here refers not only to statutory law, but also constitutional law and executive and administrative directives, like presidential orders and agency guidelines. The Constitution, the root of American law, is at heart a procedural rather than substantive document. For sure, there are grants of enumerated substantive authority, and detailed specifications about topics like elections, but the genius of the framework is that it does not seek to provide substantive answers to every governance question. Rather, it creates what is, so far, an enduring process to allow future actors to address new questions as well as rethink old ones. This process is found most notably in three places: (1) the shared and separate powers between the three branches of the federal government; (2) the concept of vertical federalism, by which the original colonies granted certain enumerated authority to a federal government but retained or reserved to the individual states the remainder of governmental authority; and (3) the Bill of Rights, the first eleven amendments to the Constitution, including the First, Fourth, and Fifth Amendments, which include many of the rights in play with AI applications, such as due process.

Wherever found, process can be good or bad. Bad process is unduly layered, slow, and diffuses or hides responsibility, and thus accountability. Good process is timely, contextual, and meaningful. It provides for unity of command, identifies dissent, offers mitigation, establishes responsibility, and addresses the pathologies of national security decisionmaking, like speed and security. Good process is also embedded in law or directive to mitigate against the tendency, in times of urgency or for reasons of expedience, to bypass key actors and avoid crucial questions by using informal process and hand-chosen participants. Because AI will, or could, transform national security decision-making, government process must address three core issues:

- When and how to operate at machine speed.

- How best to consider the long-term consequences of our AI choices as well as the short-term benefits.

- When, whether, and how to rely on black box determinations or permit algorithms to predict human behavior so that humans can act upon those predictions to take preemptive action.

A process that effectively and safely answers these three questions will pass a different kind of Turing test—the Turing test of process.

THE TURING TEST OF PROCESS

Policymakers understand the importance of operational timelines. But their sense of imminence is more Daniel Webster than Alan Turing.[3] Most policymakers have not thought through the policy implications and effects of machine speed on decisionmaking, such as the necessity of programming or delegating decisions in advance to take advantage of the capabilities AI offers.[4] This also means they are less conscious of the risks of acting at machine speed, such as not being able to recalibrate a software response based on changed circumstances or new context. Think here about the tyranny of 1914 railway timetables, of "the launch on warning" scenarios embedded in early versions of mutual assured destruction, and of Lieutenant Colonel Petrov.[5] The centaur's dilemma is how to maximize the benefit of AI tools operating at machine speed without losing control of decisions or surrendering those decisions to automatic responses devoid of the situational awareness that comes with knowing an adversary's actual rather than anticipated responses.

The key is to have a process that aligns with specific tools. That usually means the same process is not the optimum process, or even a good process, for different issues. It does not make sense, for example, to use the same process to address an Ebola outbreak as to formulate cyber-deterrence policy. Neither does it make sense to have the same process for every national security use of an AI system. The Defense Department alone has an estimated six hundred active projects; each may require a tailored process for safe and effective use. However, good process will invariably include the following:

Unity of command. In military parlance, this means subordinate commanders are seeking to accomplish the same objectives in response to the same higher command intent or purpose. With AI, this means DOD, Google, and MIT are not each making their own national security policy, but rather working toward their own objectives within a unified legal and policy framework.

Unity and clarity of message. A clear single explanation of the what, how, and why of government action along with the legal authority for the action.

The identification and mitigation of risk and dissent. Good process includes assessment of the pros and cons of options and identifies what is known and not known factually and with what degree of confidence.

Practice and exercise. Realistic exercises help to identify where policy and legal seams exist and where personality and leadership issues might arise. Exercises will also illustrate to policymakers how AI can be used, should be used, and shouldn't be used.

Responsibility. Good process fixes responsibility in a named official(s), using an identified process(es). With AI responsibility includes everything that takes place or does not take place to include the effective functioning of any technological system.

Accountable decisionmaking. Such decision is documented and transparent so that designated officials can review what has happened, appraise the results and the process, and make necessary adjustments—to policy, to process, and to the technology that informed both.

AI requires new expertise and new participants in the policy process. This may include engineers, statisticians, and software experts who can explain to policymakers and intelligence officials in plain English what it is AI can and cannot do and with what degree of accuracy. It will also invariably need to include younger, more technically savvy participants.

AI also requires a new approach to decisionmaking with more attention paid to contingency planning and response, which necessarily means with less emphasis on responsive decisionmaking. If it does not include greater emphasis on alternative futures analysis and red team scenarios, we will not take advantage of existing AI capabilities, let alone emerging capabilities. And it will require conscious regulation of the speed at which decisions are taken, and whether those decisions are allowed to occur automatically, as might be the case in certain cyber-scenarios, or require affirmative human decision, as might be the case with the release of kinetic weapons or the targeting of certain objects.

A good interagency process, for example, might include the National Institute of Standards and Technology (NIST) to identify the key technological questions, including the limits of software coding, key timelines, and milestones. The Office of Management and Budget (OMB) or the Office of Science and Technology Policy (OSTP), in turn, might run a policy process to identify the critical policy questions and breakpoints that might then result in draft legislation. An interagency lawyers' group at the National Security Council (NSC) might identify the most difficult legal questions and then create a process to resolve each or seek legislation to do so. A good AI process will also timely, contextually, and meaningfully address the following policy, algorithmic, and data-based questions:

Policy questions

- Does the U.S. government have a policy and doctrinal framework in which to apply AI, including a doctrine of deterrence and of first use, so that we are purposeful in our actions rather than random or episodic?

- Are there seams between military and intelligence uses of AI and policy expectations about how AI will be used?

- Is the U.S. government prepared to explain the actions it takes using AI, including actions not intended to become known, in order to define new norms in customary international law and to demonstrate how U.S. actions are legally or morally distinct or equivalent to reciprocal conduct by other actors? (Sound policy is often undermined by an inability or unwillingness to explain it.)

- Is U.S. policy being set at the agency level or the national level? Is it being set by individual corporate, agency, and academic actors, or in a national manner?

- Is U.S. policy being implemented and observed by U.S. businesses and academics in their conduct overseas and with foreign entities?

Algorithmic questions

- What criteria (parameters) are embedded in the original AI algorithm? Do experts and policymakers consider these parameters relevant and material to the questions presented and for which AI is used?

- Do those criteria include racial, ethnic, gender, or other sensitive categories? If so, why? Have engineers and lawyers reviewed the way these criteria were incorporated into the design of the application? How are they weighted in and by the algorithm? Are these questions reviewed and considered on an ongoing basis? (See chapter 6.)

- Are there situational factors or facts in play that might, could, or should alter the algorithmic prediction? Is the application one in which nuance and cultural knowledge is relevant? If so, has that knowledge been applied?

- What are the risks that the application has been penetrated, spoofed, or trained on poisoned data?

- How accurate is the algorithm? What confidence threshold have decisionmakers applied? What is the false positive rate? What is the false negative rate?

- When the algorithm is wrong, why and how is it wrong? What types of false positives occur? What types of missed identifications? What corrections have been made?

- Has the decisionmaker relied on factors other than those provided by the AI application? If so, what factors? What weight was given to these factors? Do these factors corroborate or run counter to the AI results? Why and how?

- Has the technology been designed to allow operators to access answers to these questions? If so, how are the answers documented? If not, why not?

Data questions
- What is the derivation and history of the data in use?
- Has the data been collected with or without consent? Why?
- Who has had access to the data?
- Is there a data chain of custody? If not, why not?
- Is there a data access registry?
- What is the age of the data?
- What would an ideal data set look like in terms of content, size, and age for the purpose at hand? How does the actual data set vary and with what potential impact?
- Is the volume of data proportionate to the task assigned?
- Has the data been stored in a secure manner commensurate with its current, as well as potential future, value? Has the data been breached? With what degree of certainty is that conclusion reached?
- Does the data set comply with established legal, policy, or ethical redlines? Are those redlines known to AI designers and operators?

- Do the answers to the questions above suggest that additional restrictions should apply to the collection, storage, use, or transfer of the data in question?

Now is the time to get the AI process right. A process that passes this Turing test is one that can answer these questions contextually, effectively build private-public partnerships in the AI community, operate day-to-day and not just in crisis, and move at machine speed when needed and it is wise to do so. If we do not get the process right—timely, contextual, and meaningful—it will not matter how good our AI is. Good process will also purposefully address the following AI challenges.

MACHINE SPEED AND MATHEMATICAL DECISION

AI may place additional pressure on decisionmakers to act in an instantaneous manner—that is, at machine speed, as has already been done in response to cyberattacks. However, AI will both assist with speed and compound its risks.

First, the combination of algorithmic intelligence and computational speed can help decisionmakers fuse relevant information faster and more effectively than humans. AI will also help decisionmakers shape and test options. The core strength of narrow AI—pattern identification, link-analysis, anomaly detection—is tailored for intelligence flags and warnings. All of which create more time for decisionmakers to process information, frame options, and make decisions.

Second, AI's impact reaches beyond cyber-operations to the full range of foreign policy contexts as well as all domains of potential conflict: maritime, air, space, and land. Thus, the ramifications of machine-speed decisionmaking could be far-reaching.

Third, AI may convey a sense of mathematical confidence, or lack of confidence, to decisionmakers, which may prove false in context. National security is an art, not a science. National security policy cannot be reduced to a mathematical formula or probability. Even if it could, one's opponent could spoof the formula. Rather, policymaking combines fact with intuition, doctrine, historical knowledge, values, and judgment about reactions and counterreactions.

In short, most national security issues do not lend themselves to formulaic response. However, machine learning is computational, and thus classifies facts or options that present policy choices as probabilities, expressed either in terms of a conclusion (there is a 76 percent chance this is a tumor), or in terms of an accuracy of instrument (AI-enabled radiology analysis is correct

76 percent of the time). Some decisionmakers covet these judgments because it makes hard decisions easier. Who can object to moving forward if there is a 76 percent chance of a policy action working? For these reasons, intelligence analysts—and directors of national intelligence—are constantly pushed to put a percentage on their judgments. And these same actors resist, resorting instead to proximate phrases like "more likely than not," or "in our judgment."[6]

There can be comfort in numbers. But there is also decisional risk on both a tactical and strategic level. Can a decision to target an individual combatant be reduced to a formula? And what if situational awareness suggests a less certain reality? Would some of the great national security judgments in history lend themselves to formulaic responses?

How would the Dunkirk evacuation operation have looked if the logistics were first run through AI applications, or the overall possibility of success or failure classified by a percentage? Would it have been possible to compute the risk to morale of not trying? Or what percentage of men on the beach were needed to prevent a subsequent invasion of the United Kingdom?

AI would certainly have helped predict the weather on June 6, and for the coming weeks. But would it have made the decision to go, or not go, any less instinctive?

And how would AI have influenced President George H. W. Bush's decision not to push on to Baghdad at the close of the First Gulf War? No doubt, the computations would have indicated a favorable prognosis for success, making it all the harder to say no.

There also seems to be a qualitative and moral difference between (1) a decision to strike a target with a Hellfire missile based on an algorithm's 76 percent–accurate predictive probability that a pattern of life reflects terrorist activity and (2) the informed judgment of the director of national security that the person is a terrorist posing imminent threat to the United States.

Fourth, with machine-driven predictions such as those generated by neural networks, decisionmakers may not fully understand the basis of their own policy choices and decisions. This will make it harder for decisionmakers to explain their choices, or it may lead them to forsake the use of a valuable security tool to augment the decisionmaking function. Daniel Kahneman received a Nobel Memorial Prize in Economic Sciences for his work identifying the differences in brain function between what he described as fast and slow thinking. Fast thinking is automatic, frequent, emotional, and unconscious. Slow thinking is logical, calculating, and deliberate. National security decisionmaking requires both. Narrow AI seems especially suited to augment national security decisionmaking, not supplant it. A timely, contextual, and meaningful decision process should and must incorporate AI functions, but also know when and how to use AI output wisely. A good process must also foster human discipline to resist over- or under-reliance on AI output.[7]

THE NATIONAL SECURITY IMPERATIVE

In *Youngstown*, the steel seizure case, Justice Robert Jackson, who served as attorney general to Franklin Delano Roosevelt (1940–41) and signed off on the lend-lease opinion, observed:

> The tendency is strong to emphasize transient results upon policies— such as wages and stabilization—and lose sight of enduring consequences upon the balanced power structure of our Republic.[8]

As with some of Jackson's other observations, he was not the first to see it or say it, but he did so with brevity, eloquence, and insight. Although Jackson was addressing wage stabilization controls, the observation is especially apt in the context of national security. Examples abound. The 1953 U.S.- and British-instigated coup against Prime Minister Mossadegh of Iran, for example, achieved its immediate objective of securing Iran's oil for Western interests and blocking Soviet ambitions in the region. It also provided twenty-five years of internal and external stability in a volatile region of the world. But in the long term, historians debate the extent to which the coup helped inspire the 1979 revolution, the seizure of the U.S. embassy, and an equally lengthy period of hostility to the U.S. and exportation of instability and terrorism throughout the Middle East. No doubt, it has also contributed, in some manner, to the sometime Iranian interest in a nuclear weapons program. For the Iranian people, one form of autocracy has followed another for over seventy years. The U.S. planning for the 2003 invasion of Iraq—in contrast to the planning for the period after Saddam Hussein's ouster—is another case in point. Of course, these and other examples may seem more apt and apparent in retrospect, as it is always easier to read history backward.

There are different reasons why the executive branch often focuses on the immediate at the expense of the intermediate and long-term. An innate American optimism is part of the equation. If you believe in your own values and exceptionalism, you may also believe that what you do will work, and work so well you need not plan out the second and third step in detail. Optimism is sometimes described as an American virtue; can-do is another way to describe the thought, with a little less suggestion of naiveté. After all, isn't the drive toward AGI partly informed by optimism, a belief that we will get there and when we do, we will be happy with the results? Indeed, national security can be a pretty grim and dreary business if you do not believe that what you do will make a positive difference.

The American electoral cycle also tends to focus policy attention and re-sults on two-year and four-year spans rather than long-term considerations. Serial issues are kicked down the road for the next person to deal with, partly because they are hard, even intractable, but also because responsibility gets passed along in two- or four-year increments. The media attention span is even shorter. It takes a deep thinker and principled leader to do the right thing for future generations at the expense of current votes and news cycles.

Values and long-term interests are also often harder to quantify and de-scribe and thus weigh in policy debates. This is especially the case where the immediate interest is measured in human lives or dollars, as against a more abstract interest in projecting legal values and stability. Finally, there is a nat-ural human tendency to procrastinate, deferring hard choices until tomorrow and pushing the costs of action or inaction into the future.

Another reason for the focus on the immediate is the national security imperative. The imperative describes the duty, desire, and focus of officials to protect the United States and its citizens from attack. Security is a, if not the, principal reason the federal government exists: to provide for the common defense. Moreover, the sense of responsibility is for most officials immediate and runs directly to the president as commander in chief. And it is a matter about which most conservative and liberal politicians would agree in concept, even if not always in execution. This is evident in war power debates, where virtually all participants, be they executive-oriented or legislative in outlook, would agree the president retains inherent constitutional authority to physi-cally defend the United States. The debate begins to vary when the president's attention moves beyond the United States to U.S. interests and lives overseas, and, to some, defense starts to look like offense.

Once we understand the national security imperative, four points rele-vant to AI emerge. First, where national security is tangibly and immediately concerned, presidents and their advisers will assert broad legal and, in some cases, moral authority to act. We have seen this with lend-lease, enhanced interrogation–torture, Iran-Contra, and the seizure of the steel mills. To the extent AI is viewed as, or comes to be viewed as, essential to national security and in an immediate way, presidents will assert broad authority to act.

Second, where officials feel a national security imperative, they will invariably overreach, unless and until the policy or legal process limits that reach. They will overreach in their efforts to access and control AI and the data that fuels AI. And there is risk they will overreach in applying its potential. Consider: if you are a counterintelligence specialist at the CIA—for example, James Jesus Angleton—and you are searching for a Soviet mole, wouldn't you err on the side of casting your net of suspicion twenty innocent persons too far rather than risk falling one spy short? That is your job and your duty, to catch spies, albeit tempered by an oath to support and defend the Constitution. Moreover, societal liberties are abstract; spies are real and concrete—unless, of course, you are an innocent subject caught in the net. Likewise, if you are looking to prevent a WMD attack in New York City, you are going to reach farther than you must or should, for fear you will otherwise not reach far enough. We should want national security actors charged with these responsibilities to reach to the limit of the law. The key is to recognize this pathology and devise a process of checks to appraise actions, validate those actions, and, where necessary, curtail them. If a lawyer never tells an official "no," the official is likely not trying hard enough to address the problem, or the lawyer is a "yes man" and not performing their duty to uphold the law and legal values. In a technology race with China, centered on AI, we should expect to see the national security imperative in play.

Third, where the law is not clear, or clearly invoked, and thus is not providing clear left and right boundaries of action, it is harder for lawyers and other actors to assess and validate executive actions. As the chapters that follow indicate, national security law was not written with AI in mind. The Defense Production Act, for example, was written with traditional Cold War defense industrial base applications in mind—not a twenty-first century AI arms race between China and the United States, where critical actors work at Google and not Los Alamos, and are named Cook and Zuckerberg and not LeMay and Nitze. Therefore, policymakers should not only approve the use of AI for security purposes; they have a duty to understand and oversee its use on an ongoing basis to identify and establish appropriate legal and policy boundaries.

BLACK BOX DECISIONMAKING

As noted, computer scientists refer to the layers of predictive computation between input layer and output layer in machine learning as the "Black Box." In many cases, if not most, operators are not sure what data or calculations the algorithm relies on in the cascade of neural networks that results in predictive outputs. The policy question is: to what extent national security decisionmakers should rely on outputs they do not fully understand, using methodologies they do not fully comprehend to take or inform national security actions. In the abstract, decisionmaking on that basis sounds absurd—or, to borrow a legal phrase, arbitrary and capricious. But we do it all the time when we rely on AI navigational tools or ticket purchase algorithms. Criminal justice decisionmakers often rely on technology they do not understand to make life- and liberty-changing decisions, like applying scientific tests to determine drug use or alcohol use. Should national security be viewed differently? There are arguments for both sides.

On the one hand,

- An AI output is not that different from a commander's or decisionmaker's intuition, which can be equally hard to identify and quantify. In the case of AI, at least, there is an immediate ability to know how often the AI output has been accurate in the past: the confidence threshold.

- We should want national security decisionmakers to use all the available tools, including technology, to advance the security mission.

- The question is not whether to use the tool, but how to do so wisely, that is, with appropriate human augmentation, validation, and confidence thresholds.

On the other hand,

- As has been seen with the use of recidivism algorithms, there are transparency issues presented where the subject of a decision cannot meaningfully question the basis of the input.

- There are also concerns, whether rooted in legal due process or not, that the AI output is not easily or readily tested and validated. By contrast, an intelligence analyst presenting a judgment can be questioned about the basis of their judgment—for example, what facts are known or unknown? It is harder to do so with an algorithm.

- Likewise, accountability is harder to pinpoint and apply. How does one challenge, or correct, or hold a machine accountable for the accuracy of its predictions? For sure, one can hold the person who designed or used the application accountable on the basis of design or command responsibility, but that can seem ethically unfair, unsound, or unsatisfying where the tool in question has been tested and adopted and used as intended, to inform decision.

- Finally, there is something undemocratic about a machine rather than a human making a decision or informing a decision, at least in the abstract, although it happens all the time, such as when judges and jurors rely on drug and DUI tests as evidence in court.

PREDICTIVE ALGORITHMS

Policymakers should also consider whether and when to use AI-generated predictive calculations to make national security decisions. Embedded in this question are subordinate questions: What level of certainty, or confidence threshold in the accuracy of the AI output, should be required for decisions to use lethal force? Keep a person off an airplane? If we are willing to make decisions based on human input that correlate to the same predictive assessment as an AI algorithm, is there an ethical difference in relying on a predictive algorithm versus human judgment?

In some jurisdictions, algorithms are used to inform parole and sentencing decisions based on predictions about future behavior, that is, the risk of recidivism. They have also been used to determine where police should patrol, based on predictions about where future crime is most likely to occur—a practice sometimes referred to as predictive policing or broken windows policing. And algorithms are used to identify candidates for jobs who are most likely to succeed based on the past performance of other candidates. Humans do the same thing, just in different ways. They rely on letters of recommendation from past and trusted sources more than they rely on references from unknown sources.

Of course, the above-mentioned questions, uses, and potential uses of AI are among the most controversial and disputed in the field. Each inspires arguments of actual and implied bias, prejudice, and due process—and, for many, an authoritarian posture as well. The point is not to endorse but to highlight that these same issues will arise in security practice, if they have not done so already, and in even less transparent form. If predictive algorithms are used to inform parole decisions and policing patterns, policymakers will ask, why shouldn't they also be used to predict such things as:

- Who should receive a security clearance, essentially a credit score for security clearances?
- Determining or informing who should be on a terrorism watch list or the no-fly list?

- Determining which persons, groups, or locales are most likely to radicalize or prove receptive to terrorist cell recruiting, by either domestic or international terrorist groups?

Thus, national security specialists must understand the legal and policy arguments for and against predictive algorithms. Imagine the U.S. government is using a remotely piloted vehicle to track a potential combatant within a designated conflict zone. Based on pattern of life analysis drawn from ten hours of video feed, an intelligence analyst offers the judgment that while there is no visual evidence of direct participation in hostilities, the analyst "believes it likely" that the person in question is affiliated with a terrorist cell based on the subject's contact with known cell members. When pressed on what "likely" means, the analyst says, "Something well above fifty percent certainty but less than a hundred percent certainty." An algorithm reviewing the same data feed offers the predictive calculation that there is a 75 percent match between the subject and the pattern of life profile of a combatant or terrorist, which is to say the confidence threshold for an algorithmic match is 75 percent, raising the possibility that there is a 25 percent chance the algorithm has not matched the pattern of life to an actual terrorist.

The on-the-scene commander has not seen the results but has been briefed on them. However, he has not been briefed on the algorithm and would not understand the algorithm if he had been briefed. That means the commander is not aware of: (1) the criteria programmed into the software to determine the "pattern of life" characteristics of combatants; or (2) the false positive rate of the algorithm, including the rate of risk that the algorithm would miss cultural cues and signals, generally, or in the specific circumstance at hand. Thus, for multiple reasons, he is not able to ask questions about the algorithmic result beyond its rate of predictive accuracy.

Questions

Should the person be placed on the target list in either or both scenarios? Is there an ethical difference between doing so in one context or the other? Does it make a difference if DOD has certified the algorithm's reliability to a percentage degree of certainty and validated the algorithm's use for LOAC compliance? Consider the pressure as well on the commander to "take the shot" when there is a 75 percent determination that the target is a valid military target. What if his intuition suggests otherwise?

This leads to a related question: Should decisionmakers set or require predictive thresholds for national security decisions such as firing a weapon in the same way the law utilizes a preponderance of evidence standard (51 percent) or a beyond-a-reasonable-doubt standard (sometimes equated to 99 percent certainty)? Alternatively, should policymakers require corroboration before algorithmic predictions are relied upon? Judges hesitate to place a percentage number on the beyond-a-reasonable-doubt standard out of concern that jurors will treat reasonable doubt as an equation. It is not. It is a judgment asking jurors to factor in all the evidence, including the demeanor evidence of witnesses, with each juror exercising their judgment and common sense in a slightly different way. What does 1 percent doubt equate to, anyway? Security decisionmakers might well resist numeric thresholds as well, out of concern they will remove the reasonable application of human judgment from decisionmaking.

Returning to the targeting scenario, it would be hard for a subject matter expert to argue with an algorithmic prediction with an 80 percent or 90 percent confidence threshold even if cultural cues might suggest a different outcome. Likewise, a commander might feel pressure to take the shot with such a high percentage prediction. Reverse the numbers, and the use of algorithmic predictions could cause commanders to hesitate to act, and fear second-guessing, even when human experience and area expertise suggest action is warranted.

Stipulating that an algorithm has been tested and validated to a degree of predictive accuracy, what are the arguments for and against predictive algorithms?

On the one hand,

- **Objectivity:** An algorithm, if properly designed, is objective in a way that humans are not. All but the most self-aware humans are susceptible to cognitive bias when addressing security decisions. Consider watch list designations to the no-fly list. It is the rare human who will not err on the side of caution when addressing a security risk. We should want this, but not when the extra caution leads to erratic or inconsistent results or embeds human bias into the decision. In theory, a Joe Friday algorithm (just the facts) would apply criteria in a neutral manner even if using social identifying descriptors we sometimes associate with ethnic, gender, or racial identity, provided those descriptors are ethically and logically relevant to the algorithm's purpose. (The question of bias is discussed in chapter 6.)

- **Augmentation:** It is hard to argue on ethical grounds that an algorithm should not be used if it is used as a tool to augment human judgment rather than replace it. Consider the difference between the sentencing guidelines when used as guidelines rather than as mandatory requirements. Guidelines that guide help ensure that sentences are fair and consistent across jurisdictions and judges, while allowing for case-specific adjustments and adjudication.

On the other hand,

- **Bias:** As will be discussed in chapter 6, there is ample opportunity for bias, including prejudice, to seep into algorithmic predictions. As the saying goes, "bias in, bias out." In security context, there is risk that policymakers will feel pressure to use all the tools available without having the corresponding knowledge or time to validate the accuracy and integrity of predictive algorithms in contexts involving life and death.

- **Specificity/individual adjudication:** An algorithm will not necessarily account for the individual characteristics, potentially novel or unique, in the context presented. Criminal sentencing, for example, is supposed to be based on the adjudication of the individual case, including mitigating or aggravating factors specific to the case. The objection to the sentencing guidelines as a mandatory standard was that they did not consider case-specific factors that were not otherwise incorporated into the reasoning behind the guidelines. The same is true with algorithms, with the added complication that the algorithm's criteria, in contrast to the guidelines, are usually not transparent to decisionmakers and, in the case of machine learning, constantly in flux.

- **Accountability:** Likewise, the use of algorithms to inform decisions lacks a ready procedural mechanism by which the user can test the reliability of the application or the subject can challenge the results. Whether this is required as a matter of law—for example, as a matter of due process—ethical principles such as reliability, accountability, and transparency likely argue in its favor.

- **Future versus past behavior:** Depending on how it is designed and how it is applied, an algorithm may be designed to predict future behavior (for example, a parole algorithm) or it may be designed to data-mine information about past behavior (for example, travel, associates). A fundamental precept of ethics and justice, as perceived through a Western lens, is that one is held to account for what they do or have done, not what they might do or what we predict they might do.

■ *Transparency:* Algorithms may be biased in their design or application. However, in the absence of transparency or a process of adjudication, there are fewer ways to see or address algorithmic bias than in the case of humans making the same predictive judgments and assessments. Transparency is also a fundamental principle of democracy and a source of moral credibility. One reason people accept the opinions of courts is that they are issued in an open and transparent manner in front of the public and with the reasons behind a decision stated in an opinion.

Values

The third purpose of law is to provide for, protect, and preserve our essential legal values. That, after all, is what the oath of office for military officers and civil servants requires: "To support and defend the Constitution."[9] However, four points bear emphasis here.

First, in the national security sphere, many of our legal values also bear national security value. In other words, the legal value contributes to the national security result. The humane treatment of prisoners of war, for example, reflects legal and humanitarian values (Common Article III of the Geneva Conventions), as well as a security value. Humanely treated prisoners are more likely to provide information to their captors. Humane treatment of an opponent's prisoners is also more likely to lead to the reciprocal humane treatment of one's own prisoners. The principles of the law of armed conflict (LOAC) more generally convey security as well as legal values. For example, the LOAC requires combatants to distinguish between combatants and noncombatants when using force; to use only the force necessary to accomplish the military purpose and then only proportionate force, which means that the unintended collateral (that is, civilian) consequences of one's actions cannot be disproportionate to the direct and concrete military advantage the use of force is intended to achieve.

Distinction, necessity, and proportionality are legal terms. But these legal concepts also reflect military common sense. Commanders know that in order to counter insurgency or terrorism, one must avoid alienating the civilian population or making enemies out of friends and neutrals. One way to avoid this is by using discriminate force and fire discipline. Likewise, the military principle known as "economy of force" is the commander's version of necessity and proportionality. Economy of force instructs commanders to use only that force necessary to accomplish the mission, thus preserving reserve capacity and an ability to meet contingencies. In short, legal values often reflect national security values.

Second, it is the responsibility of the lawyer, as advisor, not only to articulate what the law is, but also why the law is—what value or purpose the law is seeking to fulfill, protect, or preserve. The security operator should want to follow the law not just because it is the law, but because it makes security sense to do so, at least in the intermediate or long-term if not in the specific moment. This requires lawyers to understand policy objectives and purposes and not just guide with yes and no answers to legal questions. In the case of the AI technologist, understanding the purpose behind the law may result in the identification of technical solutions to what might otherwise seem like intractable legal problems.

The point is illustrated by the doctrine of command responsibility, discussed in chapter 9. The purpose of the doctrine is to ensure that armed forces remain under positive command and respect the law of war. Knowing the purpose, jurists might better conceive of different, rather than singular, ways to accomplish the goal. The law could have limited command responsibility to situations of actual direction and control (specific intent). Alternatively, the law could hold commanders responsible for everything their subordinates do or do not do (strict liability). Instead the law has evolved through international court cases somewhere in between, holding commanders responsible for the actions they direct and those of their subordinates that they should have known about and stopped (general intent). With AI, the law might include a similar principle, holding software engineers, or commanders and leaders who utilize AI tools, responsible for what they program or direct, or what might reasonably occur because of what they program or direct. One question is where to draw such a line and whom to include within it. Another question is whether such a line would have the desired effect in influencing leaders to use AI with positive control and care.

Third, the process of creating law is one way, and in many regards the most effective albeit imperfect way, to adjudicate the sometime tension in values national security presents. Indeed, many if not most debates about authority are proxy debates about values as well. In the broadest sense, national security can, but need not, create tension between physical security and liberty. Both are constitutional values. In context, a decisionmaker might place greater emphasis on one value versus the other or seek to find a balance. In drafting law, we tend to debate and adjudicate competing values more consciously and transparently than when we apply law in the national security moment. Among other things, there is generally more time to do so, more input from more players, and less focus on the immediate security objective.

AI presents many competing values, made more complex because the technical aspects of an application may not be fully understood by decisionmakers. Even if decisionmakers are inclined to consciously address competing values in the context of specific-use decisions, they may not be able to do so, or at least not in the informed and deliberative manner that public legislating *can* offer.

Finally, where values are embedded in law, rather than policy or individual decisions, they are more likely to endure and to withstand the erosive pressures that security crises bring—such as immediacy, danger, and secrecy.

TAKEAWAYS

Because the DPA and other laws were not drafted with AI in mind, they will inevitably leave questions open or unresolved. That also means that they will not necessarily or clearly define the substantive authority to act with respect to AI or the right and left boundaries of that action, for the simple reason that the drafters did not contemplate such action. It also means that one or all of the following things will happen in applying national security law to AI.

1. The government will use the law and process it has, whether it is a good fit or not, until such time as the law or process are changed. One of the lessons of national security process is that executive actors will invoke the law they have, whether it was intended for a purpose or not and whether it fits well or not. This is a product of the national security imperative. If your mission is to protect the United States from attack, the natural inclination will be to reach to find authority if you must. Former CIA and National Security Agency (NSA) director Michael Hayden calls this "playing to the edge." However, most decisionmakers do not know where the edge is, and if they are zealous about their mission, as they should be, they will push beyond the edge. That is why good process includes lawyers who not only approve the initiation of action but actively engage in appraising the subsequent results and delimiting that action— identifying the edge.

The 2015 FBI-Apple dispute and litigation regarding the San Bernardino shooter's cell phone, discussed in chapter 6, also reminds us that where national security is concerned, the government (and sometimes courts) will use the law it has—in that case, the All Writs Act of 1789. This law, which was part of the original enabling act for the federal judiciary, enables courts to issue writs (judicial orders) in aid of their jurisdiction. It does not create jurisdiction, but rather helps courts enforce the jurisdiction they already have. In any event, it is safe to say that however prescient James Madison was, Congress was not contemplating AI or iPhones at the time of the Judiciary Act of 1789, which is not to say old law is not up to new challenges. The San Bernardino magistrate judge, for example, found that the All Writs Act provided the court authority to order Apple to create software to access the iPhone, in aid of its jurisdiction to issue and enforce an FBI search warrant. However, sometimes old law applied to new technologies seems more like the pounding of the proverbial square peg into a round hole. A different magistrate judge in New York City, for example, found that the All Writs Act did not apply to search warrants involving iPhones.

This book seeks to identify potential square peg issues. It is premised on the theory that where there is a predictable need for new authority and boundaries, we should pass or amend the necessary law now or soon. If we are not able to do so, at least we will have debated the issues and values so that we know where the pitfalls are. Likewise, where the law is clear or colorable, and the government is prepared to use it going forward, it should actively contemplate doing so now. It is better to identify gaps and resolve litigation issues outside the context of crisis and immediate national security need. We have seen the consequences of not planning for and addressing known risks and legal ambiguities with the COVID-19 pandemic.

2. Constitutional law matters as does constitutional values-sorting. Because it is likely that the government will reach for constitutional authority in the absence of statutory law, and because many of the values that will likely be litigated are constitutional values, policymakers and technologists, and not just lawyers, should understand some key elements of constitutional law and structure, without spin, and before specific needs and crises color one's understanding. In this way, they will better understand and should insist upon knowing when novel constitutional arguments and theories are advanced. Understanding constitutional law, they will also more likely hold true to our enduring values.

The values embedded in the First, Fourth, and Fifth Amendments are especially relevant to AI as explained in the chapters that follow.

3. The government will, or should, also look for law to apply by analogy.
In the absence of an agreed framework for addressing AI, the government will
not only use existing law to fill the void, it will, or should, also look to other
laws to apply by analogy. In the case of international law, especially customary
international law, this can be done by executive assertion and policy alone. The
executive branch, for example, can choose, as a matter of policy discretion, to
interpret or apply the LOAC in AI contexts, and do so pursuant to the president's
authority as commander in chief and to lawful orders conveyed through the
chain of command. In the case of domestic law, it will likely require legislation,
but not always—if, for example, a concept can be implemented through a general grant of authority like IEEPA or the DPA.

One key question then is what law, or legal concepts, should apply to AI by
analogy. The chapters that follow present several concepts for consideration,
drawn from nonproliferation and arms control as well as the law of armed conflict. The principle of command responsibility, for example, applies to military
uses of AI because it is already part of military law. But shouldn't we also consider whether, how, and why the same principles might apply through adoption
and adaptation to civilian uses of AI for national security? Likewise, arms control
practice offers numerous potential analogies. Nuclear weapons practice and
history, for example, offer doctrinal, safety, and command and control lessons.
The chemical and biological weapons regimes, in turn, suggest some of the
challenges and possibilities regarding the regulation and verification of dual-
use capacities. For these reasons, these areas of law and practice are discussed
in chapters 8 and 9.

**4. If the government does not act, private actors and litigation will play a
disproportionate role in defining national policy.** Where the law is unclear or
unsettled, and the government does not seek to fill the void by analogy, amendment, or assertion, national legal policy will inevitably and eventually be shaped
by private actions and litigation decisions. Courtrooms and boardrooms are not
good locales to resolve questions of *national* security policy. But that is where
we are by default. Restated, if AI legal gaps remain, we will end up with multiple iterations of the 2015 FBI-Apple litigation over access to the San Bernardino
shooter's phone. But that litigation will seem like a Little League game compared to the litigation that will occur with AI, where the stakes are even higher
and litigation resources deeper.

Litigation is a counterproductive way to make policy. Litigation can serve as
a forcing mechanism. But litigation accents the voices and interests of a few—

the litigating parties—not those of society at large. It is called the adversarial process for a reason. The government's litigation process is also different from its policy process. It accents the views of lawyers making arguments to win cases, rather than those of policymakers addressing competing equities. Recall that some of the loudest critics of the FBI's position in the Apple dispute came from within the intelligence community. Litigation also often results in divided rather than national policy, as courts divide over outcomes. If you want informed and sound *national* security policy, better to do it in moments of calm dispassion rather than through litigation.

Alternatively, or additionally, corporations will move forward and act, because they must, to compete in the AI marketplace and because it is their fiduciary duty to do so. Corporations have not and will not wait for the government to act or to regulate. They will define the space themselves and, having done so, they will resist any countervailing effort to introduce law and regulation. And because they are nimble and narrow in doing so—in structure and objective— they will likely define the space first, before the government does, making it harder for the government and legislative process to do so. Moreover, they will do so without the tempering influence of a litigation opponent's competing interests and arguments and a judge's dispassionate review.

All of this means that we should start looking to purposefully create an AI legal architecture and do so now.

SIX

Constitutional Law

AUTHORITY TO LEGISLATE

Government authority to regulate AI starts with the Constitution. This is because legislative regulation must be tied to an enumerated grant of substantive constitutional authority, beyond Congress's general authority to legislate. Congress cannot simply dictate when, how, and for what reasons private actors may engage in AI research, development, and deployment, or how companies buy and sell data. This requires a constitutional hook. The DPA, for example, is predicated on Congress's authority "to regulate Commerce with foreign Nations, and among the several States" and to a certain extent "to make Rules for the Government and Regulation of the land and naval forces." Further, when an exercise of legislative authority is challenged, courts will look beyond mere incantation, to determine if there is a demonstrative link between a law and the underlying constitutional authority to enact that law.

This was a core challenge to the Affordable Care Act in *National Federation of Business et al. v. Sebelius* (2012), the Supreme Court's second case addressed to the act. The court asked: Was the individual mandate to buy insurance a valid exercise of Congress's power under the Commerce Clause and the Necessary and Proper Clause? A majority of the court said no. The court's reasoning is helpful in illustrating the necessity in today's Supreme Court context of demonstrating the constitutional basis for Congress (or the executive branch) to regulate an industry.

The individual mandate, however, does not regulate existing commercial activity. It instead compels individuals to become active in commerce by purchasing a product, on the ground that their failure to do so affects interstate commerce. Construing the Commerce Clause to permit Congress to regulate individuals precisely because they are doing nothing would open a new and potentially vast domain to congressional authority. . . . Nor can the individual mandate be sustained under the Necessary and Proper Clause as an integral part of the Affordable Care Act's other reforms. Each of this Court's prior cases upholding laws under that Clause involved exercises of authority derivative of, and in service to, a granted power.[1]

Nonetheless, the court went on to find that "the mandate" could be upheld as within Congress's power to "lay and collect taxes." The "penalty" for not buying insurance was analogous to a tax, the court concluded, "because it was not punitive in nature" and "[n]either the Act nor any other law attaches negative legal consequences to not buying health insurance, beyond requiring a payment to the IRS."[2]

Congress's authority to legislate and the executive branch's authority to act is a frequent subject of litigation. Further, as the Apple-FBI debate illustrates, litigation is especially likely where the government seeks to compel or direct the involuntary provision of private sector services and know-how to the government for national security reasons.

THE APPLE-FBI IPHONE LITIGATION

In December 2015, Syed Rizwan Farook and his spouse attacked a holiday party hosted by his employer, San Bernardino County, killing fourteen people and wounding seventeen. The perpetrators fled but were located four hours later. A gunfight ensued, and the perpetrators were killed. In the interim, it turned out, the perpetrators had destroyed their personal smartphones. When an iPhone 5C issued to Farook by the county was recovered in the perpetrators' vehicle, the FBI sought to access the iPhone to gather evidence, including to determine whether there were additional people involved in the attack. It was unable to do so successfully without risk of triggering a disabling feature that would permanently erase the phone's contents after ten failed attempts to enter a four-digit access code. At one point, the FBI asked the county to reset the password to Farook's iCloud account, apparently with the intent of accessing the iPhone's information in the Cloud. This had the unintended effect of preventing the iPhone from backing up the phone on the iCloud. Having obtained a search warrant from a magistrate judge in the Central District of California, the FBI asked for Apple's help in accessing the iPhone. Apple declined. The FBI then sought to compel Apple's assistance.

The magistrate issued an order pursuant to the All Writs Act, ordering Apple to provide "reasonable technical assistance to assist law enforcement agents in obtaining access to the data on the subject device." The order continued:

> Apple's reasonable technical assistance shall accomplish the following three important functions: (1) it will bypass or disable the auto-erase function whether or not it has been enabled; (2) it will enable the FBI to submit passcodes to the subject device for testing electronically via the physical device port, Bluetooth, Wi-Fi, or other protocol available on the subject device; and (3) it will ensure that when the FBI submits passcodes to the subject device, software running on the device will not purposefully introduce any additional delay between passcode attempts beyond what is incurred by Apple hardware.[3]

The All Writs Act dates to the Judiciary Act of 1789, establishing the federal court system pursuant to Article III of the Constitution. Thus, it is safe to conclude the act did not contemplate the iPhone or the internet. The All Writs Act is an enabling statute that permits courts to issue writs in aid of their jurisdiction. A writ is an order from a court. The act does not and cannot create jurisdiction that does not already exist; it is a tool to assist courts to perform their lawful functions. The magistrate's order did not elaborate on the question of jurisdiction; however, the context of the order makes clear the magistrate was seeking to enforce the prior search warrant issued under the jurisdictional authority of the court to issue warrants found at 18 U.S.C. §3102.

Apple again objected. Its CEO, Tim Cook, issued a public statement "challenging the FBI's demands," while stating, "The implications of the government's demands are chilling. If the government can use the All Writs Act to make it easier to unlock your iPhone, it would have the power to reach into anyone's device to capture their data."[4] Apple declined to follow the order and sought to enjoin enforcement of the writ. However, before the appeal was heard, the FBI withdrew its request to Apple, mooting the matter. The director of the FBI indicated the bureau had found an alternative method with which to access the phone. Press reports alternatively indicated the FBI had engaged an Israeli company to hack the phone or had paid a black-hat hacker on the Dark Web for a zero-day tool to do so. A subsequent report from the Department of Justice, Office of the Inspector General, refers to an "outside vendor . . . almost 90 percent finished with a technical solution" at the time the court order to enforce the warrant was sought. It also states that "vendor assistance . . . ultimately proved fruitful."[5]

The litigation was the most visible and dramatic chapter in a larger book titled "The Going Dark Debate." The request from the FBI, it turned out, was one of eleven pending with Apple at the time from the FBI as well as state and local authorities for assistance in accessing passcode protected iPhones thought to contain evidence of crimes of violence and child pornography. In one case in Brooklyn, New York, a magistrate judge denied the FBI's request to issue an order under the All Writs Act on the ground that the act could not be used to compel a company to modify its products and was outside the reach of the 1789 Act.[6]

There are multiple observations to draw from the San Bernardino iPhone dispute.

One, where national security is concerned, the government will seek to use the law it has. In this case, the government resorted to the All Writs Act of 1789. The more urgent the perceived need, the more unexpected or novel the government theory of law may become. Recall the earlier discussion of the national security imperative.

Two, where the law is not clear, or reasonable arguments can be made on either side, courts will vary in decisional outcome. The California magistrate ruled one way, the Brooklyn magistrate another. This can leave the law uncertain, making litigation ill-suited to resolving questions of national importance and reach. Uncertain legal authority may also cause executive hesitation and caution when speed and risk-taking are needed.

Three, litigation is a poor substitute for legislative and executive branch policymaking. Litigation accents the voices and interests of the parties, not necessarily the overriding societal interests presented. Moreover, until and only if the Supreme Court decides the question of law presented, "national security policy" will be made on a circuit-by-circuit basis, and risk becoming "circuit security policy."

Four, the government process to address litigation is not the same as the process for addressing policy. It is generally myopic in outlook and client-centered, focusing on immediate litigation needs, not long-term consequences. To illustrate, NIST, NSA, and Department of Defense were not included at the Apple-FBI litigation table. Indeed, many of the FBI's litigation positions appear to have come as a surprise to the executive branch and had broad implications regarding encryption policy generally.

Five, in retrospectives regarding the Apple-iPhone debate, some of the loudest concerns about the FBI's position were expressed by former members of the intelligence community, arguing that any vulnerability that allowed Apple to hack its own operating system could allow someone else to do the same thing with malicious motive. (Interestingly, Apple was vague throughout about whether it was technically incapable of breaking into the iPhone or simply unwilling to do so.) One should not assume that the security-liberty tension will always align as a debate between government and industry rather than one that is more nuanced between factions in both camps. That makes "us versus them" approaches and attitudes risky on substance and tactics.

Six, litigation can serve as a forcing mechanism to compel the government to make hard decisions or reach positions it is otherwise unwilling or unable to make. Where issues of national policy are resolved through litigation, the government must ensure a commensurate process of national policy decisionmaking is invoked, and not just one of litigation-decision. For example, with litigation, Department of Justice attorneys might only consult with "the client," the affected agency, rather than the interagency process.

Seven, industry and the government do not work together best in crisis, or in the context of litigation. Litigation inherently drives parties into their corners and accents differences in view rather than focusing attention on common perspectives. The American system of litigation is called the adversarial process for a reason, and it is not just because both parties are represented by counsel.

Eight, as a result, the wise policymaker and wise CEO/general counsel will spend as much time facilitating relationships between industry and Washington as they do in litigating disputes. Hopefully more. That also means they should spend more time building AI bridges and translating concerns and do so now.

Nine, the government acted before knowing or exhausting its own technical capability and potential. To the extent this was a purposeful attempt to pursue all options in parallel for security reasons, it is understandable, even commendable. To the extent the government did not understand or identify its technical options before resorting to litigation, it is not commendable, and potentially costly in terms of national security outcomes: an erased phone; an adverse court precedent; and diminished credibility carried forward to the next crisis and case. The Department of Justice inspector general concluded that organizational disconnects resulted in delay in seeking vendor assistance and stated a belief that "the emphasis on the fact that the technique would be used to assist a criminal matter could have reasonably and foreseeably led internal and external partners to limit the answers they provided to unclassified techniques only, which, if true, would have created a missed opportunity to explore all possible techniques to unlock the phone."[7]

Ten, the government makes mistakes, as it did when it requested that San Bernardino County reset Farook's iCloud password. Where time is compressed, and urgency magnified, the government is likely to make more mistakes. The government's policy and litigation tasks were made more complicated by this technical mistake. One wonders if a little more time on the front end, to survey the options, would have saved a lot more time on the back end in litigation and dispute. But deliberation is harder in moments of urgency.

Finally, the case forecasts some of the issues that will arise in the context of government efforts to involuntarily harness or regulate AI in the service of national security. For the reasons stated above, these issues might best be addressed through the policy process rather than litigation. The real and perceived stakes are higher with AI, the financial incentives and litigation assets magnitudes greater. But if litigation does occur, it will make the differences in scale and import with the Apple-FBI dispute seem like the differences between an abacus and a quantum computer. Absent a statutory framework, litigation will also be complex because it will rely on constitutional arguments based on the First, Fourth, and Fifth Amendments; arguments that are untested and, in some cases, novel.

CONSTITUTIONAL DIMENSIONS

Where individual liberties are at stake, courts will look to determine if an otherwise permissible exercise in legislative or executive authority impinges upon a constitutional right. Most relevant with AI are the rights provided by the First, Fourth, Fifth, and Sixth Amendments.

First Amendment

The First Amendment states:

> Congress shall make no law respecting an establishment of religion, or prohibiting the free exercise thereof; or abridging the freedom of speech, or of the press, or the right of the people peaceably to assemble, and to petition the Government for a redress of grievances.

The First Amendment addresses five rights: freedom of the press, speech, religion, assembly, and the right to petition the government. Every time the government, in law or practice, takes an action that can be construed as impeding, restricting, chilling, or favoring one voice or view over another, there is room for First Amendment challenge. An inventor seeking a patent, for example, might assert that the government is chilling their speech by preventing them from talking about their invention under the ISA. Consider the myriad issues as well that might arise if the government sought to review and regulate Facebook postings for foreign interference or undertook to validate the authenticity of political ads. Likewise, an AI researcher who is traveling to the United States to lecture and can't get a visa because of travel restrictions might have a First Amendment speech or association claim, as might the university that invited the person to speak. Or consider potential disputes over government funding, which, depending on how it is allocated or withheld, can create First Amendment issues. Thus, assuming jurisdiction and standing, the first question a court might ask is whether an exercise in legislative or executive authority impinges upon one of the five enumerated rights in the First Amendment. Most relevant to AI is the right to free speech.

Four takeaways warrant emphasis.

The first takeaway is that the speech clause of the First Amendment applies to corporations and to universities, including those engaged in AI research, development, and deployment. This was part of the holding in *Citizens United*,[8] in which the Supreme Court held that corporate spending on campaign ads was a form of protected political speech. Thus, the court held that Federal Election Commission (FEC) rules limiting corporate and union spending on political ads, which were not otherwise coordinated with specific candidates, violated the First Amendment.

Second, the right encompasses more than verbal or written speech, although political speech resides at its core. Court cases have consistently held that it also covers symbolic speech (for example, art and pictures), compelled speech (such as mandatory pledges of allegiance), and commercial speech (such as certain limitations on advertising). Although there are few cases on point, and even fewer that are controlling precedent, the better view is that the speech clause covers computer code. Indeed, software embodies the concept of symbolic speech. Courts liken code to musical scores and math formulas, both of which are squarely recognized as speech. However, some commentators argue code is more akin to action than speech.[9] The more complex question is not whether the amendment applies, but how and subject to what reasonable time, place, and manner regulation.[10] An even more complex question is whether machine learning–generated code is covered speech and, if so, whether it is the machine or the author of the original base code that holds and can assert the right.

Third, the right to speech is broad, but not unlimited. Courts generally permit reasonable time, place, and manner restrictions on speech where there is a compelling government interest at stake and the means of regulation are narrowly tailored to address the compelling interest. Thus, courts have upheld prohibitions and restrictions on speech that could incite violence, threaten violence, undermine good order and discipline in the military, disclose national security information, is obscene, or that undermines public safety. The most famous illustration is Justice Oliver Wendell Holmes Jr.'s example of crying "Fire!" in a crowded theater. This, he wrote, would create a "clear and present" danger to public safety.[11] However, the fact patterns in this line of cases are dated. They largely draw from antiwar and draft resistance activities during WWI and communist activities during the early days of the Cold War. By today's standards, some of the cases seem old-fashioned, almost hysterical, but not all of these cases are dated, including those dealing with the prior restraint of an article on how to build a nuclear weapon.[12] The clear and present danger test has also been replaced with the "imminent lawless action" standard from *Brandenburg*.[13] The point for policymakers and legal generalists is not that they should know the difference between a "clear and present danger" and "imminent lawless action"; most judges do not know the difference until they see it. The point is that reasonable restrictions on speech are permitted, but only where the government demonstrates a compelling need as well as a tailored nexus between restriction and need.

Fourth, the First Amendment addresses government conduct ("Congress shall make no law . . ."). There is no right to free speech as asserted against private actors, unless there is a demonstrable link between private actions and governmental conduct, such as funding, direction, or leverage, which can be shown to compel or cause the infringement on speech by a private actor. That is why private universities, private schools, and professional sports teams may require students to stand for the national anthem or face discipline without raising First Amendment concerns. Increasingly, however, scholars are asking whether the threat of legislation or regulation may create a sufficient governmental nexus to underpin First Amendment challenges where private companies take action in order to avoid additional regulation or legislation.[14] We can anticipate litigation on this question in the context of pressure to impose social media restrictions or regulate data management.

The First Amendment, of course, raises several national security issues and scenarios. The exercise of free speech, for example, can itself generate national security crises, illustrated by the 2014 North Korean cyberattacks in response to Sony's pending release of the comedic movie, *The Interview*. In less dramatic manner, the free expression of foreign policy views can complicate foreign relations. Efforts by the government to control the dissemination of national security information or know-how present classic First Amendment issues as well.

The lead Supreme Court case is *New York Times Co. v. United States* (1971),[15] "the Pentagon Papers case," in which the government sought to enjoin the *New York Times* and other papers from publishing the Pentagon Papers, a classified RAND study of the Vietnam War. The government argued that publication would cause damage to national security. The court held in a per curiam opinion (an opinion of a court, usually joined by all the judges and not identified by author) that the government had not met the "heavy presumption" against prior restraint of the press. The case stands for the proposition, among others, that where First Amendment issues are engaged, the government must do more than invoke national security. A demonstrative showing of real potential harm is required.

The eight separate opinions in the case are noteworthy for their varied definitions and treatments of "national security." The government should not take it for granted that a court will accept, or even understand, broad assertions of national security harm, based on the sort of mosaic theories that inform intelligence analysis. This might be especially true where the arguments are based on AI technologies that are hard to understand to begin with. Likewise, private actors should not take it for granted that courts, which have seen and experienced the role of intelligence and dot-connecting in a post-9/11 world, will adhere to the sort of narrow definitions of national security harm invoked in *New York Times*, and favored by the media, such as disclosures of troop movements causing certain harm. Of course, the normative "method" of prior restraint is a voluntary one. The government will approach a media outlet and request that it not disclose certain information, along with an articulation of the reasons why. Whatever the context, critical actors will need to move beyond generic statements of law and security. The situation is, of course, more complicated where an algorithm is making the disclosure or "censorship" decision.

With AI, the First Amendment might be invoked in any number of different and sometimes novel ways. For example, government use of AI favoring, or perceived to favor, one form of speech or content over another might bring challenge. This would be the case if the government used or required use of an AI algorithm to block speech, or perhaps identify speech. But what if that speech came in the form of clandestine foreign political advertising, which generated a profit for the carrier, and could not be shown conclusively to have originated from foreign sources? The government might have to reveal sources and methods of intelligence gathering. Or what if the only way to establish that such speech came from a foreign source required the disclosure of an AI-enabled and classified algorithm designed to determine the true attribution of internet code and posting? Alternatively, what if the algorithm identified speech on the internet that was perceived to support radical causes? The key distinction might hinge on whether the government-provided or -directed algorithm also shut the voice down, or could be shown to result in an equivalent chilling effect, such as arrest. A critical distinction might also depend on whether there was an additional predicate for any governmental action, such as a showing of incitement to violence or safety (shouting "fire!" in the crowded theater), or link to illicit conduct. Here, there is guidance in the form of case law distinguishing between material support for terrorism, which is subject to criminal sanction under 18 U.S.C. §2339B, and protected free speech.[16] However, courts are nuanced in finding the distinction between what is referred to as a "true threat" and political speech, satire, or internet anger-venting. Courts apply a degree of contextual analysis that is difficult, if not impossible, to code or write into generic policy.

First Amendment issues might also arise if government funding or an alternative benefit, like AI licensing, provided an advantage or perceived advantage to one corporate or political voice over another. Here the key distinction might rest on whether the government was acting in a commercial role (for example, contracting for services), or regulating with the purpose or effect of chilling or promoting a viewpoint. But what if the government contracted a company to identify communist or terroristic voices on a predictive basis, using AI algorithms and data mining, and adjust weights to predict which persons would go on to espouse such causes or engage in acts of violence? One might expect a challenge in such a case, arguing that the government was chilling free expression and engaging in the prior restraint of speech, all on a predictive basis.

One can also imagine First Amendment challenges if the government sought to prohibit the academic dissemination of ideas, or perhaps sought to compel thought. This was a First Amendment issue that simmered on the back burner during the Apple-FBI iPhone dispute. Could the government require Apple to perform a task or service by writing code or an algorithm, and, if so, could Apple, in turn, compel an individual employee to perform that same task or service? Would that be a commercial exchange or a form of compelled speech?

Questions will eventually arise as to whether artificial AI-generated voices, such as Siri, Alexa, and Watson, have free speech rights. If so, whose right is being exercised? Is it the hardware's right? The software's? The right of the person who wrote the initial AI algorithm? Or perhaps the person whose voice activated the electronic personal assistant? And does the analysis change if the device is applying a learning algorithm and thus changing the initial activating voice or rewriting code as it goes along? These are the sorts of questions law professors love and love to make up. But they are coming. However, if AI matures—as, it appears, it will—there will be more human First Amendment issues to occupy the academy before it turns to Siri.

Policymakers should also know that the First Amendment right is one to free speech, not to federal funding or to governmental benefits. The government, for example, may attach conditions to federal funding, provided those conditions do not compel, chill, or silence speech. The Solomon Amendment is a case in point.

During the era of Don't Ask, Don't Tell (DADT), 1993–2011, governing sexual orientation personnel policy in the armed forces, many law schools prohibited military recruiters from coming on campus to recruit judge advocates. The law schools were using the right of campus access to express a political view about DADT, an act virtually all lawyers would consider an exercise of free speech. (Never mind that the judge advocates barred from campus had nothing to do with the offending policy and did not pass the DADT law enforcing it. And never mind that these same law schools otherwise welcomed members of Congress and the president who enacted DADT. All of which reminds us that there is no requirement that free speech be consistent or logical, only that it be free.)

In response, the Congress passed the Solomon Amendment, withholding a significant percentage of federal research funding from any university that barred military recruiters from campus. Many schools challenged the Solomon Amendment on First Amendment grounds as a restriction on speech. Appellate courts, however, rejected this argument. The plaintiffs were free to express their views about DADT as they wished, the courts held, including by barring military recruiters from campus. But the right was to speech, not to funding. There is no First Amendment right to federal funding, the courts concluded. The government was conditioning federal funding on recruiter access, not compelling law schools to speak, be silent, or to express a view, all of which they remained free to do. Soon most, but not all, law schools reopened campus access to military recruiters. The schools that did not were largely free-standing law schools without federally supported university research programs.

The Solomon Amendment cases illustrate the importance of identifying what is speech, and what is compelled speech or compelled silence. They also clearly stand for the proposition that when appropriately tailored, the government can condition the provision of funding on the exercise of certain national security functions, such as recruiting in the Solomon Amendment context or, perhaps, limiting access to an AI lab, a code, or requiring security procedures. If the university or corporation does not want to perform those functions, they need not accept the funding. What the government cannot do is compel a private party to accept the funding and thus compel the exercise of speech. Neither can it condition the exercise of a legal right on the exercise of speech, for example, by requiring students at public schools to recite the pledge of allegiance, or a social security recipient to sing the national anthem, to receive a benefit to which they are legally entitled. Of course, the lines between compelled speech and free speech are not always clear, and even when they are, litigants may find reasons to bring challenges.

The takeaway is that First Amendment law is nuanced and case-specific. It is subject to careful, even meticulous, consideration and balancing by courts. Clear black letter lines are thus hard to draw and even harder to code. This makes AI applications driven by algorithms operating at machine speed particularly challenging in First Amendment context, which is to say, where there is a government nexus to the application in question. Social media companies have struggled to draw this line—without the burden of complying with the First Amendment—using their own centaur model of decision, a blend of algorithmic and human review.

Machine speed and the complexity of the law place a duty on policymakers and lawyers to act in a proactive manner to:

- Understand the law.

- Provide meaningful policy input into the design of algorithms.

- Adopt policy presumptions and principles within which algorithms might safely operate, including presumptions as to whether content will be protected or not.

- Include within any operating policy a meaningful process of appraisal and review, which entails conscious line-drawing as to when humans must decide and when algorithms can do so alone.

- Make purposeful, transparent, and accountable decisions that can be challenged and changed, rather than defer hard decisions to later.

Fourth Amendment

Fourth Amendment questions may arise in numerous AI and data contexts. In criminal context, for example, the government may seek to use AI-generated data or predictions as probable cause for search authorizations. In doing so, it will need to convince counsel, magistrates, judges, or all three sets of actors that AI and the results it generates are reliable. Likewise, the government may seek to offer evidence that is the product of an AI algorithmic search, requiring the government to lay a foundation for its admissibility as well as authenticate its accuracy and reliability. (In other words, comply with Federal Rules of Evidence 401, 402, and 403 and *Daubert*,[17] the Supreme Court case governing the admission of expert scientific evidence.) A defendant will likely seek its exclusion on the opposite grounds. One question is how much background courts will require on AI methodology before admitting machine learning outputs into evidence or to predicate search warrants. A second question is how much discovery courts will allow, or require, into the underlying algorithms and reasoning behind AI-based evidence.

Where AI data is used at criminal trial as evidence by the prosecution, a defendant may also assert a Sixth Amendment right to question the author of the algorithm. The Sixth Amendment provides that "In all criminal prosecutions, the accused shall enjoy the right . . . to be confronted with the witnesses against him." This right is understood to encompass the right to cross-examine witnesses at trial. An algorithm is not a witness, but in *Crawford*,[18] the Supreme Court held that the right to cross-examine witnesses extends, in some cases, to certain out-of-court "statements" introduced at trial, including statements to the police (as was the case in *Crawford*) as well as "statements that were made under circumstances which would lead an objective witness reasonably to believe that the statement would be available for use at a later trial." Significantly, the court subsequently held that certain lab reports were testimonial, and thus the technician or scientist who compiled the report was subject to examination. Before *Crawford*, many of these statements were admitted into evidence as business records or under generally recognized exceptions to the hearsay rules. In the absence of clarifying guidance from the court, lower courts have struggled to apply *Crawford* to documentary data and information later introduced as criminal evidence, such as lab reports and photographs. That is to say, it is applied in inconsistent manner and on a case-by-case basis. AI-generated information, later used as evidence, is fertile ground for *Crawford* challenge, including litigation over just who or what is "bearing witness." The software, the learning algorithm, the computer scientist who wrote the code, and the official who initiated the input are all candidates.

In civil context, private parties may challenge government efforts to collect data as violating their Fourth Amendment rights. For example, one can anticipate challenges to the government's authority to collect and hold data for AI purposes. Parties may also challenge international agreements seeking to regulate, curtail, or verify the use of AI in U.S. labs and industry. As a result, a specialist in AI law and policy must understand the basic parameters of Fourth Amendment search and seizure law. This will allow AI technologists and their lawyers to spot and avoid issues when possible and mitigate risks when not.

Fourth Amendment law starts with the language of the amendment. This may appear an obvious point. However, policy or litigation advocates often start with a theory or perspective regarding the Fourth Amendment rather than the text. In assessing the strength of an argument, policymakers should understand how far from the text and mainstream interpretation they are. The Fourth Amendment states:

> The right of the people to be secure in their persons, houses, papers, and effects, against unreasonable searches and seizures, shall not be violated, and no Warrants shall issue, but upon probable cause, supported by Oath or affirmation, and particularly describing the place to be searched, and the persons or things to be seized.

Not surprisingly, given the text, the threshold question for national security and criminal specialists is, often, will or does the government's action(s) amount to a search or seizure? In general, an action is a search for Fourth Amendment purposes, if (1) the government is seeking to find evidence of a crime that has, will, or is in the process of being committed; (2) the government is seeking to enforce civil or administrative rules and regulations; or (3) the government is targeting a U.S. person's communications or property within the United States for intelligence purposes where the person is suspected of being an "agent of a foreign power." "Agent of a Foreign Power" is broadly defined in the Foreign Intelligence Surveillance Act (FISA) and includes "lone wolves" and terrorist organizations as well as traditional intelligence actors.

The next threshold question is whether the search or seizure is reasonable. This depends on whether the person in question has a subjective expectation of privacy that is objectively reasonable in the place, object, or communication searched. This judicially crafted test from *United States v. Katz* (1967)[19] has been carried forward in numerous criminal cases since. Where a person has a reasonable expectation in privacy, the government is required to have probable cause to overcome that expectation. In criminal context, probable cause is addressed with both a substantive and procedural standard. Probable cause is generally defined as specific and articulable facts that will lead a reasonable person to conclude that a crime is, has been, or will be committed. That is the substantive test in federal practice. It is usually validated in the form of a warrant issued by a magistrate judge or a district judge. That is the procedural requirement.

In the case of overseas searches of U.S. persons or property, a warrant is not required, in part because courts cannot figure out where jurisdiction would rest to issue such a warrant. But at least one circuit court has held that an overseas search of a U.S. citizen's property must be reasonable to survive a motion to suppress in a criminal trial.[20] In the case of a search for foreign intelligence purposes within the United States, the government is required to get a FISA order. Finally, the Supreme Court held in *Verdugo-Urquidez* that the Fourth Amendment does not apply to "the search and seizure by United States agents of property owned by a nonresident alien and located in a foreign country." The "people" in the Fourth Amendment refers to "a class of persons who are part of a national community or who have otherwise developed sufficient connection with this country to be considered part of that community."[21]

The requirement for a warrant or order is not absolute. Courts have created and recognized exceptions to the requirement, including in exigent circumstances and searches incident to arrest. Courts have also consistently held that consent obviates the need for a warrant. Questions involving consent usually hinge on: (1) whether consent was, in fact, given, as in the case of a mandatory banner on a computer consenting to search as a condition of use; (2) whether consent was voluntary; (3) whether consent was valid, as in the case of a co-tenant or co-owner providing search authorization for shared space; or (4) the scope of the consent granted. Most important for AI, with respect to external or stored data, courts have relied on the so-called Third-Party Doctrine to address many Fourth Amendment questions.

The Third-Party Doctrine posits that if someone has voluntarily shared information with a third party, like a bank or a communications provider, then the person no longer has a reasonable expectation of privacy in that data, in the same way that if you share a secret with a third party, it is no longer a secret. The doctrine is based on two cases from the 1970s. In *United States v. Miller*,[22] the defendant was charged with tax evasion. To prove its case, the government subpoenaed Miller's banks for canceled checks and deposit slips. Miller sought to exclude the evidence on Fourth Amendment grounds, asserting the government was required to demonstrate probable cause and obtain a warrant before searching the records. The Supreme Court disagreed. The court concluded that the records were business records of the banks, not Miller's confidential communications. Moreover, his checks and deposit slips were necessarily exposed to bank employees in the ordinary course of business. That is how checks work. Therefore, Miller did not possess a reasonable expectation of privacy in the records.

The second case, *Smith v. Maryland* (1979),[23] involved a robbery suspect who subsequently harassed the victim via telephone and by driving by her home. To prove that the suspect was contacting the witness, the government placed a pen register on the suspect's telephone. It did so without a warrant. (A pen register records all of the numbers "dialed" out on a phone, in this case at the central telephone office. A trap-and-trace device "traps" all incoming calls and traces and records the number from which the calls originated.) When the suspect, Smith, subsequently challenged the admission of the evidence as a violation of the Fourth Amendment, the Supreme Court held that the suspect did not have an objectively reasonable expectation of privacy in the numbers he called, because he had voluntarily shared those numbers with the telephone company for placement and billing purposes. The court also relied on the long-standing and related distinction in Fourth Amendment law between the content of a communication and its transmission data, which, at least at the time, was equated to the difference between an envelope address and the contents within the envelope. (Note the use of metaphor.) As a result, while the law provides some Fourth Amendment protection for calling data, a pen register or trap-and-trace placement requires a showing of "relevance to an investigation" to obtain a court order; it does not require probable cause of a crime.

Two additional questions frequently arise in Fourth Amendment search context. However, these questions should not be conflated with the threshold constitutional questions about what is or is not reasonable or private under the Fourth Amendment. First, was/is the government authorized to collect and search for the information/data in question, and has the authorization process, if any, been properly invoked? In other words, whether the subject of collection has a reasonable expectation of privacy over information or not, the collection of that information may nonetheless exceed government authority. For example, the CIA is prohibited by statute from exercising any internal police or subpoena power. However, courts have also held that if the government has lawfully collected or received information and lawfully retains it, there is no longer a reasonable constitutional expectation of privacy with respect to subsequent searches of that information.

However, this leads to a second question: Is the data in question subject to other legal limitations or prohibitions? Regardless of whether a person retains a Fourth Amendment interest in information held by the government or not, the information may be subject to additional statutory, executive, or judicial protections. Statutory rights, for example, are found in the Privacy Act of 1974 and the Health Insurance Portability and Accountability Act (HIPAA), which impose limitations on how information can be shared, with whom, and when. In addition, executive directives regulate the way intentionally collected and incidentally collected information is stored, retained, and disseminated, if at all. These are known as minimization rules and procedures. Judicial orders may, in turn, delimit the information searched, retained, and disseminated in a case, as with a criminal search warrant, or do so on a programmatic basis as in the case of the 702 FISA program and court rulings. State governments may, for example, wish to legislatively delimit how license data and pictures may be used for AI data—that is, facial recognition—purposes by the federal government. Likewise, the government may wish to regulate how AI data sets are collected, stored, used, and shared.

The strength and logic of the Third-Party Doctrine is found in the distinction between content and data, as reflected in the envelope analogy. However, commentators have criticized the concept of third-party "waiver" from the outset. The problem, which courts have consciously overlooked, at least until *Carpenter*, is that telephone customers do not really have a choice as to whether they turn over the numbers they dial to their provider, or their cell phone location to a cell phone relay tower. It is voluntary only in the sense that it is knowing. The party can decline to place a call if they wish, turn off their smartphone, or perhaps use carrier pigeons to communicate instead. But the arrangement is no more voluntary than the contract of adhesion one signs for a washer and dryer, or the airplane ticket establishing the take-it-or-leave-it terms of acceptance. The adhesive nature of the doctrine has not caused courts much concern over the years.

The analysis breaks down further as old law meets new technologies, especially big data, algorithms, and machine learning. First, as noted, the doctrine dates to *Smith v. Maryland*, a 1979 case. Thus, the case and the court did not contemplate or account for the internet, the Internet of Things, or data mining. *Smith* is a rotary phone case. Second, the ubiquity of today's data has come to concern courts—the amount of data as well as the government's ability to access it, mine it, and connect it to other data and to do so retroactively. This has led to distinct but related lines of cases involving iPhones and GPS tracking, around which Fourth Amendment law now uncertainly orbits.

In 2014, in a case called *Riley*,[24] the Supreme Court addressed a split among lower appellate courts as to whether the government could search an iPhone incident to arrest. The case hinged, in part, on legal metaphor. Was an iPhone more like a container or a key to someone's home? The metaphor is important because long-standing doctrine provides that the police can search containers—like wallets and suitcases—found on a person incident to arrest. This is viewed as reasonable, because the purpose is to identify suspects, find contraband, and preserve evidence as well as protect officers and bystanders from the presence of hidden weapons. However, some courts, including my own in *Wicks*,[25] concluded that an iPhone was more akin to a key offering access to a person's home than it was to a wallet offering access to a person's identity. And this key provides access not only to the "home," but to a person's computer, their pictures, and a record of their communications (their filing cabinets); in other words, what the Fourth Amendment textually refers to as "houses, papers, and effects." Moreover, if the Fourth Amendment protects anything at all, courts agree it protects the sanctity of the home from unreasonable government searches. In *Riley*, the Supreme Court sided with the key rather than container analogy, holding that a separate warrant, or lawful predicate, was required to search an iPhone incident to arrest.

A different case, *Jones*,[26] involved the GPS tracking of a suspected drug dealer. Much like the Third-Party Doctrine, the Plain Sight Doctrine posits that if you leave something in plain sight, including yourself, you do not have an objectively reasonable expectation of privacy in that item, including from having that item surveilled as it moves about, like a car or a person (that is, visually but not physically searched) or an item left on a counter in a home that is otherwise lawfully entered. On this basis, and sound logic, it is not unreasonable for law enforcement officers to follow someone without a search or arrest warrant when the person is in public view. It is the same reason that one does not have a reasonable expectation of privacy from being seen on government video cameras in Times Square, train stations, and so on. The person in question is voluntarily placing themselves in plain view. However, to save resources and to avoid detection, law enforcement officers sometimes resort to GPS tracking rather than expending the manpower necessary to follow a person. This can be done by attaching a beacon to a vehicle or bag, for example, or it can be done by determining where a cell phone connects to cell phone towers. (Depending on context, including whether a person is seeking to evade surveillance, as many as twenty trained officers may be necessary to successfully follow someone.)

In *Jones*, the Supreme Court threw up a cautionary flag. Enough may be enough. Jones was a suspected gang member and drug dealer in Washington, D.C. The police decided to track his movements by placing a GPS device on a vehicle registered to his wife. The police obtained a warrant in the District of Columbia, which required installation within ten days. However, on the eleventh day the police attached the GPS device to the vehicle in Maryland. They proceeded to track Jones over four weeks. In 2005, Jones was charged with a series of drug offenses, but was acquitted of all offenses except one conspiracy charge on which the jury was hung (divided). Jones was subsequently convicted of the charge at retrial, in part based on the GPS tracking evidence placing Jones in the vicinity of drug activity. He appealed. In a plurality opinion (one in which a majority of the court agrees on the result, but not the reasoning), a unanimous court held the evidence inadmissible. The court did so based on a majority conclusion that the police had trespassed on Jones's property rights in placing the GPS device on his vehicle, aware that the police had exceeded the geographic and temporal limits of their warrant. However, five justices went further by suggesting in concurrence, but not in the majority opinion, that the case should have been decided based on Jones's reasonable expectation of privacy, because "longer-term GPS monitoring in government investigations of most offenses impinges on expectations of privacy."[27] The import was clear: the *Smith* stool was wobbling and might fall over.

Jones suggests that the Supreme Court is not comfortable with the aggregation of information that big data allows, because it undermines the content versus data distinction in Fourth Amendment law. One may move about in the open without expectation of privacy, providing a cell phone or GPS signal to one's carrier. But at some point, there may be such an aggregation of data as to effectively turn that data into content about one's life—one's friends, one's place of worship, one's dietary patterns, and so on.

One also wonders whether the outcome would have been different if the government had engaged in the exact same tracking but using gumshoes. Perhaps a lurking concern behind *Jones* is that GPS makes it too easy for the government, exposing not just Jones, but all of us, to perpetual tracking without a warrant or probable cause. Restated, the expenditure of human capital may serve as a demonstrative measure of reasonable suspicion in a way that running an algorithm against stored data does not, a form of de facto rather than de jure probable cause.

Jones also suggests that the Supreme Court may realize that while the Third-Party Doctrine may make sense in the context of a bank transaction or a communications carrier, it may not make sense with big data, AI, and the Internet of Things. Most customers understand that it would be hard to run a bank or a communications carrier without tracking the customer's transactions. Caveat emptor. A reasonable person should be on notice that a bank or communications carrier would retain such data and need to transfer some of that data to others to function. The intrusion is also finite. What may seem reasonable when applied to bank records or credit cards, however, looks a lot less so when the same data may be going to multiple parties, many of them unknown to the users/senders and many times without the data subject knowing it is happening. This may occur because the receiver shares the data with additional parties, or because the same data is being transmitted through multiple devices. In the IoT era, the Third-Party Doctrine may feel more like "The Unknown and Multiple Parties Doctrine."

This brings us to *Carpenter*—the case that might knock the Third-Party stool over. It is also a case, like *Youngstown*, that is so central to national security practice going forward that policymakers and lawyers must learn it and know it. It will be cited for all sorts of propositions, some accurate and some not. Specialists will need to know the difference.

Carpenter and an accomplice Sanders were convicted of nine armed robberies in and around Detroit in 2011. They were convicted, in part, based on evidence obtained from cell-site location information (CSLI) placing their cell phones near the crimes on the dates and times in question. The government collected data for Carpenter covering 127 days, and for Sanders covering 88 days. The court acknowledged that the government did so

> pursuant to a court order issued under the Stored Communications Act of 1986 (SCA). The SCA, which covers wire and electronic communications stored or communicated by Internet Service Providers, requires the government to show 'reasonable grounds' for believing that the records requested are 'relevant and material to an ongoing investigation.'"[28]

Carpenter challenged the admission of the cell-site data on the basis that he had a reasonable expectation of privacy in the data, and thus the government required a warrant supported by probable cause to overcome that expectation, not mere relevance to an investigation under the SCA. *Carpenter* cited *Jones*.

The Sixth Circuit disagreed, affirming the conviction. The Circuit Court distinguished *Jones* on two grounds. First, the government did not invade Carpenter's privacy or property to obtain the data. The data was classic third-party information. Second, the data was not particularly sensitive or private.

> GPS devices are accurate to within about fifty feet, which is accurate enough to show that the target is located within an individual building. . . . But here the cell-site data cannot tell that story. Instead, per the undisputed testimony at trial, the data could do no better than locate the defendants' cellphones within a 120- (or sometimes 60-) degree radial wedge extending between one-half mile and two miles in length.[29]

When the Supreme Court took the case for review, there was much anticipation, with commentators unsure whether the court would treat *Carpenter* as a straightforward application of the Third-Party Doctrine, as the Sixth Circuit had, or was looking for an opportunity to expand on *Jones*.

The court decided *Carpenter* in June 2018.[30] The court divided 5-4 with the four "predictable liberal" justices in the majority and four of the five "predictable conservative" justices in dissent. However, the deciding fifth vote came from Chief Justice Roberts rather than Justice Kennedy. The court concluded the acquisition of Carpenter's CSLI was a Fourth Amendment search. Therefore, the government was required to obtain a search warrant under the higher criminal constitutional probable cause standard ("some quantum of individualized suspicion") rather than the lower statutory standard of the SCA ("reasonable grounds" that the records are "relevant and material to an ongoing investigation"). In reaching this conclusion, the court stated that the cell-site records "lie at the intersection of two lines of cases . . . which inform our understanding of the privacy interests at stake." One line of cases (*Jones*-GPS) is addressed to a person's physical location and movements. The other line, the court noted, addresses what "a person keeps to himself and what he shares with others," citing *Smith* and *Miller*. The court then went on to distinguish these lines of cases before placing *Carpenter* into the *Jones* rather than *Smith* line of analysis.

The court argued that *Miller* and *Smith* did not rely solely on the act of sharing information with a third party, but also considered the "nature of the particular documents sought" while also asking "whether there is a legitimate expectation of privacy concerning their contents." In this regard, the court noted the government had acquired 12,898 location points "cataloguing Carpenter's movements—an average of 101 data points per day. . . . Cell phone location information is detailed, encyclopedic, and effortlessly compiled," the court wrote, it is "easy, cheap, and efficient. . . . We therefore decline to extend *Smith* and *Miller* to the collection of CSLI." The ubiquitous nature of cell phone data also addressed the second line of cases, dealing with a person's movements in plain view. Because cell phone carriers typically keep cell-site records for five years, the court concluded, "Whoever the suspect turns out to be, he has effectively been tailed every minute of every day for five years."

The dissent treated the case as a straightforward application of *Smith* and *Miller* and property law.

> Cell-site records, however, are no different from the many other kinds of business records the government has lawful right to obtain by compulsory process. Customers . . . do not own, possess, control, or use the records, and for that reason have no reasonable expectation that they cannot be disclosed pursuant to lawful compulsory process.

Moreover, "[t]he government acquired the records through an investigative process enacted by Congress. Upon approval by a neutral magistrate and based on the government's duty to show reasonable necessity . . ."[31]

The majority took pains to state that it was not overruling the Third-Party Doctrine (the "doctrine applies to telephone numbers and bank records; it is not clear whether its logic extends to the qualitatively different category of cell-site records"). The majority's qualifying caveats are extensive, almost apologetic. "Our decision today is a narrow one."

> We do not disturb the application of *Smith* and *Miller* or call into question conventional surveillance techniques and tools, such as security cameras. Nor do we address other business records that might incidentally reveal location information. Further, our opinion does not consider other collection techniques involving foreign affairs or national security.

Finally, the court reminds, the "ultimate measure of the constitutionality of a governmental search is 'reasonableness.'"

Carpenter, however, *is* new law. Since 1979, the Third-Party Doctrine has applied as doctrine. A majority of the court has now signaled a desire to look at the privacy implications of big data and the aggregation of data on a case-by-case basis and, perhaps, technology-by-technology basis. That *is* new. And it has implications for AI systems. Nor is it clear what the limiting principle is that might distinguish five years of cell-site data from five years of facial images drawn from security cameras or scraped from Facebook. The court's limitations notwithstanding, *Carpenter* may still be the case that pushes the Third-Party stool over. It is teetering, not just because of what the court wrote, but because those who follow emerging technologies and AI know what is coming. The court has constructed a careful aggregation paradigm for playing in the data waves without going over one's head. The rest of us see the digital tidal wave offshore.

Why does all this matter to AI? Because AI is the tidal wave, and it will raise a myriad of Fourth Amendment issues. Among other things:

1. AI-generated results will serve as a predicate for probable cause.

2. AI will search data sets, training and otherwise, that may themselves be the product of a government search and subject to Fourth Amendment analysis.

3. AI, computational capacity, big data, and the IoT may change our personal as well as legal perceptions about what is "reasonable" in terms of the breadth and depth of what can be derived from data and not just content.

4. If the Third-Party Doctrine disappears, in part, or in whole, a large volume of AI data *may* disappear with it, depending, of course, on

what if anything replaces the doctrine. For example, training data for machine learning that is currently collected and used pursuant to the Third-Party Doctrine may be in jeopardy or be challenged, like license photos for facial recognition.

5. The government may search for workarounds, such as purchasing data as a commercial actor rather than "seizing" it.

The doctrine may linger in uncertain limbo, subject to incremental litigation making it harder to proceed with new AI architectures, as AI actors become cautious about using Third-Party data. Alternatively, uncertainty could drive policymakers to provide clarity in executive policy or legislation.

Carpenter, not *Smith*, now becomes a, and perhaps the, new pivot point. Civil plaintiffs and criminal defendants will seek to tie the government's use of data aggregation and new technologies to the court's descriptions of CSLI as "detailed, encyclopedic, and effortlessly compiled," or "easy, cheap, and efficient." "[W]hen the government tracks the location of a cell phone, it achieves near perfect surveillance, as if it had attached an ankle monitor to the phone's user . . . police need not even know in advance whether they want to follow a particular individual, or when."[32] The government, in turn, will seek to limit *Carpenter* to CSLI only, and otherwise test, push, and explore the court's apparent openness to exceptions for foreign affairs, national security, and "conventional surveillance techniques and tools." All sides, of course, will also argue that *Carpenter* is a narrow case (as the court said), not relevant and not on point to the technology or use at hand. They just will do so at different times and for different reasons.

This means that if the government is going to continue down the AI road for law enforcement and intelligence purposes, as it is, will, and must, it should offer a viable legal doctrine to replace the Third-Party Doctrine, and, in light of *Carpenter*, sooner rather than later. If the government does not do so, and do so in a persuasive way that courts accept, the courts, and ultimately the Supreme Court, will do so, case by case and slowly over time. That will make it harder to invest in and operate AI applications in a consistent and predictable manner. Another possibility is that judicial concerns about the aggregation of data—expressed in the context of criminal law cases challenging the Third-Party Doctrine, may prompt Congress to consider additional statutory rules and rights over data collected by the government (for example, license photos) or available to the government (for example, the internet) beyond what might be required by constitutional law.

One problem with deferring to judicial review is that the courts are inconsistent on Fourth Amendment law, especially when "new" technology is involved. And, as *Carpenter* illustrates, issues are rarely definitively resolved rather than deferred. Consider the civil litigation challenging the government's use of section 215 of the PATRIOT Act to collect metadata. As is well known now, shortly after 9/11, the government started to collect and store metadata from carriers on millions of calls, querying the data for connections going three hops out from the original seed call. (See *Klayman v. Obama*[33] and *ACLU v. Clapper*.[34]) The government did so on the basis that the information was third-party information for which there was no reasonable expectation of privacy. It relied on section 215 for authority to collect the information as business records "relevant to an authorized investigation." What was the relevant investigation? All ongoing investigations or future investigations of terrorist incidents for which the metadata from millions of calls might prove useful in finding suspects or eliminating suspects. Most lawyers know that relevance is an elastic as well as low standard, but this was a creative and elastic argument.

The U.S. District Court in the District of Columbia found that the civil plaintiffs would likely prevail on their Fourth Amendment claim at trial, and thus granted a preliminary injunction against the government collecting metadata from the plaintiffs. It was unreasonable, the court held, in part because the government could not demonstrate that it was necessary, as the government could not point to a single terrorist attack that had been stopped because of the program. In contrast, the U.S. District Court for the Southern District of New York ruled on the same law and essentially the same facts that the program was reasonable and therefore constitutional. What was reasonable, the court determined, was not measured by attacks stopped, but the degree to which the program helped the government connect the dots and prevent future acts of terrorism. The information helped to isolate leads, eliminate leads, and better create an overall threat mosaic. In the end, the relevant appeals courts, the Second Circuit and the D.C. Circuit, concluded that the government had exceeded its statutory 215 authority. Thus, they did not ultimately define the constitutional boundaries of the metadata problem presented—that is, rule on what is reasonable and unreasonable in the IoT metadata age when it comes to public expectations of privacy.

Here are the takeaways.

Most Fourth Amendment law is practiced by government attorneys in criminal, intelligence, and civil contexts. Government actors will look to agency authorizing rules and guidance, as well as scenario-specific legal concurrences from internal lawyers. General counsel, in turn, will look to case law and good-faith extrapolation of case law interpretation to determine where to draw the Fourth Amendment lines. The law that applies is found in the Constitution, statute, case law, and executive directives. Oversight comes in the form of congressional inquiry, academic commentary, and litigation in criminal cases or where plaintiffs can establish standing to pursue civil privacy claims.

This means that courts are likely to set the left and right Fourth Amendment boundaries as to what is permitted, in the context of issuing warrants, orders, and reviewing programs, or when reviewing motions to suppress the admission of evidence at trial. Absent clear left and right boundaries in case law, or changing boundaries, one of two things is sure to happen, or maybe both. Depending on personalities and cultures, government lawyers may be more cautious and incremental in their advice. This is problematic, because operators need clear guidance to build programs, collect data, and use data. Whatever its flaws, the Third-Party Doctrine before *Carpenter* provided a relatively clear line of demarcation between what is reasonable and what is not. Alternatively, or as well, lawyers may become consumed with the national security mission, saying yes to everything, and essentially acting without meaningful boundary or at least out to Mike Hayden's edge of the law.

This has its own consequence, including the risk that courts or the Congress will snap the law back in response, curtailing the authority to act, but without the sort of nuanced knowledge of how the U.S. government uses data to train AI or for national security use. Most Fourth Amendment litigation occurs in criminal cases involving motions to suppress evidence with courts applying the heightened standard of criminal probable cause to the facts. One detects an increasing judicial unease with the aggregation of data. This may spill over into how courts look at civil challenges to the use of AI for national security reasons, such as watch lists and sanctions enforcement. One key question is whether, when, and how the aggregation concern will topple the Third-Party Doctrine. Another alternative is that Congress will do so itself by establishing statutory boundaries to data collection, use, and retention.

The question arises: when it comes to AI and the Fourth Amendment, does the executive branch want to roll the judicial dice or fill the vacuum itself first through executive policy or a legislative framework? One problem courts will have is that they are limited to the record of trial and the evidence before the court as they try to capture in judicial amber the moment in time in which an AI machine-learning algorithm searches data or seizes data. Case law is inherently incremental, as courts are limited to deciding the case or controversy before them. Usually they do so in a cautious or narrow manner, conscious that a different set of facts might change the analysis and thus they should not reach too far. Wouldn't it be better for the government to offer a doctrinal replacement for the Third-Party Doctrine on the basis not only of all the facts known to the government, in and out of court, but also knowledge of what is coming down the AI road?

One option is to set the Third-Party Doctrine aside and return to first principles and a fresh look at three questions:

1. What is *reasonable* in the context of big data analytics, IoT, and AI?

2. What *authority* should the government have to collect, analyze, retain, and disseminate information for law enforcement, intelligence, AI training, and "in case we need it" reasons?

3. Subject to what statutory and procedural limitations and *safeguards*, before, during, and after?

The answer starts with the Fourth Amendment and the meaning of "reasonable." Here, "originalists," who, in theory, focus on the text of the Constitution alone, and "realists," who interpret the Constitution as a living document reflecting evolving societal norms, might share common ground. For "reasonable" is a fixed textual word, but necessarily one with evolving and contextual meaning. What is reasonable in a military barracks, for example, may be unreasonable in a civilian home.

One need not try to figure out the precise moment when an AI application becomes a search or a seizure, or whether review of a training data set is a search or something else. Rather, one might ask, is it reasonable, knowing what we know about AI and knowing the procedures the government has put into place, to ensure proper use of data sets, algorithms, and their results? What makes it reasonable? What makes it unreasonable? Here, one might note that AI itself may be its own best safeguard, providing a mechanism to determine when, why, and how government actors have accessed and used AI capacities. One area where AI systems already outperform humans is in spotting anomalies, including, presumably, if used to determine when government actors access data or systems outside ordinary practice and need.

The goal is purposeful policy choice and accountable decisionmaking regarding who is using data, how, and subject to what limitations. Whether determined by courts, legislators, or policymakers, a factors approach to what is reasonable might best address security and privacy while keeping pace with technological change.

A factors approach to what is reasonable might include the following elements:

Place of intrusion. What is being searched? Is it data or content? A home, a phone, a room, a vehicle? And, if it is data, how much, in terms of depth and breadth? Is it specific to a person—that is, personally identifiable information? This is consistent with the Supreme Court's existing distinction between searches that penetrate the home—for example, infrared intrusion—and searches that do not—such as flyovers.

Duration of intrusion. What is the duration of the intrusion? For how long is a person being tracked by GPS or how far back is data being reviewed and analyzed regarding a person's communications or movements? Much as the law incorporates statutes of limitation beyond which a person need no longer fear prosecution, "reasonable" search parameters might adopt the same concept, with a parallel concept that the more serious the investigative purpose or predicate, the longer the permitted scope of historical data review.

Purpose of the intrusion. What is the underlying predicate for the use of the data?

Degree to which the individual has demonstrated an intent to protect and preserve the privacy of the search object, data, or act in question. Did the individual in question encrypt their communications; turn off their phone or location marker; use passcodes; take measures to minimize third-party disclosures; and did the individual personally post, send, or tweet the information into cyberspace? The Stored Communications Act uses a similar framework, for example.

Degree to which the search implicates or impinges on other constitutional rights. Here the primary concern is First Amendment speech.

Clarity with which the underlying activity is authorized, by statute, and statutory procedures followed. While a statute cannot make an otherwise unconstitutional act constitutional, it can reflect a societal sense of what is objectively reasonable.

Degree to which the initiation and continuation of the search is subject to judicial or other independent review. In this regard, *Jones* seems a more problematic case than *Carpenter*. Law enforcement authorities did just what they were supposed to do in *Carpenter*. They obtained a court order for business records from the cell-site carrier; the time covered was coterminous with the period of the crime spree; and, perhaps most important, the order was not open-ended: it was subject to review by the court if it did not bear fruit and was for a time certain. In contrast, the *Jones* GPS was conducted without prior approval, was ongoing and continuous, and was not subject to ongoing review and validation.

————

The problem with a factors approach is that it does not always produce clear or predictive guidance. One court may find 122 days of cell-site records too long, while another is not bothered at all. One might also consider whether a court has, in fact, identified and applied factors rather than an "I do not like what I see" approach.

The strength of a factors approach is that it accounts for new technology, evolving norms, and changing contexts. It also can serve as a lever to compel disciplined process and review by executive actors and subsequent appraisers. Moreover, factors can impose discipline on what otherwise may be an instinctive or snap process. Where the government is shown to have genuinely walked through relevant factual and legal factors, courts will give greater deference to executive decisions; the government also tends to reach better results. A factors approach also tends to find its own equilibrium, as case law acts like the weighted adjustments that occur during AI machine learning. However, the process is a bit slower!

In any event, we should have this debate now, so that we might better and sooner reach our legal equilibrium.

Fifth Amendment

The Fifth Amendment may present the most varied potential challenges to the use, or directed use, of AI by the government. It provides, in relevant part: "No person shall . . . be deprived of life, liberty, or property, without due process law; nor shall private property be taken for public use without just compensation."

Three potential issues are immediate. First, do the government's actions violate an individual's, university's, or corporation's right to Fifth Amendment procedural due process, for example, by imposing an obligation or a restriction, or depriving a person of life, liberty, or property, without due opportunity to be heard and, presumably, challenge the basis for the action, including perhaps the use of an algorithm in doing so? This might arise in a myriad of AI scenarios, such as the use of AI algorithms to target individuals for collection or attack; the use of AI to model and apply control lists, including the no-fly list and IEEPA sanctions lists. Second, AI may present issues of substantive due process, where an AI application reflects bias toward, or has a disproportionate impact on, a suspect or protected class of persons based on categories like gender, race, or religion. As discussed below, "bias" may be intentional—for example, in the case of a facial recognition tool designed to identify males. It may also be unintentional and hidden, as in the case of tainted or stale data, or design function. Third, the Fifth Amendment authorizes the taking of private property "for public use," provided the government pays just compensation. Understanding that most of the AI research in the United States is conducted by industry and academia, imagine that one such entity creates a process or algorithm of national security importance. The takings clause would seem to suggest that the government could seize the property for public use, provided it paid just compensation for doing so. To state the obvious, this would present values as well as valuation issues.

There are two types of constitutional due process: substantive and procedural. Substantive due process is largely addressed to the fair and equal treatment of similarly situated persons and groups. Civil rights, such as the equal right to vote and to education, are a product of substantive due process, derived from the Fifth, Thirteenth, and Fourteenth Amendments, for example. Procedural due process is just that: the process that is constitutionally required, if at all, before the government can deprive someone of their life, liberty, or property.

PROCEDURAL DUE PROCESS

For many courts, procedural due process analysis starts with *Matthews v. Eldridge*.[35] This is a 1976 case involving the adjudication of disability benefits under the Social Security Administration Act. When Matthews was denied benefits without a hearing, he sued the commissioner of Social Security, Eldridge. The Supreme Court held that Matthews was entitled to a hearing. In doing so, the court created a three-part balancing test for determining whether a person has received procedural due process: (1) the importance of the interest at stake; (2) the risk of an erroneous deprivation of that interest because of the procedures used and the probable value of additional procedural safeguards; and (3) the government's interest.

Courts have subsequently applied *Mathews* in other contexts, including national security contexts, such as the administration of the no-fly list.[36] Remarkably, the executive branch has itself apparently applied *Matthews* in national security contexts, such as military targeting, where it has not previously been applied. This occurred in a 2010 Office of Legal Counsel opinion addressed to the targeting of dual U.S.-Saudi citizen Anwar al-Awlaki, where the Justice Department concluded that under *Matthews*, no further process was due before the president, as commander in chief, authorized a missile strike to kill al-Awlaki pursuant to the law of armed conflict.[37] For sure, process was due, but not due process. The process that was due was the rigorous but ordinary process of target review by military lawyers and decisionmakers. al-Awlaki was killed by a drone strike in 2011.

There is an AI lesson here, going forward. Where AI is used in national security context, courts will likely apply due process principles to AI results. Therefore, the executive branch will need to be able to articulate how and in what manner the plaintiff or accused has been able to reasonably challenge those results, and if not, why not. Where process is due, courts will look to the executive branch to provide it, and if the executive branch does not, courts will likely do so themselves. And, if they do so, they will look in the first instance to *Matthews*. Unless, of course, the government believes there is a more apt test than a Social Security disability case! The executive branch should now affirmatively consider where, when, and how to apply process to AI questions, including due process (that required by the Fifth Amendment) to national security decisions using AI.

A Fifth Amendment issue might also arise where foreign actors are prohibited or restricted in accessing U.S. universities. This was an issue in litigation involving the so-called Trump administration travel bans. Depending on the role of private industry in such applications, private industry may be sued as well on a tort basis, or sue the government, raising questions of liability, indemnity, and insurance, among others. In a related, but distinct, legal manner, an individual may challenge an AI application on the ground of equal protection—for example, in the application of the training sets for machine learning on a theory that the algorithm biased a protected class of people. This has already occurred in the case of algorithms used for bail hearings and to predict recidivism risks for parole candidates, where litigants have argued there is an inherent bias against African Americans based on training data and algorithm design.[38] One might expect similar challenges where AI is used to identify national security threats, and the results reflect actual or perceived bias against certain religions, races, or nationalities. Machine learning and black box neural networks may pose special challenges. Can one effectively challenge a result without knowing and understanding the algorithms involved and what happens within the black box of machine learning? One might also ask if, under *Crawford*, the subject of AI-generated evidence may insist on examining the software engineer. The government can, of course, mitigate against such challenges on the front end in the way it designs algorithms and selects data sets as well as in the manner it commits to explaining which algorithmic features were selected and why. Policymakers and lawyers should ask about the design of algorithms and insist on plain English answers. If they don't, courts likely will.

BIAS AND SUBSTANTIVE DUE PROCESS

Bias is often associated with the human application of stereotypes or prejudices to an ethnic, gender, racial, or other identity group. Such bias is evident, for example, in the manner that the government of China uses AI tools such as facial recognition to track, control, and discriminate against Uighurs. In U.S. law, these categories are generally recognized as "suspect classes" of persons under the equal protection clause of the Fifth Amendment, as applied to the federal government, and the Fourteenth Amendment as applied to the individual states. That means that any application of the law that discriminates against one or more suspect classes of persons—that is, treats them differently from the populace as a whole—if challenged in court, must pass either a strict scrutiny test, intermediate test, or rational basis test, depending on the class. Race receives strict scrutiny, requiring the government to show a compelling government interest for the discriminate treatment and that the means used are narrowly tailored to accomplish that interest. Gender is subject to intermediate review, in which case the disparate treatment must further an important government interest and do so by means that are substantially related to the interest.

For AI, however, bias might be defined in broader terms as a witting or unwitting (conscious or subconscious) predisposition that can undermine the accuracy of an AI application or output. Bias also addresses a range of cognitive tendencies that can undermine objective analysis and technical accuracy, such as groupthink, confirmation bias, anchoring bias, and so on. Significantly, in AI context, bias also refers to unintentional design and data flaws that can undermine the objective and predictive accuracy of AI outputs. Unintentional bias is often difficult to discern, because it is embedded in the design of an AI system or in the data used to train an algorithm. Where bias goes unseen, decisionmakers may subsequently place undue reliance on AI outputs that do not warrant such reliance because they are predicated on biased input. This can have pernicious security effect in at least two ways. It can undermine confidence in and support for national security decisionmaking through the generation of a disproportionate number of false positives. And it can result in the failure to identify authentic threats to security in a timely manner, where, for example, bias in the design of a search algorithm makes it accurate in identifying male suspects, but incapable of finding and accurately identifying female suspects. It can also raise constitutional due process concerns.

Whether subject to litigation or not, the government is bound to follow the requirements of the Fifth Amendment and do so in good faith. It should wish to do so because an AI application that can withstand Fifth Amendment scrutiny is likely to be more accurate in its function than one that cannot. Moreover, not all bias presents Fifth Amendment concerns, just as not all process must accord with "due process." The Fifth Amendment and case law presents the constitutional standard. Thus, technologists, policymakers, and lawyers should ask in each context what process is appropriate and if there is unintended bias embedded in a system, and if so, why and where. To do so, it is helpful to consider where and how bias might arise.

Data and Design Bias
Technical bias might derive from data sets or algorithms that rely on flawed or dated information. For example, an algorithm intended to identify potentially successful job applicants might rely on past successful job performance as an indicator of future successful job performance, and derive from that data certain preferred hiring characteristics, such as age, school, and experience. However, such a data set might rely on dated data, for example, from a period when women, minorities, or foreign nationals were not full participants in the relevant employment market, and thus exclude at least 50 percent of the potential workforce. Likewise, such data might unwittingly incorporate human bias, perhaps in the form of a past company policy to only hire persons from certain schools. This might have seemed an objective criterion at the time the company adopted the policy, but it necessarily incorporates any socioeconomic bias and other biases of the college admissions process at the time. Thus, in this search, the algorithm might exclude candidates who might perform even better than the "successful job performer" set from the past. Similar concerns have been raised about algorithms designed to inform parole decisions by predicting future recidivism or bail risk, which may rely too heavily on socioeconomic status and neighborhood locations as predic-

tive criteria or self-fulfilling criteria. The police anticipating more crime in certain neighborhoods will patrol those neighborhoods in greater force and thus make more arrests, identify more crime, and in the process reinforce confidence in the algorithm's capacity to predict criminal conduct. One can and should debate the validity of using such algorithms— and there are active debates—but all sides should be able to agree that factors that might skew data should be identified and either eliminated or mitigated.

One can imagine how similar bias might migrate into data sets designed to train machine learning AI to predict terrorism recruitment or threats. First, the data may rely too heavily on international actors versus domestic actors, due to the domestic considerations, the perceptions of the designers, or dated data. Second, there will not be as much data, in contrast to an Amazon shopping algorithm or YouTube push algorithm, thus human actors may put too much credence in the reliability of the predictive output they receive. As a general matter, the more data that is used to train a predictive algorithm the more accurate the result. As a result, if an algorithm trained to predict risk of terrorism is trained on males with beards, it will be better at locating and identifying people with beards. Subsequently, more males with beards will likely be identified as potential terrorists and more males will be found to be engaged in suspicious activities, thus validating the algorithm and the choice of criteria. Third, the algorithm may omit an important class of potential actor—potential female actors—given the dearth of prior female perpetrators.

This example demonstrates that the risk is not just in false positives, the focus of much bias analysis to date, but in the potential failure to identify credible risks—false negatives. For example, disparities in facial recognition data between males and females may lead to higher inaccuracies in identifying female subjects. This has an equal protection and fairness component if it results in an increase in the number of false positives, for example, the number of innocent female travelers identified for extra screening or questioning at airports. But it has security implications if it results in an inability to track and locate known security subjects or threats—for example, a search for a wanted person on London CCTV camera feeds.

Bias may also arrive in the form of design ambiguity. This might occur when the reasoning behind a match is necessary to understand the value or import of the match. To illustrate, consider the queen who asks, "AI, AI on the wall, who is the fairest of them all?" "Bias" in this context comes in the form of the computer engineer's predisposition regarding the meaning of the word "fair," or perhaps on whether the algorithm is programmed to use the most prevalent use of the term "fair" in the first instance. The queen may be surprised when the answer comes back "Learned Hand"—a judge known for his commitment to even-handed process. In national security context, a similar problem may arise with an algorithm designed to assess risk. What is risk? An algorithm will almost certainly incorporate the fears, tolerances, and perceptions of its designers. The problem may be aggravated when the algorithm is both human-generated and machine-generated—a centaur—making it all the harder to transparently see where and how cognitive bias might have entered the system.

Unwitting Human Bias

Unwitting human bias may also affect AI accuracy, by which is meant the unintentional infusion into an application of human preferences, stereotypes, values, or knowledge. Returning to the risk algorithm, an engineer might apply engineering principles to a risk equation. Richard Posner has done just this in assessing terrorism risk by using a law and economics model to factor the financial costs of preventing terrorist attacks.[39] The result is a mathematical equation ($\frac{p}{1-p} > \frac{b(d) + d + w(p,d)}{a}$), a logical choice for a computer engineer. However, the equation does not account for human behavior, which is informed not only by the calculation of objective zero-sum costs, but also the emotional impact of fear. Embed Posner's equation or model into software code, and the user would not know the algorithm was using a law and economics model to assess risk, unless of course the design was transparent or policymakers affirmatively asked.

Similarly, engineers may design algorithms to search for particular words or phrases, which may make sense if one is searching for persons engaged in radicalizing internet users. But without deep cultural and language knowledge, a computer scientist might design a search using the wrong terms as features. Phrases like "the bomb," "knock 'em dead," and "kill it" all mean one thing in youthful American vernacular, but quite a different thing to an algorithm searching for terrorist profiles on the internet. Imagine the same scenario using foreign languages. Likewise, an engineer designing an algorithm to search for white nationalists and domestic terrorism may not know the import of "the fourteen words" and thus unwittingly design an algorithm that misses a potential data threat stream.

Intentional Bias

Scientists, operators, and decisionmakers may use AI facial recognition tools or predictive algorithms to target disfavored or vulnerable groups. Algorithms can be designed to identify and select certain real and perceived social identity descriptors associated with race, gender, sexuality, national origin, religion, disability, and so on. With this capacity, for example, facial recognition technology can identify and track certain ethnic groups, as is the case in China, where AI is used to identify persons with "Uighur characteristics." Although clearly pernicious in the profiling of Uighurs—or, more accurately, a band of physical characteristics Chinese state security services associate with Uighurs—one ethical question is whether the purposeful uses of social identity descriptors are ever appropriate AI search parameters. The ethical answer may depend in part on the purpose for which social identity descriptors are used, as well as how one defines "profiling" and how one defines "search parameter."

On the one hand, there are qualitative differences between the reactive versus predictive uses of social identity descriptors. For example, using a suspect's description, including social identity descriptors, in response to a credible predicate makes sense. Of course, one needs to consider that the initial social indicator that might trigger the use of an AI application may itself be affected by cognitive, societal, or personal bias, including conditioned expectations. It is also common practice. If one is using facial recognition to search for a known suspect—or, in a less pejorative sense, a person identified in an Amber alert—you would not expect law enforcement or national security services to employ race-gender-or-age-neutral input or an algorithm incapable of searching for the specific or reported characteristics of the victim or suspect. To place the point in pure national security context, if one searched video feeds for one of ISIS leader al Baghdadi's wives who was suspected of having fled the Idib compound in 2019, there is nothing inherently unethical about using an algorithm that is "biased" in favor of identifying a female gait, or a person with the skin tone or facial structure associated with one of al Baghdadi's wives, provided such characteristics were credibly linked to the wife. From an ethical standpoint, national security officials and law enforcement officials have a duty to use all lawfully available tools to accomplish the security mission. One potential challenge to individually based suspect descriptions is that to the extent social identities are fluid rather than fixed, they may be difficult to code and for officials to implement fairly and accurately.

On the other hand, using a suspect category to identify persons who might engage in an unlawful act on a predictive basis using social identifiers—absent a credible predicate in the form of reasonable suspicion/probable cause—is an exercise in bias. National security specialists should eschew such an approach on national security grounds and not just legal grounds. First, security resources being finite, it follows that resources used in this manner are resources that cannot be used to address credible leads elsewhere. Second, where a suspect group—or, for that matter, any group—feels unfairly "targeted," members of the group will be less likely to share the sort of information that leads to credible threats.

Use of racial and other social identifying descriptors is also inherently risky. One can imagine how intentional and unintentional human bias might enter the equation as a computer scientist embeds what they believe are the characteristics of a race or ethnicity into facial recognition software. Race and ethnicity are inherently ambiguous terms, like "fair" and "risk," covering a wide continuum of blended skin tones and hues, hair colors, and so on. Bias may also occur unwittingly in machine learning applications that may not be designed to rely on social identity descriptors, but nonetheless rely on such characteristics within the neural network black box. In both cases, such bias can lead to both the under and over inclusion of the targeted group, as race, ethnicity, and even gender are malleable concepts. Thus, it may have unintended discriminatory effect if, for example, facial recognition technology results in a high rate of false positives for persons of color or women.

Clear "black letter" rules are easier to identify and enforce than contextual rules. In other words, it is easier to prohibit racial profiling by eliminating race as an algorithmic parameter altogether than to restrict such use to "appropriate uses passing the strict scrutiny test." Even were the strict scrutiny test understandable and employable at the tactical level of AI design and deployment, invariably the wider the use of a method the more likely the predicate will be misunderstood, misapplied, or abused. This phenomenon is seen with the different ways in which America's nineteen thousand police forces approach the question of profiling today even where judges would tell you the law, if not its implementation, is clear on what is permitted and not permitted. This concern is compounded because many AI applications designed to recognize social identifying descriptors, especially gender, are inconsistent in their application. Facial recognition technology has proven more accurate in identifying male and Caucasian faces than faces of females or people of color. Developers dispute the accuracy of this reporting, but so far, the dispute is about degrees of variance, not its presence. Finally, social identifying descriptors are easy to spoof or disguise if it is known that an application or security force is searching for such descriptors and the target audience seeks to evade detection. Thus, AI security applications that rely on social identifying descriptors alone run the risk of error.

It is easy to be for national security and against profiling. But where AI and security are concerned, one should avoid blithe, dogmatic, or simple answers. There is great variance in the quality, nature, and purpose of AI applications. Thus, an absolute prohibition might eliminate essential security tools, just as unregulated use of such terms might encourage the sort of profiling that undermines security and degrades public trust. What, then, is the answer? One answer is sound process—timely, contextual, and meaningful. "Timely" means at the point where input can most effectively influence outcomes—which, in turn, means at the design phase, testing phase, and deployment phases of AI development. "Contextual" means specific to the tool and use in question and with actual knowledge of the tool's purposes, capabilities, and weaknesses. "Meaningful" means independent, impartial, and accountable. More specifically, the person using or designing an application should not also validate its ethical design or use. In addition, to the extent feasible, the system's parameters should be known or retrievable. The system should be subject to a process of ongoing review and adjustment. The rules, if any, regarding the permissible use of social identifying descriptors, should also be enunciated and clear. Finally, the answer is also found in asking the right questions, which policymakers should want to ask not just for legal reasons, but for security effect:

- Who designed the algorithm at play and subject to what process of review?

- Are the algorithm's selection criteria known? Iterative? Retrievable in a transparent form? If not, why not?

- Does the application rely on a neural network? If so, is there risk that the system will rely on parameters that are unintended or unknown to the designers or operators? Is it possible to identify those potential parameters? How high is the risk? Is the risk demonstrated? How is the risk mitigated?

- Is the input query or prompt asking for a judgment, a fact, or a prediction? Is the judgment, fact, or prediction subject to ambiguity in response?

- Do the criteria include real or perceived racial, ethnic, gender, or other sensitive categories of social identity descriptors? If so, why? And have engineers and lawyers reviewed the way these criteria were weighted in and by the algorithm, as part of the design function and on an ongoing basis? In accord with what process of validation and review?

- Are there situational factors or facts in play that might, could, or should alter the algorithm's predictive accuracy?

- Is the application one in which nuance and cultural knowledge is essential to determine the accuracy of the AI application? To properly query the AI application?

- Are the search terms and equations objective or ambiguous in character? Can they be more precise and more objective? If not, why not?

- Was the algorithm trained on similar or apt data for the function for which it is being used?

- What is the application's false positive rate? What is the false negative rate?

- Is there disparity shown in the confidence threshold as between classes of persons based on racial characteristics, ethnicity, and gender, and so on? If so, are there logical and objective reasons for such disparity?

- What information corroborates or disputes the determination reached by the AI application? Is the application of the AI designed to allow for such real-time assessment? If not, is that based on operational necessity, or simply one of design? If not, is there a process for such assessment that occurs after the fact?

THE TAKINGS CLAUSE

A third due process inquiry is likely to arise in AI context: does government action deprive an actor of property without just compensation? The Fifth Amendment Takings Clause states: ". . . nor shall private property be taken for public use without just compensation." The classic takings scenario involves the appropriation of land to build public works, for example, a highway. However, in AI context, it may involve the use or diversion of private industry capacity pursuant to the DPA, ISA, or other authority. A taking can be partial in terms of time or use. There are five questions that generally arise:

1. Does the government have the authority to engage in the act or actions in question?

2. Did the government "take" property, for the purpose of the clause? If so, in what sense? Did it seize the property? Impinge on its value or use? For how long?

3. Was the property taken "for public use?"

4. Is "just compensation" warranted? If so, pursuant to what method of valuation? Is the value uncertain, speculative?

5. In accordance with what process will these questions be addressed?

The key question may be the first: does the government have statutory authority to direct a U.S. company or academic institution to provide AI capacity or services in the first place, or, perhaps, seize or use data? Where a legislative authority is ambiguous, and the president can credibly assert that he is also relying on an enumerated or implied Article II authority, a court may more likely defer to an executive branch national security determination. A court will offer even greater deference if the Takings Clause has been followed, including an established and fair process for assessing just compensation. Equally important in national security context, a court will more likely abstain from enjoining the action in question at the outset of litigation. All of this is illustrated by the seminal *Youngstown* case.

YOUNGSTOWN

Youngstown explores national security separation of powers. Arguably, it remains the most important case for defining the limits of the president's powers to address national security within the United States, and specifically his power to regulate industry for national security reasons. For these reasons, it is among the most frequently cited cases in security practice. Therefore, policymakers and lawyers must know what it says, and, just as important, what it does not say. Because you can be sure someone will stretch or confine its reach for tactical rather than objective analytical reasons.

Faced with the prospect of a labor strike in the steel mills in April 1952, during the Korean War, President Truman directed secretary of commerce, Charles Sawyer, to "take possession and operate the plants and facilities of certain steel companies." The April 8 order listed over eighty such companies. As its basis, President Truman cited "the authority vested in me by the Constitution and laws of the United States, and as President of the United States and Commander in Chief of the armed forces." Notably, while the president relied on "the laws of the United States," he did not specify which laws, including three that addressed labor disputes.[40]

The Taft-Hartley Act, which Congress passed in 1947, included provisions for addressing and resolving labor disputes. However, the bill passed over President Truman's veto and the president stated that, under the act, "the union has already done more, voluntarily, than it could be required to do under the Taft-Hartley Act." Section 18 of the Selective Service Act authorized the president

> to take immediate possession of any plant, mine, or other facility where he determines that it is in the national interest of the national security for the government to obtain prompt delivery of any articles or materials the procurement of which has been authorized by the Congress exclusively for the use of the armed forces.[41]

However, the act included procedural requirements for congressional authorization and advisory board consultation, which ran counter to the president's sense of urgency conveyed in his radio and television address on the steel mill seizures. "We do not need further delay and a prolonging of the crisis. We need a settlement and we need it fast."[42] Finally, the president did not rely on Title V of the recently passed Defense Production Act—the section that provided a labor dispute mechanism.[43]

The affected companies sued Secretary Sawyer, seeking to enjoin enforcement of the president's order. The plaintiffs won in district court. The D.C. Circuit then stayed the trial court's injunction by a vote of 5-4, with the court sitting en banc; however, the D.C. Circuit conditioned its ruling on the parties immediately seeking Supreme Court review, bucking the issues presented to the Supreme Court. The government did so on May 2, 1952. The court granted the case and heard oral argument on May 12 and 13, just ten days later. After five hours of oral argument and three weeks of deliberation, the Supreme Court issued its decision on June 2, 1952. Ruling 6-3, the court removed the stay and held for the plaintiff steel companies, upholding the district court's injunction barring implementation of the order.

The clarity of the decision was diluted somewhat by the six different majority opinions, a lead opinion written by Justice Black and five separate concurrences. The distinction between these opinions is found in the absolute versus nuanced nature of the analysis. Justice Black concluded emphatically that the president did not have authority to seize the steel mills.

The president's power, if any, to issue the order must stem either from an act of Congress or from the Constitution itself. There is no statute that expressly authorizes the president to take possession of property as he did here. Nor is there any act of Congress to which our attention has been directed from which such a power can fairly be implied. . . . Even though theater of war be an expanding concept, we cannot with faithfulness to our constitutional system hold that the commander in chief of the armed forces has the ultimate power as such to take possession of private property in order to keep labor disputes from stopping production. This is a job for the nation's lawmakers, not for its military authorities.[44]

Justices Frankfurter and Jackson found the question more nuanced: "The considerations relevant to the legal enforcement of the principle of separation of powers seem to me more complicated and flexible than may appear from what Mr. Justice Black has written," Frankfurter wrote. There were, for example, circumstances where presidential authority might be derived from an established practice acquiesced to by Congress, creating a "gloss" on executive power. Nonetheless, he agreed with the result.

Justices Vinson, Minton, and Reed dissented. After first reviewing the context of the Korean War and Cold War, they expressed the view that the president's enumerated constitutional authorities must include a seizure authority in times of emergency.

Accordingly, if the president has any power under the Constitution to meet a critical situation in the absence of express statutory authorization, there is no basis whatever for criticizing the exercise of such power in this case. . . . Under [the majority's] view, the president is left powerless at the very moment when the need for action may be most pressing and when no one, other than he, is immediately capable of action.[45]

However, the case is best known for Justice Jackson's separate opinion and separation of powers paradigm.

1. When the president acts pursuant to an express or implied authorization of Congress, his authority is at its maximum, for it includes all that he possesses in his own right plus all that Congress can delegate.

2. When the president acts in absence of either a congressional grant or denial of authority, he can only rely upon his own independent

powers, but there is a zone of twilight in which he and Congress may have concurrent authority, or in which its distribution is uncertain.

3. When the president takes measures incompatible with the expressed or implied will of Congress, his power is at its lowest ebb, for then he can rely only upon his own constitutional powers minus any constitutional powers of Congress over the matter.[46]

Jackson concluded that the president's seizure of the steel mills fell into his third category, as the president had not relied on one of the three statutes noted above. Then, after reviewing each of the president's independent constitutional powers, Jackson concluded that the president acting alone did not have authority to seize the mills. With respect to one of those authorities, Jackson wrote,

There are indications that the Constitution did not contemplate that the title commander in chief of the army and navy will constitute him also commander in chief of the country, its industries, and its inhabitants. He has no monopoly of "war powers," whatever they are. While Congress cannot deprive the president of the command of the army and navy, only Congress can provide him an army or navy to command. It is also empowered to make rules for the "government and regulation of land and naval forces," by which it may, to some unknown extent, impinge upon even command functions.[47]

Justice Jackson's concurrence remains the most succinct and eloquent statement of the constitutional authority of the president in a system of separate and shared powers with the Congress.

TEN *YOUNGSTOWN* TAKEAWAYS

As happens when there is both a dearth of Supreme Court guidance and an equal thirst for clarity, one might make too much of a case. It is also possible to draw too little, dismissing the case as addressed to a different time and place. *Youngstown* is in both categories. What, then, are the key takeaways in AI context from *Youngstown*?

A narrow holding. The case stands for a narrow proposition—in the context presented, the president did not have authority to seize and operate a defense industry (steel plants) pursuant to his constitutional authority alone, where the Congress had provided alternative statutory means to accomplish the same goal.

With broader implications. One can also find a line of argument in the dissent (for sure) and the Jackson-Frankfurter majority concurrences (by implication) that hints at broad commander in chief power that might, in a different context—where there was no statutory alternative, or impediment—permit the president to seize and operate a defense industry for national security reasons. Depending on who is holding the door (that is, doing the analysis), the door to presidential authority is ajar, agape, or there is just the hint of light emanating from beneath a closed door.

The case occurred in time of war. While at least one justice, Frankfurter, noted that it was not a time of declared war, all the justices acknowledged the gravity of the national security context. The backdrop, in other words, for an expanded view of presidential authority appeared compelling. And yet, the court, and the courts, were prepared to decisively rule against the president's action.

There were alternatives. However compelling the backdrop, a majority of justices noted in one way or another that there were statutory alternatives—perhaps less desirable, but alternatives nonetheless—available to the president to address the labor dispute. That means *Youngstown* is not a pure constitutional case. Moreover, as commentators have noted, though it was not explicitly stated in the court's opinions, there was, in fact, a national shortage of steel but a sufficient supply to keep the defense industry running. Both points bore out in subsequent events. Having lost in *Youngstown*, President Truman rescinded his steel seizure order and availed himself of the labor dispute mechanism provided in Taft-Hartley. The war continued with no apparent impact on national security from the strikes or delay.

Litigation is an uncertain and imperfect mechanism to validate executive assertions. Litigation, of course, is one way to validate the government's national security arguments, assertions, and actions. However, one wonders sometimes whether the government might not be better advised to validate those assertions in advance of litigation. The government was confident it would win the *Youngstown* case. Less confident parties often avoid litigation, to rule out the potential of an uncertain and potentially adverse outcome. AI offers fertile litigation potential for the reasons stated throughout this book. There are private parties and property involved. And there is a lack of statutory clarity. The question in any given context is whether legislation or litigation offers more potential risk or benefit as a path to resolution. But where one can count legislative votes, one cannot do the same with judges, beyond analyzing past opinions and framing arguments accordingly.

Youngstown *is not a DPA case.* Because the government cited the DPA in its brief, and one justice addressed the DPA, it is possible to read *Youngstown* as a trimming of the president's DPA sails. However, this is an example of reading too much into the case. In its brief and at oral argument, the government relied almost exclusively on the president's constitutional authority, not his statutory authority, to seize the steel mills. The executive branch only argued a general statutory basis for its actions, the argument that the president was acting consistently with statutory purpose, not pursuant to a specific statute. In other words, the government made this a constitutional case about the president's authority as commander in chief and chief executive. Some commentators argue this was a tactical error on the part of the government. Indeed, unless one reads the underlying statutes, in particular the Selective Service Act, it is not evident in the court's opinions that Congress had statutorily anticipated a strike-shutdown scenario. But Congress did anticipate the prospect of labor disputes in the defense industry and gave the president statutory authority to address it. If *Youngstown* was a power grab, it was a grab contemplated by Congress by other means.

Thus, only one justice addressed the DPA in concurring. That was Justice Frankfurter, who stated,

> But it is now claimed that the president has seizure power by virtue of the Defense Production Act of 1950 and its amendments. And the claim is based on the occurrence of new events—Korea and the need for stabilization, and so on—although it was well known that seizure power was withheld by the Act of 1947 and although the president, whose specific requests for other authority were in the main granted by Congress in Title V of the Defense Production Act, entitled "Settlement of Labor Disputes," pronounced the will of Congress "that there be effective procedures for the settlement of labor disputes affecting national defense," and that "primary reliance" be placed "upon the parties to any labor dispute to make every effort through negotiation and collective bargaining and the full use of mediation and conciliation facilities to effect a settlement in the national interest."[48]

In other words, Title V of the DPA did not grant the president authority to seize the steel mills. In fairness, the government did not argue that it did. The government's brief refers to the DPA only once, tangentially.[49] In any event, the title in question, Title V of the DPA, was subsequently repealed.

Low ebb or dry land? The Supreme Court returned to the *Youngstown* paradigm and the president's commander in chief authority in *Hamdan*, a Guantanamo Bay habeas corpus case. The question in *Hamdan* was whether the president, as commander in chief, could convene military commissions to try non-privileged belligerents for war crimes. A majority of the court found that the president did not have authority to do so absent congressional authorization, and where "there is nothing in the text or legislative history of the AUMF [Authorization to Use Military Force] even hinting that Congress intended to expand or alter the authorization set forth in Article 21 of the UCMJ" [for establishing military commissions].[50]

The interesting observation, for our purposes, is that the court included a footnote, suggesting that under *Youngstown*, the president was bound by Congress's action, and thus, under Jackson category 3, the president was not at a low ebb of authority, he was on dry land without authority to act on his own.

> Whether or not the president has independent power, absent congressional authorization, to convene military commissions, he may not disregard limitations that Congress has, in proper exercise of its own war powers, placed on his powers. See *Youngstown Sheet & Tube Co. v. Sawyer*, 343 U.S. 579, 637 (1952) (Jackson, J., concurring).

The question thus remains open as to just what authority the president has when acting in category 3 in any given context.

Courts view themselves as constitutional guardians and stewards of the bill of rights. This is not a surprising conclusion, but it is an observation that should not be lost on litigators who may want to turn to litigation and the courts, rather than Congress, to establish or validate executive powers. As Justice Jackson elegantly said in *Youngstown*, "Such institutions [of free government] may be destined to pass away. But it is the duty of the court to be last, not first, to give them up." Most judges think the same way, and as an "institution of free government," the Constitution comes first in judicial order, not the executive branch or president.

Courts and, more important, the judicial system, can move fast. When judges believe, or are persuaded by the parties, that the national interest demands it, courts can move fast. Recall that *Youngstown* progressed from the president's executive order to the district court, circuit court of appeals, and Supreme Court oral argument and decision *in less than two months*. Moreover, this was not an easy case that lent itself to prompt resolution and a singular per curiam opinion. Lower courts can also leverage the judicial system to prompt more expeditious review through use of injunctive power and, as the circuit court did here, conditioning their decisions on the parties seeking Supreme Court review. There are lots of reasons to avoid litigation, but speed need not be one of them if ***both*** parties are prepared to effectively make the case for speed.

Finally, some of the president's more important AI tools are, or may be, Youngstown strong. Reading the underlying statutory authority provided to the president to address labor disputes at the time, including that provided in the Selective Service Act, the breadth of the president's authority to seize all or part of the defense industrial base for national security reasons is extraordinary. Here is the text of section 18 of the Selective Service Act as passed in 1948:

> (a) Whenever the president after consultation with and receiving advice from the National Security Resources Board determines that it is in the interest of the national security for the government to obtain prompt delivery of any articles or materials the procurement of which has been authorized by the Congress exclusively for the use of the armed forces of the United States, . . . he is authorized, through the head of any government agency, to place with any person operating a plant, mine, or other facility capable of producing such articles or materials an order for such quantity of such articles or materials as the president deems appropriate. . . .
>
> (c) *In case any person with whom an order is placed pursuant to the provisions of subsection (a) refuses or fails—*
>
> . . .
>
> *The president is authorized to take immediate possession of any plant, mine, or other facility of such person and to operate it through any government agency, for the production of such articles or materials as may be required by the government.* [Emphasis mine]

That was then, and this is now. It is hard to imagine a similar grant of authority today, outside the context of the Cold War, or Korean War. Or is it? The DPA is broad in its reach, and it is reauthorized every five years. Thus, in theory, it reflects a contemporary congressional view of what the law should be, and not just one rooted in 1950s Cold War thinking. Private industry may wish to seek clarity to avert such assertions or ensure a more predictable landscape. To the extent the president wishes to assert broad constitutional authority as commander in chief and chief executive to use and regulate AI for national security purposes, he may find a broader legislative mandate to do so in the DPA than one might immediately imagine. Indeed, as discussed in the next chapter, commentators and industry actors seemed to accept such an interpretation during the COVID-19 pandemic. The president might also receive additional authority from Congress, if requested, perhaps in the context of tensions with China. In either situation, he would subsequently be operating at the zenith of his authority in *Youngstown* category 1. When, and whether, such an assertion would be well founded is the subject of the next chapter, which addresses some of the principal statutes relevant to AI.

SEVEN

Statutory Regulation of the National Technology Industrial Base

This chapter examines statutory law potentially applicable to government use or regulation for national security purposes of AI developed or controlled by private U.S. actors. "Potentially applicable," because most of this law is incomplete, episodic, and was not drafted with AI in mind. As with cyberspace, where policymakers have found that the Communications Act of 1934 did not contemplate the full range of social media issues presented today, AI actors will find the statutory regime does not always contemplate or answer critical questions.

U.S. export control regimes, for example, found in statutes like the Arms Export Control Act and the Export Controls Act of 2018, which repeals and replaces the Export Administration Act of 1979,[1] clearly reach sensitive AI technologies. The central policy question is whether the control lists promulgated under these laws are effectively calibrated to cover the range of technology transfer necessary to protect U.S. national security in the context of AI development by U.S. adversaries and potential adversaries. Specific sector authorities, like the Robert T. Stafford Disaster Relief and Emergency Assistance Act,[2] might apply, as is, to AI technologies in a given sector or with respect to a specific country. The Federal Power Act,[3] for example, provides the Federal Energy Regulatory Commission with emergency power to "require by order

such temporary connections of facilities and such generation, delivery, inter-
change, or transmission of electric energy as in its judgment will best meet
the emergency and serve the public interest." There is no apparent textual
reason why these powers would not apply to a national emergency requiring
the diversion of resources to AI applications for national security reasons. But
these statutes have, heretofore, been used for grid and blackout failures and
without apparent, or at least public, consideration of other national security
contexts. The act was not drafted and passed with AI in mind. Thus, there has
been no legislative or executive dialogue to alert or prepare stakeholders and
the public for their use in AI context, even if their plain text would appear to
permit such use.

In short, statutes such as these, traditionally used for one purpose, may
be used in new AI contexts as well, where the text permits. They also provide
metaphor as to how AI might otherwise be regulated more broadly. The Land
Remote Sensing Policy Act of 1992 (recodified and amended by Pub. L. 111-
314),[4] for example, could serve as a model for how to condition licenses in
other national security sectors and for other purposes. The act authorizes the
secretary of commerce to license commercial satellites and do so in a manner
to preserve national security and uphold international obligations, including
those in the Space Treaty discussed in chapter 9. The law requires the secretary of commerce to consult with the secretary of defense "on all matters
affecting national security." The law is implemented through regulations permitting commerce to condition licenses through the exercise of "shutter control." Shutter control can take the form of (1) limiting the resolution quality of
commercial satellites; (2) prohibiting flight or pictures over certain locations;
or (3) actual shutter control by prohibiting pictures from being taken or released at a certain time or in a certain location. In practice, this latter form of
shutter control has been invoked only once (during Operation Enduring Freedom at the outset of U.S. operations in Afghanistan after 9/11). Proponents of
the commercial satellite industry object to shutter control on First (speech),
Fourth (seizure), and Fifth (due process and takings) Amendments grounds.
However, experience suggests that abstract concerns about the government's
reach and overreach may prove less alarming in practice. One takeaway is
that Congress might better condition the government's authority to address
private sector concerns rather than prohibit use of government authority outright, thus allowing factual context and good process to inform practice.

Three existing laws would seem most apt in defining the limits and authorities of the government with respect to AI in the absence of more spe-

cific or tailored laws: the International Economic Emergencies Powers Act (IEEPA), the Invention Secrecy Act (ISA), and the Defense Production Act (DPA). Because we are moving from identifying general principles of constitutional law that might be applicable in AI contexts to relevant provisions of law, the ensuing analysis and detail is more granular and specific than in previous chapters.

INTERNATIONAL EMERGENCY ECONOMIC POWERS ACT

The International Emergency Economic Powers Act (IEEPA), 50 U.S.C. 1701–1708, is not a technology statute and it is not addressed to the defense industrial base. It is a trade and sanctions statute that authorizes the president by executive order to seize and/or freeze the assets of foreign nations and persons within the United States or under U.S. control, to include transactions only momentarily under U.S. control as international transactions in U.S. dollars are cleared via the New York Federal Reserve Bank in New York City. It also authorizes the president to prohibit certain or all financial transactions with certain foreign states, persons, or entities. The statute is administered by the Office of Foreign Assets Control (OFAC) at the Department of the Treasury. However, decisions to list an entity are policy decisions made by the policy community, and ultimately the president, based on open-source as well as classified information. The president may invoke the statute in response to

> . . . any unusual and extraordinary threat, which has its source in whole or substantial part outside the United States, to the national security, foreign policy, or economy of the United States, if the president declares a national emergency with respect to such threat.[5]

National emergencies are declared pursuant to the National Emergencies Act, 50 U.S.C. 1601–1651.[6]

The normal process of implementation is for the policy community to frame policy objectives and purposes, usually through the NSC process. Treasury/OFAC, with interagency input, will then implement the policy direction in the form of an executive order for presidential signature. (Notice and comment are not required under the Administrative Procedures Act.) The order is published in the Code of Federal Regulations (CFR) and implemented with Treasury/OFAC regulations, licenses, and enforcement.

The IEEPA is relevant to AI, because it is a nimble and discretionary executive tool with which the president may limit transactions with foreign states and entities for national security reasons. Thus it provides the underlying basis for sanctions against Syria, Iran, and North Korea, among other states. The authority has also been used to impose secondary sanctions on people and entities that trade with countries or entities in violation of direct sanctions. While the language of the statute invokes the specter of "unusual and extraordinary threats," practice indicates that use of the statute is, in fact, ordinary. Moreover, there is no textual reason this authority would not reach transactions involving AI and other technologies with national security impact. The executive branch, for example, might use IEEPA to regulate or prohibit U.S. companies from assisting authoritarian states with AI applications used for domestic surveillance.

Where the president acts pursuant to his own constitutional authority as well as that delegated by Congress—in this case, in the IEEPA—he is said to act at the zenith of his authority under *Youngstown*. It is also a matter of constitutional logic. In AI context, it is important, because where the president acts pursuant to congressional authorization as well as his own authority, the executive branch is more likely to prevail when challenged than when it acts alone, even where the exercise of authority is novel.

INVENTION SECRECY ACT

The Invention Secrecy Act (ISA), 35 U.S.C. 181–188, is a Cold War–era statute (1952) that authorizes the government to impose a secrecy order on certain inventions in the interest of national security. Specifically, "if, in the opinion of the Atomic Energy Commission, the secretary of a Defense Department, or the chief officer of another department or agency so designated, the publication or disclosure of the invention by the publication of an application or by granting of a patent therefor would be detrimental to the national security," that officer shall notify the commissioner of patents and the "commissioner shall order that the invention be kept secret and shall withhold the grant of a patent for such period as the national interest requires." Secrecy orders may be issued for up to one year and are subject to renewal on an annual basis upon notification by the requesting agency, or for shorter periods, if requested.

The ISA comes with several enforcement mechanisms. In the event information about a covered invention is published or disclosed, or an application for a patent for a covered invention filed in a foreign country, the invention may be treated as abandoned by the Patent and Trademark Office (PTO). In addition, violation of the act with knowledge of a secrecy order carries a potential criminal penalty of a US$10,000 fine and imprisonment of not more than two years. Appeals of secrecy orders may be taken to the secretary of commerce and from there to the court of federal claims or the U.S. court of the district where the claimant resides. In both cases, the courts have authority to issue protective orders to hear appeals of secrecy orders in a secure manner.

The law is implemented through the PTO within the Department of Commerce and is triggered by an application for a patent. According to media reports,[7] the principal agencies involved in ISA reviews are the Defense Threat Reduction Agency, NSA, Department of Justice, and Department of Homeland Security (DHS). These same reports indicate that by 2012 there were approximately 5,300 such orders, with a high-water mark of just under a hundred issued in 1998. At least one commentator has suggested that the way for academics to circumvent the law is to preempt it by publishing research before filing for a patent or by seeking a foreign patent first.

The ISA would seem directly on point in the event a U.S. corporate or academic entity created an algorithm or AI application with security importance the public disclosure of which could undermine national security. This might be the case, for example, if disclosure would alert adversaries to an emergent U.S. capability or lead to the possible theft or copycat emulation by an adversary. The question is not whether the law would apply to AI. It clearly does. The questions are whether, when, and why the government might invoke its authority with respect to AI and subject to what litigation risks. Another policy question is whether the government should hold additional authority, beyond the patent process, to protect technology and know-how in the research and development stage before or outside the context of patent applications. These are at root policy questions. However, they also present process and legal questions to the extent they implicate the government's ability and authority to determine what is occurring within industry and academia in the first place. The government cannot very well invoke the ISA if it does not know whether an invention is in the research pipeline. The process questions include whether key agencies and offices, like the Patent Office, understand the national security applications and implications of AI well enough to implement the statute, and whether they have received sufficient policy guidance from relevant agencies to timely trigger the process of ISA review.

Consistent with the Takings Clause, the law provides for a right to compensation for use of the invention by the government. Thus, another string of legal questions addresses the extent to which an inventor is entitled to compensation where an invention is not used by the government but where the inventor is otherwise barred by a secrecy order from taking an invention to market. Embedded in this issue is the question of valuation, which can be highly speculative before an invention is deployed and thus before it realizes its market potential. There are also questions of secrecy, First Amendment rights, and courtroom procedure, each potentially raising due process concerns about the right of private stakeholders to receive a fair opportunity to present their case. A second string of legal questions considers the extent to which the government can look within academia and industry to determine what is occurring to better determine when and whether to invoke the ISA or other authorities. This is one of the central AI questions posed by the Defense Production Act (DPA).

NATIONAL TECHNOLOGY INDUSTRIAL BASE

Historically, U.S. military deterrence plans have been driven by offset strategies. An offset strategy seeks ways to counteract a competitor's advantages versus trying to match strength for strength.[8] The United States adopted two offset strategies during the Cold War to address real and perceived Soviet advantages in personnel and battlefield hardware as well as eventual Soviet parity in the number of ICBMs. Each was based on the strength and advantages of the U.S. defense industrial base. As described by the Department of Defense:

> The first offset strategy occurred in the 1950s as the Soviet Union reached parity with the United States on conventional weapons. The United States turned to tactical nuclear weapons for conventional deterrence. The second offset occurred in the 1970s and 1980s as strategic nuclear parity was reached, and the United States turned its focus to building an advantage in conventional guided munitions."[9]

As indicated, these offset strategies were directed at the Soviet Union in Cold War context. The U.S. response came in the form of technological advantages in developing and producing weapons, specifically artillery shells, mines, and missiles in the 1950s, and precision guided munitions in the 1970s and 1980s.

In 2016, the United States adopted a third offset strategy, which continues in concept if not expressly in name.[10] It is different from the previous strategies in six ways, each of which will test the scope of the government's legal authority to regulate and access AI technology.

First, the third offset strategy relies on technology to do more than enhance weapons and munitions. It is intended to augment human decision, intelligence capacity, communications, and logistics.

Second, it relies on a commercial sector that reaches beyond traditional defense contractors and is global in form. Thus not all the same assumptions about mission alignment and compatibility necessarily apply between the Department of Defense and AI industry actors as pertains to traditional defense contractors.

Third, it is intended to offset the strengths of a variety of potential adversaries, both state and non-state, as opposed to a single adversary.

Fourth, it is directed not just to the perceived numeric advantages of potential opponents, such as Soviet conventional forces, but to potential opponents' advantages in asymmetric warfare—for example, Russian information operations.

Fifth, AI will play a critical role in the third offset strategy. The Department of Defense has said so:

> The third offset's initial vector is to exploit all the advances in artificial intelligence and autonomy and insert them into DOD's battle networks to achieve a step increase in performance that the department believes will strengthen conventional deterrence. The offset includes technological leaps . . . but it's really about operational and organizational constructs based on doctrine, training and exercises that allow the joint force to operate with such technologies to achieve an advantage.[11]

Sixth, and finally, this offset will spill over into many aspects of national security beyond traditional defense areas, including homeland security, balance of power grand strategy, and national security decisionmaking.

To achieve this third strategic offset, the United States government will rely on four national security assets: (1) an unmatched national technical intelligence capacity; (2) a robust university educational and research system; (3) the presence of much of the advanced information technology industry in the United States; and (4) an established defense industrial base. To meld and utilize these assets, the U.S. government has relied on the legislative tools Congress has provided with respect to the defense industrial base (DIB). However, these tools do not provide a cohesive legal framework and were not drafted with AI in mind. They were also largely enacted at a time of relative Cold War unity of purpose across parties and between government and industry. Neither is it a foregone conclusion that the United States will sustain these advantages or use them wisely, effectively, and purposefully.[12] The phrase "DIB" is derivative of the Cold War and connotes images of military hardware, like tanks and aircraft, as well as material resources like steel. However, the term is, in fact and law, broadly defined. Congress has amended the enabling statutes to include "national technology" and "critical technology" within the scope of the DIB.[13]

Constitutional authority for Congress to regulate the national technology and industrial base is found in the Commerce Clause, the Rules Clause, and the Necessary and Proper Clause, among other places. As *Youngstown* explored, the president's constitutional authority derives from his role as commander in chief, chief executive, and the Take Care Clause, among others. When it comes to the DIB, the primary law the president is taking care to faithfully execute is the Defense Production Act (DPA). However, chapter 148 of Title 10 should not be overlooked.

Title 10, Chapter 148

Title 10 is the federal code addressed to the U.S. Armed Forces and the Department of Defense. Chapter 148 of the title helps set congressional policy regarding the DIB and reinforces authority found in the DPA. The chapter states:

> The secretary of defense shall develop a national security strategy for the national technology and industrial base. . . . Such strategy shall be based on a prioritized assessment of risks and challenges to the defense supply chain and shall ensure that the national technology and industrial base is capable of achieving the following national security objectives: [providing] systems capable of ensuring technological superiority over potential adversaries [and] the development, production, and integration of information technology within the national technology and industrial base.

From an executive perspective, such statements of congressional policy are considered as persuasive, but not positive enabling authority. Nonetheless, executive lawyers cite language like this to argue the president is acting at least consistent with, if not pursuant to, congressional policy and intent. This is not quite *Youngstown* category I, but it is something more than category II. Moreover, congressional policy is clear: the secretary *shall* provide for the development, production, and integration of information technology within the national technology and industrial base. That includes AI.

Chapter 148 provides positive enabling authority to do so. Section 2507, for example, authorizes the president to collect data to administer and enforce chapter 148. Specifically:

> The president shall be entitled, by regulation, subpoena, or otherwise, to obtain such information from, require such reports and keeping of such records by, make such inspection of books, records, and other writings, premises or property of, and take sworn testimony of, and administer oaths and affirmations to, any person as may be necessary or appropriate, in the president's discretion, to the enforcement or the administration of this chapter and the regulations issued under this chapter.

While expansive, this section is subject to scope and exhaustion limitations. First, the president is required to issue regulations "ensuring that the authority of this section will be used only after the scope and purpose of the investigation, inspection, or inquiry to be made have been defined by competent authority." Second, the regulations shall further provide that the data collection authority will only be used if it is "assured that no adequate and authoritative data are available from any federal or other responsible agency." This section is noteworthy because it duplicates and reinforces similar authority in the DPA and because it provides limitations on that authority offering safeguards against government overreach and potential grounds for litigation.

Defense Production Act

The Defense Production Act, 50 U.S.C. 2061–2171, is the principal executive authority to "shape defense preparedness programs and to take appropriate steps to maintain and enhance the domestic industrial base." It provides four essential authorities:

- Authority to prioritize contracts and allocate resources.
- Authority to incentivize research, development, and production capacity in support of national defense and homeland security.
- Authority for the Committee for Foreign Investment in the United States (CFIUS) and through the committee a mechanism for protecting the U.S. technological supply chain.
- Authority to gather information to uphold and administer the DPA and to assess the U.S. industrial base to support national defense.

The DPA was enacted in 1950 during the Korean War (and Cold War) with the purpose of providing a mechanism to ensure the "supply [of] materials and services for the national defense and to prepare for and respond to military conflicts." This declaration of policy was amended in 1992 to include within its statement of security purpose, "natural or man-caused disasters, or acts of terrorism within the United States."[14] The act was also amended to reach energy supplies, emergency preparedness, and critical infrastructure—in other words, to reach beyond traditional Cold War industrial base disciplines. Thus, on a strategic level, the act is intended to be used to mobilize the nation's industrial base to meet national security challenges. On a tactical level, the act is intended to provide specific security resources that would otherwise not be produced or not be produced in the volume or on the timeline required.

Since original passage, the DPA has included a five-year sunset clause for a majority, but not all, of its provisions. (At times, the reauthorization of the DPA has sunset on a shorter and longer timeline, for example, when the act was continued to accommodate a later congressional debate and extension.) The act has been reauthorized fifty-three times, most recently in 2019.[15] Thus, reauthorization serves as one safeguard against government overreach. It also provides ongoing opportunity to amend or adjust the DPA to address AI applications or ambiguities. Policymakers should do so in a purposeful rather than default manner with AI in mind.

TEXT AND SCOPE

The DPA defines domestic industrial base as

> Domestic sources which are providing, or which would be reasonably expected to provide, materials or services to meet *national defense* requirements during peacetime, national emergency, or war. [Emphasis added.]

National defense includes

> . . . any *systems and assets, whether physical or cyber-based, so vital to the United States* that the degradation or destruction of such systems and assets would have a debilitating impact on national security . . . [Emphasis added.]

Notably, in the context of the COVID-19 pandemic, the term also includes "critical infrastructure," which in turn includes "national economic security and national public health or safety."[16] This definitional daisy chain indicates the DPA has broad scope and clearly reaches AI, if those who wield its authority wish it to reach AI. Further, the act applies in peacetime as well as periods of national emergency and war.

The act also has teeth. It carries potential civil and criminal sanction (not more than one year of confinement and up to a US$10,000 fine) for willfully failing to perform a required act or an act prohibited by the statute, or willfully disclosing information the president deems is confidential under the act.[17] It also provides an enforcement forum, by granting jurisdiction to U.S. federal district courts over "violations of this act or any rule, regulation, order, or subpoena thereunder, and of all civil actions under this act to enforce any liability or duty created by, or to enjoin any violation of, this act or any rule, regulation, order, or subpoena thereunder."[18]

The act had seven titles. Four have been repealed—II, IV, V, and VI—while Titles I, III, and VII remain good law.

TITLE I. PRIORITIZATION AND ALLOCATION AUTHORITY

Title I authorizes the president to prioritize contracts to promote the national defense as well as allocate materials, services, and facilities to promote the national defense.

Allocation of Materials, Services, and Facilities
Under section 101(a) of Title I, The president is authorized

> (1) to require that performance under contracts or orders (other than contracts of employment), which he deems necessary or appropriate to promote the national defense, shall take priority over performance under any other contract or order, *and for the purpose of assuring such priority, to require acceptance and performance of such contracts or orders by any persons he finds to be capable of their performance*, and (2) to allocate materials, services, and facilities in such manner, upon such conditions, and to such extent as he shall deem necessary or appropriate to promote national defense. [Emphasis added.]

Section 101(b) further provides that "this section [allocation authority] shall not be used to control the general distribution of any material in the civilian market unless the president finds" (1) that the material is a scarce and critical material essential to national defense; and (2) the requirements for national defense cannot otherwise be met. Section (b) is a limitation on the president's authority, but it also illustrates the DPA's potential breadth. Section 101(c) provides distinct prioritization and allocation authority "in order to maximize domestic energy supplies." This section, in contrast to the national defense authority in subsection (a), requires three presidential findings antecedent to its use. The law presents threshold questions relevant to AI that are related to the scope and reach of the law and the meaning of services.

Scope and reach. From first passage, section 101(a) has been viewed as a broad grant of authority, with some referring to it as a "commandeering" authority, granting the government the power to take over and run defense industries. However, there are at least two apparent and material questions regarding the scope of Title I authority. (1) Could the president direct a company to accept a government contract (perhaps for AI services) or is the authority limited to prioritization of existing contracts and orders? (2) How far can the president go in directing the allocation of materials, services, and facilities?

The meaning of services and other terms of art. The act does not clearly define the meaning of *services*. Absent clarity, technology firms may choose to litigate the applicability of the DPA to requests for AI services, rather than provide them.

INTERPRETATION

The plain language of section 101(a), Title I, authorizes the president to require performance "under contracts and orders." This appears to be the core intent of the section titled "Priority in Contracts and Orders." It is less clear whether the language "to require acceptance and performance of such contracts and orders" only applies to existing contracts or orders (prioritization) or also applies to new orders or distinct orders. The phrase "such contracts or orders" refers back to "under contracts or orders . . . to promote the national defense." This could be read to mean *existing* contracts and orders, as suggested by the use of the word "under" and by the preceding phrase "and for the purpose of assuring such priority." Or it could be read to mean "contracts or orders to promote the national defense"—full stop, without caveat, meaning any such contract, new or existing. The distinction is important. Were the section read to only apply to existing contracts, an AI company that wished to avoid the application of DPA prioritization and direction could forgo national defense contracting and decline the order.

On the one hand, the legislative history supports an expansive reading of Title I. As quoted in a Department of Justice Office of Legal Counsel Memorandum, the House Report accompanying the original version of the bill described this authority as "broad and flexible." More significant, the language of the House Report seems to encompass both the prioritization of existing contracts and the acceptance of new contracts:

> The powers granted under section 101(a) would include the power to issue orders stopping or reducing the production of any item; orders to prohibit the use of a material for a particular purpose or for anything except a particular purpose; and orders to prohibit the accumulation of excessive inventories. . . . Section 101(a) would authorize the president to require filling certain orders in preference to other orders, or *requiring the acceptance and performance of particular orders*. [Emphasis added.][19]

It is significant that this legislative history distinguishes between the authority to prioritize and the authority to require acceptance. Interestingly, however, the floor debate in 1950 was about price controls, not the apparent authority to compel the acceptance of contracts. The absence of debate—"silent legislative history"—can be interpreted both ways. The authority was not controversial. Or perhaps it was not addressed because it was not perceived as part of the bill. But it was. Academic commentary at the time suggests so. One article, for example, addressed the need to preserve economic freedom by preserving respect for the sanctity of contract and encouraging voluntary rather than mandatory controls. "The sole limitation on most of the controls provided for in the new act is that they be 'necessary or appropriate to promote the national defense,'" commented one academic.[20]

Executive branch interpretations of the authority appear to cut in both directions. The Code of Federal Regulations (CFR) implementing regulations for the Department of Commerce indicate that the authority is mandatory with respect to new contracts, but also provide several exceptions, which seem to negate any obligation to fulfill contracts beyond *existing* contracts and orders. The regulations state:

> 700.3(b) Persons receiving rated orders must give them preferential treatment as required by this regulation. *This means a person must accept and fill a rated order for items that the person normally supplies.* [Emphasis added].

However, there are exceptions to mandatory acceptance, including the delimiting language above, "that the person normally supplies." The exceptions are found in §700.13 15 CFR VII, "Acceptance and Rejection of Rated Orders":

(a) Mandatory acceptance (1) except as otherwise specified in this section, a person shall accept every rated order received and must fill such orders regardless of any other rated or unrated orders that have been accepted.

(b) Mandatory rejection [is required under certain conditions where the recipient cannot comply].

(c) Optional rejection. Unless otherwise directed by Commerce, rated orders may be rejected in any of the following cases as long as a supplier does not discriminate among customers: (1) . . . *If the order is for an item not supplied or a service not performed* . . . [Emphasis added].

A rated order is defined as a "prime contract, a subcontract, or a purchase order *in support of an approved program* issued in accordance with the provisions of this regulation." Thus, one can conclude that whether this authority reaches both new and existing requests, it is best read as only applying to existing *programs*—those designated by the cabinet secretaries with delegated authority. This suggests doubt that the government could identify an emergency need, and from scratch use Title I of the DPA to require acceptance of an order and priority treatment outside an existing program. This conclusion is supported by paragraph (1) above, permitting optional rejection where the order "is for an item not supplied or a service not performed." It is also supported by the predicate regulatory language compelling acceptance "for items that the person normally supplies."

To the extent the CFR regulations are ambiguous, even confusing, President Obama's Executive Order 13603, "National Defense Resources Preparedness," of March 16, 2012, was not. (This is the most recent presidential executive order directed to the DIB generally, which remains in force as of January 2020.) The order cites, as underlying authority, both the DPA and the president's constitutional authority, including as commander in chief. This is an exercise in *Youngstown* drafting, seeking to place the president's directive at the zenith of authority, that is, that delegated by the Congress in the DPA and that found in the Commander in Chief Clause. The critical language (with emphasis added) for understanding the executive branch's interpretation of section 101 is found in section 201 of the order.

Sec. 201. Priorities and Allocations Authorities:

(a) The authority of the president conferred by section 101 of the act, 50 U.S.C. App. 2071, *to require acceptance* and priority performance of contracts and orders . . . is delegated to the following agency heads:

(1) the secretary of agriculture with respect to food resources, food resource facilities, livestock resources, veterinary resources, plant health resources, and the domestic distribution of farm equipment and commercial fertilizer;

(2) the secretary of energy with respect to all forms of energy;

(3) the secretary of health and human services with respect to health resources;

(4) the secretary of transportation with respect to all forms of civil transportation;

(5) the secretary of defense with respect to water resources; and

(6) the secretary of commerce with respect to all other materials, services, and facilities, including construction materials.

(b) The secretary of each agency delegated authority under subsection (a) of this section (resource departments) shall plan for and issue regulations to prioritize and allocate resources and establish standards and procedures by which the authority shall be used to promote the national defense, under both emergency and non-emergency conditions.

There is also ambiguity found in the act regarding the president's allocation authority. However, here the ambiguity derives from the absence of modern usage rather than the statutory language, which is broad. As noted, the president is authorized to allocate materials, services, and facilities "to such an extent as he shall deem necessary or appropriate to promote national defense" provided he makes the antecedent findings in section 101(b). This is the kind of expansive language presidential lawyers sneak into bills when no one is looking. But the authority appears not to have been used to allocate resources at least since the Cold War and perhaps even the Korean War, when President Truman used the act to allocate petroleum and steel for defense purposes. For sure, the act has been "used" continuously since 1951 to "allocate" civilian airliners and freighters to the Civil Reserve Air Fleet, but on a contingency basis. Most recently, President Trump delegated allocation authority to the secretary of agriculture, stating in an executive order:

Secretary of Agriculture shall use the authority under Section 101 of the Act, . . . to determine the proper nationwide priorities and allocation of all the materials, services, and facilities necessary to ensure the continued supply of meat and poultry, consistent with the guidance for the operations of meat and poultry processing facilities jointly issued by CDC and OSHA.[21]

But this appears to have been an effort to create leverage with state and local authorities as well as with unions in response to the closing and potential closing of certain meat packing plants impacted by COVID-19, an invocation without use to encourage the plants to remain open. What remains uncertain is whether the executive branch would exercise the policy and legal will to assert "general distribution authority" of a material or commodity "in the civilian market," as President Truman did during the Korean War, *and* whether America's corporate actors would accept such an exercise without political, policy, and litigation resistance. The pending advent of a COVID-19 vaccine may provide answers to this question.

Six observations arise.

First, in the view of the executive branch, DPA section 101 authority extends beyond traditional defense functions and beyond the Department of Defense. The language of the act supports this reading, which is also reflected in executive interpretation and now in practice as well with the president's episodic invocation of the act during the COVID-19 pandemic not just to address medical supplies but also the supply of meat.[22]

Second, to the extent that there is statutory ambiguity as to whether section 101(a) applies to new contracts as well as to "supplies a provider does not ordinarily make," the corporate targets of President Trump's episodic invocation of section 101(a) during the COVID-19 pandemic have not as of June 2020 contested the legality of the orders in public or in court. Of course, those same companies, GM and 3M, had also expressed an intention to act before the DPA was invoked, and thus they may have been acting out of a sense of corporate social responsibility, not a sense of legal obligation. Moreover, while the president invoked the act the government did not use it and in fact order the companies to act. However, it is noteworthy that many experts assumed the president possessed the power to order the acceptance of new contracts as well as broad authority over the allocation of medical supplies and medicines.[23]

Third, the president has delegated his authority to six cabinet departments. (Generally, Title III of the United States Code and the chief executive authority permit the president to do so unless it is an authority that only he can exercise, for example, the pardon power, or the Congress prohibits the president from re-delegating the authority, such as section 303(a) discussed below.)

Fourth, the operative language of E.O. section 201 differs from that in

DPA section 101. The E.O. is more precise; a plain reading of the E.O. would appear to cover new contracts. This is also reflected on agency websites providing DPA guidance. The DHS/FEMA website asks: "When should a rated order be used?" The response: "Use of rated orders should not be limited to solving known supply problems or *for compelling acceptance of a contract by a reluctant supplier.*"[24] [Emphasis added.]

Fifth, the president has stated that "the authority shall be used to promote national defense, under both emergency and nonemergency conditions," a concept not found explicitly in the DPA.

Finally, and significantly in AI context, the order does not identify cyberspace, information technology, or commercial information technology within the scope of paragraph 201. For sure, it is possible that the secretary of commerce could, or might, assert authority in these areas within the category of "all other materials, services, and facilities." But one would have thought that considering the importance of this segment of the economy to national security, as well as the potential for resistance and litigation, any such delegation would be express. Moreover, later treatment in President Obama's Cybersecurity E.O. 13636 suggests that if the president intended to reach AI, or commercial information technology generally, he would have clearly stated so.

Executive orders do not have "legislative history" to fall back on. But issuance of E.O. 13636, "Improving Critical Infrastructure Cybersecurity," almost a year later (February 12, 2013) offers insight into how we should interpret E.O. 13603. In the later order, the president directs the secretary of homeland security to "use a risk-based approach to identify critical infrastructure where a cybersecurity incident could reasonably result in catastrophic regional or national effects on public health or safety, economic security, or national security." However, the same section also states, "The secretary shall *not* [emphasis added] identify any commercial information technology products or consumer information technology services under this section." The intent behind this limitation is not stated. Thus, it is not clear whether this restriction reflects a substantive conclusion that these entities do not qualify as critical infrastructure; a reflection of the complexity of regulating the commercial information technology sector; a reflection of divided views and disagreements on how this section and authority might apply; or perhaps the product of strong lobbying by certain companies on privacy grounds, as media reports suggested.

DEFINITIONAL QUESTIONS

One additional definition is important in considering how the DPA might apply to AI capabilities in the private sector. *What is the meaning of "services"?* The question is apt, considering the statute's express statement excepting "contracts of employment." Recall that section 101(a) is titled "Allocation of Materials, Services, and Facilities." Titles usually do not determine statutory meaning; however, "services" is used again in subsection (2) and is defined as "any effort that is needed for or incidental to the development, production, processing, distribution, delivery, or use of an industrial resource or a critical technology item. . . ."

The act goes on to define critical technology as including "any designated by the president to be essential to national defense."

It warrants repeating, critical technology is defined with reference to what the president designates as "essential to the national defense." In contrast, "employment contract" is not defined in the DPA. Thus, a court would most likely use the plain dictionary definition of the terms "employment" and "contract." These terms are defined, for example, by Merriam-Webster as "an activity in which one engages or is employed seeking gainful employment" and "the condition of having paid work and a binding agreement between two or more parties," respectively.

The definitional distinction between "employment" and "services" bears emphasis, considering the San Bernardino Apple-FBI litigation and the likelihood of similar disputes in the future. The DPA appears to distinguish between services and employment. Therefore, one might better conclude that the government could not compel Robert Oppenheimer to work at or on the Manhattan Project. However, once he was employed by the Manhattan Project, the government could use section 101 to prioritize the Manhattan Project's work and direct that the Manhattan Project provide a service that might draw on Oppenheimer's knowledge and skills, pursuant to his existing employment contract with the project.

PROCESS AND PRACTICE

Internal DPA process is opaque and often classified. However, public sources, including law, regulation, and directive, offer a start point to making the DPA accessible to generalists, as has debate about use of the DPA during the COVID-19 pandemic.

Application of Title I of the DPA involves five layers of law and regulation: the Constitution, the DPA, executive order, implementing regulations, and departmental and agency internal regulations and memoranda. In ordinary practice, the system is implemented using the Defense Priorities Allocation System (DPAS). In general, DPAS is administered by the Department of Commerce (DOC), Bureau of Industry and Security. However, DOC has delegated many of the DPAS authorities to other agencies. In addition, the DPA, in some instances, requires certain process, such as presidential determinations with respect to sections 101(b) and 303, and thus is not subject to regulatory deviation. And, of course, the president's own direction takes legal precedence over agency direction, as evident during the pandemic.

The president has delegated certain DPA authorities pursuant to Executive Order 13603 (Obama), as well as on a more limited basis with Executive Orders 13909, 13910, 13911, and 13917 (Trump).[25] First, E.O. 13603 delegated 101(a) authorities to six cabinet secretaries with respect to six specific areas. However, exercise of this delegated authority "may be used only to support programs that have been determined in writing as necessary or appropriate to promote the national defense" as determined by the secretaries of defense, energy, and homeland security. Specifically:

> . . . the authority delegated by section 202 of this order may be used only to support programs that have been determined in writing as necessary or appropriate to promote the national defense:

> - by the secretary of defense with respect to military production and construction, military assistance to foreign nations, military use of civil transportation, stockpiles managed by the Department of Defense, space, and directly related activities;

> - by the secretary of energy with respect to energy production and construction, distribution and use, and directly related activities; and

> - by the secretary of homeland security with respect to all other national defense programs, including civil defense and continuity of government.

The Department of Commerce has delegated authority to four agencies to place priority-rated contracts and orders: Defense, Energy, DHS, and GSA. The Department of Commerce and these agencies can also place priority contracts for the use of other agencies. The Department of Defense uses two DPAS industrial priority ratings—DX and DO. DO is used for orders "critical to national defense" and requires the approval of the undersecretary of defense for acquisition, technology, and logistics. DX-rated orders are used for orders of the "highest national defense urgency" and must be approved by the secretary or deputy secretary of defense.[26] DX-rated orders have equal priority and take precedence over DO orders. Likewise, DO orders have equal priority and take precedence over regular commercial contracts. As illustration, the following programs were designated DX as of April 2017:[27]

Department of Defense
National Reconnaissance (Program 390)
Integrated Ballistic Missile Defense System

Department of the Navy
Presidential helicopters (VH-3D, VH-60N)
Fleet Ballistic Missile Weapons System, Trident System
Program 341

Department of the Air Force
Space-Based Infrared System (SBIRS) High
Intercontinental Ballistic Missile, Minuteman III
B-2 Stealth Bomber
VC-25A presidential aircraft

Joint Service
Mine Resistant Ambush Protected (MRAP) vehicles
National Security Agency Program
Counter Radio-Controlled Improvised Explosive Device Electronic
     Warfare (CREW)[28]

While the Department of Defense is the primary user of the system, applying the "critical to national defense" DO rating to approximately 300,000 contracts per year, the authority is used episodically by a range of agencies and by DHS on a regular basis. The breadth and potential range of this authority is illustrated with reference to the 2011 Defense Production Act Committee (DPAC) report.

The "priorities authority has been used to support, for example, hurricane and flood preparedness and response activities; Homeland Security Technology Programs; emergency preparedness activities related to the 2009 H1N1 flu virus; the Greater New Orleans Hurricane and Storm Damage Risk Reduction System program (by the U.S. Army Corps of Engineers); the International Safeguards, Second Line of Defense, and Nuclear Counterterrorism Incident Response programs (by DOE's National Nuclear Security Administration);

the Geostationary Operational Environmental Satellite, R-Series Program (DOD's NOAA); and the Terrorist Screening Center program (DOJ/FBI)."[29]

DHS/FEMA guidance and reporting indicates that DHS primarily uses rated orders to ensure on-time performance of contracts and to address supply chain problems.

Where the statutory elements are otherwise met, DPA Title I authority may be invoked for foreign contracts and for the benefit of foreign nations. This was the case, for example, with the 2003 decision to provide DX prioritization to the supply of Precision Lightweight GPS Receivers to British military forces in Iraq. In addition, DPA Title I authority includes pass-through authority. If the prime contractor receives a DX-rated order, it can, in turn, require priority treatment from subcontractors working on the same-rated order.

Finally, as required by the DPA, E.O. 13603 directs each agency with delegated authority to "issue regulations to prioritize and allocate resources and establish standards and procedures by which the authority shall be used to promote the national defense, under both emergency and nonemergency conditions. . . ." Four agencies have issued regulations, including the Departments of Agriculture, Health and Human Services, and Transportation. The Department of Commerce, Bureau of Industry and Security, amended existing regulations, which cover the Department of Defense as well as Commerce.

In ordinary practice, policy oversight is provided by the Defense Production Act Committee (DPAC), and its subordinate interagency working groups. Much of the DPAC's work is conducted at the working group level on either an interagency basis or an as-needed agency basis. Under section 722(b) of the DPA, the DPAC advises the president on the effective use of DPA authorities in support of national defense. Seventeen departments and agencies are members of the DPAC, which is chaired by the director of the Federal Emergency Management Agency (FEMA). Since 2011, the DPAC has issued an annual report on "government contingency planning for events that might require the use of the priorities and allocations authorities," which "provides recommendations for effective use of priorities and allocations authorities and provides recommendations for improving information-sharing among federal departments and agencies relating to the use of priorities and allocations authorities."[30] This report serves as a third safeguard on governmental use of the DPA, along with judicial review and periodic congressional reauthorization.

The report is currently submitted under the signature of the administrator of the Federal Emergency Management Agency, as delegated by the secretary of DHS. One question for Congress to consider in the context of COVID-19 is whether to require additional transparency from agencies regarding their use of the DPA beyond what can be discerned from the president's executive orders, DPAC reporting, and contract announcements.

Section 2502 purports to establish a National Defense Technology and Industry Base Council (NDTIBC), in a manner modeled on the National Security Council. The NDTIBC is "comprised of the secretaries of defense, energy, commerce, labor, and such other officials as may be determined by the president." However, the act also states:

> (d) ALTERNATIVE PERFORMANCE OF RESPONSIBILITIES. Notwithstanding subsection (c), the president may assign the responsibilities of the council to another interagency organization of the executive branch that includes among its members the officials specified . . .

The DPAC includes those specified members and thus removes any issue regarding whether the president is complying with the law or acting consistently with it, in theory preserving the constitutional position that the president is free to determine the process by which he receives advice, a point made evident during President Trump's response to COVID-19. The president might also oversee implementation of the DPA and DPAS using the National Security Council process, the military chain of command, or, informally, with the affected cabinet secretaries. In other words, if the process does not work, the president can change it.

Under President George W. Bush, the DPAC was chaired on a rotating basis by the secretaries of defense and homeland security. However, the 2014 Defense Production Act Reauthorization amended the DPA to provide that "the chairperson of the committee shall be the head of the agency to which the president has delegated primary responsibility for government-wide coordination of the authorities in this act."[31] President Barack Obama appears to have placed the secretary of homeland security in this role. *Appears*, because E.O. 13603 does not expressly do so, but does so by implication. Thus, the order states: "The secretary of homeland security shall: . . . (2) provide for the central coordination of the plans and programs incident to the authorities and functions delegated under this order, and provide guidance to agencies assigned functions under this order, developed in consultation with such agencies."

OTHER DPA PROVISIONS: TITLE III AND TITLE VII

Most commentary on the DPA is addressed to Title I's prioritization and allocation authority. This is true of the Annual DPAC Report to Congress as well. This makes sense. Title I is a frequently used provision of the DPA. It is also the authority most likely to be used in an emergency. And it is the authority most likely to be subject to litigation because of its potential scope and reach. However, other provisions of the DPA are important as well.

Title III authorizes the provision of incentives through loan guarantees (301), direct loans (302), purchase commitments and purchases (303(a)), and subsidy payments (303(c)) to provide industrial capacity in support of national defense and homeland security. Title III includes establishment of a fund to carry out the provisions of the title that appropriated $64 million in fiscal year 2020. Specifically, the Title III program provides "the president broad authority to ensure the timely availability of essential domestic industrial resources to support national defense and homeland security requirements, through the use of highly tailored economic incentives."[32] Invocation of the program requires the president to make seven determinations, including:

1. That the resource or technology is essential for national defense.

2. Industry cannot or will not provide needed capacity in a reasonable time without DPA Title III assistance.

3. Title III incentives are the most cost-effective, expedient, and practical alternative for meeting the need.[33]

The law prohibits the president from delegating these determinations. The program is overseen by the deputy assistant secretary of defense for manufacturing and industrial base policy, reporting to the undersecretary of defense (acquisition, technology, and logistics). The DOD executive agent for the program is the air force, specifically, the Title III office at Wright-Patterson AFB. There were twenty-eight publicly listed Title III projects in 2017, covering subjects such as thermal, solar, and lithium batteries; nanotechnology; and rocket motors. Thus, in immediate practice this authority has been used for specific scarce defense resources or capacities for which there is not a ready supply or broad market; however, it could be used on a more systemic industry basis, as experts have argued in the context of medical supplies and a vaccine during the COVID-19 pandemic.[34]

Title VII of the DPA includes several provisions addressing operation of the DPA. Section 702 provides definitions of key terms. Section 706 grants federal district courts jurisdiction over civil and criminal proceedings for violations of the act or its regulations, including the power to enjoin the government or enforce provisions of the DPA. This provision reflects Congress's anticipation that use of the DPA might necessitate a judicial forum for dispute resolution as well as enforcement mechanism. However, in practice, there is a surprising lack of litigation with most of the lead substantive cases dating to the 1950s, following passage of the act and initial efforts to implement its provisions.[35] Section 707 provides recipients of DPA orders liability protection "for damages or penalties for any act or failure to act resulting directly or indirectly from compliance with a rule, regulation, or order issued pursuant to this Act, notwithstanding that any such rule, regulation, or order shall thereafter be declared by judicial or other competent authority to be invalid." The better reading of this text is that it covers contract liability, but not state or federal tort liability. The word "tort" does not appear in the language. Moreover, if the DPA were intended to preempt state tort law, judges would look for an express textual statement of such intent.

Title VII also provides additional authorities to study, shape, and influence the defense industrial base. Section 722 provides the statutory underpinning of the defense industrial base system, which, in turn, is the statutory foundation for the DPAS, the DPAC, and the DIB information system. Title VII, section 721, also serves as the statutory enabling authority for the Committee on Foreign Investment (CFIUS). (The committee was established by President Ford in 1975 by executive order and pursuant to executive authority. It was given statutory authority in 2007.) The committee is the principal executive vehicle for regulating foreign control and investment in the United States that could impair national security. The committee is formally comprised of nine cabinet members and five members of the president's national security staff; however, in practice, the committee is run by staff, usually at the assistant secretary level, and includes formal and informal members, advisors, and as-needed agency representation. The director of national intelligence is required to provide either a general threat assessment or a thorough analysis of any threat about each covered transaction.

Pursuant to Title VII, as amended by the Foreign Investment Risk Review Modernization Act of 2018 (FIRRMA), the committee is required to review "any merger, acquisition, or takeover that is proposed or pending after August 23, 1988, by or with any foreign person that could result in foreign control of any United States business, including such a merger, acquisition, or takeover carried out through a joint venture." Companies may affirmatively seek review by filing a notice with the committee and thus mitigate the risk of unilateral CFIUS review after a transaction is underway. The law requires CFIUS to safeguard confidential information provided by businesses during the review process. During the period 2008–15, the committee received on average 116 notices of transactions per year, with a high of 147 in 2014 and a low of 65 in 2009. During this same period, the committee conducted 333 investigations with a high of 66 in 2015 and low of 23 in 2008. The annual reports do not indicate the number or nature of mitigation steps taken in each case or generally; however, the reports indicate that 42 notices of transaction were withdrawn after CFIUS receipt and 62 during investigation. Since 1990, the president has blocked six transactions outright, all involving in some manner Chinese firms or investors, in most cases involving the acquisition of semiconductor or communications firms.[36]

Title VII provides statutory deadlines for the committee's work. Notably, the law provides tight timelines for each step of the process measured in days; ten days to review and accept a notice; thirty days to take action in regard to a notice; forty-five days to conduct an investigation, which time can be extended by fifteen days at the request of an agency head or deputy head; and fifteen days for the president to take action following the completion of a CFIUS investigation or referral of the matter by CFIUS to the president. The president is not bound by the committee's recommendations. Where the committee does not meet its deadlines, or a subject company believes the government has acted outside its authority, CFIUS process is subject to court review under the Due Process Clause of the Fifth Amendment, among other bases. In contrast to the DPA more generally, there is ample CFIUS case law with which to derive additional guidance regarding interpretation of this DPA title. Finally, FFRMA expanded CFIUS jurisdiction to expressly include real estate transactions, critical infrastructure, critical technologies, and businesses that maintain or collect sensitive personnel data of U.S. citizens. It is too early to tell how the expanded authority of FFRMA will change CFIUS practice, although an increase in use and litigation is likely. Moreover, CFIUS review is one area where policymakers will want to ensure AI policy is aligned with AI practice and appropriate AI expertise assigned to the committee.

Section 708 provides for voluntary agreements between government and industry, where the work of industrial partnerships might otherwise raise antitrust or other fair business practice concerns. "Before a voluntary agreement may take effect, the attorney general is required to make a written finding that conditions exist which may pose a threat to the national defense or its preparedness programs and that voluntary agreements are necessary to help provide for the national defense."

The DPA provides two authorities that may bear on recruiting critical expertise for government AI work. Section 703 provides agency heads waiver authority to hire persons outside the competitive civil service system and without regard to the general schedule (GS) pay scale. However, salaries are still capped at the GS-18 rate (now calculated at the senior level, which replaced the grades of GS-16 through GS-18; senior level, or SL, paygrades are, in theory, designated for government employees with specialized expertise who are not otherwise performing management functions associated with the senior executive service (SES). Government pay scales are not competitive with the sort of NFL salaries many AI innovators and engineers are receiving in the private sector. A first-year PhD in computer science can make as much as US$600,000 as a software engineer at a leading commercial technology firm. In contrast, a similarly situated PhD joining a federally funded research and development center (FFRDC) can expect to make one-third or less of that amount.[37] Using this special 703 authority and the GS-18 rate, a government employee could, at best, make US$207,000—the highest possible level of ES-I (2019). Of course, an entry-level employee would not likely receive the benefit of a 703 waiver for this purpose. Although not addressed in the DPA, in other contexts, such as the Public Health Service and the military, the government possesses statutory authority to provide signing bonuses and incentive payments to recruit and retain expertise. Thus, it is possible for policymakers to construct even greater incentives to attract AI talent than is currently contained in the DPA. The government could also make greater use of the Intergovernmental Personnel Act (IPA), which authorizes the assignment of employees of state and local governments, colleges and universities, and federally funded research and development centers, among other organizations, to the federal government for up to two years with the concurrence of the employee and sending entity. The IPA includes reciprocal authority for federal employees to work at universities and state and local authorities.[38]

Section 710(e) provides presidential authority to establish a National Defense Executive Reserve (NDER), which, in theory, could serve as a cadre of executives from critical defense industries and sectors to serve in the federal government during periods of emergency. The original concept appears to have contemplated use of the NDER as a traditional reserve to backfill government positions vacated by military deployments. However, the law and implementing regulations permit use of this authority in other ways, such as to augment government capacity with civilian expertise in the event of a national defense emergency.

The NDER authority dates to the original DPA, but has been used only intermittently since the 1950s. There are few NDER benchmarks along the internet way. In 1957, President Eisenhower addressed a full auditorium at the Department of Commerce at the National Defense Executive Reserve Conference.[39] In the 1980s, there were GAO reports addressing the decline and dysfunction of the NDER, although it is evident from the few reports available that there were still NDER units at several agencies. However, over time, the NDER slid into disuse. Executive Order 13603 "reestablished" the NDER. The order delegates authority over the program to the secretary of homeland security, including issuance of necessary guidance, which, in turn, was delegated to FEMA. FEMA had already issued interim NDER guidance in 2007, which appears to remain in effect. There is no accessible listing of NDER units or members within the government, a transparency gap the Congress should consider closing. Recall of NDER members requires a determination of a "national defense emergency." Executive Order 13603 delegates this authority to the secretary of homeland security and precludes re-delegation of the determination. It is evident from this procedure that President Obama, at least, perceived the NDER as most relevant in a homeland security context, but the law does not compel such a limitation. As in other contexts, one can designate an emergency in one context, but not another. In other words, logical or statutory consistency is not required.

SECTION 705 AUTHORITY TO INQUIRE AND SURVEY—INDUSTRIAL BASE ASSESSMENTS

The AI field has been described by some commentators as ungovernable. One reason it is hard to govern is that it covers many different fields and capabilities. It also is spread over a breadth of private and academic actors, many acting in secrecy to protect intellectual property and profit potentials. This makes section 705 worthy of special comment as an authority that could be used to collect information about AI R & D and to forecast milestones and pending breakout moments. Thus, depending on whether and how it is used, it could be as important as Title I or the CFIUS provisions of the DPA. But its use in this manner could come with challenge and controversy.

Section 705 states:

The president shall be entitled . . . by regulation, subpoena, or otherwise, to obtain such information from, require such reports and the keeping of such records by, make such inspection of books, records, or other writings, premises or property of, and take the sworn testimony of, and administer oaths and affirmations to, any person as may be necessary or appropriate, in his discretion, to the enforcement or administration of this act and the regulations or orders issued thereunder.

The section is broad and flexible in scope and can be used in support of any provision of the DPA. The authority can also be used independently of other sections of the DPA to "obtain information in order to perform industry studies to assess the capabilities of the U.S. industrial base to support national defense."

The authority is used frequently by the Department of Commerce[40] and would seem a logical authority for determining and assessing AI developments relevant to national defense in both industry and academia. However, there are scope and exhaustion requirements before the executive branch can resort to the authority. It may only be used after the scope and purpose of an investigation is defined and "it is assured that no adequate or authoritative data are available from any federal or other responsible agency." As with other DPA sections, the authority can be enforced with reference to the criminal sanctions in sections 706 and 705(c), as well as through the judicial power of contempt. Significantly, the section protects trade secrets, under threat of criminal sanction, which is one reason use of the 705 authority is opaque. Section 705(d) states:

Information obtained under this section, which the president deems confidential or with reference to which a request for confidential treatment is made by the person furnishing such information, shall not be published or disclosed unless the president determines that the withholding thereof is contrary to the interest of the national defense, and any person willfully violating this provision shall, upon conviction, be fined not more than US$10,000, or imprisoned for not more than one year, or both.

Finally, reminiscent of debates in the context of PATRIOT Act enforcement, there is an express right to consult counsel in response to a subpoena issued under this section.

The section 705 survey authority is well established, but not regarding AI and especially AI applications found outside traditional defense disciplines. More to the point, many AI companies are not part of the Cold War defense establishment. As discussed in chapter 10, Google's primary commercial interest is not national defense contracting. Neither is AI a defense function or weapon—it is a universal capacity.

As was evident from original passage of the DPA, section 705 challenges American concepts of commercial and regulatory freedom. President George H. W. Bush recognized as much when he signed the Defense Production Act Amendments of 1992 into law, including amendments enhancing the 705 authorities. His signing statement reflects this tension:

> Collecting industrial base data from America's companies through the means provided in section 705 would intrude inappropriately in peacetime in the lives of Americans who own and work in the nation's businesses. Such intrusion is neither necessary to meet U.S. national defense needs nor would be consistent with the liberties of those who own and work in America's businesses. Accordingly, I direct the affected heads of executive departments and agencies not to use subpoena, search warrant, or other intrusive techniques under the authority of section 705 of the Defense Production Act, implementing section 722 of the act without the specific approval of the president. They will proceed instead to seek information from America's businesses on a voluntary basis. However, the provisions of section 705 may be used to support other programs and other provisions of the Defense Production Act, in accordance with current delegations of authority under section 705.

This statement highlights the existence of the authority, but also its potential to generate controversy and litigation.

Section 705 does not present the same ambiguities as section 101. It is clearly written and the authority it presents is strong. It is also reinforced by chapter 148, section 2507, discussed at the outset of this chapter. Where the executive branch, in fact, follows the law, the president would act at the zenith of his *Youngstown* authority. That means that if one believes the potential reach of the DPA goes too far, statutory amendment and not litigation is the better course. Two issues warrant debate and resolution—now. One is technical, the other philosophical. The technical question is: If the government is going to collect information from private companies, as it already does, are there additional safeguards and limitations on doing so that should be put in place? The philosophical question is: To what extent, if at all, should the government use its authority to inquire into the activities of private companies engaged in AI research?

The DPA provides surprisingly broad authority to the president and executive branch to prioritize, allocate, incentivize, and survey critical technology related to national defense. The authority is "surprising," because the plain language is expansive in its scope and reach, especially in a context where private rights and property are at issue. But in many regards, the scope of this authority is untested either by the government, which has not pushed as far as the statutory language might allow, or by private industry, which has not litigated where it might. Perhaps all sides are hesitant to push too far or too hard and risk a litigation loss, choosing to assert preferred constitutional positions while seeking accommodation in practice. This might be especially true with respect to critical commercial AI technologies. But the executive branch could do so, and there is no apparent legal impediment to the president doing so. The language of the critical enabling laws and regulations reach this sector.

Efforts to use the DPA to reach beyond traditional DIB actors or use the DPA in new ways risks litigation. Indeed, the DPA contemplates litigation and enforcement in granting jurisdiction to federal district courts over DPA disputes. Six challenges are likely:

1. The authority is being used beyond the predicate necessity of "national defense."

2. The authority being used does not meet the statutory or regulatory requirements of the DPA.

3. Use of the authority violates the individual's or institution's First Amendment rights.

4. Use of the authority violates the individual's or institution's Fourth Amendment rights.

5. Use of the authority violates the individual's or institution's Fifth Amendment rights.

6. The authority has fallen into disuse, if it was ever used, and is no longer extant under the doctrine of desuetude.

If litigated, courts will weigh the language of the statute along with practice and legislative history. Where language is plain, many judges will go no further.

If litigation is likely, as it is, regarding the reach of the DPA into academic and industry AI, it is preferable to test the reach of the law now, rather than at a moment of crisis or need in the years ahead. In this regard, the FBI-Apple iPhone litigation may provide the model and the deterrent. The government is not always at its best, and most nuanced, in times of crisis. At such times, it is more likely to overreach or focus exclusively on immediate needs than on long-term consequences. Litigation also risks the disclosure of trade secrets and milestones, not necessarily in court but perhaps in media responses and commentary. In the context of the PATRIOT Act and FISA Amendments Act, it has taken time, now almost two decades, to find something of a security-privacy equilibrium. As with software code, Congress patches the law. Of course, an even better course is to find a common understanding between parties based on shared interests, and—where helpful—embed that under-standing in legislation, perhaps in the form of a DPA reauthorization.

TAKEAWAYS

DOD has taken a lead role in the development of U.S. government AI capabilities and policies, both by design and default. However, while the DPA is known to logisticians and defense contractors, it is not within the core competencies of national security law and practice. Therefore, absent additional legislation, the DPA is the authority the government is likely to use to harness AI for national security purposes. This would include instances where private industry or academia is unwilling or unable to contract with the government to meet AI goals and needs. Here are ten takeaways.

   1. The edge of the law. The term "defense industrial base" is defined broadly in statute and clearly covers a full range of critical technologies, including those associated with national security innovation like AI. Likewise, the DPA includes broad authority to investigate, inventory, incentivize, and use technology; however, the government does not appear to have used the DPA to the limits of the law. Policymakers and lawyers will want to make purposeful decisions about when and whether to push to the edge of the law.

   2. The DPA includes safeguards on its use and abuse. While the DPA has been referred to as a commandeering authority and some business critics imply that the law provides for centralized (that is, socialist) government control of the economy, the law includes important safeguards. These include jurisdiction in federal court over enforcement of the act as well as disputes arising under the act. The government is required to report on its use of the act. Most important, the majority of the act expires unless reauthorized by Congress every five years. Moreover, while the act allows the president to prevent hoarding and price gouging, "no provision of this Act shall be interpreted as providing for the imposition of wage or price controls without the prior authorization of such action by a joint resolution of Congress."[41]

3. DPA and DPAS process. The DPAS has operated under multiple models of policy direction. There is a tendency between administrations to change process as well as personnel. However, government-industry as well as government-academic relationships take time to develop where trust does not necessarily derive from shared goals and background, where DIB relationships are not long-standing, and companies are less dependent than traditional defense contractors on government contracts. To this end, in 2015, the Defense Department opened a liaison office in the Silicon Valley, the Defense Innovation Unit Experimental (DIUx, now DIU). If one wants to reach AI through the DPA and DPAS process, one needs to understand who the critical actors are. If the critical AI actors are not present, then they should be added to the process or purposefully and consciously excluded. The government should take care to distinguish between what works and what does not work, making clear in each context to distinguish between process, the law, or the people involved. The government should also give process that does work the time to grow bureaucratic roots and culture. One area that does not "work" is the government contracting cycle, which is too slow and burdensome to operate at AI pace and appeal to most industry actors.

4. Responsibility and accountability. Under E.O. 13603, responsibility is diffuse. Seventeen different agencies are members of the Defense Production Act Committee. That is the same number of agencies and entities that are members of the intelligence community. However, where there is a director of national intelligence to coordinate and, in theory, lead the intelligence community, there is no comparable position within the DIB DPAS system. Clearly, the secretaries of defense, commerce, and DHS are among the critical actors. Interagency responsibility is diffuse as well. Under E.O. 13603, for example, "The National Security Council and Homeland Security Council, in conjunction with the National Economic Council, shall serve as the integrated policymaking forum for consideration and formulation of national defense resource preparedness policy and shall make recommendations to the president on the use of authorities under the act."

Presidential directives are often written in an inclusive manner to win agency concurrence and leave to context and practice resolution of issues. If one wants to know who the actual members of the National Security Council are, for example, one does not just look to the law, or to presidential directives; one looks at White House pictures to see who is in the room (not quite the lost art of Kremlinology, but important nonetheless in determining actual process and whether lawyers are in the room). The same may be true of defense production policy and the DPA. On paper, at least, the lines of responsibility are unclear and accountability uncertain. This is potentially problematic where DPAS issues become controversial or require specialized expertise. Hard issues may linger in the interagency process without resolution. Moreover, except for the secretary of defense, it is hard to imagine members of the NSC, HSC, or NEC will view DPAC policy as a primary responsibility warranting substantial time and bureaucratic capital.

5. **Clarify Title I authority.** DPA practice is not transparent. It is not evident, for example, or publicly evident that the authority in Title I has been used to initiate and prioritize contracts that are independent of existing designated programs. Thus, it is not evident how the exception in the regulations for "item[s] not supplied or a service not performed" has applied or will apply. It would be better to know in advance than in a moment of crisis. Nor is it evident whether the lack of compelled practice reflects a legal judgment on the reach of the authority, the absence of a necessity for its use, or caution about litigation risk.

6. **The DPA is used in all contexts.** Title I and the DX rating have been used in direct support of warfighting and in both emergency and nonemergency but timely contexts. Thus, the authority was used to speed MRAP production during the Iraq and Afghanistan Wars, but also used in the 1970s to preserve Chrysler's capacity to produce the M1 Abrams tank at a time of economic trouble for the company. It has also been invoked to address some aspects of the COVID-19 pandemic.

7. **Transparency.** The exercise of DPA authority over AI is not transparent. Designated programs or generically listed programs like "NSA Program" or "Program 341" might involve AI applications. Without further transparency, policymakers will struggle to shape law and policy. Internal executive actors and/or the Congress should request more transparent reporting and briefing in this area. Transparency is especially important where the government is seeking to influence or direct private conduct, and the validity of the government's legal basis for acting is subject to validation and litigation.

With or without litigation, government use of the DPA for AI purposes will necessitate clear and careful explanation as to what is intended and why. This is evidenced by headlines about E.O. 13603, when it was issued in 2012, for example, "Executive Order 13603—How Dangerous Is It?" And "Obama's E.O.

13603 Reintroduces Slavery to America." For sure, some of this commentary reflected partisan politics and internet hysteria. But it also reflects a society that is less trustful of its elected and appointed leaders and government overall. As the phrase might go, this is not your father's DPA—or your grandfather's. The clearer the law the less opportunity there will be both to litigate and to assert that the government is acting beyond the law. And where national security genuinely warrants, we should want the law to be clear and effective. Therefore, policy actors should consider carefully the opportunities ahead to clarify the law and educate key constituencies. One place to start is with the reauthorization and potential amendment of the DPA. New uses of the DPA may be controversial; clear communication is as important as legal authority.

8. Litigation. The DPA has not been used or tested in AI context, and thus, for that reason alone, it is likely to generate dispute and litigation. Neither has the scope of certain sections been tested in other contexts, such as the allocation authority in section 101(b). Title I authority has primarily been used by the Department of Defense to prioritize defense contracts. There is no question that the law provides for such prioritization, and there is a long track record of doing so. However, there is less practice outside of DOD in using Title I authority, including in less traditional national security fields. However, other agencies, especially DHS, are increasing their use of DPA Title I authority for preparedness and disaster response. Based on this practice, some companies may take the view that to the extent the DPA is read to provide a "commandeering"—that is, directive authority beyond existing contract prioritization—such authority has either lapsed or was not intended to apply to them in the first place. Whether such arguments are well founded or not, litigation is likely, given the stakes involved.

The clearer the law is on such matters, the more likely parties will reach agreement without litigation. Likewise, where the law is clear and there is dispute, courts are more likely to uphold well-founded interpretations and decisions applying the law, and do so in a consistent manner. Conversely, the more ambiguous the law and past practice, the more likely courts will substitute their independent judgment on the scope of the law in exercising their jurisdiction to resolve disputes, especially where private property rights are at issue. Varied case law results in less certainty about how the law will apply in future and different contexts.

9. The litigation tie-breakers cut in both directions. When law is ambiguous, subject to litigation, and ambiguity is not resolved through legislative history—in other words, the law could go either way—judges often turn to doctrines of legal deference in applying the law. This is similar to the way finders of fact use burdens of proof to resolve uncertainty in criminal and civil cases. The *Chevron* Doctrine, for example, is a form of such deference whereby courts, in theory, defer to an agency's interpretation of its "own" statutes, unless that interpretation is arbitrary or capricious, even if the court might have ruled in a different way with a clean slate. The political question doctrine is another deference doctrine, whereby courts defer to the decisions of the political branches on matters that are textually assigned and ordinarily addressed by those branches, such as use of the war power. Regarding whether Title I is mandatory with respect to new contracts or the reach of 705, courts might well look to the *Youngstown* or *Chevron* as "tie-breakers." Executive branch lawyers looking to place the president's exercise of authority over AI into *Youngstown* category 1 (zenith) will likely look to the DPA to do so. Likewise, opponents of such use will likely look to the DPA to demonstrate that Congress did not contemplate such use and thus the president is in category 2 or 3 (low ebb or dry land).

However, because the DPA is a criminal statute, courts might also look to the rule of lenity, which generally provides that where criminal sanctions are implicated, ambiguities in the law should be resolved in the defendant's favor. While the adage that "ignorance of the law is no defense" remains true, if a court determines a reasonable person could not understand what the law required, fundamental fairness might suggest application of the rule of lenity.

10. Personnel law and policy. If AI is an integral ingredient in national security, the government needs to prepare now for a future where large numbers of AI specialists or skill sets are required in government. This will inevitably require greater pay and hiring flexibility. Incentive comes from the opportunity to perform public service and work on governmental applications. However, background investigations and comparatively low pay may impede recruitment. Additional thought and more conscious risk management about security waivers is needed. What is also needed in the AI personnel context is thoughtful, deliberate, conscious, and accountable choices. So, too, the government could well make wider use of personnel incentive mechanisms.

EIGHT

Arms Control by Analogy

Lawyers, like policymakers, search for metaphor when trying to understand or frame issues. This is evident in the context of cyberspace, where lawyers have asked, and debated, whether cyberattacks should be treated like acts of war, espionage, covert action, crime, or electronic vandalism, and, if so, when. Fixed, predictable, and reliable paradigms have proven elusive.

The next two chapters consider whether there is additional law or principles from other security regimes we should adopt, adapt, and apply by analogy to AI. This chapter considers whether there are lessons to learn and apply from the U.S. arms control experience involving nuclear, biological, and chemical weapons—arms control metaphors. The chapter is also intended to give generalists an overview of Cold War arms control history so that they might more effectively identify lessons to apply as well as critical distinctions. To proponents and skeptics, aspects of arms control are theological. This chapter does not espouse a doctrinal view of arms control, which may be viewed as doctrinal in itself. Let us also stipulate up front that verification is imperfect. States cheat. Sometimes they are caught and sometimes they are not caught. The Soviet Union continued its biological weapons program after becoming a party to the Biological Weapons Convention (BWC) in 1972 and was not definitively exposed until 1992. States are also presumed to cheat when sometimes they do not. Iraq was thought to have certain WMD programs in violation of UN sanctions before the U.S. invasion of Iraq in 2003. But such weapons were not found. Saddam Hussein, it appears, was engaged in a balance-of-power ruse with Iraq's immediate neighbors. In this same vein, we will stipulate that "trust, but verify" is U.S. doctrine and not subject to genuine dispute or debate as a policy precept.

Further, many but not all arms control advocates and skeptics will agree that the question is not just whether a control instrument worked or did not work as intended. The more objective question is whether the net result, however imperfect, was or is better than if there had been no treaty, law, or verification mechanism at all. Did the instrument, for example, make it harder to build or hide weapons or weapons capacities? Did the instrument contribute to stability? Did it reduce the risk of a weapon's use? It is a strawman argument, to ask whether there should be verification or whether verification is ever foolproof. Yes and no. Arms control may be an exercise in optimism. But it is also a national security tool that should inform AI policy.

Finally, in contrast to the DPA, which, on its face, applies to the defense and technology industrial base generally, most arms control efforts are specific to the arm or weapon addressed. That means arms control is not directly or immediately applicable to AI (outside the AI used within covered weapons or in conflict). Thus, one cannot simply make the necessary textual and doctrinal changes in all the necessary places—*mutatis mutandis*—and cover AI. But arms control is potentially instructive. The question is how and with what degree of risk management and certainty should states, including the United States, or other relevant parties seek to prohibit or regulate AI using arms control lessons and methods.

THE NUCLEAR ARMS RACE

If AI presents positive attributes and applications, it also presents national security risks. One such risk is an arms race between the United States, China, Russia, and potentially, regional actors like Iran. There have been arms races before. Robert Massie[1] and others documented the race to produce dreadnought battleships as part of the competition between the United Kingdom and Germany during the decade before World War I. Launched in 1906, the *Dreadnought* all-big-gun battleship was so superior in speed, armor, and armament to the next-in-class vessel it replaced that its arrival had the unintentional effect of zeroing out, or near zeroing, Britain's numeric naval advantage. It was also built in fourteen months, a remarkable pace at the time.[2]

The race was on to build dreadnought-class ships. As recounted by Giles Edwards, "We Want Eight and We Won't Wait" was a popular public slogan. "The admiralty had demanded six ships; the economists offered four," Winston Churchill is said to have quipped, "and we [Parliament] finally compromised on eight."[3] By the outbreak of World War I, the Royal Navy had forty-nine capital ships (not all dreadnoughts) to the Imperial German Navy's twenty-six. Equally important, as an unintended consequence, unable to keep pace with Britain and concerned with the ground threat posed by Russia's immense manpower, Germany turned to building up its army and to submarines as its primary naval weapon with which to challenge Britain.

No arms race, of course, was more important than the race to weaponize the atom, between Nazi Germany and the Allies.[4] That race occurred during the period of impending war in the 1930s and during World War II. State survival was at stake. Thus, there were fewer, if any, incentives or opportunities for internal, external, or self-regulation, beyond those imposed by the limits of knowledge, secrecy, and resources. In hindsight, one can wonder at the absence of introspection or hesitation on the part of some of the scientists. Only one Manhattan Project scientist, Józef Rotblat, is understood to have resigned from the project based on ethical concerns about weaponizing the atom and its potential use. He did so after it became clear that the Germans would not develop an atomic weapon.[5]

The Manhattan Project scientists pushed on. At the time of the Alamogordo test in July 1945, the scientists were not sure what would happen. Some scientists placed bets on whether the Trinity Test would work, and if so, with what kiloton yield. Two bombs were dropped on Japan—in part because they represented the entire U.S. inventory, and in part because they represented two different fission designs. Little Boy was the uranium-235 weapon dropped on Hiroshima. It had a yield of approximately fifteen kilotons of TNT. Fat Man was the plutonium weapon dropped on Nagasaki with a yield of twenty-one kilotons of TNT.

There is room for historical debate over when, whether, and how the first atomic weapons were used. Should the United States, for example, have demonstrated the power of the weapons in Tokyo Harbor first, as Edward Teller argued, before targeting cities? Should Japan have been given more opportunity to surrender before the second weapon was dropped on Nagasaki? Should more overtly military targets have been struck, away from population centers? But it is hard to take issue with the project itself. This was an arms race that had to be run and won, at least until the war was won.

Japan's surrender and America's atomic weapon monopoly in 1945 arguably offered a moment for pause and reflection. Historians debate whether an atomic arms race was inevitable at this point, or the product of a failure of imagination and of political and policy will to achieve a different result and work toward it. But it was not for lack of trying. In late 1945, the victorious powers created the United Nations Atomic Energy Commission (UNAEC), operating under the auspices of the UN Security Council. Its purpose was to advise the council on the destruction of all atomic weapons and the peaceful uses of nuclear energy under UN supervision.

In late 1945, Secretary of State James Byrne commissioned *A Report on the International Control of Atomic Energy*, which came to be known as the Acheson-Lilienthal Report, after its primary State Department sponsor, Undersecretary Dean Acheson, and the study's chairman, David Lilienthal, chairman of the Tennessee Valley Authority.[6] (Much of the report was understood to have been written by Robert Oppenheimer, one of the five report consultants.) The report argued for international control and regulation of atomic energy for peaceful purposes under the auspices of an International Atomic Development Authority. The report implied that the United States would eventually give up atomic weapons, but was not specific on when or how. The U.S. representative to the United Nations, Bernard Baruch, subsequently proposed a plan to the UNAEC for international control of atomic energy.

The Baruch Plan called for the destruction of the U.S. inventory of atomic weapons, international inspections to verify that states were not engaged in atomic weapons–related activity, and the prospect of security council sanctions against states engaged in prohibited activities. Moreover, permanent representatives to the security council would be barred from using their veto power over such sanctions. The Baruch Plan was not adopted. The Soviet Union objected. Whether the United States was actually prepared to give up its weapons monopoly was a moot issue, as the Soviet Union was not prepared to concede to the United States such a monopoly. Neither was it prepared to surrender its veto or accede to international inspections. It was forging ahead through espionage and research with its own weapon.

The atomic arms race entered a third, more permanent phase, the Cold War. The chronological events of the race are generally known and remembered as the sides sought military advantage, or a deterrent, in the form of more advanced weaponry, increased numbers, or both. On both sides, policy was spurred by real and perceived risks. In 1949, the USSR conducted its first atomic weapons test. It had the bomb. In 1952, the United States tested its first thermonuclear weapon, with almost seven hundred times the explosive power of the weapon dropped on Hiroshima, the equivalent of ten thousand kilotons of TNT. The Soviet Union followed in 1953. In 1957, the USSR launched the first orbital satellite, *Sputnik*. The United States rushed to follow suit; however, the first U.S. attempt to launch a satellite resulted in an explosion on the launch pad. The first U.S. ICBMs were deployed in 1959, the same year the Soviet Union deployed its first ICBM. The Polaris submarine-launched ballistic missile (SLBM) arrived in U.S. inventory in 1963, as did the first Soviet SLBM.

Both sides also deployed tactical nuclear weapons to offset real and perceived advantages of the other in conventional arms and geography. In the case of the United States and NATO, this took the form of tactical missiles and munitions (the first offset) to stem a Soviet invasion of Western Europe, such as the ten-ton yield W54 nuclear warhead used with munitions fired from the Davy Crockett recoilless gun. For its part, the Soviet Union deployed tactical nuclear weapons (cruise missiles, bombs, and torpedoes) in and around Cuba in 1962 to defend against a U.S. invasion. Thus, by the mid-1960s, the deterrence equation was established, with each side depending on some combination of bombers, ICBMs, tactical nuclear weapons, and submarines to deter attack and perhaps respond.

A corresponding political and doctrinal stability was more evasive. As the micro-races for tactical advantage proceeded, doctrine fluctuated. The "bomber-gap" of the 1950s and "missile-gap" of the early 1960s were fictional, spurred in part by domestic politics and the sort of faulty intelligence that derives from fixed assumptions and cognitive biases. At the height of the "missile-gap," the time of John F. Kennedy's election as president in November 1960, the Soviets had "just four SS-6 missiles" deployed. "In other words, there was a missile gap, even a deterrent gap, and the ratio in forces was nearly ten to one—but the gap was in our favor."[7] And while the strategic triad was set, the number of weapons deployed was not. Both sides sought to find and create advantage with new weapons and delivery systems, like Multiple Independently Targetable Reentry Vehicles (MIRVs), introduced on the Minuteman III in 1970, and Anti-Ballistic Missile (ABM) systems, as well as by increasing the numbers of each.

Arms Race Observations for the AI Generalist

Although the general outlines of the race may be remembered by its bench-marks, much is forgotten or unknown to the generation of scientists, policy-makers, and lawyers who work on AI today. Seven points warrant emphasis.

First, while it is understood that U.S. national security policy during the Cold War pivoted around the Soviet Union and colored how many, if not most, foreign policy events were perceived, the degree to which the Cold War, in turn, pivoted around the nuclear arms race is less evident. Nuclear doctrine and security were taught at every college and university, not just in the 1950s and 1960s, but into the 1980s. In the words of Thomas Powers: "In the 1980s, nuclear weapons dominated discussions of national security affairs to a degree that specialists under the age of, say, fifty would find baffling."[8] As a corollary, to someone who is over the age of fifty and has seen the influence of nuclear weapons during the Cold War, it is baffling today that more attention is not paid to AI and its certain impact on national security.

Second, students of the Cold War arms race may assume that the concept of mutual or finite deterrence, known popularly as Mutual Assured Destruction (MAD), emerged naturally, instantly, and collectively from the obvious, apparent, and rational thought that after Hiroshima and Nagasaki, strategic nuclear weapons should never be used again. As an early nuclear strategist Bernard Brodie concluded,

> Clausewitz argued that war is violence, but controlled violence in pursuit of some national objective. "National objectives" cannot be consonant with national suicide. There is no use talking about a mutual exchange of nuclear weapons, as being anything other than national suicide.[9]

But this was not U.S. doctrine during the Cold War. As Fred Kaplan recounts in *The Wizards of Armageddon*, U.S. doctrine at various times contemplated and incorporated counterforce and first strike scenarios as well as finite deterrence, which came in the form of the certainty that enough of either side's weapons would survive a surprise first strike to guarantee the destruction of the other side's major cities in response.

Rational people contemplated the irrational. In a 1954 speech, Chairman of the Joint Chiefs of Staff Admiral Arthur W. Radford said the following:

> What does all this mean? It means that atomic forces are now our primary forces. It means that actions by other forces, on land, sea, or air are relegated to a secondary role . . . nuclear weapons, fission, and fusion will be

used in the next major war. Availability of fissile material, the economy of its use, the magnitude of its destructive effects, and the flexibility of its use makes it the primary munition of war. Victory will come to the side that makes the best use of it.[10]

That the speech was given behind closed doors at the Naval War College suggests it was not purely or even primarily intended for Soviet consumption, but rather actually reflected a statement of U.S. military planning and doctrine. On becoming secretary of defense in 1961, Robert McNamara was stunned to learn that the U.S. war plan for responding to a Soviet first strike, known as the Single Integrated Operations Plan (SIOP), included the launch of missiles at China, with the potential loss of 175 million lives. This was *not* an option if, for example, China were somehow complicit in a Soviet attack; this was *the* plan. In addition to Secretary McNamara, only one service chief objected to the plan. As recounted by Kaplan, Marine Commandant General David M. Shoup, who earned the Medal of Honor at Tarawa, "stood and said, 'Sir, any plan that kills millions of Chinese when it is not even their war is not a good plan. This is not the American way.'"[11]

Third, the Chinese, in Kaplan's words, "have never played the nuclear arms race game."[12] Spurred by General MacArthur's threats to use U.S. nuclear weapons during the Korean War as well as the Taiwan Straits Crisis (1954–55), China launched its own nuclear weapons program in the 1950s with help from the Soviet Union. China tested its first nuclear weapon in 1964. It deployed its first ICBM in 1967. However, rather than compete with the Soviet Union and the United States, China maintained a doctrine of assured retaliation. The doctrine is, apparently, predicated on three factors. First, China has a declared policy of no first use of nuclear weapons. Second, the strategic objective is one described by Western analysts as assured retaliation or "minimum deterrence." The third factor is centralized command and control.[13]

Whereas Soviet and U.S. war-gaming and planning sought to calculate the potential destruction in lives and cities in any nuclear exchange, Chinese doctrine was and is thought to be based on the calculation that a lower level of certain destruction is good enough. Estimates of the numbers of Chinese nuclear weapons from the 1960s to the 2000s were in the low hundreds, and perhaps even lower. Chinese doctrine, then and now, is characterized as "lean and effective." A 2017 RAND Corporation study on Chinese deterrence refers to a 2013 Chinese think tank study, which in turn concludes that Chinese strategy is captured by a 1957 quotation from Chinese premier Zhou Enlai:

Developing nuclear strength is chiefly to resolve the [nuclear] "existential" problem, and the scale should not be too great; China is developing nuclear weapons to oppose nuclear threat, not to engage in a nuclear arms race with the nuclear states.[14]

The precise number of Chinese weapons today is not known or declared, in contrast to those of Russia and the United States. However, it is estimated to be in the low hundreds, and in 1966 may have been as low as forty ICBMs and SLBMs, which surely means fewer before that year. However, it is possible that Chinese doctrine and numbers will change, considering India's nuclear weapons capacity and rivalry, North Korea, and China's pursuit of great power status. As during the Cold War, nuclear weapons remain a symbol of great power status, as far as China is concerned.[15]

Fourth, the U.S. response to the arms race and nuclear weapons at times verged on hysteria—perhaps with good reason, but hysteria nonetheless. This was reflected in drills that had school children shelter under their desks in the event of a nuclear attack. It was also reflected in the fallout shelter industry. Federal and state tax deductions were provided for the installation of backyard fallout shelters. In 1961, at the height of the shelter craze, the Kennedy administration asked Congress for US$100 million in fallout shelter funding. It received US$169 million. (A funding adjustment reminiscent of Churchill's quip about Parliament funding the dreadnought class of vessels). In New York City alone, there were nineteen thousand fallout shelters.

Fifth, at various times, nuclear weapons were maintained on a hair trigger, or close to one. For example, during the years 1961 to 1990, the United States kept a nuclear command and control aircraft airborne twenty-four hours a day. It also kept SAC flights on airborne alert until 1968. "The alert flights were stopped following accidents, particularly those at Palomares [Spain] and Thule [Greenland]; the rising cost of maintaining SAC bomber force constantly on airborne alert; and the advent of a responsive and survivable" ICBM force.[16]

Sixth, at various times, the world came close to the intentional use of nuclear weapons, as in the case of the Cuban Missile Crisis and Indo-Pakistan crisis of 1998.[17] The United States and Soviet Union also came close to the erroneous launch of nuclear weapons on at least two occasions recounted earlier, involving National Security Advisor Zbigniew Brzezinski (1979) and Lieutenant Colonel Petrov (1983). The William J. Perry Project states that "there have been thirty-three broken arrow incidents officially confirmed by the Pentagon. . . . A 'broken arrow' is an accidental event that involves nuclear weapons, which does not risk nuclear conflict between states."[18] Not all, even most, involved the risk of detonation as opposed to loss. But some did. And surely there are more, the Soviet Union—now Russia—not being known for its transparency on such matters.

Seventh, in the aftermath of Hiroshima and Nagasaki, there was some introspection and retrospection on the part of the scientific community, but not much. Robert Oppenheimer, James Conant, and Enrico Fermi argued against the testing and adoption of thermonuclear weapons in the early 1950s. (The position may have contributed to later accusations that Oppenheimer held Communist sympathies leading to the loss of his security clearance.[19]) But Fermi continued to work on the weapon nonetheless. In 1955, eleven scientists, including ten Nobel laureates and Bertrand Russell, wrote an open letter—the "Russell-Einstein Manifesto"—calling for peaceful resolution of disputes to avoid a nuclear war. The presentation of the resolution did not change many government minds, but it did lead to the creation of the Pugwash Conferences addressed to nuclear weapons and other WMD risks, and thus arguably contributed to the advent of the arms control process. However, for every Einstein or Rotblat, there seems to have been an Edward Teller, who ardently argued for the development of the hydrogen bomb. "That I have spent my life working on weapons, I have not the least regret," Teller said during a 2007 interview. "I succeeded. I believe that by building the H-bomb, I contributed to winning the Cold War without bloodshed."[20] In short, arms race constraint did not come from the academic community, which seemed to embrace the individual components of the race—the mini-races for each weapon—with patriotic as well as scientific vigor. The academic community also embraced the pursuit of nuclear arms doctrine, bringing game theory and economic analysis to the exercise. The combination of national security, scientific inquiry, and career advancement is a powerful mix.

Conclusions

One question with AI is, where are we now? Is this the 1930s? Are we at a Baruch Plan moment in 1947? Or are we past that point, plunging headfirst into an AI arms race? The temporal and technological context is, of course, different. AI is not a weapon, per se, it is a collection of technological capacities. Moreover, governments do not have a monopoly over its development, regulation, and use. A Baruch Plan would not work for AI, even if there was governmental will to regulate and control AI in such a manner. Moreover, the leading edge of research and development is found in industry and academia. Can an "arms race" be averted? The question drives the work of some of the leading AI think tanks.

The answer, however, is already evident. Governments, as well as industry and academic actors, have identified AI as a transformative security technology, equal to if not more transformative than nuclear weapons, aviation, and submarines. AI offers both the prospect and the threat of a transcendent and perhaps permanent security advantage to first movers. States are responding by overtly spending billions of dollars on AI, and perhaps more in secret, including on autonomous weapons development. They are also incorporating AI into national security policy, such as the third offset strategy.

Whether we like it or not, a technology race is here. The national security imperative makes it inevitable and essential for states to keep pace. But that does not mean that states, industry, and academic actors cannot or should not adopt or impose controls. The purpose of this chapter is to describe some of the previous efforts to control arms, from which lessons and options for the regulation of AI might be derived, understanding that AI, as opposed to LAWS, is more like "electricity" or "energy" than an arm. This discussion starts with efforts to control the last "most" transformative weapon.

NUCLEAR WEAPONS REGIME

The Nuclear Weapons Regime—as used here—is the body of international and domestic law intended to regulate control of, proliferation of, and the potential use of nuclear weapons. Arms control, in turn, includes four essential substantive elements: reduction, elimination, renunciation, and regulation. It also includes several procedural elements, including doctrine, command and control, verification, and confidence building measures.

At first glance, the nuclear regime seems the most apt to AI because of the potential impact of AI to transform the national security landscape, as nuclear weapons did before. Moreover, AI may have the potential, like nuclear weapons, to pose an existential threat to states. Therefore, it is worth exploring how nuclear arms are similar and dissimilar. Of course, similarity or dissimilarity in one regard does not necessarily mean AI should be treated as nuclear weapons are or were. Two concepts warrant attention: (1) command and control, and (2) first mover or first strike advantage.

Key Concepts Compared and Contrasted
COMMAND AND CONTROL

AI and nuclear weapons present command and control issues and questions based on their potential first strike capacity and the speed with which the systems operate.[21] In the case of a Soviet nuclear first strike, the president was estimated to have minutes in which to verify the occurrence of a launch and decide how to respond. In the case of a launch from a submarine, the timeline could be shorter. Of course, tactical nuclear weapons can present even shorter timelines. News stories indicate that doctrine calls for a four-minute window of decision; however, as the 1979 Brzezinski incident suggests, "in practice" the window is as wide as the president or his immediate advisors make it, but no longer than the flight time of an incoming missile. The estimated flight time of an ICBM from North Korea to Los Angeles, or from Russia over the Arctic to most U.S. cities, is publicly estimated at twenty or twenty-five minutes.

Such time pressures placed, and place, a premium on determining in advance who has authority to order a response and in accordance with what legal principles and doctrine. It also necessitates decisions about the pre-delegation of authority, if at all, to make decisions in the event the chain of command is disrupted or, in the vernacular of the Cold War, "decapitated." Deterrence, the logic went, would be achieved through the promise of mutually assured destruction and the continuity of government functions.

AI applications, of course, present parallel time constraint pressures, but these constraints are measured in nanoseconds or microseconds, not minutes. (A nanosecond is one-billionth of a second; a microsecond is one-millionth of a second.) This sort of time pressure is already present in cyberspace where algorithms and people are said to engage in instantaneous hand-to-hand combat attacking and defending systems. Any hesitation or delay can prove fatal to the system at stake and whatever infrastructure the system controls. Pre-delegation to humans and to machines in the form of code is essential, as is advance doctrinal agreement without which decisionmakers will not know what to code or delegate.

Outside cyberspace, AI may determine when and whether a weapon system is fired. Pre-delegation, in this context, is likely to come in the form of policy guidance on whether and when an AI capacity can be programmed to automatically and instantaneously act in offense or defense. As in the nuclear context, this creates the necessity to establish and apply doctrine. It also creates the necessity to ensure the integrity of the command and control system, to validate any triggering information, and to do so before it is too late to do so.

However, there are critical distinctions between nuclear weapons and AI command and control. To start, in U.S. practice, there is a culture of safety and security surrounding the command and control of nuclear weapons unlike any other in the U.S. military. Attention to detail is exacting; accountability expected. This is hard to do in a security environment where the likelihood of use is low, but the necessity for constant and immediate vigilance is high. But it is generally done well. And, when it is not, there usually are consequences. This was the case, for example, in June 2008, when both the secretary of the air force and the chief of staff of the air force were relieved of duties (a.k.a., fired) by the secretary of defense after a string of incidents suggesting a declining security culture within the air force nuclear weapons community.

Likewise, the command of the nuclear triad is precise and practiced. It is clear within the chain of command who has authority to do what and in accordance with what procedures. This is one of the reasons former secretary of defense Rumsfeld changed the chain of command nomenclature for nuclear command and control from one known as the national command authority (NCA) to one specifying the president/commander in chief and secretary of defense by name and position. It seems a semantic point, but it is not, if one is building a system of known, accountable, and responsible command. With nuclear weapons, there is not only a human in the loop: that human is specific, named, and thus accountable. And, just to be clear, invariably there is more than one human in the loop.

In contrast, AI is an enabling capacity, not a weapon. As MIT's Harvey Sapolsky pointed out with respect to the development of the Polaris missile, it is a lot easier to build a weapon as well as an esprit de corps and a culture of safety and security around a weapon system than it is around a class of technology or a concept. Therefore, it is inapt to compare nuclear command and control to AI command and control, generally. A more apt analogy may be offensive and defensive cyber-weapons. But here, less is known about command and control, and the culture of command and control, than with nuclear weapons. Nor is there a publicly expressed and understood doctrine of use and deterrence. The unclassified *Summary of the DOD Cybersecurity Strategy* of September 2018 comes closest.[22] Going forward, one question with respect to national security applications of AI is whether—and, if so, how— the United States should define the culture surrounding the command and control of AI. Should it be more FBI coat-and-tie or Apple beanbag-chairs-

and-lattes? It is not too early to start defining a purposeful delegation doctrine and culture of AI command and control, as well as safety, within the government generally or within select institutions or programs.

THE FIRST MOVER/FIRST STRIKE DILEMMA

Nuclear weapons and AI both present real and perceived strategic and tactical advantages to the beneficiary of any breakout capacity. The fear and consequences of a breakout first emerged in the race for atomic weapons during World War II. It continued during the Cold War, with both sides fearing the consequences of the other side achieving technological or numeric superiority in a manner that inferred supremacy, and thus the potential threat of a first strike or the necessity of submission. This fueled the arms race as both sides developed new weapons—atomic, hydrogen, neutron; new and better delivery means—ICBMs, SLBMs, MIRVs; and greater numbers of platforms with each step intended to prevent the adversary from obtaining an irrevocable lead or advantage while keeping the other side from perceiving an intent to break out or break away. Each step was also seemingly oblivious to the possibility that at some point enough was enough to ensure the survival of an adequate force to guarantee a sufficiently destructive response and thus deter any incentive for the other side to strike first.

In this contest, perception could be as important as reality. If the opponent was perceived to have the upper hand, it could have the same strategic consequence as the situation where the opponent did have the upper hand. In this way, the perceived bomber-gap of the 1950s and the perceived missile-gap of the early 1960s fueled U.S. efforts to develop and deploy more and better weapons systems, which, in a cyclical fashion, compelled the other side to do the same, all the while distorting perceptions about intent and fears of a first strike. Why, for example, would the United States need or want more bombers or missiles, the Kremlin might have asked in 1960, when the United States already held a decisive advantage? More accurate knowledge and transparency, it turned out, could help limit arms race incentives and risks. It also eventually incentivized arms control measures and the introduction of confidence building measures to reduce the risk of a breakout or an erroneous decision to launch.

With AI, the concept of a breakout is usually referred to as "first mover advantage." However, depending on the capacity, a first mover may, in theory and logic, also be a last mover if the AI application has the capacity to overwhelm and control an opponent's AI. First mover advantage is usually contemplated in the form of the first state to achieve human-level machine intelligence in a narrow area—or, more decisively, with a capacity to switch from task to task in response to external influences. But it may come in the form of a narrow AI capacity, perhaps one designed to disable other AI capacities or penetrate command and control mechanisms. Or, as some states worry, it may come in the form of an AWS advantage. One might extrapolate certain parallels from the nuclear and Cold War context, including how the fear of an opponent's breakout fueled the arms race but also incentivized arms control.

Just as the arms race engendered fears of a breakout and the strategic consequences that would follow, there are concerns that the state that first achieves an AI breakout capacity may seek to use that capacity to control or disable another state's or actor's AI capacity and defense. Nuclear strategy sought to deter and respond to the first-strike risk in three related ways. The first was with doctrine. The doctrine of MAD was predicated on the short, but not insignificant, lag time between launch and strike in a nuclear weapons scenario, giving the recipient of a first strike time to respond. The second way was technological, to build a military capacity that was redundant and could survive a first strike. This was the nuclear triad. The third way was to deploy so many weapons the enemy could never be sure it would destroy all of them, or enough of them, to avoid a devastating response. This resulted in what felt at times like an inexorable climb in the number of weapons, all to ensure that something would survive to guarantee a response that would make any first strike suicidal. MIRVs and ABMs were therefore thought destabilizing, because they raised the possibility that one could successfully execute a first strike and then defend against a diminished retaliatory strike, provided you were willing to risk (and accept) the destruction of cities and the death of millions.

Similarly, AI superiority or supremacy, as the military uses those terms, seems inherently destabilizing. Because AI superiority carries the potential to decisively cripple or overwhelm an opponent's military AI capacity and is potentially instantaneous in its effect, it reintroduces the theoretical risk and advantage of a first strike. But in contrast to a nuclear first strike, an AI first move could come without warning or time lag. It could also overwhelm or subvert any responsive AI capacity, at least in theory, either driving a state to the use of kinetic weapons or compelling some form of surrender or submission. This is a recipe for an arms race, for miscalculation, and for escalation. It is also a scenario that needs a thoughtful and conscious doctrinal response.

CRITICAL DISTINCTIONS

An important distinction between nuclear weapons and AI is that while both are capacities, nuclear weapons and their dual-use companion, nuclear energy, are defined and finite capacities. We know what a nuclear weapon looks like and we have seen, or can model, what it can do. We can register and trace nuclear attribution signatures. Therefore, we know what we are trying to control, limit, and verify. AI, in contrast, is a constellation of capacities and applications. It is easier to control a finite resource than an unknown or infinite resource. Which is not to say it is easy, just easier.

The nuclear regime is also subject to arms control measures. AI is not. But that was not always the case. It emerged as the United States and other states and actors sought to reduce the risk of nuclear war using arms control and law as tools. The question is posed, does the ensuing arms control regime offer relevant analogies to AI and the AI arms race?

Confidence Building Measures

The first successful mutual steps to control the risk of nuclear weapons during the Cold War involved confidence building measures (CBM). This occurred after the Cuban Missile Crisis, when both sides realized how close to nuclear war the United States and the Soviet Union came. It was closer even than the participants realized at the time. Among other things, the USSR deployed tactical nuclear weapons to Cuba, and Communist Party Chairman Nikita Khrushchev authorized their use by Soviet forces in the event of an invasion. At one point, a U.S. invasion was contemplated, even imminent. Not only had members of the Executive Committee of the National Security Council (ExComm) argued in favor of an invasion if the USSR did not remove its intermediate range missiles from Cuba, the ExComm also agreed, in principle, to an invasion if a second U-2 was shot down. A first U-2 had been shot down on the initiative of Cuban air defense forces and perhaps Fidel Castro, not at the direction of Soviet commanders or the Politburo. In other words, nuclear war might have started based on the decisions of an air defense battery commander or the decisions of a proxy state leader.

In a second incident, the U.S. Navy sought to "signal" to a submerged Soviet submarine to surface using practice depth charges.[23] Unaware that the depth charges were practice rounds, the submarine commander thought his vessel was under attack and that war had broken out. The Soviet captain considered two options: surface and surrender, or launch nuclear tipped torpedoes at the destroyers. By chance, the submarine flotilla commander, Vasili

Arkhipov, was aboard this vessel. Therefore, the captain needed the concurrence of not only the political officer, but the flotilla commander to launch a nuclear weapon. The presence of Arkhipov was fortuitous. The captain and political officer wanted to launch torpedoes; Arkhipov did not. He eventually persuaded the vessel's captain to surface to receive orders from Moscow. At this point, the officers discovered the U.S. vessels were signaling, not attacking.

In March 1963, the United States proposed the creation of a "hotline" between Moscow and Washington. A "Memorandum of Understanding Between the United States of America and the Union of Soviet Socialist Republics Regarding the Establishment of a Direct Communications Link" followed in June. The agreement led to the establishment of two full-time dedicated telex machines running between the Pentagon and Communist Party Headquarters. (Telex was a mode of communication that relied on electric current to transmit point-to-point signals from one teleprinter to another using hole-punch paper printouts. Printers would answer back before messages were transmitted, providing additional security beyond encryption. The telex system was used widely in international communication from the late 1950s until the 1990s.) The machines were staffed twenty-four hours a day and messages conveyed up the chain of command upon receipt. In 1967, the White House received a terminal. In 1971, 1984, and 1988, agreements were concluded to modernize the hotline. The telex lines were replaced by satellite communications, fax machines, and, in 2006, e-mail. According to the State Department website, the communications link proved its worth during the 1967 Six Day War and 1973 Arab-Israeli War, where it was used to "avoid possible misunderstandings regarding U.S. fleet movements." However, as a general matter, use of the hotline is not publicized.[24]

The hotline serves multiple purposes. It can be used for signaling intention and to avoid misunderstanding. It allows for confidential communications "free from the public posturing that makes crisis de-escalation difficult." It avoids having to work through intermediaries when and if heads of state wish to communicate directly. And, of course, it is fast, secure, and reliable. Other states have established hotlines as well. China has hotlines with Russia (1998), the United States (1998), South Korea (2008), India (2008), and Vietnam (2008). India and Pakistan (2011) and South Korea and North Korea have established hotlines as well.[25]

As the Cold War progressed, additional CBM measures were added to facilitate stability by building confidence in verification regimes, preventing surprise, and providing for trusted lines of communication at times of crisis.

Noteworthy examples include the 1992 Open Skies Treaty, which provides overflight privileges for U.S. and Russian aircraft, among others, over each other's territory.[26] Another example is the International Atomic Energy Agency (IAEA) Inspection Protocol and corresponding verification and inspection agreements; and what might loosely be called the nuclear "Rules of the Road"— informal understandings among certain states defining expectations about conduct. Military attaches, for example, were, and are, permitted a certain amount of access for the purposes of overt spying.

Elimination and Renunciation

The United States and USSR were not alone in desiring CBM to reduce the threat of nuclear weapons. The international community did as well. This took its most lasting form in the negotiation and conclusion of the Nuclear Nonproliferation Treaty (NPT), which opened for signature in 1968 and entered into force in 1972. Its impetus is rooted in nonproliferation as well as the dynamics of the Cold War arms race. Whether called arms control, nonproliferation, or both, the theory behind the NPT is twofold. The fewer states with nuclear weapons the less likelihood of a nuclear war, incident, or theft. Likewise, the fewer weapons and warheads the less risk of unintentional war, incident, or theft. The essential bargain contained in the treaty is between weapon states and non-weapon states. The non-weapon states agree to forgo the development and deployment of nuclear weapons in exchange for the weapon states committing to share their nuclear know-how and technology for peaceful purposes as well as a commitment to "pursue negotiations in good faith on effective measures leading to the cessation of the nuclear arms race at an early date and to nuclear disarmament, and on a treaty on general and complete disarmament under strict and effective international control" (NPT, article VII).

The treaty has a mixed record as a nonproliferation tool. Critics note that the NPT did not stop signatory North Korea from withdrawing, testing warheads, and joining the nuclear weapons "club." Syria sought to join the club as well, when in 2007 its clandestine nuclear weapons facility was destroyed by Israeli bombers. (Israel, which is generally understood to have obtained nuclear weapons capacity in the later 1960s, was never a signatory to the treaty.) Thus, since 1972, the number of nuclear weapon states has grown from six (United States, Russia, China, United Kingdom, France, Israel) to nine (including India, Pakistan, North Korea). In addition, the treaty provides cover to states that may wish to pursue clandestine weapons programs or preserve the capacity to do so, by providing a "lawful" basis to pursue nuclear energy resources "for peaceful purposes" along with a commitment from the weapon states to help, such as Russia's help to Iran at the Bushehr power plant. Interpretive disputes also remain over whether the weapon states, especially Russia and the United States, have worked in good faith toward nuclear disarmament as well as whether article VII is a commitment to reduce arms or completely disarm, as the text seems to suggest—a return to the Baruch Plan.

On the other hand, the NPT establishes a clear line of demarcation between nuclear energy and nuclear weapons. Four states have given up their nuclear weapons or programs (former Soviet republics Ukraine, Kazakhstan, and Belarus—as well as South Africa). It is doubtful that these states did so out of a sense of legal obligation to the NPT; however, they certainly did so, consistent with the NPT, and the NPT provided the mechanism with which to verifiably do so. Moreover, the NPT helped to establish a normative expectation against the development and possession of nuclear weapons.

Perhaps most important, the NPT provides the legal framework, including a verification annex and mechanism, to police and verify the line of demarcation between peaceful nuclear endeavors and weapons production. To regulate the NPT regime, the international community turned to the IAEA, which operates under UN auspices. The suggestion for such an agency originated at the national level with the U.S. and President Eisenhower's "Atoms for Peace" speech at the UN in 1953. The agency was subsequently created in 1957.

Today, IAEA

> . . . safeguard activities are applied routinely at over nine hundred facilities in seventy-one countries. . . . At least thirty countries have nuclear power reactors. There are scores of other major facilities containing nuclear material in over seventy countries that are "safeguarded" under IAEA agreements with governments.

The IAEA has safeguard agreements with 145 states. These IAEA activities include reviewing the completeness and correctness of state declarations, the placement of seals and cameras in nuclear facilities, and field inspections. In addition, but separately from its NPT safeguard work, the IAEA undertakes special investigations at the request of the UN Security Council—as in the case of Iraq, pursuant to UNSCR 687, following the First Gulf War. A sense of the scope and nature of the IAEA activities is suggested by the following 2015 agency statistics:

- 1,286 nuclear facilities and locations outside facilities were under IAEA safeguards.

- 2,118 in-field inspections, 623 design information verifications, and 64 complementary accesses (the term of art to describe access provided to the IAEA pursuant to an additional protocol to a Safeguards Agreement for verifying compliance) were conducted, constituting 13,248 calendar days in the field.

- The agency verified approximately 23,300 seals that had been installed on nuclear material, facility equipment, or agency safeguard equipment at nuclear facilities.

- By the end of 2015, the agency had 1,416 cameras connected to 863 systems operating at 266 facilities.[27]

However, in the end, the IAEA Safeguards Regime is essentially a coalition of the willing. As the IAEA itself points out, ultimately, the strength of the IAEA safeguard system depends upon three interrelated elements:

- The extent to which the IAEA is aware of the nature and locations of states' nuclear and nuclear-related activities.

- The extent to which IAEA inspectors have physical access to relevant locations for the purpose of providing independent verification of the exclusively peaceful intent of a state's nuclear program.

- The will of the international community, through the UN Security Council, to take action against states that are not complying with their safeguard commitments to the IAEA.[28]

Domestic legal efforts to regulate the peaceful transfer of technology, consistent with the NPT, are reflected in section 123 of the Atomic Energy Act and corresponding 123 Agreements between the United States and states receiving peaceful nuclear energy assistance. These agreements are overseen by the National Nuclear Security Administration (NNSA)—a specialized agency within the Department of Energy with expertise in nuclear matters. In U.S. law, the leading program to eliminate the risk of nuclear weapons is the Department of Defense Cooperative Threat Reduction Program, known by its popular name Nunn-Lugar for its two 1991 principal bipartisan senatorial cosponsors. The legislation was inspired, in part, by Senator Nunn's question to General Secretary Mikhail Gorbachev following an aborted coup by hardline Soviet officials in August 1991: "Did you retain command and control of nuclear weapons during the coup?" According to Senator Nunn, "Gorbachev did not answer," implying the answer was no.[29] The legislation was originally opposed by conservative members of the Senate, but it subsequently passed 86-8 after briefings on the imminent collapse of the Soviet Union.

As suggested by the agency charged with its implementation, the Defense Threat Reduction Agency (DTRA), as well as the act's original name—the Soviet Threat Reduction Act—the program was first addressed to the states of the former Soviet Union and was intended to help Russia and former Soviet republics dismantle and destroy nuclear weapons and vehicles to minimize the threat that these weapons might fall into nefarious hands. During the period 1994–2013, the program deactivated 7,616 warheads out of declared 13,300; 926 ICBMs out of declared 1,473; and 498 ICBM silos out of declared 831. In 2003, the Nunn-Lugar Expansion Act extended the program's authority beyond the former Soviet Union to the rest of the globe.[30]

The principal critiques of the program are: (1) that it creates a market for the weapons it is designed to reduce and thus raises the cost of destroying or dismantling weapons; and (2) because money is fungible, money the United States spends implementing the program is money the host government does not need to spend, and thus the United States and its taxpayers are subsidizing the defense budgets and responsibilities of other countries. The rebuttal is twofold. First, most of the recipients of DTRA aid would not otherwise spend their defense money on Nunn-Lugar activities. Second, proponents ask rhetorically, is the United States—and the world—better off having spent the money to take these weapons out of circulation than it would have been if it had not spent the money to take these weapons out of circulation? Clearly, the former, as fewer weapons and materials means less risk of illicit acquisition by state and non-state actors, or mistaken launch. Additional threat reduction programs are addressed to border control and detection of radiological devices, and efforts to acquire and degrade weapon-quality fissile material.

Reduction

The United States and Soviet Union also sought to reduce the risk of nuclear war by reducing the number of weapons and the number of weapons kept on alert. While likely the least apt arms control mechanism for current AI, reduction is addressed here for the sake of completeness and because policymakers might wish at some point to consider numeric limits on LAWS and other AI systems. At the close of World War II, the Soviet Union raced to obtain atomic weapons capacity. It did so in 1949. The United States, for its part, raced to obtain an adequate means to ensure delivery of its nuclear weapons in the event of a Soviet first strike or ground invasion of Europe. This started with a drive to increase the number of long-range bombers. The goal was to have enough bombers survive an initial conventional or nuclear attack to ensure there were enough aircraft left to launch and to reach their target destinations in the Soviet Union. Greater numbers, in theory, would deter any incentive to engage in a first strike. Both sides attempted to track the other side's bomber production and capability with this prospect in mind.

The development of intermediate range and intercontinental ballistic missiles changed the calculus behind first strike potential and incentives. In theory, the right number of missiles with the right accuracy could knock out enough of the opponent's offensive capability to make a first strike feasible. Further, the flight time of an ICBM, in theory, made this a possibility if you could catch the opponent's deterrent capacity on the ground, in hangars, and in silos, or at least enough of them so that your own retaliatory destruction was "acceptable," whatever that meant. (That significant elements of the U.S. and Soviet national security establishments seemed to have thought such destruction acceptable, as Fred Kaplan recounts, should give pause when considering whether government national security actors are best suited to alone regulate the military uses of AI.)

One solution to the ICBM risk was greater numbers of delivery vehicles and missiles. Another solution was to harden the silos, creating doubt about just how many would survive. Yet another solution was mobility. Mobility was initially found in rail- and vehicle-transported missiles. Intuitively, if you made your missiles harder to find, more of them would survive a first strike. Unless, of course, the opponent built and launched so many more missiles that they could saturate their target lists.

The introduction of SLBMs in the early 1960s again changed the calculus and opened the door wider to the possibility of arms reduction. Because they were harder to find, and you could never be sure you would, submarine-launched weapons guaranteed for both sides that a sufficient number of warheads would survive a first strike to ensure mutual destruction and thus deter any possible incentive for a first strike. It thus became possible, in the context of the triad, for both sides to calculate with sufficient certainty just how many weapons and platforms, and of which type, would be needed to accomplish this goal.

There followed a series of arms control reduction treaties, including:[31] the Strategic Arms Limitation Treaty (SALT I), 1972; Anti-Ballistic Missile Treaty

(ABM), 1972; SALT II, 1979; Intermediate-Range Nuclear Forces Treaty (INF), 1987; Strategic Arms Reduction Treaty (START I), 1991; START II, 1993; START III, 1997; Strategic Offensive Reductions Treaty (SORT), signed 2002/ratified 2003; and New START, 2010, which limits both sides to 1,550 strategic nuclear warheads and 700 strategic delivery vehicles. In February 2018, the United States and Russia each announced that it had complied with the terms of the treaty, which would expire in 2021 absent the parties agreeing on an extension. With U.S. withdrawal from the INF, New START remains the last arms reduction treaty in effect with Russia.

After 1972 and the conclusion of the NPT, these reductions had the added advantage, and presumptive purpose, of fulfilling at least part of the obligation of the weapon states to work toward disarmament. Although it is fair to also say that détente, cost, and a search for stability drove the process, and not necessarily NPT obligations.

Regulation

The most apt connection between arms control and AI may be in the area of regulation. Cold War arms control started with regulation, which is to say, efforts to limit the risks from nuclear weapons as well as their testing. These efforts are also noteworthy because they occurred at a time when the parties were not prepared to reduce the nature or number of their weapons. Both sides remained on a near-war footing. Nonetheless, they wanted to reduce the unintended risks of weapons use and proliferation. This started in 1963 with the Limited Test Ban Treaty. The treaty, originally between the United States, Soviet Union, and United Kingdom, prohibits nuclear weapons tests "or any other nuclear explosion" in the atmosphere, in outer space, or under water. The treaty does not distinguish between peaceful tests and other tests because of the difficulty in distinguishing between the two for verification purposes. In addition to seeking to limit the arms race, the treaty has, as its goal, the prevention of radiological debris crossing national borders. The treaty is of unlimited duration and is open to all states to join. As of 2017, there were 107 states parties. China and North Korea are not parties.

A follow-on treaty, the Comprehensive Nuclear-Test-Ban Treaty (CTBT), was negotiated in 1996 in the context of the UN Conference on Disarmament (CD). As the title suggests, the treaty prohibits nuclear weapons tests or any other nuclear explosions. There are 166 states parties to the treaty as of January 2017. However, under the terms of the treaty, it does not enter into force until the 44 states who were members of the CD in 1996 and possessed nuclear energy or research facilities ratify the treaty. As of January 2017, China, Egypt, India, Iran, Israel, North Korea, Pakistan, and the United States are not parties. In 1999, the U.S. Senate voted down a resolution offering advice and consent to ratification by a vote of 51-48. Nonetheless, many states adhere to the prohibition as a matter of policy, including the United States, which has observed a testing moratorium since 1992.

The argument for the treaty is that it establishes a black letter international norm and moratorium on all testing, removing any debate as to whether any future test is lawful or not. In addition, the treaty includes a robust on-site verification annex and regime.

The arguments against the treaty, at least from a U.S. perspective, include the likelihood that the treaty will never go into effect because of the requirement in article XIV that certain states become parties. Thus, by becoming a party, the United States would limit its own testing options without a corresponding commitment from other critical states. That is because signatories are bound by the principle of treaty law found in the Vienna Convention on the Law of Treaties not to defeat the object and purpose of the treaty pending its entry into force (article 18). In addition, opponents argue the treaty is not verifiable, its international enforcement mechanisms are unworkable, and that the United States will at some point need to test its nuclear weapons to verify that they remain functional or to deploy new systems using methods beyond AI and other modeling.

The Outer Space Treaty may offer the most useful analogy for AI regulation for three reasons. First, it covers an important domain and global commons that is also subject to AI proliferation risk. Second, it addresses the question of liability where private actors are as likely as government actors to create risks and cause harm. Further, it does so in a way that does not require precise individualized attribution, but rather relies on geographic attribution. Article VI of the treaty provides:

> States parties to the treaty shall bear international responsibility for national activities in outer space, including the moon and other celestial bodies, whether such activities are carried on by governmental agencies or by non-governmental entities, and for assuring that national activities are carried out in conformity with the provisions set forth in the present treaty. The activities of non-governmental entities in outer space, including the Moon and other celestial bodies, shall require authorization and continuing supervision by the appropriate state party to the treaty. When activities are carried on in outer space . . . by an international organiza-

tion, responsibility for compliance with this treaty shall be borne both by the international organization and by the states parties to the treaty participating in such organization.

This provision has an interesting pedigree. The treaty was the product of negotiations starting in 1962 and ending with the signing of the treaty in 1967. The negotiating parties agreed on the notion that the exploration of space as a global commons should be open to all states; however, the Soviet Union did not want to recognize the right of private parties to participate in the exploration of space, a position apparently rooted in political doctrine as much as security principle. Given the state of space exploration at the time, private activities did not seem an immediate issue, which, on the question of liability, resulted in a compromise between the negotiating parties. The text would not preclude private enterprises from participating in the exploration of space, but neither would the treaty expressly recognize them. Thus, when it came to liability, "each state party from whose territory or facility an object is launched" would be held liable for damage to another state, without specifying the source of "the object."[32] The liability provision has been generally accepted. There are 105 states parties (the term of art for treaty parties) to the treaty, including China, Russia, and the United States.

Another Space Treaty provision warrants review as well. Article IX of the treaty is addressed to "cross-contamination." This is the risk that in exploring outer space, states might return to Earth with harmful "extraterrestrial matter." The treaty does not specify how, but requires parties to "conduct exploration of the Moon and other celestial bodies . . . so as to avoid their harmful contamination and also adverse changes in the environment of the Earth resulting from the introduction of extraterrestrial matter and, where necessary, parties shall adopt appropriate measures for this purpose." According to one report, "most countries try to adhere to guidelines set forth by the Committee on Space Research (COSPAR) . . . an international organization of scientists that comes up with standards for how to clean a spacecraft" and handle space samples brought back to Earth.[33]

Finally, the treaty is instructive because it was agreed to before countries other than the United States and Soviet Union had a stake in the space race, and thus it reflects a scenario like AI, where there are principal state actors but other states hold a shared interest in the safe and secure use of AI for national security as well as other purposes.

Conclusions

Necessity to study other arms races. At the height of the Cold War, grand strategy and nuclear studies were taught at virtually every university and were a staple part of think tank programs and war college instruction. Today they are less frequently studied. Equally important, AI as technology, as a strategic instrument, and as a precursor to a new arms race is not studied with the frequency and depth as the nuclear arms race once was. It should be, if AI will play as transformative a role in national security as nuclear weapons have. An AI arms race will use some, perhaps much, of the vernacular of the nuclear arms race. That is the arms race we know best. Therefore, AI specialists should be conversant in its history, trajectory, and terms. They should also determine which of those lessons and applications from the nuclear arms race are most apt to AI by analogy. Depending on one's perspective on arms control, the following "lessons" warrant AI consideration.

Agreement is sometimes possible at moments of great, even greatest, tension. Many of the principal arms control agreements were negotiated and ratified at moments of great tension, like the Hotline Agreement in the wake of the Cuban Missile Crisis. Moreover, such agreements, whether they come in the form of CBM or limitations, may be most needed at such times. Small steps can lead to bigger steps. Bilateral efforts can become multilateral in effect.

Lasting and effective agreements need not be legally binding. Effective agreements tend to bind through mutual interest, not necessarily law. The U.S.-Soviet/Russian hotline agreements are a case in point.

States are more likely to give up numbers and set limits than they are to surrender capacities. This is reflected in the SALT, START, and SORT line of agreements. It is also reflected in the Outer Space Treaty and Test Limit Treaties. Initial efforts at AI regulation, therefore, might most fruitfully focus on limiting the risk of AI and the domains in which it is deployed and employed, rather than seeking to prohibit classes of activity or research altogether.

Perfect should not be the enemy of good enough. One of the flaws in ratification of the CTBT is its requirement that all forty-four members of the CD with nuclear energy capabilities or research centers become parties before the CTBT enters into force. That makes logical sense, if the ban is intended to be comprehensive. But it does not make political sense, in a context where known outliers will remain outliers. Moreover, a treaty in force can help to define customary international law and thus help bring pressure on outlier states by more clearly identifying such states as acting outside international law and norms as the Ottawa Treaty illustrates. (See the discussion of the Ottawa Treaty in chapter 9.)

Accountability. There is a military aphorism, "You get what you inspect, not what you expect." One lesson of the nuclear arms race is that doctrine did not always reflect the principles critical actors expected, as in 1961, when Secretary McNamara learned that SIOP-62 included China as part of any nuclear exchange with the Soviet Union. Critical actors should not assume they know how AI is being used and incorporated into the U.S. national security infrastructure and in accordance with what doctrine of use and control. Likewise, university presidents and general counsels should not assume AI research and development is safe, necessary, or protected from external threats, like theft and intelligence penetration. They should determine that it is.

Command and control. One lesson of the Cold War arms race is that it is not too early to consider the doctrine and command structure that should govern national security uses of AI. To be sure, they are being considered on an episodic basis, as in the case of AWS. But one does not yet see the depth of study of questions of pre-delegation that one saw during the development of nuclear weapons. Which AI capacities should be delegated to human decisionmakers? Which to predetermined software responses? And which to machine learning algorithms that evolve and change?[34]

A culture of security and safety. Policymakers on an agency basis and a government basis should make conscious choices about when, how, and in what form to develop a culture of security and safety around AI, as has been done with nuclear command and control, which is to say, one consciously defined by training, esprit de corps, and unit or bureaucratic cohesion across the policy, legal, and technical disciplines. With a defined culture comes a corresponding opportunity to routinize commitment to doctrine, safety, security, accountability, and responsibility. Culture need not be risk-averse. The National Clandestine Service and the Marine Corps have different and defined cultures, which presumably are not risk-averse. They also have defined professional norms and expectations. In the absence of a conscious choice to do so, the likely outcome is a stovepipe approach to AI, with each system, application, or user defining its own rules and culture across academia, industry, and within the government. The result will likely range from a series of special access programs, which will minimize oversight and appraisal, to open labs and dialogues, which will enhance creative energy but also open the door wider to security and safety risks.

Limitations and prohibitions. It seems premature to consider AI reduction as a driving imperative. However, it is not too early to consider questions like (1) what is the unit of measure—that is, what is the technology or activity being limited? (2) How might such limitations be verified? For example, there could be limits, or prohibitions, on:

- the number of human-in-the-loop, or more likely human-out-of-the-loop applications in the area of weapons;
- systems connected to kinetic weapons, cyber-weapons, or nuclear weapons;
- the deployment of AI national security systems into space;
- the deployment of AI systems onto or into designated critical infrastructures offensively or defensively;
- the use of certain data; or
- limitations on and controls for connecting AI to the internet, if any.

Of course, years-long negotiations on the meaning of "delivery system" in the SALT and SORT contexts may appear routine and easy, compared to defining concepts like "human-in-the-loop" or "AI." Indeed, an international definition of "human-in-the-loop" would serve stability by ensuring states do not inadvertently or intentionally talk past each other while agreeing to opaque commitments to keep a "human-in-the-loop."

The NPT may suggest one model for alleviating the downside risks of AI. States that are concerned with the use of AI as a weapon, weapon enabler, or national security tool may choose to express this concern in the form of a treaty forsaking their own development, deployment, and use of such capabilities. These same states, with or without LAWS programs, may also agree to forgo certain types of research or types of weapons, such as those weapons that do not require a human-in-the-loop to launch.

Likewise, states might forgo efforts to achieve certain AI capabilities. Such a treaty commitment would not prevent states from doing so. But it could raise the threshold for doing so, not only by making it clear that states that did so were running counter to international norms, but by imposing trade sanctions on states and companies that conducted research and development outside the parameters permitted by the treaty.

"Crowdsourcing" regulation and compliance. The sheer volume of data available today makes nuclear monitoring and verification challenging due to the signal-to-noise ratio. Likewise, one challenge in regulating AI is to verify compliance with any regulation in an easily hidden dual-use field. Efforts to crowdsource through NGOs and other individual non-state actors may be especially apt to AI and warrant further study. The availability of public data allows non-state actors, including NGOs, to track supply chain activities and transportation manifests. Trade-related data, for example, includes import declarations, export declarations, tenders, customs reports, and transportation manifests, most of it electronically accessible. Subscription services track this information, and algorithms can search it for indications of illicit technology or other transfers.[35] In this regard, new computational applications, including and especially AI, may help to aggregate information, identify patterns, and spot anomalies, as well as help policymakers distinguish between fact and fiction. This may be particularly apt where verification necessarily must extend to commercial and academic fora.

In short, with AI, there are new opportunities to crowdsource nonproliferation verification and do so with "public technical means" rather than national technical means. AI may further these efforts in this and other contexts with its ability to aggregate and collate information and identify anomalies. Of course, these same capabilities might also be applied to AI regulation and verification.

Verification agencies and mechanisms. Consideration of the NNSA domestically and the IAEA internationally may help test the proposition presented by MIT's Kenneth Oye and others that single-issue agencies, such as the FAA, the NTSB, and the FDA, are more effective in implementing safety and regulatory regimes than multi-mission agencies with similar tasks. It is a lot easier to build esprit de corps around a singular mission than multiple missions that compete for funding and leadership attention. This is reflected in the difference between the Department of Homeland Security and the Marine Corps, for example. At the same time, single-issue policy agencies can tend toward the myopic. It is not too early to consider what such an agency should look like and whether it should have policy as well as safety, security, and oversight responsibilities. As with the IAEA, the core logistical questions would include matters of funding and personnel. The substantive questions would abound and include matters of jurisdiction, protection of trade secrets and intellectual property, and search authority, for which the Chemical Weapons Convention (CWC) might serve as metaphor.

Loopholes. The experience of arms control generally is that if there is a textual loophole, states will find it and use it. The more black letter the line, the easier it is to verify. Of course, AI may be the perfect cheater, able to spoof verification and feed favorable data to other machines.

CBM. Policymakers should also consider what confidence-building measures might serve to avert or mitigate an AI arms race, undue escalation, or prevent miscalculations, perhaps in the event AI-enabled technology does not work as intended. There are two core AI questions: (1) what would CBM look like in AI context? (2) would states or the private and academic interests they affect be willing to accept them? The first question may be the easier of the two. To facilitate verification, and as a CBM, states or industry may want to require, in some manner, that an AI system connected to critical infrastructures or with transborder reach be declared and/or subject to public identification through coding or other known signatures.

Liability. Especially at a time when it is not clear in what direction AI is heading, states may be less likely to agree to absolute prohibitions and bans. They may be more willing to agree to delimit the boundaries of any AI race, because it is in their self-interest to do so, in a test ban manner. It may be in their self-interest, because parallel competitors are on an equal footing (now), there is risk in the unknown, or they wish to remove a domain or area from the burden of AI competition. There also may be shared interest in establishing rules of liability before individual states have a specific interest in shifting the cost and burden of liability elsewhere. International liability could vary as well by being pegged to the implementation of domestic licensing and safety inspections. It is easier to align later domestic law with an already existing international regime than it is to align international law with a myriad of different domestic regimes, which often results in the international regime adopting a lowest-common-denominator approach that is more exhortation than proscription. Additional study and consideration of the Outer Space Treaty liability regime is warranted.

BIOLOGICAL AND CHEMICAL WEAPONS AND THE CHALLENGE OF DUAL USE VERIFICATION

The Biological Weapons Convention (BWC) and the Chemical Weapons Convention (CWC) arguably represent the broadest and most successful attempts to prohibit the manufacture, stockpiling, and use of a type of weapon, and do so on a multilateral and global basis. However, where the BWC verification regime and results are generally ineffective, the CWC regime has proven more effective and therefore warrants attention. That is because the CWC includes a functional verification mechanism and oversight bureaucracy that is generally accepted by industry. Because AI is not a weapon but rather an array of technological fields and subfields, it presents distinct dilemmas involving private ownership, including those involving on-site verification and intellectual property protection. The challenge of verifying code is especially daunting. For this reason, efforts to regulate and then eliminate biological and chemical weapons might prove instructive.

Background

Nations and theologians have sought to regulate the use of specific arms in battle since the Second Lateran Council of 1139, which sought to prohibit use of the crossbow (albeit only against Christians). Although the crossbow had existed since ancient times, including in China and Greece, it was the advent of the steel bolt and its impact on humans that prompted the effort at prohibition.[36]

The Battle of Solferino in June 1859 is often cited as the beginning of the "modern effort" to regulate the means and methods of warfare for humanitarian reasons. The battle pitted French and allied Sardinian-Piedmontese forces against Austrian forces in Lombardy (northern Italy). The battle was one chapter in the Italian unification wars. The battle was the last in which the opposing forces were personally commanded by the monarchs involved—Napoleon III, Vittorio Emanuele II, and Franz Josef. Although it nominally resulted in a French victory, there were over forty thousand casualties on both sides, with most of the wounded and dead being left on the battlefield after nine to fifteen hours of fighting. A Swiss businessman named Henri Dunant visited the battlefield when the fighting was over and was so moved by the suffering of the wounded that he started a campaign to create relief societies across Europe. These societies became chapters of the Red Cross—and, in Switzerland, the International Committee of the Red Cross (ICRC). Dunant also campaigned for states to negotiate a convention for the care of the wounded and dead in warfare. This resulted in the first Geneva conference and convention in 1864.[37] Because so many of the conventions and instruments that regulate warfare were subsequently negotiated in Geneva or in The Hague, commentators tend to bifurcate international humanitarian law into a Hague and a Geneva line of law. The Hague line of law is generally addressed to the regulation of the means or methods of warfare. The Geneva line of law is generally addressed to the rights and obligations of combatants and noncombatants in armed conflict. Combined, the field is commonly known as international humanitarian law (IHL), as well as the law of armed conflict (LOAC) or the law of war (LOW).[38]

In U.S. practice, and most countries' practice, IHL/LOAC bring together three areas of law: (1) international treaty law; (2) customary international law

(CIL); and (3) domestic law. Treaty law is textual and generally only binding on the states parties to a treaty. Customary international law reflects the practice of states performed out of a sense of legal obligation. Customary international law is harder to determine, because it is based not on text but on practice. Further, CIL is created by the assertion of states that they are doing something out of a sense of legal obligation, but scholars and governments rarely agree on the point at which an assertion becomes a norm versus merely an unlawful act. But CIL is just as much law as treaties, and depending on circumstance is subject to war crime prosecution and other sanctions. The United States, for example, is not a party to Additional Protocol I to the Geneva Conventions, but recognizes many of the protocol's textual statements of law as customary principles of law binding on all states. By illustration, in the absence of treaty text, the international law of cyberspace is largely defined by customary international law norms, if it is defined at all. The *Tallinn Manuals* (I and II) are an effort by scholars to say what the law is; however, the manual is nonbinding; it does not reflect state views. International law is also dependent on domestic law, for many—if not most—treaties are not self-executing. That means they are subject to domestic state processes of ratification as well as domestic implementing legislation before they become effective for the state in question.

The interlocking nature of all three areas of law is illustrated with respect to chemical and biological weapons. The Biological Weapons Convention and the Chemical Weapons Convention prohibit the manufacture, possession, and use of such weapons. However, the conventions by their terms rely on states parties to pass implementing legislation to enforce the terms of the treaties. U.S. implementing legislation is found in Title 18, sections 175–78 (Biological Weapons and Anti-Terrorism Act of 1989, Pub. L. 101-298 (1990)) and sections 229–29F (Pub. L. 105-277, CR for 1998). It is this domestic law that binds U.S. actors and subjects them to potential criminal sanction in the event of violations. In addition, virtually all international lawyers would agree that customary international law prohibits the manufacture and use of biological or chemical weapons in armed conflict. A slightly less inclusive group would also say that the use of such weapons is *jus cogens* (compelling law), which means universally prohibited and presenting a peremptory norm. Peremptory norms are subject to universal jurisdiction to prosecute, provided a nation's domestic law permits such prosecution. Piracy and slave-trading fall into this category, which is why pirates captured off the coast of Somalia have been tried in U.S. as well as European courts, without otherwise having a geographic nexus to the location, the victim, or the perpetrator of the crime.

In U.S. practice, the modern era in the regulation of armed conflict and the rules of war dates to the Lieber Code—the Civil War Code drafted by Professor Franz Lieber and issued under Abraham Lincoln's signature as General Order 100 to Union forces. The code promulgated rules on the treatment of the wounded, prisoners of war, and saboteurs and spies. Humane treatment was prescribed in the first two instances, summary execution in the latter. The code also prohibited the use of "poison weapons." Lieber was motivated, in part, by his own experience in the Prussian Army, including being wounded at the Battle of Waterloo. His three sons also fought in the Civil War, two for the Union and one, who died at the Battle of Eltham's Landing during the Peninsular Campaign, for the Confederacy.

The 1899 "Hague Declaration on the Prohibition of the Use of Projectiles with the Sole Object of Spreading Asphyxiating Poison Gas" is arguably the first "modern" effort to outlaw a specific weapon of war: poison gas. It was signed and ratified by all the major powers later engaged in World War I, except the United States. The 1907 Hague Convention on Land Warfare reiterated the prohibition, stating in Article 23 of Declaration IV, ". . . it is especially forbidden to employ poison or poisoned weapons." Even more states joined this second Hague Conference and declaration, including the United Kingdom, France, Germany, Russia, and the United States.

The Hague Conventions of 1899 and 1907 notwithstanding, World War I demonstrated the limits of international law in the context of state and regime survival. The Germans first introduced the use of chlorine gas during the Second Battle of Ypres, Belgium, in April 1915. In contrast to the machine gun or tank, gas was not an effective weapon. There were countermeasures to the use of gas, such as gas masks. Gas is also difficult to use because it is subject to the elements, especially wind, and is indiscriminate in its effect, targeting civilians and advancing troops as well as the enemy. Nonetheless, it was widely and continuously used. By war's end, an estimated 1.3 million soldiers from the allied and central powers had been killed or wounded by gas.

World War I spurred new efforts to regulate the means and methods of warfare. This started with the Versailles Treaty, which prohibited the defeated central powers from manufacturing or importing poison gas. The Geneva Protocol of 1925 affirmed the treaty prohibition on using poison gas. It also affirmed that the prohibition was customary in nature, and thus binding on non-signatory states. In addition, it extended the prohibition to include the use of bacteriological weapons. Germany, Britain, and France became parties to the protocol, but each also reserved by declaration the right to use such weapons in the event an opponent used such weapons first—a concept known as belligerent reprisal. Japan and the United States did not become parties before World War II. In the case of the United States, which supported negotiation of the protocol, the instrument fell victim to the same isolationism that earlier doomed the League of Nations. The protocol was submitted to the Senate in 1926, but not ratified. It was submitted again in 1970 and ratified in 1975. The Kellogg-Briand Pact of 1928 went even further, not just seeking to delimit the use of weapons, but to prohibit war itself.

Thus, at the outbreak of World War II, there was both a prohibition on the use of chemical and biological warfare and, in theory, a prohibition on war itself. Germany, of course, used poison gas during the Holocaust, and Japan used gas and biological agents against detainees in China. Germany also developed three nerve agents, which were produced and loaded in artillery shells and aircraft bombs.[39] However, with the notable exception of the Japanese, who used gas in China, chemical and biological agents were not used on World War II battlefields, in a war during which, to state the obvious, the combatants did not recognize many limits—if any—on the use of weaponry or violence. No doubt this reflected, in part, a sense of legal obligation or prohibition. However, it is as likely that the stronger influence was the fear of reprisal. Reprisals are generally unlawful in warfare and are considered war crimes, such as the killing of civilians in response to acts of sabotage. However, belligerent reprisal recognizes the right of a state to engage in what would otherwise be an unlawful act to address and stop an offending state's precipitate unlawful act, provided the reprisal is otherwise necessary and proportional—that is, necessary to stop the offending act and does not cause undue harm beyond that necessary to stop the offending act. Belligerent reprisal is thus the wartime equivalent of peacetime countermeasures.

Like World War I before it, World War II spurred new efforts to regulate warfare and hold those responsible for violations of the law accountable. This was most notably done in the context of the Nuremberg Trials and Tokyo War Crimes Trials. New impetus was also given to an absolute prohibition on the manufacture and use of biological and chemical weapons.

The BWC

The BWC represents the first instance in which the global community agreed to give up a weapons capability, which is to say the possession of the weapon and not just its use. However, before the BWC, the United States first unilaterally renounced biological weapons in 1969 as a matter of policy.[40] Specifically,

President Nixon announced and directed that the United States renounce the use of lethal biological agents and weapons and all other methods of biological warfare. He also directed that U.S. research be limited to defensive measures and that the United States dispose of its existing weapons. The decision was preceded by extensive internal debate, resolved only by the president's personal involvement and commitment. As recounted by Jonathan Tucker, the U.S. decision was not motivated by altruistic or moral self-interest, but by pragmatic national security interests as well as the personal reasons of the president. In the context of the Vietnam War and protests at home, President Nixon wanted to be seen as a man of peace aware of the public's general repugnance toward biological weapons. He was also satisfied that the U.S. nuclear capacity would serve as a deterrent to any use of biological warfare.

After President Nixon's decision, the United States and Russia, along with the then-16 other members of the Conference on Disarmament, concluded negotiation of the 1972 BWC Convention, which entered into force in 1975. As of May 2020, the BWC has 182 states parties. However, 17 states have either not signed and/or ratified the BWC, including Syria, Egypt, Israel, and South Sudan. The United States ratified the BWC in 1974 and became a party in 1975.

The core undertaking is found in Article I, which states:

Each state party to this convention undertakes never in any circumstances to develop, produce, stockpile, or otherwise acquire or retain:

1. Microbial or other biological agents, or toxins whatever their origin or method of production, of types and in quantities that have no justification for prophylactic, protective, or other peaceful purposes;

2. Weapons, equipment, or means of delivery designed to use such agents or toxins for hostile purposes or in armed conflict.

The convention further required parties to destroy existing stocks of weapons or divert them to peaceful purposes. In addition, parties may not transfer "or in any way assist, encourage, or induce anyone else to acquire or retain biological weapons." Parties are required to take the national measures necessary to implement the convention, to consult "to solve problems with the implementation of the BWC," to request the security council investigate alleged breaches of the BWC, and assist states that have been exposed to the dangers of biological weapons.

It is interesting and odd that Article I does not expressly prohibit the use of biological agents or toxins as weapons. Such a prohibition is implicit, for surely one cannot use something they do not produce or retain. In any event, this textual loophole was sealed in 1996, when the parties confirmed at the 4th Review Conference that Article I prohibited the use of biological agents as weapons, which conclusion is now part of the treaty's negotiating and review history.

As outlined by the Nuclear Threat Initiative (NTI), there are several challenges with implementation of the BWC, which parallel challenges with AI.[41]

First, the convention presents many dual-use verification and breakout issues. Because some agents and toxins have legitimate peaceful purposes, such as the development of vaccines, they are not banned or prohibited outright. Thus, "compliance is measured in terms of intent" rather than possession, which is often difficult to determine and verify. Further, advances in bioscience and biotechnology have introduced new agents to a wider, more diverse group of state and non-state actors.

Second, "in contrast to chemical and nuclear weapons, only small quantities of biological agents are initially needed to produce amounts that have great military significance."

Third, "biological agents can be produced rapidly and eliminated rapidly (sometimes in a matter of hours)."

Fourth, and most important, for all these reasons the BWC does not have a verification regime. The parties sought to address this omission through adoption of Confidence Building Measures at subsequent review conferences. These include the exchange of information on research centers and laboratories working with high-risk biological materials; the promotion of scientific contacts and exchanges; the declaration of legislation, regulations, and other measures; the declaration of past activities related to offensive and defensive programs; and the declaration of vaccine production facilities.[42]

These verification challenges were highlighted in 1992, when a Russian defector revealed that the Soviet Union/Russia had continued a clandestine and large-scale biological weapons program after joining the BWC. Russian President Boris Yeltsin confirmed this fact the same year. Challenges in verification returned in the context of Iraq, where critical actors, including the United States, believed Iraq had resumed a clandestine BW program. Lack of BWC verification confidence is also reflected in ongoing issues surrounding retention of multiple strains of the smallpox virus.

Smallpox was declared eradicated by the World Health Organization in 1980, the year of the last known case of naturally occurring smallpox in

Somalia. In the United States, routine smallpox vaccination ceased in 1972. Nonetheless, the United States, Russia, and the World Health Organization (WHO) decided in the 1990s to retain stockpiles of multiple strains of the smallpox. The strains are held at singular sites monitored by the WHO, one at the CDC in Atlanta, the other at the Vector Institute in Novosibirsk, Russia. Such retention would clearly be prohibited by the BWC if the samples were used as a weapon or retained for offensive weapons research. However, both states have argued, in the face of international pressure from "destructionists," that the samples should be retained for two reasons. First, they may be needed for public health purposes as a potential source of vaccine from natural or synthetic smallpox. Second, they serve as a hedge against states or non-state actors "breaking out" a real or synthetic strain of smallpox as a weapon. The arguments for and against these decisions, as well as the bureaucratic nature of internal U.S. government disagreements, may be instructive in the AI context.

CONCLUSIONS

The BWC illustrates five points.

1. Prohibitions alone may be ineffective, or at best uncertain, without an effective verification mechanism.

2. If there is a textual loophole, lawyers will find it and states will exploit it. Where terms are hard to define or capture, as in the case of emerging technologies, states will want to incorporate binding mechanisms to clarify and amend agreement gaps, as in the case of the BWC conference of the parties.

3. States will hedge their bets if they lack confidence in the underlying regime and prohibition. This is illustrated with respect to the Soviet/Russian non-compliance with the BWC, but also with the continuing controversy over the retention of the smallpox virus.

4. In the absence of an effective verification regime, the parties turned to a series of CBM, including lab visits and declarations. A nascent AI regime might incorporate similar measures.

5. Even where a verification regime is inchoate or ineffective, it can drive up the risk of discovery and the cost of violation; in such cases, absolute and black letter prohibitions are easier to verify than intent-based prohibitions.

The CWC

In contrast to the BWC, the CWC arguably offers an effective verification regime. Indeed, the BWC and CWC in some regards represent bookends on the continuum of verification possibilities and challenges. That is not to say the CWC is without challenges. These challenges are instructive, because the verification issues associated with biological agents and chemicals are arguably more akin to AI than those presented by nuclear weapons. Where states have a monopoly on nuclear weapons, biologics and chemicals have many legitimate uses and their manufacture, use, and study are widely dispersed across industry and academia. Moreover, nuclear energy is a dual-use capacity that is heavily regulated and harder to conceal.

The CWC prohibits the possession, use, transfer, or stockpiling of chemical weapons. It also requires parties to declare and destroy any chemical weapons within their possession or on their territory. And it prohibits parties from engaging in preparations to use chemical weapons. The treaty addresses the dual-use nature of chemicals by dividing chemicals into three categories and imposing different rules and thresholds for each.

Schedule 1 includes toxic chemicals or precursors that generally have limited or no purposes not prohibited by the CWC. Only a hundred grams of this material may be produced per year for medical, pharmaceutical, or defensive testing purposes, provided it is declared and subject to verification.

Schedule 2 includes chemicals that pose significant risk because they could be used for chemical weapons, but also have legitimate uses and are not produced in large enough quantities to undermine the CWC. Schedule 2 chemicals must be declared, are subject to verification, and may not be exported.

Schedule 3 covers chemicals that have been used as chemical weapons but also have large-scale uses not prohibited by CWC. These chemicals are subject to declaration and inspection if produced in quantities of more than thirty tons per year per plant, site, or facility.

In addition to the listed chemical schedules, the CWC applies to any toxic chemical, regardless of how it is made, that has a purpose prohibited by the treaty. This is known as the "general purpose criterion," and, in theory, allows amendment and adaption of the lists of scheduled chemicals as needed. There are 193 states parties to the convention, including Russia and Syria. Egypt, Israel, North Korea, and South Sudan are not states parties (as of May 2020).

The UN Conference on Disarmament began negotiation of a chemical weapons treaty in 1980. The effort was spurred by the Iran-Iraq War, 1980–88, which saw the widest use of chemical weapons in warfare since World War

I. The CWC was concluded in September 1992 and opened for signature in January 1993. The negotiations were supported by the Ronald Reagan and George H. W. Bush administrations, which authorized United States signature of the treaty in January 1993, making the United States an original party to the CWC. President Bill Clinton subsequently submitted the CWC to the Senate for advice and consent to ratification in November 1993, which consent was received in April 1997.

The core general obligations of the CWC are found in Article I:

1. Each state party to this convention undertakes never under any circumstances:

   a. To develop, produce, otherwise acquire, stockpile, or retain chemical weapons, or transfer, directly or indirectly, chemical weapons to anyone;

   b. To use chemical weapons;

   c. To engage in any military preparations to use chemical weapons;

   d. To assist, encourage, or induce, in any way, anyone to engage in any activity prohibited to a state party under this convention.

2. Each state party undertakes to destroy chemical weapons it owns or possesses, or that are located in any place under its jurisdiction or control, in accordance with the provisions of this convention.

3. Each state party undertakes to destroy all chemical weapons it abandoned on the territory of another state party, in accordance with the provisions of this convention.

4. Each state party undertakes to destroy any chemical weapons production facilities it owns or possesses, or that are located in any place under its jurisdiction or control, in accordance with the provisions of this convention.

5. Each state party undertakes not to use riot control agents as a method of warfare.

The obligations are much like those found in the BWC. However, in contrast to the BWC, the CWC includes a verification regime and enforcement mechanism. States parties are required to declare the possession of chemical weapons (Article IV) as well as chemical weapons production facilities. Pursuant to the verification annex, an international organization—the Organization for the Prohibition of Chemical Weapons (OPCW)—is charged with overseeing and verifying the destruction of chemical weapons and the destruction or conversion of chemical weapons production facilities.

The treaty includes five verification mechanisms, each of which might inform an AI regime.

First, as already reviewed, the CWC provides an annex, dividing named chemicals into schedules, each with its own rules and limitations. The parties therefore know what is and is not covered and prohibited.

Second, the CWC provides for ongoing routine inspections by the OPCW of declared facilities in the private and public sectors of states parties. Based on the treaty as well as OPCW guidelines, there are detailed rules involving the conduct of inspections, including inspection rate, notification, duration, and access. "From April 1997 to October 2017, the OPCW conducted over 6,600 inspections on the territory of over eighty-six states parties."[43]

Third, the CWC provides for challenge inspections of facilities suspected of violating the treaty, perhaps because they are not declared, or they are suspected of producing prohibited substances or amounts.

Fourth, Article X authorizes the OPCW to investigate the alleged use of chemical weapons pursuant to a challenge inspection or at the request of a state party against whom chemical weapons are alleged to have been used.

Fifth, the CWC includes a confidentiality annex, which, as the title implies, is intended to safeguard trade secrets disclosed pursuant to the OPCW verification regime and more generally the intellectual property of companies exposed to CWC inspection.

The confidentiality annex assigns "primary responsibility" for the protection of confidential information to the director-general of the OPCW. It creates a presumption against the public disclosure of information obtained during inspection, which information can, with limited exception, only be released with the consent of the party "to which the information refers." The annex further provides procedures governing the employment of OPCW staff to protect confidentiality, measures to protect information during inspections and in OPCW control, and procedures in the case of a breach of confidentiality.[44]

For a treaty with the support of three administrations across parties, the ratification process was contentious. It was not until April 1997 that the Senate voted to consent to ratification 74-26, with twenty-eight conditions to ratification. (The Constitution requires a two-thirds super majority vote of 67 to pass a resolution of ratification to a treaty.) Opposition to the treaty was led by Senator Jesse Helms and the wing of the Republican Party generally opposed to arms control treaties. Opposition centered on: (1) the treaty's prohibition on the use of riot control agents (RCA) as a weapon of warfare; (2) concerns over the efficacy of the verification regime with respect to hostile states; (3) the sharing of intelligence with the OPCW; and (4) Fourth Amendment and trade secret concerns regarding inspections of U.S. industry. The latter three of these issues are, of course, directly relevant to AI. The Senate's concerns were addressed in multiple ways.

First, the U.S. Intelligence Community indicated that it "believed that the CWC verification regime would detect militarily significant cheating and deter states from acquiring chemical weapons."[45] In addition, the Senate conditions included a number addressed to the safeguarding of U.S. intelligence information shared with the OPCW.

Second, the U.S. chemical industry participated in the negotiation of the CWC as observers, through trade associations and other affinity groups. Thus, "industry" was aware of and generally comfortable with the CWC before it was presented as a fait accompli to the Senate. The chemical industry was also aware that the CWC required parties to phase in restrictions on trade with the chemical companies of non-party states. To address industry concerns, the Senate included a condition that in the event a U.S. company withheld consent to a challenge inspection, the United States government would obtain a criminal search warrant before allowing the inspection. A condition was also included stating that in the event confidential business information was disclosed as part of the inspection process, U.S. financial contributions to the OPCW would be withheld as punishment.[46]

With respect to RCAs, the administration agreed to keep in force President Ford's 1975 executive order permitting the use of RCAs with presidential authorization in "'defensive military modes to save lives,' including rescuing air crews downed behind enemy lines and reducing the need to use lethal force when civilians were used to screen attacks."[47] Later, in 1999, in the context of passing domestic legislation to implement the CWC, the administration also agreed to Senator Helms's legislation dissolving the Arms Control and Disarmament Agency (ACDA) as an independent agency and moving its functions to the Department of State.

In addition, to address both trade and verification concerns, the Senate included a condition hinging U.S. ratification to the continued vitality of the Australia Group, a group of like-minded states working together to regulate trade related to chemical and biological weapons.[48] First, the Senate attached a declaration stating that the collapse of the Australia Group would constitute a fundamental change in circumstances affecting the object and purpose of the convention. Second, the president is required to certify to Congress on an annual basis that the Australia Group "remains a viable mechanism for limiting the spread of chemical and biological weapons–related material and technology," and that group members "continue to maintain an equally effective or more comprehensive control over the export of toxic chemicals and their precursors [and other materials and agents covered by the convention] . . . as that afforded by the Australia Group as of the date of ratification. . . ."

The Australia Group emerged in 1985 in response to a UN investigation determining that Iraq used chemical weapons during the Iran-Iraq War and that "materials for its CW program had been sourced through legitimate trade channels."[49] In addition to seeking to uphold international prohibitions on such weapons, the group helps align each state's domestic regulations through parallel control lists, to close CW and BW loopholes. It also removes incentives to favor one's domestic industry over others with more permissive rules and interpretations. The group consists of forty-three members, including the EU (as of May 2020).

The United Nations 1540 Committee seeks to accomplish on a global scale the same objectives as the Australia Group. The 1540 Committee is an ad hoc UN Security Council Resolution (UNSCR) committee established pursuant to paragraph d.(4) of UNSCR 1540 (2004). Resolution 1540 addresses the proliferation of nuclear, biological, and chemical weapons. Acting under chapter VII of the charter—that is, with the full authority of the security council—the committee is charged with overseeing implementation of UNSCR 1540. The committee is relevant to the nuclear, biological, and chemical regimes because UNSCR 1540 is legally binding and provides an additional level of sanctions support to the CWC, BWC, and NPT frameworks. It is also relevant because it is specifically addressed to non-state actors as well as state actors. It seeks to align export controls on a global basis in the same manner that the Australia Group does on a like-minded basis. The 1540 Committee is also supposed to review the domestic implementation of UNSCR 1540 sanctions and serve as a forum in which to publicize issues; but the committee does not have the authority to promulgate control lists and suffers from the same dynamics that affect the UN and security council generally.

Beyond the CWC, BWC, and NPT context, the 1540 and Australia frameworks illustrate some of the strengths and weaknesses of a tiered system of technology export controls that is dependent on the interface and implementation of domestic, regional, and global export controls. The result is an imperfect Venn diagram, with each higher level becoming more porous and subject to national interests overriding collective global interests, but without it, domestic controls would simply serve to limit or affect domestic industries.

United States implementing legislation for the CWC was enacted in October 1998 (Pub. L. 105-277, October 21, 1998). The law provides criminal and civil penalties for, and federal jurisdiction over, any person violating the law's prohibition on developing, producing, acquiring, using, or transferring chemical weapons. Attempting or conspiring to do so violates the law as well. In addition, the law provides a detailed framework implementing the CWC's inspection regime. Among other things, this regime provides for facility agreements between the OPCW and U.S. plants and facilities, which

Shall—
(1) Identify the areas, equipment, computers, records, data, and samples subject to inspection;
(2) Describe the procedures for providing notice of an inspection to the owner, occupant, operator, or agent in charge of a facility;
(3) Describe the timeframes for inspections; and
(4) Detail the areas, equipment, computers, records, data, and samples that are not subject to inspection.

The law also requires advance notice of inspections as well as limits on the number of and agency representation of U.S. government employees accompanying OPCW inspections. For example, no EPA or OSHA employees may accompany a technical inspection team. In other words, the CWC inspection regime cannot be used to enforce other legal requirements. Moreover, "The owner or the operator, occupant, or agent in charge of the premises to be inspected may withhold consent for any reason or no reason" (sec. 305, Pub. L. 105-277). In such cases, the U.S. government may obtain an administrative search warrant from the relevant U.S. district court where the government satisfies the court that the inspection request meets the requirements of the CWC. A warrant is not required with consent. In the case of challenge inspections, a criminal warrant establishing probable cause is required, as a challenge inspection is necessarily predicated on a suspicion that the CWC has been violated, which violation would also likely be criminal under U.S. law.

To protect trade secrets, the law specifies that unless required by the CWC, no inspection

Shall extend to

- Financial data;
- Sales and marketing data (other than shipment data);
- Pricing data;
- Personnel data;
- Research data;
- Patent data;
- Data maintained in compliance with environmental or occupational health and safety regulations; or
- Personnel and vehicles entering and personnel and personal passenger vehicles exiting the facility.

The law also provides a FOIA exemption over any confidential business information reported to or acquired by the U.S. government under the convention. The president is required to submit an annual report to Congress on inspections, to include, among other things, the number and costs of inspections, a description of any industrial espionage or misconduct by inspectors, and "the identity of parties claiming loss of trade secrets, the circumstances surrounding those losses, and the efforts taken by the U.S. government to redress those losses" (sec. 309). Finally, the law provides the president with authority to "deny a request to inspect any facility in the United States in cases where the president determines that the inspection may pose a threat to the national security interests of the United States" (sec. 307).

As Syria demonstrates, the CWC verification regime is imperfect. Syria has been a member of the CWC since 2013; however, its regime has repeatedly used chemical weapons against its own citizens and regime opponents during the Syrian Civil War, both before and after it joined the CWC. The CWC did not prevent the Assad regime in Syria from acquiring or using chemical weapons. Neither did it constrain Russia's toleration, and perhaps support, of such use of chemical weapons.

Russia, a party to the CWC since 1997, has on at least two occasions used chemical agents to attack—and in one case, murder—former intelligence officers residing in the United Kingdom. The first incident, in 2006 in London, involved the use of the isotope polonium-210, which, as trace analysis revealed, could have affected thousands of bystanders and air travelers. The second incident occurred in 2018, in Salisbury, and involved an attempt to kill former FSB officer Sergei Skripal with the military grade nerve agent BZ through surface contact on the ex-agent's front door. The CWC mechanisms allowed the government of the United Kingdom to quickly and persuasively determine the source of the chemical agent. The CWC also served as a basis for a consistent international response to the Russian delict, in the form of sanctions and expulsions.

Further, the OPCW does not have the resources or authority to conduct the full range of inspections contemplated by the verification annex. Many of the verification provisions are predicated on state party self-inspection. In addition, while the CWC provides for challenge inspections undertaken by the OPCW, no state has requested a challenge inspection, including in Syria.[50] This may reflect a silent agreement among the parties not to use the mechanism, rather than use it and risk a tit-for-tat escalation of challenge inspections. Whatever the motivation, the challenge mechanism has not been used and thus tested as a mechanism that might warrant emulation in an AI context.

New compounds, including synthetic compounds, also present challenges. A strength of the compliance regime is its reliance on agreed lists of precluded or restricted chemicals, reinforced by UN sanctions and the Australia Group. There is clarity and breadth in such a process. However, the CWC prohibitions are not limited to listed compounds, and the treaty mechanism for adding compounds to the lists through the general-purpose criterion in article II is underused out of concern that the listing of new compounds will alert state and non-state actors to new and dangerous compounds and formulas. In addition, it is possible to avoid some of the limitations in the CWC regime through the manufacture of chemicals that only become restricted when blended, as is the case with binary chemical weapons.

At the same time, the CWC has had success. Under the auspices of the CWC/OPCW, eight parties have declared possession of chemical weapons and destroyed those weapons with OPCW verification. Fourteen parties have declared former chemical weapons production facilities and have had those facilities destroyed or converted with OPCW verification. Moreover, the 193 states parties to the treaty cover 98 percent of the chemical industry. In addition, the OPCW conducts approximately 240 voluntary inspections per year. The fact that the OPCW also identifies ten to twenty "issues requiring further assessment" per year and has an acronym to define the concept—IRFA[51]—can be interpreted as either a positive sign of a functioning verification regime or indication of continuing loopholes and risk. All of this makes it harder, but not impossible, for parties to hide or break out a chemical weapons capability. It also makes it harder for other states to do so, because the OPCW regime is supplemented by the 1540 Committee process and the Australia Group.

In addition, the CCW/OPCW provides a functional "off-the-shelf" mechanism to respond to situations like Syria. If not the OPCW, what other entity could immediately and credibly conduct over ten assessments and five major missions to Syria during 2013–15 to remove and destroy declared chemicals and twenty-seven declared chemical weapons production facilities? Of course, therein is the verification problem. Absent intelligence regarding the undeclared production or use of chemical weapons, a challenge inspection, and access by the OPCW, it is difficult to know what is occurring.

TAKEAWAYS

Further, and detailed, study of the CWC is warranted. The CWC merits further study as a potential analogy for the regulation of AI. Among other things, the treaty includes a functional verification regime for a dual-use industrial capacity. In addition, the regime received industry acceptance for on-site inspections, including of computers and data. AI specialists should consider the following:

- Which, if any, parts of the CWC model might work with AI?

- What has worked well with on-site verification? What has not worked well? Would CWC-style verification work with AI algorithms and code?

- Have any genuine Fourth Amendment or Fifth Amendment concerns arisen in U.S. verification practice? How were they resolved and what are the lessons learned?

- Has the confidentiality annex worked? Have trade secrets been lost or exposed, and if so, have there been effective remedies and adjustments made to the regime?

- Why hasn't the challenge regime been used? Is the problem with the CWC challenge regime or challenge regimes in general?

- Most important, is it possible to conduct an on-site (or remote) inspection in a field defined by cyberspace, algorithms, and code?

Is it time to consider an Australia Group for AI? Effective arms regulation does not require a treaty. It requires like-minded states. Is it time to start considering an Australia Group for AI disciplines and applications? If so, which countries or entities should be in the group and what role should it play? And what would these like-minded countries seek to regulate and control?

In U.S. practice, successful arms control efforts require presidential leadership. This is almost always the case regarding Senate ratification of major treaties; however, it is also true within the U.S. government, where the president's direct involvement proved critical to overcoming bureaucratic, especially military, opposition and in changing long-standing doctrinal understandings about the biological and chemical weapons involved. In the case of the CWC, three U.S. presidents were directly and personally involved.

Public relations are also critical to any arms control effort. That is the case both internally, with respect to negotiating constituencies, including industry, and externally with the public at large.

Winning industry support for regulatory efforts. Although the data set is small, private industry is more likely to support efforts to regulate and inspect industry applications where industry is represented at the treaty negotiating table. This is normative in many negotiating settings. Industry is even more likely to support such efforts where the instruments in question privilege the commercial interests of states parties over those of non-states parties. Proponents of AI regulation should consider what mechanisms can be used to influence industry support for international regulation, as trade sanctions against non-states parties were used in the CWC context.

Distinctions between the CWC and BWC. The CWC is a more viable regime than the BWC, in part, because

- Ongoing review conferences adjust and update the chemical schedules. Thus the text is not locked in a moment in technological time.
- The treaty is backed up by a robust verification regime and bureaucracy, which is perceived by objective parties as neutral.
- The verification regime works, in part, because it is underpinned by a functional intellectual property annex. Trade secrets are protected on paper *and* in practice.

Of course, there are also other reasons for the different level of success with each treaty. One reason the CWC is easier to verify is that chemical weapons generally require larger amounts of precursor elements than do biological weapons, and thus it is easier to detect illicit supplies of chemicals than biological agents. It is easier to conceal a strain of synthetic smallpox than thirty tons of chlorine. Thus the core technological question for AI arms control, by analogy, is what if anything can be verified that is embedded in code and how would such a regime work.

Verification and AI. There is surprisingly little literature in the AI field on verification mechanisms. However, before decisionmakers can decide on a policy of control, if any, they need to know what can be verified and what cannot, in both a context of transparent and willing access or one of compelled, restricted, or denied access. How, for example, can states and regulatory bodies verify the function and use of code? How can they do so when code is evolving or can be designed to mask its true function? If not with code, are there other mechanisms that could be used to verify AI use or function?

Matthew Mittelsteadt, a scholar at Syracuse University, suggests a number of possibilities, including:

- Behavioral pattern analysis, to determine if a human or a machine has made a decision.
- Traffic analysis, to determine if an AI system is linked to a support system, like GPS.
- The use of coding signatures and cultural watermarks.
- The designation of verification zones and dark zones within AI systems, permitting secure code beyond the reach of external observation and transparent code open to external inspection.
- The use of instructional checkpoints, which interface between AI applications and subsystems to verify use or delimit use through software application.
- Confidence building measures, like the sharing of software, software signatures, or the downloading of use data on a real-time or retrospective basis.
- Tamper-proof and tamper-evident software using algorithm hashing and obfuscation.
- The measurement of electrical loads and signatures, including baselines.
- The measurement of Van Eck Radiation, to detect use, or perhaps the scale of use, at a declared or undeclared location.

These ideas may or may not be viable in a given context. However, if arms control and CBM mechanisms are to offer effective metaphor for AI, further technical development in the verification area is essential.

NINE

The Means and Methods of War

ADDITIONAL ANALOGIES AND
POTENTIAL APPLICATIONS

This chapter considers six international humanitarian law subjects from which one might extract potential lessons to apply to AI by analogy. The Ottawa Treaty is a successful example of a grassroots effort in the face of great power reluctance to regulate a weapon: antipersonnel land mines. The law of armed conflict (LOAC) distinction between lawful ruse and unlawful perfidy may offer apt metaphor given the ease and risk with which AI can be used to mask attribution and engage in voice and image mimicry. A different set of LOAC principles addresses efforts to uphold and comply with the law in armed conflict, a context (combat) where counterpressures, fatigue, and fear make it harder to embed and enforce principles in practice. Three principles are addressed: (1) the duty to test weapons for compliance with the law; (2) the duty to instruct personnel on the law; and (3) command responsibility for the actions of one's subordinates, including with respect to (1) and (2). The doctrine of command responsibility may have specific resonance with some of the challenges presented by the human-in-the-loop challenges of certain AI applications, suggesting at least one model for establishing responsibility and accountability in peacetime, as well as war and everything in between. Finally, the chapter considers the rules applicable to LOAC targeting, asking two questions. First, should AI change the way lawyers interpret the principles of proportionality and military objective? Second, in addition to the existing LOAC target prohibitions, should AI prompt the inclusion of additional prohibitions on the use of some or all lethal autonomous weapons systems?

THE OTTAWA TREATY AND THE POWER
OF PUBLIC PERSUASION

The 1997 Convention on the Prohibition on the Use, Stockpiling, Production and Transfer of Antipersonnel Mines and Their Destruction—more widely known by its popular name, the Ottawa Treaty—as its title suggests, prohibits states parties from "using, developing, producing, otherwise acquiring, stockpiling, retaining, or transferring to anyone, directly or indirectly, antipersonnel land mines, or to assist, encourage, or induce, in any way, anyone to engage in any activity prohibited to a state party under the convention" (article 1).

In addition, the treaty requires states to identify, remove, and dispose of land mines on their territory within ten years of becoming parties—with the assistance of other parties, if requested. An antipersonnel land mine (APL) under the convention is defined as

> a mine designed to be exploded by the presence, proximity or contact of a person. . . . Mines designed to be detonated by the presence, proximity, or contact of a vehicle as opposed to a person, that are equipped with anti-handling devices are not considered antipersonnel mines . . ." (article 2.1).

As of May 2020, there were 164 parties to the convention, including Australia, the United Kingdom, and Canada. Thirty-six UN members are not parties to the treaty, including the United States, Russia, China, Iran, Israel, and India.

The treaty is credited with helping to reduce the number of APLs that maim or kill civilians each year in conflict zones and former conflict zones. It has spurred twenty-nine states to eliminate APLs from their weapons inventory and dispose of all APLs on their territory. The treaty has also established a norm against the use of APLs, whether that norm is accepted as customary international law or not. However, the treaty has shortcomings.

First, critical actors are not parties. For the United States, this reflects a national security determination that it could not meet its defense commitments on the Korean Peninsula, and potentially elsewhere, without the presence of

APLs in the DMZ and in contingency reserve. In the DMZ, for example, it is estimated that the two Koreas have deployed over a million land mines, which is one estimate of North Korean land mines alone. Thus, even if the United States were a party to the treaty, it could not meet its obligations in the context of its alliance with South Korea and corresponding joint command structure. Because of this U.S. practice and that of other states, the United States takes the view that the Ottawa Treaty does not reflect customary international law binding on non-states parties.

Second, the treaty is limited by its terms to APLs and does not cover mixed munitions, which are munitions designed for use against both vehicles and personnel, like cluster munitions, or anti-vehicle mines. These munitions kill or maim thousands of civilians notwithstanding their designation as mixed or anti-tank/vehicle.

Third, the treaty lacks a compliance mechanism. There is no Ottawa OPCW. This means that where parties have fallen behind on their ability to identify, collect, and destroy APLs on their territory, there is no central authority or mechanism to obtain technical or financial assistance.[1]

Fourth, this also means there is no standing enforcement and verification mechanism. Some states parties continue to use APLs, while others stockpile APLs or discuss doing so in the event of a security need. Turkey, for example, continues to maintain hundreds of thousands of APLs along its border with Syria, a border over which thousands of refugees, as well as combatants in Syria, regularly cross or attempt to cross. Parties to Libya's conflict have also deployed APLs. And it is likely that other states may do the same where there is a real or perceived threat of invasion. Russian aggression in Crimea and Eastern Ukraine, as well as against Georgia and the Baltic states, may yet place additional pressures on the Baltic states parties to reconsider their commitment to the treaty, or at least the prospect of reserving a right to deviate in the case of security exigency. Indeed, Russian aggression may affect the degree to which the Baltic states are willing to sign on to absolute prohibitions in other contexts as well.

Finally, the Ottawa Treaty applies to states parties and not to non-state actors. Thus, it has had no bearing on the widespread use of IEDs, a form of APL, by non-state actors in Syria, Iraq, Afghanistan, and Yemen, among other places. It would be naïve to think that many, if any, of these non-state actors would follow treaty or customary international law if it applied. The point is, one significant limitation of some treaty-based mechanisms is their inapplicability to private actors. Of course, the use of IEDs by non-state actors might violate other law of armed conflict norms, like distinction, murder, and indiscriminate killing, which are subject to criminal enforcement.

What makes the Ottawa Treaty potentially of interest in AI context, beyond the general lessons about arms control it offers, are its origins and its effect on U.S. practice. The original efforts to negotiate a land mine treaty occurred within the structure of the UN Conference on Disarmament (CD) in Geneva. Thus, the negotiations consisted of the usual UN parties as well as the accompanying dynamics of UN structure. The CD, one might say, was not a coalition of the willing or like-minded states, but rather a UN conference with all the disincentives that break consensus and drive UN efforts to lowest common denominators and division.

Certain states sought to avoid this dynamic by taking the negotiations outside the UN to what was essentially a conference of the willing. Canada agreed to host the process, which was spurred by the personal interest and commitment of Canadian foreign secretary Lloyd Axworthy.[2] This process coincided with—and was, in part, a product of—two parallel events. The first, and most important, was a grassroots effort starting in 1991 by individuals and NGOs to pressure states and the international community to ban land mines. The most visible, but not only, NGO in this effort was the International Committee to Ban Land Mines (ICBL), led by Jody Williams, which would receive the Nobel Peace Prize in 1997 for its efforts. The campaign was supported by a letter-writing campaign and popular figures such as Diana, Princess of Wales.

At the same time, and in parallel, several states were on their own banning APLs under domestic law. This started with Belgium in 1995, which banned the use of APLs but not their stockpiling. Austria was the first state in 1996 to prohibit APLs outright, including their possession. It was also an Austrian diplomat, Dr. Werner Ehrlich, who proved instrumental in drafting and providing treaty text at decisive diplomatic moments, when ideas needed to move from concept to text to move forward.

Ottawa is also noteworthy because while the United States did not join the treaty for its own (and South Korea's) security reasons, Ottawa nonetheless influenced U.S. practice. Among other things, in 1997 the United States adopted a policy of only using APLs that automatically self-destruct and to limit APL use to Korea.[3] Indeed, most APLs in U.S. inventory disarm or self-destruct within four hours, and thus do not remain a persistent threat to either civilians or combatants. The exception to U.S. policy is on the Korean Peninsula, where South Korea uses extensive persistent minefields to deter invasion from North Korea—and, if need be, channel attacking forces.

As noted, one critique of the Ottawa Treaty is that it did not reach mixed munitions like cluster munitions. As a result, a similar grassroots effort was undertaken in 2006 with respect to cluster munitions. Like Ottawa, the process started within the UN Conference on Disarmament but moved outside the process under the auspices of the government of Norway when UN roadblocks impeded progress. A Convention on Cluster Munitions was concluded in 2008 and entered into force in 2010. As of May 2020, there were 108 parties, including Australia, Canada, the United Kingdom, as well as Afghanistan and Iraq. However, this effort is arguably less successful than Ottawa. In contrast to Ottawa, there was a less effective grassroots campaign in terms of size, impact, and visibility. Equally as important, many state actors are not prepared to forgo the stockpiling and potential use of cluster munitions, which are used to protect downed pilots, to protect a fixed location from being overrun, and to stop or channel armored vehicles, as might be necessary to stop a Russian invasion into the Baltic states, the Caucasus states, Ukraine, or even Scandinavia. Thus, certain states are not parties to the convention, including China, Latvia, Estonia, Finland, Georgia, and the United States, which was able to forgo APLs as a policy commitment in part because of its capacity to use mixed cluster munitions. Moreover, the prohibition on cluster munitions is defined to permit the use of munitions that meet size and submunition limitations so long as each submunition has a self-destruct or self-deactivation capacity.

Conclusions

- Four factors saw the Ottawa Treaty materialize from concept in 1991 to treaty in 1997—remarkable speed for a multilateral treaty: (1) an NGO champion, the ICBL; (2) a state champion, Canada; (3) a diplomatic champion, Dr. Werner Ehrlich; and (4) a public relations champion, Princess Diana. Each contributed to a groundswell of public and governmental support for a treaty. One question is, who will be the Henri Dunant or Jody Williams of AI regulation?

- International efforts to regulate technology, including land mines and cluster munitions, can influence policy even when and where critical states do not join binding treaties. Ottawa is a case in point, influencing, as it did, U.S. land mine policy.

PERFIDY AND RUSE

A ruse is lawful trickery. Or, more precisely, as defined in U.S. military manuals, "acts which are intended to mislead an adversary or induce him to act recklessly but which infringe no rule of international law applicable in armed conflict."[4] The original and classic ruse, in every sense, was the Trojan Horse. D-Day also offers numerous examples of lawful and successful ruses, designed to fool or confuse the Germans as to the time and location of the Allied cross-channel landings. This included the use of inflatable tanks and aircraft (a ruse still used today); the assignment of George Patton to command a fictitious army group aimed at Calais; and, on D-Day itself, the use of metal particles to mimic aircraft formations on radar, and mini-paratroopers with firecrackers to simulate parachute drops.

Defined broadly, perfidy is treachery, the "killing or wounding treacherously individuals belonging to the hostile nation or army."[5] At its core, the prohibition on perfidy seeks to outlaw the use of protected symbols to gain an opponent's confidence in order to kill them. Thus, article 37(1) of Additional Protocol I defines perfidy as "acts inviting confidence of an adversary to lead him to believe that he is entitled to, or obliged to accord, protection under the rules of international law applicable in armed conflict, with intent to betray that confidence." The *DOD Law of War Manual* defines perfidy in a similar manner, stating, "The key element in perfidy is the false claim to protections under the law of war in order to secure a military advantage over the opponent. The claim must be to legal protections."[6] Classic examples of unlawful perfidy involve the use of internationally protected symbols to gain advantage over an opponent like use of a false flag of surrender or the donning of a Red Cross or Red Crescent emblem. However, perfidy reaches more than protected symbols, and more than combatants. It is also generally viewed as treacherous to use assassins, assassination being a form of treacherous killing, although there is no general agreement on what exactly assassination means. Further, the prohibition reaches, or rather protects, "individuals belonging to the hostile nation" and not just members of its military, if the Hague Convention remains good law. In addition, perfidy bars the wearing of the uniforms or emblems of neutral countries not party to a conflict.[7]

There is debate about whether and when an adversary can wear the uniform of one's opponent. The *DOD Law of War Manual* takes the view that POWs can lawfully wear an adversary's uniforms to effect escape and "outside of combat."[8] Article 23 of the 1907 Hague Convention prohibits the "improper" wearing of an enemy combatant's uniform. In contrast, wearing an opponent's uniform in combat is viewed as treacherous. But there is ample debate on what is considered "outside of combat" and the degree to which an adversary's uniform can be worn to gain the element of surprise. At a minimum, while it may not be a war crime under the rubric of perfidy, it does expose the perpetrator to the loss of combatant status and potential exposure as a spy. This was the case with the German soldiers under the command of Otto Skorzeny, at the outset of the Battle of the Bulge, who wore American uniforms and sought to sow confusion and chaos behind American lines by cutting communications lines and misdirecting traffic. Skorzeny was later charged with a war crime for these acts but acquitted for lack of direct evidence that he gave the command for German soldiers to wear U.S. uniforms while in combat rather than for purposes of infiltration and deception. One defense witness was a British Special Operations Executive (SOE) member who testified that SOE agents wore German uniforms as disguise behind enemy lines. However, eighteen German soldiers captured during the battle wearing American uniforms were executed after brief military trials.

There remains active debate among experts on whether the wearing of an adversary's uniform is a war crime, or just risky under foreign law. It is unresolved, in part, because the major powers that tend to drive the law of armed conflict may have a foot in both camps. There are media pictures of special forces units from multiple countries dressed in local attire to blend in during the conflict in Afghanistan. Local attire may also be the "uniform" of the adversary if, for example, one is fighting the Taliban. The circumstance is somewhat like cyber-debates, where the law remains opaque because the driving states are not quite sure whether they want offense or defense to prevail, and thus they leave the law vague, permitting some contextual choice.

Virtually no commentators—or, for that matter, U.S. policymakers—push back on the prohibition on using protected symbols. Other black letter law applications of perfidy may at times seem a bit oxymoronic. If the overall purpose of international humanitarian law is humanitarian, wouldn't it minimize civilian suffering to permit the assassination of key actors, which might otherwise help to end a conflict? However, the perfidy prohibition makes more sense in this context if one considers the two root purposes of the prohibition. First, the law is intended to capture, perhaps in dated terms, concepts of fair play and chivalry. In this regard, it is noteworthy that the 2015 *DOD Law of War Manual* includes "honor" as one of the core principles of the law of armed conflict, along with distinction, necessity, and proportionality.[9]

Second, the law is intended to protect civilians. Were assassination permitted, then civilians would be inherently suspect, and the distinction between combatants and noncombatants harder to find and enforce. The debate thus returns to the meaning of assassination and whether there is a principled difference between targeting an opposing military leader with a precision munition, a sniper's rifle, or a car bomb. Perfidy is also prohibited because, in the words of the 1956 manual, "Treacherous or perfidious conduct in war is forbidden because it destroys the basis for a restoration of peace short of the complete annihilation of one belligerent by the other."[10]

Conclusions

What do perfidy and ruse have to do with AI?

First, of course, the law of perfidy and ruse applies to AI-enabled weapons systems and techniques just as it applies to any other weapon or effort to deceive the enemy. One cannot use AI capacities to mimic Red Cross call signs or mimic the voices of aid workers. However, it may be less obvious how the law might apply in the context of camouflage and concealment. Might a drone be camouflaged to look like an Amazon delivery vehicle or a recreational toy? Wearing an adversary's uniform may take on new meaning in the the context of weapons systems designed to look like an adversary's, or that are an adversary's, because they have been captured and are now controlled by the opponent through AI and cyber means. Is this a form of wearing the opponent's uniform? And should such conduct be permitted under the law of armed conflict? Policymakers should actively consider these questions before there is a need to do so. Addressed in the abstract, policymakers will focus on long-term interests and consequences, such as stability, rather than the short-term interests that are paramount in the context of specific operational decisions and moments of crisis.

Second, should cyberattacks in the form of phishing or other methods be treated like a Trojan Horse or perfidy? At this time, they are treated like the former; indeed, some cyberattacks are known as "Trojan Horses." But is that the right rubric going forward, where the potential risks of AI-enabled cyberattacks are greater? Should there be legal redlines, for example, that prohibit acts that inherently undermine stability, or the ability of commanders to responsibly command? Should the use of malicious bots—software applications that can rapidly run repetitive scripted tasks such as denial of service attacks, or other methods of attack that mask attribution—be treated as one more cyber-challenge or as akin to wearing the uniform of a neutral party, which is perfidious under the law of armed conflict?

Third, what about AI applications that undermine stability, in peace as well as in war, and in between? For example, should it be viewed as perfidious to interfere with, or run a false flag operation against, a state-to-state hotline? What about interfering with nuclear command and control or systems that help to predict weather or alert civilians to emergency circumstances? Or human-in-the-loop links to lethal autonomous weapons systems (LAWS)? Should these systems be off limits from AI intrusion, and if so, should those restrictions apply in peace as well as in war and everything in between? And in any event, would any of this be detectable or verifiable before it was too late, in which case post-facto sanction alone would be the primary deterrent?

The law of ruse and perfidy is narrow and applies solely to international armed conflict. However, the perfidy-ruse distinction may offer an important line of analysis as states, and other actors, determine when and how to regulate the capacity of AI applications to mimic, trick, and commandeer other states' or actors' tools. In peace, as well as in conflict, certain values and functions may be so inherently important to stability that critical actors may wish to draw redlines around what are permitted and prohibited actions in AI space by determining now what would constitute unlawful perfidious conduct. The policy question presented is whether states should consider applying a rule of perfidy and ruse to AI now, before states have sufficiently developed a capacity that would discourage the identification of redlines later. These questions are not rhetorical, with the answer presumed, but intended to prompt conscious consideration of the new risks that come from AI's potential to deceive.

ADHERENCE TO THE LAW OF ARMED CONFLICT/IHL

Many have said that the difference between an armed mob and a professional army is discipline. Discipline is rooted in leadership and law. International law seeks to minimize human suffering in warfare and promote adherence to the law in numerous ways, including requirements that new weapons be tested for compliance with the law, military personnel be trained in the law, and commanders be held responsible for the conduct of those they lead.

Adherence to these and other IHL norms occurs, if it occurs at all, because states have a reciprocal interest in their application; states care how they are perceived, especially if they seek alliance; the participation of some states in military operations is contingent on compliance with international law; and because there is an effective, or possible, means of domestic or international enforcement. A disciplined, law-abiding armed force is also more effective in accomplishing the mission than one that is not.

In U.S. military practice, leadership is the backbone of good order and discipline. Military law and regulation reinforce leadership by establishing a code of conduct and means of enforcement. Thus, the Uniform Code of Military Justice (UCMJ) serves two core national security interests: justice and good order and discipline. Additional criminal sanctions for grave breaches of the law of armed conflict are found in Title 18, section 2441. The question posed in this subsection is whether some of these principles should be adopted and adapted to apply, in relevant manner, to national security uses of AI, and if so, when and in what manner.

New Weapons Review

Article 36 of Additional Protocol I to the Geneva Conventions states:

> In the study, development, acquisition, or adoption of a new weapon, means, or method of warfare, a high contracting party is under an obligation to determine whether its employment would, in some or all circumstances, be prohibited by this protocol or by any other rule of international law applicable to a high contracting party.

According to the International Review of the Red Cross, "The aim of article 36 is to prevent the use of weapons that would violate international law in all circumstances and to impose restrictions on the use of weapons that would violate international law in some circumstances, by determining their lawfulness before they are developed, acquired, or otherwise incorporated into a state's arsenal."[11] Biological and chemical weapons, for example, are weapons that would fall into the first category. They would violate international law in all circumstances, not just because they are expressly prohibited by treaty and customary international law, but also because they are inherently indiscriminate in their effect. The use of munitions whose fragments are not detectable by X-ray also fall into this category, because they cause undue suffering. In contrast, the use of white phosphorus or lasers might be lawful or unlawful, depending on how they are used. Their use as antipersonnel weapons, for example, to burn and to blind, is outlawed for causing undue suffering. However, if used to mark targets, for example, to help pilots or artillery observers distinguish between civilian and military objects, they are lawful.

Indeed, proponents of discriminate warfare should want to encourage their appropriate use.

Scholars and states debate where nuclear weapons fall on this continuum. On the one hand, opponents argue nuclear weapons are inherently indiscriminate and disproportionate to any lawful military objective because they cause undue suffering. On the other hand, proponents conceive of the possibility they could be used in a tactical manner that is necessary, discriminate, and proportionate to the military objective and need at hand, such as destroying a bunker or channeling an invasion force. They further posit that they are necessary for stability as a belligerent reprisal deterrent to an opponent's use of WMD.

What about AI? Interestingly, article 36, which was included in the protocol opened for signature in June 1977, appears to have contemplated some form of future AI and autonomous weapons systems (AWS). The 1987 ICRC commentaries state:

> The use of long distance, remote control weapons, or weapons connected to sensors positioned in the field, leads to automation of the battlefield in which the soldier plays an increasingly less important role. The countermeasures developed as a result of this evolution, in particular electronic jamming (or interference), exacerbate the indiscriminate character of combat.[12]

Although the United States is not a party to protocol I, it recognizes article 36 as reflecting customary international law. Indeed, the United States conducted weapons reviews before the adoption of article 36. The United States has implemented the requirements of this provision in, among other places, Department of Defense directives. DOD Directive 5000.1, the Defense Acquisition System, states:

> The acquisition and procurement of DOD weapons and weapons systems shall be consistent with all applicable domestic law and treaties and international agreements . . . An attorney authorized to conduct such legal reviews in the department shall conduct the legal review of the intended acquisition of weapons or weapons systems.[13]

The directive further establishes a process for conducting reviews as do department regulations for each of the military services with respect to the procurement of new weapons systems.

The *DOD Law of War Manual* states that the review "should consider three questions to determine whether the weapon's acquisition or procurement is prohibited: (1) whether the weapon's intended use is calculated to cause superfluous injury, (2) whether the weapon is inherently indiscriminate, and (3) whether the weapon falls within a class of weapons that has been specifically prohibited."[14]

In 2012, DOD issued a directive addressed specifically to Autonomy in Weapons Systems (3000.09, November 21, 2012). The directive (1) establishes DOD policy and assigns responsibilities for the development and use of autonomous and semiautonomous functions in weapons systems, including manned and unmanned platforms, and (2) establishes guidelines designed to minimize the probability and consequences of failures in autonomous and semiautonomous weapons systems that could lead to unintended engagements.

Further, the directive establishes DOD policy regarding AI in weapons systems, including the following:

a. Autonomous and semiautonomous weapons systems shall be designed to allow commanders and operators to exercise appropriate levels of human judgment over the use of force.

  (1) Systems will go through rigorous hardware and software verification and validation and realistic system development and operation test and evaluation . . .

  (2) . . .

  (3) In order for operators to make informed and appropriate decisions in engaging targets, the interface between people and machines for autonomous and semiautonomous weapons shall:

  ▪ Be readily understandable to trained operators.

  ▪ Provide traceable feedback on system status.

  ▪ Provide clear procedures for trained operators to activate and deactivate system functions.

  ▪ . . .

  ▪ . . .

  ▪ . . . be designed such that, in the event of degraded or lost communications, the system does not autonomously select and engage individual targets or specific target groups that have not been previously selected by an authorized human operator.

  ▪ Human-supervised autonomous weapon systems may be used to select and engage targets, with the exception of selecting humans as targets, for local defense to intercept attempted time-critical or saturation attacks for:

☐ Static defense of manned installations.

☐ Onboard defense of manned platforms.

- Autonomous weapons systems may be used to apply nonlethal, non-kinetic force, such as some forms of electronic attack, against material targets in accordance with DOD Directive 3000.3 [Policy for Non-Lethal Weapons].

The directive also states that semiautonomous weapons systems applying kinetic or nonkinetic force or autonomous weapons designed to apply nonlethal, nonkinetic force, "must be designed such that, in the event of degraded or lost communications, the system does not autonomously select and engage individual targets or specific target groups that have not been previously selected by an authorized human operator," unless by the undersecretary of defense for policy, the undersecretary of defense for acquisition, and the chairman of the Joint Chiefs of Staff before formal development and again before fielding. The directive assigns responsibilities, and thus accountability in the review of autonomy in weapons systems, to include the DOD general counsel for legal review in accordance with article 36 and Directive 5000.1. It follows that DOD/GC must ensure it has personnel capable of doing so and doing so upstream at the R&D stages. Security specialists should want such review, not just because it is the law, but because it will help ensure applications work as intended.

There are several interpretive questions regarding the application of article 36 and its customary norm.

First, what is the meaning of new weapon and how should it be read in conjunction with the clause that follows, "means or method of warfare"? The ICRC commentaries take the view that, when read together, "the words 'methods and means' include weapons in the widest sense, as well as the way in which they are used."[15] Thus, the Australian application of the article defines weapons broadly to include "an offensive or defensive instrument of combat used to destroy, injure, defeat, or threaten. It includes weapon systems, munitions, submunitions, ammunition, targeting devices, and other damaging or injuring mechanisms."[16] The ICRC Guide to the Legal Review of Weapons indicates that review should also extend to new uses for weapons or modifications to existing weapons, or weapons that are new in the inventory of the country involved.

The second question regarding new weapons review is what is required. There is general agreement that the requirement covers the normal anticipated use(s) at the time of evaluation. States are not required to foresee and evaluate how a weapon might be misused or used for unintended purposes. The review is also contextual. Modeling can be used or actual firing, in the case of kinetic weapons. According to the ICRC, the review is supposed to be multidisciplinary, taking into account "military, legal, environmental, and health-related considerations."[17] Where necessary, the review is intended to result in modification or cessation of the weapon's development, or appropriate training and guidance—for example, in the case of a munition like riot control agents, which might have both lawful and unlawful uses. Commentary also points to the importance of testing weapons at each stage of the development process and not just prior to deployment or fielding. This is the better course because of the difficult budget and bureaucratic challenges of canceling or modifying a weapons program after it is fully developed. Finally, there is general agreement that a state is not required to make its review or findings public for reasons of security.

Conclusions

Should AI applications be subject to some form of "new technology" review? The new weapon requirement presents a potential template for AI applications outside the construct of weapons systems. Six questions immediately arise.

1. Should states be required to test AI technologies or components for compliance with the law prior to development and deployment?

2. If so, should entities other than states, such as corporations and academic labs, also be required to engage in new AI review? At what stages of research and development?

3. If so, with what law or regulations should AI comply? In the absence of agreed law, should states be required to meet certain safety and security standards and to assess the risk of unintended consequences?

4. Should such a requirement apply to AI generally, hardware and software, just national security applications, or just to a subset of AI associated with kinetic and cyber-weapons? The question is like that posed by the meaning of new weapon. Line drawing with AI is more complex than with weapons, but here one might ask whether one could reasonably distinguish be-

tween AI applications. One might also distinguish between systems that are attached to critical infrastructures, like the internet or the energy grid, and those that are not.

5. Should states be required to publish their regulations providing for such testing generally, or just for article 36 purposes?

6. Should an international organization like the OPCW or IAEA, or a nonprofit like IANA/ICANN, in internet context, oversee the conduct of such safety and security testing and do so on a confidential basis?

If so, or in any event, who should be held responsible and accountable for new AI technology and applications? As a matter of internal U.S. process, the *DOD Directive on Autonomous Weapons* suggests the following questions: Who, or what institutions, should approve AI research and development? In LOAC context, what does "appropriate levels of human judgment over the use of force" mean, and should the United States return to a policy of no first use of AWS without a human in the loop? In the context of autonomous and semiautonomous weapons systems, the key decisional actors are the undersecretaries of policy, research and engineering, and acquisition and sustainment, as well as the chairman of the Joint Chiefs of Staff. Should additional decisionmakers outside the department in question also be involved? And, in private and academic context, which actors should be involved, responsible, and accountable? In industry, the responsible actor is presumably the CEO. But should law or regulation expressly require general counsel concurrence, or a decision of the board of directors? In academia, should AI be subject to internal review board review, or general counsel approval?

Start with transparency. As a first step, states might consider publishing regulations that apply to the safety and security testing of AI. As noted, there is no requirement to publish the results of a new weapons review. This makes sense. If there were a requirement, states would either decline to test weapons or lie about the results out of concern that they would reveal security capabilities or vulnerabilities to potential adversaries. However, the law might usefully require states to publish their regulations regarding new weapons review as a first step toward verifying compliance with the overall requirement. Few states do so, which leaves one to wonder whether states generally adhere to this requirement or not. Moreover, without publication of state regulations, it is hard to determine whether there is agreement on what the law requires, how it applies, and thus also determine if there are gaps and fissures.

Former deputy secretary of defense Robert O. Work has described five AI building blocks or components to the third offset strategy.[18]

1. Autonomous deep learning systems

2. Human-machine collaboration

3. Assisted human operations

4. Human-machine combat teaming

5. Autonomous weapons

The legal policy question presented is how the "new weapons" requirement should be adopted and adapted to each of these functions in the context of specific projects and programs. A second question is whether the Department of Defense should publicly state how it will comply with article 36 in the context of these five scenarios. In doing so, the United States can help to establish customary international law on the matter as well as pressure other states to make their procedures public.

TRAINING

Most law of war treaties include requirements to implement those treaties through training specific to the treaty as well as through domestic enforcement mechanisms. This practice dates to the 1906 Geneva Convention. These provisions are sometimes general, as in the case of common article 1 to the four 1949 Geneva Conventions, which states: "The high contracting parties undertake to respect and to ensure respect for the present convention in all circumstances."

This article is viewed as creating a requirement for training and enforcement "to ensure respect for the convention." (Contemporary disputes in interpretation revolve around the extent to which this article imposes on parties an obligation to ensure their allies—with whom they share intelligence and weapons, for example—are adhering to the law in the conduct operations.)

Other requirements to train are more specific, like the obligation found in article 144 of the 1949 Geneva Convention IV, "Relative to the Protection of Civilian Persons in Time of War," which seems to require civilian training, if possible, in addition to military training:

The high contracting parties undertake, in time of peace as in time of war, to disseminate the text of the present convention as widely as possible in their respective countries, and, in particular, to include the study thereof in their programs of military and, if possible, civil instruction, so that the principles thereof may become known to the entire population.

This is an extraordinary undertaking, creating skepticism about the obligation being operational law rather than aspirational concept. Perhaps the most useful statement of the duty to train personnel in the law is found in article 83 of AP I (Additional Protocol I) to the Geneva Conventions, which makes it clear that the obligation should be tailored to one's duties and responsibilities:

> In order to prevent and suppress breaches, high contracting parties and parties to the conflict shall require that, commensurate with their level of responsibility, commanders ensure that members of the armed forces under their command are aware of their obligations under the conventions and this protocol.

The United States implements its obligations under these and other treaties through the DOD Law of War Program, DOD Directive 2311.01 E., 2011. Among other things, the program recognizes that the United States should adhere to these requirements not just because it is obliged to do so, but because it makes military sense to do so. Principles of law requiring distinction between combatants and noncombatants and the humane treatment of detainees reflect national security values. Adherence to these values can protect one's own forces when the law is applied in reciprocal manner as well as encourage detainees to share information. In the context of counterinsurgency or counterterrorism operations, adherence helps to keep the affected population friendly, or at least neutral rather than hostile. Adherence to the law generally also leads to wider domestic support for the military. Consider how Abu Ghraib and My Lai served as turning points in public perceptions about the Iraq and Vietnam Wars. Adherence to the law and training on the law also garner and sustain allied support for U.S. operations.

Parties to treaties, of course, may go beyond any required obligation. The DOD Law of War Program does so. For example, the secretary of defense has directed that:

> The heads of the DOD components shall make qualified legal advisers at all levels of command available to provide advice about law of war compliance during planning and execution of exercises and operations;[19]

The commanders of the combatant commands shall . . . ensure all plans, policies, directives, and rules of engagement issued by the command and its subordinate commands and components are reviewed by legal advisers to ensure their consistency with this directive and the law of war.[20]

In addition, as is generally known, the military provides case-specific rules of engagement to supplement the general principles of the law of armed conflict, which always apply.

Although the obligations to train are textually clear, several genuine questions arise. First, when is training required? The better view, based on both the text of Protocol I and state practice is that training is required in peacetime as well as during wartime, and on an ongoing basis. But treaty text could be more expressive on this point.

Second, how specific is the required training? Again, the text could be clearer. Protocol I states, "commensurate with their level of responsibility." However, it is not clear, nor expressly required, that training occur on the record or be conducted by lawyers.

Third, whatever the obligation, it is also clear that in conflict, training is only effective if violations that deviate from training are addressed, corrected, and, where appropriate, disciplined.

Finally, however clear or unclear the requirement to train is with respect to states, it is far less clear with respect to non-state actors and parties. According to the ICRC, "Article 19 of Additional Protocol II, applicable to Non-International Armed Conflicts, states that the protocol 'shall be disseminated as widely as possible,' and this provision binds armed opposition groups." To address this potential loophole, there are cases where parties in conflict have agreed on a bilateral basis on an obligation to disseminate and adhere to the law of armed conflict.[21]

Conclusions

Beyond the application of AI in contexts where the law of armed conflict applies, should international and domestic law require training on AI or the law of AI? Such training might encompass safety, security, and law, as well as include an express acknowledgment of responsibility and accountability—in effect, a chain of custody for the proper use of the AI in question.

Taking article 144 of Geneva Convention IV as a model, U.S. policy, U.S. law, or international law might also require the training of civilians as well as military personnel in AI applications to warfare. Under current U.S. practice, civilians receive virtually no formal or required training in the law of armed conflict. Rather, the training that is received is informal and on-the-job in the form of advice and memos. As a matter of domestic law and regulation, if not international law, this could and should be changed. Why not require something similar for AI? States might also consider a requirement for legal or ethical training for persons engaged in AI research and development in industry and academia based on the IHL model. Required training could cover algorithmic functions, bias, data, predictive probability, and law.

States might also agree to require publication of any national requirements to provide training, thus creating pressure on other states to do the same.

Finally, proponents of AI should consider the lessons learned from the DOD law of war program. The program is not only implemented out of a sense of legal obligation. It is implemented because adherence to the law results in greater public support and sustainment for military operations, underpins allied support and assistance to U.S. military operations, and is the foundation upon which the reciprocal application and enforcement of the law depends. It also leads to better national security results. It also makes military sense. Disciplined soldiers are more effective.

Command Responsibility

As noted above, protocol I and customary international law hold commanders responsible for "ensuring that members of the armed forces under their command are aware of their obligations under the conventions and this protocol." Among these obligations is the principle of command responsibility. Command responsibility includes five elements.[22]

Individual responsibility. All members of an armed force are responsible and accountable for upholding the law of armed conflict; not just commanders. This means that following superior orders is not a defense to violating the law of armed conflict. In U.S. practice and law, an order is presumed to be lawful unless a reasonable person would know it was unlawful, in which case the recipient has a duty not to follow the order.

Commanders are responsible for war crimes they knew of or had reason to know of and did nothing to stop. The most important case in this line of law is the *Yamashita* case.[23] General Tomoyuki Yamashita was one of Japan's most successful and revered commanders, known as the "Tiger of Malaya" for his conduct of the Malayan campaign and capture of Singapore. In 1944, he was in charge of holding and defending the Philippines from General MacArthur's Allied forces. After the war, Yamashita was charged and tried before a U.S. military court-martial in Manila for the war crimes of troops under his command, including mass murder, torture, and rape. Yamashita was not charged with committing, directing, or ordering the offenses himself. Nevertheless, the court concluded that Yamashita was culpable for the offenses of his subordinates, because he ". . . unlawfully disregarded and failed to discharge his duty as a commander, to control the operations of the members of his command, permitting them to commit brutal atrocities . . . and he . . . thereby violated the laws of war." Yamashita was convicted and hanged.

The *Queenfish* case addresses the commander's responsibility with respect to process. In the case,[24] the commander of a U.S. submarine was court-martialed for torpedoing, in 1945, the Japanese ship *Awa Maru*. At the time, the passenger-cargo vessel was marked as a hospital ship and transported urgent supplies and medicines to Allied POWs held in Japanese camps. In exchange, the vessel received safe passage from the U.S. Pacific Command, despite the possibility that the vessel would also be used to transport war material and personnel to and from Japan during its outbound and return voyages. The Pacific Command sent multiple encrypted and clear messages to fleet submarines to provide safe passage. One message stated: "Let pass safely the *Awa Maru* carrying prisoner of war supplies. She will be passing through your areas between March 30 and April 4. She is lighted at night and plastered with white crosses." The *Queenfish* received the message, but the message was not specific as to location or route. A more detailed message was not read by the commander, although it was read by his communications officer. Later, the *Queenfish* was advised by other submarines that there were targets in her area near the Taiwan Strait, and she proceeded, in dense fog, to engage a vessel the commander believed to be a Japanese destroyer. It was the *Awa Maru*.

There was one survivor. He was picked up by the *Queenfish*, at which point Commander E. Elliott Loughlin learned he had torpedoed the *Maru*. He reported what had occurred. The *Queenfish* was ordered to port and Chief of Naval Operations Admiral Ernest Joseph King eventually ordered, "Detach Loughlin from his command and have him tried by general court-martial." A subsequent court-martial acquitted Loughlin of culpable inefficiency in the performance of duty, and disobeying orders, but found him guilty of a third offense of dereliction of duty "for negligence in obeying orders." Loughlin was sentenced to a letter of admonition from the secretary of navy,[25] while Admiral King ordered that Loughlin not command submarines again. However, in due course, Loughlin commanded a squadron of submarines and eventually served as, and retired with the grade of, rear admiral. Two Navy Crosses for

Loughlin's prior wartime service as well as successful postwar service as the Naval Academy's athletic director no doubt contributed to his rehabilitation.

There are few cases in this area, and one needs to take care not to draw too much from a single case. Nonetheless, there are lessons to learn from the incident, some of them relevant to AI. The *Queenfish* case, like the *Yamashita* case, is cited for the proposition that commanders are responsible for the actions of their commands, whether they hold the specific intent to commit the underlying delict or not. In Loughlin's case, he was convicted, in part, for having an ineffective process in place to ensure compliance with orders. No doubt, as well, wartime pressure to continue the safe transit of supplies to Allied prisoners in Japanese camps contributed to the charging decision. Process matters in exercising command authority or failing to do so. The Pacific Command did not repeat the safe passage warning to the officers of the *Queenfish* during its operational briefing but relied on message traffic alone to communicate the safe passage order. Lacking visibility in the fog, the officers of the *Queenfish* relied on radar to profile the *Awa Maru* along with its speed and direction. The *Awa Maru* was running fast and low in the water, like a destroyer, rather than zigzagging like a merchant vessel, which dovetailed with what the officers were predisposed to expect from a hostile naval vessel (confirmation bias). And, of course, there was the fog of war, both literal and in the sense that Clausewitz meant.

Commanders must take reasonable measures to prevent violations of the law of armed conflict. The requirement to take "reasonable measures" is found in the case law and statutes of the International Criminal Tribunals for the Former Yugoslavia (ICTY) and Rwanda (ICTR), as well as in the Rome Treaty establishing the International Criminal Court. However, article 86 of Protocol I purports to require commanders to take "all feasible measures within their power"—a higher standard and one with additional elements of proof. The United States has adopted the "reasonable measures" standard since the *1956 U.S. Army Field Manual on the Law of Land Warfare*. The 2015 *DOD Law of War Manual* applies this standard as well, stating:

> Commanders have duties to take necessary and reasonable measures to ensure their subordinates do not commit violations of the law of war. Failures by commanders . . . can result in criminal responsibility.[26]

In the *Queenfish* case, there was no evidence the commander saw the communications granting the *Maru* safe passage, but the communications had been received. The commander was found responsible for his failure to have established proper procedures on his vessel for the handling of such communications.[27] Thus, *Queenfish* can be viewed as a "reasonable measures" case as well as one upholding the commander's duty to know of the actions of his subordinates.

Civilian command responsibility. Although the principle of command responsibility is most often articulated with reference to military command and commanders, recent case law in the context of the ICTY and ICTR make clear that the concept can extend to civilian command responsibility for the actions of military subordinates. The ICRC Commentaries, for example, state:

> Not only military personnel but also civilians can be liable for war crimes based on command responsibility. The International Criminal Tribunal for Rwanda, in the *Akayesu* case in 1998 and in the *Kayishema* and *Ruzindana* cases in 1999, and the International Criminal Tribunal for the Former Yugoslavia, in the *Delalic* case in 1998, have adopted this principle.[28]

These principles are reinforced at the head of state level by the arrest and subsequent trial before the ICTY of former Serbian president Slobodan Milosevic for war crimes associated with the Balkan Wars of the 1990s, as well as of Radovan Karadzic, the former president of the breakaway Republika Srpska, who was convicted in 2016 of multiple war crimes. (Milosevic died in 2006, before the completion of his trial; Karadzic was convicted of genocide, crimes against humanity, and violations of the laws and customs of war and sentenced to forty years of confinement.)

Investigation and prosecution. Finally, lawyers generally agree that the doctrine of command responsibility includes the duty of the command to investigate credible assertions of war crimes and to hold accountable those responsible for war crimes. The issues that are usually debated here are whether the predicate for "investigation" has been met, and then whether the country in question has engaged in a credible investigation and effort to hold responsible parties accountable. There is a tension, of course, between victims and outside observers, who view "conviction" as synonymous with "investigation," in contrast to military authorities, who view the obligation as requiring good faith investigation and, where appropriate, prosecution. In U.S. practice, this requires proof beyond a reasonable doubt of each element of an offense in an open and fair trial.

Finally, the Uniform Code of Military Justice, the criminal code applicable to members of the U.S. Armed Forces, does not have a provision on command responsibility. However, it accomplishes the objectives embodied in the principle of command responsibility through punitive Article 92, which covers, among other things, failure to follow orders and dereliction of duty.

Conclusions

If AI is used in armed conflict, the command responsibility question is clear. Lawyers and technologists can argue about who should be held responsible when software does not work as intended. But in conflict, the commander will and should be held responsible, if he knew of, or had reason to know of, violations of law, including that a weapon or system would not work as intended, was not working as intended, or did not work in a manner consistent with the law of war. As *Yamashita* established, ignorance, willful or otherwise, is not a defense.

One question is whether the United States should seek to refine the law regarding how command responsibility does, or should, apply to AWS specifically, or AI generally, by adopting and adapting the principles of command responsibility to AI applications. If commanders are responsible for how AI-enabled systems function, they are more likely to devote the resources necessary to validate code, require training, and understand the operational uses and limitations of AI systems. This can be done by changing domestic law, or by asserting, as a matter of legal obligation, certain requirements in customary international law. Policymakers may want to do so not just because they believe in good order and discipline, but because they want better security outcomes.

More broadly, one might ask: should the United States, other countries, or other actors, such as NGOS, seek to develop and expand the concept of command responsibility, including civilian responsibility, to better address AI applications in warfare, gray zones, and peacetime? AI may especially warrant development of a doctrine of civilian command responsibility in times of peace and war.

THE PRINCIPLES OF TARGETING

Since the advent of the digital age, lawyers and operators have been debating the application of the law of armed conflict to the cyber-domain. The discussion over when and whether a cyber-event rises to the level of "armed attack," and thus gives rise to a right to kinetic or other self-defense, seems to attract inordinate attention. U.S. public policy regarding armed attack in cyberspace appears to be "we will know it when we see it," and we will continue to reserve the right to respond with a full array of policy options—cyber, kinetic, and other. The *Tallinn Manuals* (I and II) are an effort by scholars to come to grips with some of these questions from the perspective of international law. Scholars in public, and operators in less public settings, also debate how and whether the core principles of targeting should apply in cyberspace in peacetime, or in that peculiar gray-space within the cyber-domain, which is neither war nor peace, but marked by hand-to-hand cyber-engagement.[29]

One question for military law and doctrine presented by AI is whether the targeting principles should apply in a different manner to AI and AI-enabled tools than they already do to kinetic and cyber-operations. For sure, one of the strengths of the targeting principles is that they are principles, and thus adaptable to different contexts. But while the definitions may be the same, and must be the same, principles often apply differently in different contexts. The Fourth Amendment is a case in point. The text of the amendment is static; however, what is "reasonable" will vary depending on circumstance.

Proportionality

How might the LOAC principles apply differently with AI? Start with proportionality, which is defined in the *DOD Law of War Manual* as "the principle that even where one is justified in acting, one must not act in a way that is unreasonable or excessive."[30] In applying this principle to kinetic operations, military lawyers and commanders weigh military advantage against the potential unintended consequences. If there is time to do so, as in the case of planned or static targets, sophisticated modeling is used, incorporating attack azimuths, angles of attack, fuse type, and so on. Where there is less time, as in the case of targets of opportunity or infantry pop-up targets, military actors rely on practice and experience in evaluating relative advantage and proportional effect.

Stuxnet illustrates that it is a lot harder to make these judgments when dealing with technological weapons that persist and for which the only real model of effect will occur when they are used. With Stuxnet, for example, it was possible to determine the kinetic effect on centrifuges. It was also possible to assess whether the air-locked introduction of malware might jump the rails. But it was much harder to predict what would happen if the malware jumped the rails. It did, which is one reason the virus was discovered and one reason the weapon might be used again by others. Simply put, cyber-modeling is not as accurate and reliable as explosive radius analysis for kinetic weapons. There are more variables, including the unpredictable role of humans and the persistent nature of some cyber-weapons.

AI-enabled tools, or AI-enabled weapons, may present some of the same challenges and in magnified manner, especially if one is talking about weapons that are persistent or that can act on their own, to escape and evade with human level intelligence. That is one reason that the Defense Directive 3000.9 states that in the event of a loss of communications, autonomous systems will not operate autonomously against targets not previously selected by an authorized human operator. There are questions ahead: Where a weapon has autonomy and autonomous features, is it good enough to weigh the proportional effect of a weapon's use based on modeling and prediction? Or should there be some additional burden of proof to demonstrate the safe or proportionate use of the weapon? These are among the questions an article 36 review might consider. The question posed here is whether the doctrine of proportionality should evolve to address AI-enabled systems as well. A further question is whether AI, which is "brittle" now, will ever be subtle enough to make the sort of intuitive, situational, and judgment-based decisions many proportionality assessments require in combat. This might happen, for example, when an engagement is anticipated to present a low-level of risk to noncombatants, but in reality and in the moment presents a higher risk of casualties.

Military Objective

The principle of military objective may present challenges as well. The DOD manual defines military objective as "persons or objects that may be made the object of attack. Certain classes of persons and objects are categorically recognized as military objectives . . . other objects are assessed as to whether they meet the definition of 'military objective.'"[31] This principle is easy to apply in the case of World War II–type targets, like tanks, aircraft, and factories producing armaments (although cover and concealment may make it harder to discern the true nature of a target). But the line is less clear when one is considering less traditional objects. This is illustrated with respect to the 2016 debate about whether oil trucks transporting fuel to market from ISIS-occupied Syria and Iraq were lawful military objects subject to attack. On the one hand, scholars and the government pointed out that there was a direct link between the selling of the fuel on the Turkish black market and the financing of ISIS's terrorist operations. The tankers, in effect, had been appropriated by ISIS. On the other hand, other scholars pointed out that the fuel was being transported in civilian vehicles with civilian drivers who had been engaged in this smuggling activity before ISIS occupied the region, and likely would be again after ISIS was gone, if they or the vehicles survived to drive another day.[32]

If AI is the transformative military technology of the twenty-first century, what constitutes a military object where AI is concerned? Does that make MIT an AI munitions factory? How far down the supply chain is the law, and are commanders prepared to go in targeting "military AI"? Or is the concept of military objective irrelevant and does the answer turn, as it sometimes does with civilians, on whether the entity is directly participating in hostilities? If one contemplates a potential target continuum, one might put an autonomous weapon system on one end, and on the other end, an R & D lab at a federally funded research and development center. But where along the continuum might one put the privately owned cloud in which the AI-enabled weapon stores essential data? And if the majority of AI R & D is being conducted in private industry and at universities, when do those facilities become more like World War II ball-bearing factories and less like schools?

It is doubtful that governments will spend, or have spent, much time contemplating these questions in advance of conflict—and, were they to do so, even more doubtful that they would choose to reveal their thinking on these questions. They should. At the very least, the question warrants internal review and clarity at a time free from the pressures and consequences of conflict. It is at times of relative stability that policymakers have time and space to deliberately consider the intermediate and long-term consequences of any doctrinal shift or drift, whereas crisis tends to focus decisionmaking on immediate impacts and needs.

Prohibitions and Redlines

In addition to providing core targeting principles, the LOAC also includes absolute, or black letter rules. These include prohibitions on attacking hospitals, cultural and historic sites, and religious sites, among others. However, like most law, black letter rules have exceptions. For example, the misuse of a protected target—such as the use of a school or hospital to store arms or command military operations—does not immunize the site from attack. Rather, it can make it a lawful military object of attack; however, the value of attacking the target and its necessity must be reconsidered in light of the presence of civilians and civilian objects. The proportionality analysis will change as well: are the collateral consequences of attack unreasonable or disproportionate to the concrete and direct military advantages of attacking the target? This reveals one of the strengths of the principles: they adapt to context. This makes sense; otherwise, bad actors would use protected sites with impunity. Instead, sites are exposed to appropriate attack and the perpetrators to investigation and potential prosecution for having used a protected site in such a manner.

The first question presented in this subsection is whether states and non-state actors should consider specific black letter rules, including prohibitions, regarding AI-enabled systems, before AI is fully integrated into weapons and weapons systems and thus before states have too large a stake in the outcome of their own research and development to restrict or prohibit any real and perceived AI advantages. As discussed, one possible redline might incorporate the principles contained in DOD Directive 5000.1, including the statement that "systems will not operate autonomously against targets not previously selected by an authorized human operator." The Defense Department has stated that "DOD does not currently have an autonomous weapon system that can search for, identify, track, select, and engage targets independent of a human operator's input."[33] This, too, might provide the basis of an international redline, albeit one that is hard to verify. Other redlines might address:

- Linking AI to certain weapons, including nuclear weapons.
- Deploying AI-enabled systems, or autonomous systems into certain domains, such as space.
- Requiring traceable feedback from and to any weapon relying on AI-generated target data or queuing. This might include the capability to determine whether targeting decisions were made at machine speed or human speed.
- Designating additional sites and objects as inherently nonmilitary in nature, provided they are not used for military purposes.

A further question is whether states and non-state actors who are not engaged in AI weapons development, or the AI arms race, might nonetheless seek to regulate the field or impose specific prohibitions. This is the subject of various expert group meetings convened under the auspices of the UN and the Convention on Certain Conventional Weapons (CCW).

The CCW was opened for signature in 1980 and entered into force in 1983. As the title—Convention on the Prohibitions and Restrictions on the Use of Certain Conventional Weapons which May Be Deemed to Be Excessively Injurious or to Have Indiscriminate Effects, as Amended on 21 December 2001—indicates, the purpose of the treaty is to create a framework for banning or restricting the use of weapons that cause undue suffering or are indiscriminate in nature. Protocol I to the treaty, for example, adopted with the treaty along with Protocols II and III, consists of one sentence: "It is prohibited to use any weapon the primary effect of which is to injure by fragments which in the human body escape detection by X-rays." Protocol II and Amended Protocol II (May 3, 1996) are addressed to minimizing the impact of mines and booby traps on civilian populations by prohibiting, among other things, the deployment of booby traps that look like toys or are attached to dead or wounded persons. The protocol also requires the recording of the placement of mines and booby traps. Protocol III prohibits the use of incendiary weapons against civilians and civilian objects. Protocol IV (July 30, 1998) prohibits the use of laser weapons designed to blind. Protocol V is addressed to the explosive remnants of war and the duties of combatants to protect the civilian population and humanitarian missions following the conclusion of conflict (November 28, 2003). The treaty entered into force in 1983 and has 125 parties, including China, Russia, and the United States, which are also parties to the amendments and protocols to the treaty.

Based on a 2013 decision of the parties, an informal group of experts has met since 2014 to consider a potential ban on LAWS. In 2017, a more formal Group of Governmental Experts (GGE) was established to consider the topic, indicating an intent, at least in diplomatic circles, to stick with the topic. The talks have been popularly characterized as an effort to ban "killer robots."

So far, the GGE has met approximately twice a year. Four positions have emerged. First, certain states generally associated with the one-time non-aligned movement, but notably including China, have advocated on behalf of a binding legal restriction on LAWS. At the September 2018 GGE meeting, twenty-six states favored this position. Second, other states, largely associated with the EU, favor a political declaration regarding LAWS, but not an outright legal prohibition. A third group of states favors requirements for positive human control over critical functions of weapons systems. And a fourth group of states is opposed to a prohibition, legal or political, and generally favors, at least in diplomatic context, some form of autonomous weapons review akin to, but not necessarily required by, article 36. Of course, there is fluidity between the positions as well as within the positions. Russia and the United States might both be characterized as being against a LAWS ban, but their positions, outlook, and interests are hardly aligned. In addition to divisions on fundamental positions, the talks have also revealed differences and difficulties in defining key terms such as "human-in-the-loop" and LAWS itself. Nor has the experts group begun to ponder, and thus resolve, how in any event such a ban would be verified.

In short, efforts at regulating LAWS in the context of the CCW continue but will likely evade agreement. Those states and entities that wish to regulate

AWS might do well to consider some of the lessons learned from the Ottawa Treaty.

TAKEAWAYS

Don't wait to act. Like-minded states and private parties do not need to wait for the United States, China, or the UN to regulate AI. The Ottawa Treaty demonstrates at least one path forward in the absence of great power involvement.

Address the hard LOAC questions now when there is time and space to deliberate. The LOAC, including the principles addressed in this chapter, necessarily applies to AI applications used by the military to the same extent that they already apply to other military tools and weapons in and out of armed conflict. Therefore, military practitioners would be wise to consider now how these principles apply to military uses of AI and whether they apply in the same or a different manner than with current systems and weapons. Fifty-nine years elapsed between the *Department of the Army Field Manual, The Law of Land Warfare* (1956) and the *Department of Defense Law of War Manual* (2015). The United States can ill-afford to wait to consider these AI questions, because other countries and actors will, with or without U.S. input, which one hopes would accent democratic values in the use of AI. Moreover, while states are not likely to agree to prohibitions, as the LAWS debate at the UN illustrates, they may agree on controls and limitations on use, especially before such uses are fully developed, deployed, and embedded in doctrine.

Apply the LOAC as analogy where apt. The LOAC is also ripe with potential metaphor for the regulation of AI more generally. Lawyers and policymakers should purposefully consider whether to adopt and adapt LOAC principles to civilian settings as well as contexts outside of armed conflict. In particular, as adapted, these principles might require: (1) that new forms of AI used for security purposes be reviewed for compliance with the law, including constitutional law; (2) that states distinguish in civilian practice, as they do in military conflict, between lawful trickery, disguise, and deceit (ruse) and unlawful trickery, disguise, and deceit (perfidy); (3) legal training by those who use AI, including training on bias and data management; and (4) a doctrine that holds civilians, like military commanders, responsible for the use of AI in some or all contexts.

TEN

Completing the Template

ETHICS, CODES, GUIDELINES, AND
CORPORATE SECURITY RESPONSIBILTY

This chapter looks at mechanisms other than law for identifying and regulating AI risks. Three mechanisms are considered: (1) ethics, including the codes of conduct associated with law, engineering, computer engineering, computer science, and addressed to AI; (2) internal review boards (IRBs), the principal academic mechanisms for reviewing the ethical implications of research and the conduct of experimentation; and (3) corporate social responsibility (CSR), the social science term used to describe the voluntary manner by which corporations may seek to promote philanthropic, environmental, or other societal interests. What is it about the history and use of these mechanisms that AI policymakers and lawyers should know in order to consider their potential use to supplement an AI legal regime? This chapter also explains why reliance on ethics or CSR alone is inadequate to maximize the benefits and minimize the risks of AI.

ETHICS

Commentators are quick to observe that AI poses ethical challenges, but not as quick to detail those challenges or identify their solutions. AI ethical questions tend to derive from three sources: (1) the use of AI in decisionmaking;

(2) data management; and (3) bias. Ethics are the principles that should, or could, guide moral choice in security decisionmaking when the law is silent or inadequate. Thus decisionmakers face an ethical dilemma when they have a choice between lawful paths presenting varying and often competitive virtues as well as positive and objectionable consequences. One difference between law and ethics is that law, in theory, is binding and thus removes the element of choice unless the law offers options, which may create its own ethical choice between legally available alternatives. A decision to follow the law is itself an ethical choice.

National security lawyers have a professional responsibility to understand and identify the ethical questions and dilemmas associated with AI-enabled systems and machines. The state bar rules that govern attorney licensing require this as part of what it means to exercise reasonable competence and diligence.[1] The rules also unequivocally charge lawyers with addressing ethical matters in their role as advisors, so long as they distinguish between what is law and what is ethical choice.[2] The lawyer who is not conversant with AI will not be invited into the decisionmaking room and will not hold their place in that room. Nor will they be consulted at the research and development stage of AI system creation. Thus they will be left to answer legal and ethical questions at the use stage, if they are asked at all, when there are fewer opportunities to ask the right questions and even fewer opportunities to guide AI applications to preferred outcomes through technical, doctrinal, or ethical input.

Ethics, as the National AI Commission and Defense Innovation Board have noted, is also what will (or could) distinguish American, or democratic, use of AI from the authoritarian use of AI. For example, embedded in corporate policies and law, ethics will help determine the extent to which U.S. companies partner with authoritarian regimes in the development and deployment of AI systems used to monitor and control domestic populations. The ethical use of AI will help to attract AI talent to, or keep AI talent in, the United States, including in industry, academia, and government. Ethics will also encourage security and economic alliance from like-minded governments and entities. Conversely, the perception that the United States is using AI in an unethical manner will deter AI talent from working in the United States and hinder international cooperation. Finally, the transparent and ethical use of AI will more likely garner public trust and support, leading to the sustained commitment needed to maximize the security and economic advantages of AI and to mitigate the risks.

Ethical choice will supplement legal requirements, or, where policymakers cannot agree on policy or law, fill the vacuum. One ethical approach, in the absence of a comprehensive law or policy framework, is to adopt principles for lawyers to apply generally to each scenario, much as the law of armed conflict (LOAC) does not seek to address every possible combat scenario with a rule, but rather requires the application of the five binding principles of distinction: distinction, necessity, proportionality, minimization of suffering, and military objective.[3] The Defense Innovation Board, for example, recommended that DOD not deploy AI until an application is demonstratively responsible, equitable, traceable, reliable, and governable, principles that were adopted by the Department of Defense for combat and noncombat functions in February 2020. To this list, one might add the notion that policymakers and lawyers should not approve the use of an AI application until they purposefully determine how the following additional principles apply.

Agency. The right to decide how one's image or data is used and by whom, or at minimum to know how and by whom it is being used so that one can choose to decline consent, withdraw consent, or mitigate the consequences.

Privacy. Privacy is defined differently by different people, as well as differently by the same people in different contexts. In U.S. practice, privacy is often defined in relationship to the government, as is suggested by the continuous debate over the reach of the Fourth Amendment. In contrast, in Europe, privacy is commonly defined with respect to other persons. European governments generally have broad surveillance authority, but individuals have the right to regulate and reclaim their individual identity on social media using mechanisms such as the right to be forgotten. In authoritarian context, privacy takes on an altogether different meaning with or without the exercise of individual agency, where the interests of the state and of order usually prevail over individual privacy.

Privacy requires conscious consideration and accountable choice regarding (1) how, by whom, and for what purpose data is aggregated; (2) how, by whom, with what purpose, and with what degree of notice data sets are collected and stored; (3) the application of security safeguards commensurate with the AI value of data, not necessarily the value at the time of which it was collected; and (4) whether data is allowed to be sold or transferred overseas. Data is forever. Once obtained and stored outside the jurisdiction of U.S. law and policy, foreign entities and governments are free to use that data in consistence with their principles of privacy rather than our own.

Accountability. With accountability comes responsibility, and with responsibility comes care. With each AI application, policymakers and lawyers should ask, who is authorized to make a request? According to what standards? According to what process of review? And with what record of use? In addition, they should ensure there is a method in place to determine algorithmic design and to record its accuracy. And where AI is used to augment decision, there should be a statement on the record as to how this is/was done, just as a judge ensures that a confession was corroborated by independent evidence.

Accuracy. Designers and users of AI have a duty to ask who has validated the accuracy of the data or AI in use. We can stipulate that it would be unethical to knowingly use corrupted data, such as data intentionally altered to fool a training algorithm. But do these same actors have a responsibility to ensure the reliability of data based on its age, size, or relevance, which can also lead to inaccurate results? For example, we know that facial recognition applications are less accurate in the case of women and minorities, in part because some facial recognition algorithms are trained on data that is principally drawn from male images. One can see as well that the age of data can make a difference if an algorithm is trained on images that do not capture current reality. Military planners would not use old satellite photos of coastal defenses to plan an amphibious assault. Likewise, there is risk if there is too little data in which to train an algorithm. This is a particular risk in national security contexts, where, for example, intelligence specialists are often searching for novel or rare data matches, such as a singular propeller sound or a new missile launch. Likewise, intelligence data training sets may be unusually small, as one might imagine in the case of images of an opponent's missile inventory, or the voices of reclusive foreign leaders.

Equality. In cases where it is legal to collect data, one should also ask if it is ethical to do so based on the principle of equality. Are disfavored or disadvantaged groups treated differently for reasons not related to empirical need or programmatic purpose, and if so, why? One might also ask if the data that we are using for AI development is derived from unwitting or unwilling subjects or through contracts of adhesion, and if so, whether that matters.

Equality arises as an ethical consideration in another way. Do the benefits of AI accrue to nation-states and individuals in a fair and proportionate manner? The equitable issues are easiest to see outside the national security context, where, for example, in the medical field, AI-driven algorithms have proven better than humans at detecting tumors and screening for diabetic blindness. Are these benefits available on a need basis, or based on financial means and power?

Professional Codes and Ethical Principles

In addition to determining which ethical principles should apply to AI, lawyers and policymakers should be cognizant of, and where necessary follow, relevant professional codes. Several ethical codes apply to AI R & D and deployment when conducted by members of a covered profession. Two codes are directly apt. The National Society of Professional Engineers (NSPE)[4] promulgates a code of ethics for engineers that applies to the engineering profession generally, which is to say, mechanical, civil, electronic, and chemical engineers. The code includes numerous relevant provisions.

"Fundamental Canons" 1 and 6, for example, state:

> Engineers, in the fulfillment of their professional duties, shall: (1) hold paramount the safety, health, and welfare of the public. . . . (6) conduct themselves honorably, responsibly, ethically, and lawfully so as to enhance the honor, reputation, and usefulness of the profession.

In the category of "Rules of Practice," the code states:

> (1) Engineers shall hold paramount the safety, health, and welfare of the public (a) if engineers' judgment is overruled under circumstances that endanger life or property, they shall notify their employer or client and such other authority as may be appropriate. . . . (f) engineers having knowledge of any alleged violation of this code shall report thereon to appropriate professional bodies and, when relevant, also to public authorities, and cooperate with the proper authorities in furnishing such information or assistance as may be required.

This language is broad in scope and thus, even where binding, is too vague or general to guide or direct outcomes presenting complex or competing values, as opposed to conduct that is squarely off-code, like financial self-dealing. The NSPE also hosts an advisory hotline. Thus, engineers with AI questions could draw from a common base of advice were the hotline prepared to provide such advice. However, the majority of posted NSPE ethics opinions are addressed to topics such as conflicts of interest and service as an expert witness. AI or related terms do not appear in the index or opinion headers.

Not all states have integrated the NSPE code into their licensing requirements. Where states have done so, observance of the code is a professional requirement the violation of which can lead to license suspension or revocation. This is similar to the Model Rules of Professional Responsibility for lawyers promulgated by the American Bar Association (ABA). They are "model" and advisory unless and until adopted as a state bar licensing requirement, at which point they are binding. This also means that ethical requirements can vary from state to state based on how the rules are, or are not, amended when adopted or interpreted.

Specialized fields of engineering also promulgate ethical codes. Some are expressly voluntary. Others use directive language like "shall" rather than "should," but are drafted in hortatory or exhortatory manner. The most important such code for AI is the Institute of Electrical and Electronics Engineers (IEEE) Code of Ethics. IEEE is the primary professional association for industry and academic professionals in computer science, electronics, and electrical engineering. Like the ABA, membership in the association is voluntary, and like the ABA, there are approximately 400,000 members.[5]

The IEEE code of ethics states, in part:

> We the members of the IEEE, . . . do hereby commit ourselves to the highest ethical and professional conduct and agree:
>
> 1. To hold paramount the safety, health, and welfare of the public, to strive to comply with ethical design and sustainable development practices, and to disclose promptly factors that might endanger the public or the environment; . . .
>
> 2. To improve the understanding by individuals and society of conventional and emerging technologies, including intelligent systems.

This is general stuff. Moreover, "strive to comply" in an ethics document is like a UN resolution that "calls on" states to take "appropriate" action, designed to make states feel good, but require little in return. The IEEE, however, has done something more. The executive director of the IEEE issues an ethics newsletter to members and academics working in the AI field. In 2016, the IEEE addressed eight issue areas with respect to AI in the form of a public discussion draft and then final draft of "Ethically Aligned Design: A Vision for Prioritizing Human Wellbeing with Artificial Intelligence and Autonomous Systems" (2019). The document addresses numerous AI ethics issues, including transparency, accountability, and black box components. However, many of the issues remain in question rather than answer form in a document that is intended to be part of an iterative conversation.

Other professional codes may apply by implication to the use of AI. This might be the case, for example, for doctors working with AI applications, like the Indian ophthalmologists, referenced in chapter 2, treating diabetic blindness. In such cases, the doctors would be bound by the applicable medical code of conduct and licensing requirements, as well as the Hippocratic oath. Likewise, a government doctor, maybe at NIH, CDC, the VA, or in the military, might have cause to work with AI, perhaps with disabled veterans, bringing the operation of medical ethics to AI applications.

Lawyers working with AI would refer to the Model Rules of Professional Responsibility or state bar equivalent. None of the rules are directly on point. But some are relevant, including Rule 2.1 (Advisor), which states: "In rendering advice, a lawyer may refer not only to the law but to other considerations such as moral, economic, social, and political factors that may be relevant to a client's situation."

In other words, where AI is concerned, lawyers should not limit their advice to the authority to act and the left and right boundaries of that action, but also advise on the legal values involved and preferred outcomes. In doing so, the lawyer should clearly distinguish between what is legal advice and what is legal policy, ethical, or policy advice. (Legal advice tells the client whether they can do something. Legal policy and ethical advice tell the client whether it is a good idea to do something, as well as whether there is a better, safer, or more effective way to accomplish the same goal.)

Rule 1.6 (Confidentiality of Information) requires a lawyer, among other things, to "make reasonable efforts to prevent the inadvertent or unauthorized disclosure of, or unauthorized access to, information relating to the representation of the client." Lawyers and firms have struggled to determine just what this means in the context of cyber-security with the professional bar slow to provide specific and concrete advice. Imagine now how this rule might be tested and applied to AI-driven link analysis and the thirst for data to inform machine learning.

The obligation to protect confidential information and the capacity to do so in an AI environment relates as well to Rule 1.1 (Competence) and Rule 1.3 (Diligence). Whether lawyers like it or not, they must be comfortable with AI and competent in its use, not least because AI is increasingly used to search for and screen discovery documents. National security lawyers, however, have a greater obligation to competently understand the strengths and limitations of AI for security use and decision if they are to advise national security policymakers and operators.

Finally, Rule 1.4 (Communication) and Rule 1.13 (Organization as Client) address such issues as (1) who is the client; (2) who speaks for the client within an organization; and (3) when the client or the lawyer can or must make a decision. Machine learning–driven AI presents myriad opportunities to complicate these rules, especially when an AI application is providing the crucial decisional output. In such context, the rules will need to be clear whether the lawyer or the client is ultimately responsible for the decision as well as the way AI informed or made the decision. The rules may also need to specify when a human must make the decision as opposed to deferring to an AI algorithm.

In addition to ethical codes, there are several statements of ethical principles issued by members of the scientific research and civil society groups addressing AI, including its security use. Scholars cite two documents in particular.

The 2017 Asilomar AI principles were developed in conjunction with a conference hosted by the Future of Life Institute at the Asilomar Conference Center in California. Approximately one hundred attendees comprised of practitioners in science, engineering, and ethics drafted the twenty-three principles. "Principle 6: Safety" states: "AI systems should be safe and secure throughout their operational lifetime, and verifiably so where applicable and feasible." "Principle 9: Responsibility" states: "Designers and builders of advanced AI systems are stakeholders in the moral implications of their use, misuse, and actions, with responsibility and opportunity to shape those implications." "Principle 12: Personal Privacy" states: "People should have the right to access, manage, and control the data they generate, given AI systems' power to analyze." As these examples illustrate, the principles are both indeterminate ("where applicable and feasible") and specific (the right to manage and control personal data).

In 2018, a broad coalition of civil society organizations under the umbrella of the Public Voice Coalition issued a statement of Universal Guidelines for Artificial Intelligence in conjunction with the International Conference of Data Protection and Privacy Commissioners. The preamble addresses the purpose of the document:

> We propose these universal guidelines to guide the design and use of AI. These guidelines should be incorporated into ethical standards, adopted in national law and international agreements, and built into the design of systems. We state clearly that the primary responsibility for the AI systems must reside with those institutions that develop and deploy them.

Twelve guidelines follow, including:

(1) Right to Transparency. All individuals have the right to know the basis of an AI decision that concerns them. This includes access to the factors, the logic, and the techniques that produced the outcome.

(2) Right to Human Determination. All individuals have the right to a final determination made by a person.

(4) Accountability Obligation. Institutions must be responsible for decisions made by an AI system.

(6) Data Quality Obligation. Institutions must ensure data provenance, quality, and relevance for the data input into algorithms. Secondary use of data collected for AI processing must not exceed the original purpose of collection.

(9) Cybersecurity Obligation. Institutions must secure AI systems against cybersecurity threats.

(12) Termination Obligation. An institution that has established an AI system has an affirmative obligation to terminate the system if it will lose control of the system.

The guidelines have no legal or governmental standing and are not binding. However, like the Asilomar principles, they warrant the attention of policymakers for three reasons. First, they highlight some of the strengths and weaknesses of existing law and ethical codes. Clearly, the proponents of these documents do not feel that existing law effectively addresses the AI ethical questions presented, if at all. Second, while not necessarily offering the collective or consensus views of their professions, they do offer insight into views within the profession, demonstrating that whatever we might generally think about the ability and desire of engineers or academics to self-regulate, professional perspective is not singular or monolithic. There is a substantial component of actors within these fields concerned about AI's direction that seeks further regulation. Third, and most important, the guidelines offer a framework for considering an AI legal regime. A comprehensive legal regime must at least consider each of the guideline headers, which means purposefully include or exclude language addressing the guideline presented.

Assessment

Previous chapters underscored the importance of law in regulating AI. Law does not guarantee wise choices, but it can improve the odds of having a process that will lead to such choices and that the process is used. Moreover, law can reach across constituencies and compel, where policy encourages and ethics guide. That is a necessary thing where interests are disparate. The legislative process can also serve as an effective mechanism to adjudicate competing values as well as validate risks and opportunities.

However, law is not a panacea. Law is not enough when there are gaps in the law due to lack of a federal nexus, interest, or the political will to legislate. So, too, law may be too much if it imposes regulatory rigidity and burdens when flexibility and innovation are required. Substantive law can also have unintentional reach, especially when it seeks to regulate emerging technologies through substantive rather than procedural mechanisms. The third-party doctrine is a good example of law that has not kept pace with technology.

Sound ethical codes and principles can fill legal gaps. First, they can help to identify professional concerns before they become legislative concerns. A prudent legislator or regulator would be wise to watch the ethical debates within the IEEE and ABA to forecast the sorts of issues policymakers and legislators should address with AI. Second, while complicated, the processes for amending ethical codes, whether at the IEEE or ABA, are faster and more certain than the legislative process. Third, in any event, policymakers and legislators need to be familiar with the ethical codes so that law and ethics work in parallel and complementary manner rather than at cross-purposes. Most important, the codes provide a framework in which engineers can bring safety and security concerns forward to public or policy attention; indeed, there is an obligation to do so. Thus, whether the law favors safety or security or both, there is no excuse for engineers working in AI fields not to identify safety and security concerns involving AI. That is what NSPE Rule of Practice 1 requires. ("Engineers having knowledge of any alleged violation of this code shall report thereon to appropriate professional bodies, and when relevant, also to public authorities.") The follow-up question for government, industry, and academic policymakers is: Do their institutions provide an effective mechanism in which to do so?

Ethics alone, however, are inadequate to regulate AI. First, many of the relevant ethical codes do not bind—at best, they guide. "Strive to comply" is not a rigorous standard. Moreover, voluntary codes do not hold up well against prevailing professional incentives. They do not compete well, for example, with the financial incentives of industry or the Everest complex of academia, the desire to be the first to break new ground. Just ask an engineering professor at MIT, Caltech, or Carnegie Mellon: which is the stronger incentive—the IEEE ethical code or the desire to be first to the patent or publication finish line? Consider as well Asilomar principle 18, "AI Arms Race," stating: "An arms race in lethal autonomous weapons should be avoided." The principle may be sound, based on the risks inherent in technology arms races, but the principle is clearly aspirational, not operational. An AI "arms race" *has* started. Moreover, the Asilomar principles do not apply to the parties that matter most—the national security actors and drivers within governments around the world—nor does the principle offer insight on how to avoid a race.

Second, ethical codes are usually too general to effectively guide. For example, Asilomar principle 5, "Race Avoidance," states, "Teams developing AI systems should actively cooperate to avoid corner-cutting on safety standards." This reads more like a warning than a principle of conduct. Specific examples are not provided. By further example, the Model Rules of Professional Responsibility for lawyers, which, when adopted as bar rules, *are* binding, require lawyers to take "reasonable" steps to safeguard client confidences (rule 1.16). But what does that mean in the digital age, and is the answer the same, or should it be the same, for a solo practitioner and a large, well-resourced law firm? A more meaningful approach might adopt the one-time practice of the bar authority in the United Kingdom, which not only promulgates an ethical code, but at one time included with each principle five to ten "indicative behaviors" illustrating adherence to the principle: concrete and specific steps practitioners should take (or not take) to fulfill the ethical obligation. AI ethicists might consider a similar approach for academia and industry. For example, when it comes to shortcuts, what shortcuts and safety standards did the engineers who drafted Asilomar principle 5 have in mind and what are the indicators that such shortcuts are in use and what steps should be taken to avoid them?

Third, where ethical codes are binding on a profession, they tend to reflect a lowest common denominator of agreement, the basement of permitted conduct, not its ceiling. The Model Rules of Professional Responsibility tell lawyers what not to do—for example, steal money from clients or disclose confidences. They do not say much about achieving justice or effective representation. Even when codes are not binding, it is hard to find clear agreement. Asilomar principle 18, for example, only advises against a LAWS arms race, not arms races generally, or the potential risks of human-in-the-loop and human-out-of-the-loop scenarios.

Finally, ethical codes accent the views and interests of single disciplines—for example, engineers or lawyers. Moreover, they may not represent the views of the profession at large. Rather, they accent the views of the members of the profession who have opted into the professional associations involved and, in particular, the views of members who are part of the constitutive process of drafting and approving rules, just as the views of Google and Apple at the decisional level may or may not represent the views of rank-and-file employees. Thus, even when the codes get it right, they have less reach. Moreover, they do not reflect the sort of values adjudication that occurs with the passage of law, where multiple views and objectives are, in theory and sometimes in practice, debated and validated.

Conclusions

1. Lawyers have a duty to apply ethical principles to AI and not just legal requirements.

2. There are multiple entry points for ethical choice and input with AI, in each component area of an AI application—software, algorithm, hardware, operator, and designer—and in each stage of development and use—research, design, development, and employment.

3. There are no generic or singular answers to AI ethics questions. One size does not fit all, nor the application of one principle. If the Department of Defense has six hundred different AI projects, as the National AI Commission reports, there are likely six hundred different ways to approach the ethical questions and dilemmas described below.

4. Getting AI ethics contextually right places a premium on timely input and good process—so the right lawyer is in the right place at the right stage of development to provide the right input.

ACADEMIC ETHICS

In academia, ethical regulation generally comes in one of four forms, if it comes at all.

First, as discussed, professional codes may apply to professors and researchers who are licensed to practice in those fields.

Second, research is subject to ongoing formal and informal peer review. A lab colleague may take issue with how an experiment is structured, or with the contents of a proposal, and guide the proponents in a different direction or insist on referral to a more formal process of review. In some cases, peer review takes the more specific but still informal manifestation of a professor or institution declining to participate in a study. Peer review becomes more formal when institutions decline to fund research or publish its results in peer-reviewed journals, the lifeblood and raison d'être of many academics.

This type of informal "regulation" is illustrated by Dr. Jiankui He, a biophysics researcher in China who in 2018 announced that he had cloned the first gene-edited babies. According to media accounts, Dr. He sent e-mails to his mentor at Stanford University describing his work. The mentor responded by e-mail, encouraging Dr. He to submit his research to the internal review boards of his university and the participating hospital. The e-mail exchange included kind words of the sort that might be viewed as courtesies by the sender and encouragement by the recipient. Stanford University subsequently investigated the contact between three Stanford professors and He, concluding:

> . . . the Stanford researchers expressed serious concerns to Dr. He about his work. When Dr. He did not heed their recommendations and proceeded, Stanford researchers urged him to follow proper scientific practices, which included identifying an unmet medical need, securing informed consent, obtaining institutional review board (IRB) approval, and publishing the research in a peer-reviewed journal. Finally, the reviewers found that Stanford researchers were told by Dr. He that he had secured IRB approvals for his work.[6]

The case illustrates the shortcomings of informal review. The mentor did not have legal authority over Dr. He, only persuasive authority. In the end, Dr. He ignored the advice and, according to media reports, the Chinese government found He forged the ethical review documents. After a period of house arrest, in December 2019, in a closed Chinese criminal trial, He was convicted of forging ethical review board documents and sentenced to three years confinement and a fine of US$430,000.[7]

Third, regulation also comes in the form of grant requirements and restrictions. Here, the grantor, which is often the government, can condition how the money is spent and not spent. However, the reality is, most grants do not impose ethical requirements or limitations beyond those already contained in law or imposed through operation of the common rule pertaining to the conduct of human research—but they could. With the coming AI summer, now may be the time for the National Science Foundation, and other major government grant organizations, to consider whether it is time for a common rule for AI research and development.

A fourth mechanism for regulating academic research is known as an internal review board (IRB).

Finally, as the He case illustrates, criminal law is a definitive and ultimate mechanism of academic "regulation."

Internal Review Boards

The procedural mechanism for reviewing the ethical conduct of research at universities is an IRB. In the case of federally funded research, grant recipient institutions are required to have an IRB review any research involving human subjects. This is binding as a matter of federal law and regulation, and is known as the Common Rule.[8] It is binding because it derives from a requirement in the National Research Act of 1974. It is a rule because it is implemented by the Department of Health and Human Services using the Code of Federal Regulations. And it is common because it applies to all federal agencies awarding research grants and funding, including the Department of Defense. However, the rule is limited in two ways. It is only binding in the case of federally funded research and it only applies to research and experimentation involving humans.

Prohibitions on certain human research and restrictions on the manner in which experimentation is approved and conducted derive from the Nuremberg Code and its successor statements of principle. The Nuremberg Code is a product of the experience of World War II and the horrific use of concentration camp prisoners for inhumane medical experiments, which came to light during the Doctors Trial (1945–47). Twenty of the twenty-three defendants were medical doctors. Some defendants argued their actions were justified on the basis of security, such as the use of subjects to test the capacity of pilots to survive in North Sea waters. To rebut this defense, the prosecution called on medical testimony from an American doctor, Andrew Ivy, who outlined three principles of ethics concerning experimentation with human beings. The "good of the state" argument was rejected by the tribunal. Sixteen defendants were found guilty. Seven were hanged. However, security did bend principle in the case of Japanese experiments with biological agents on Chinese prisoners in Manchuria. The responsible military and medical personnel were not tried for war crimes; in exchange, they provided the United States information thought useful in the context of the coming Cold War with the Soviet Union.[9]

In 1947, the judges hearing the Doctors Trial cases issued the Nuremberg Code, a statement of principles involving medical research and human rights, derived from the trial. The code begins by stating: "The voluntary consent of the human subject is absolutely essential." The code goes on to include such additional principles as exhaustion of remedies ("The experiment should be such as to yield fruitful results for the good of society, unprocurable by other methods or means of study, and not random or unnecessary in nature"); minimization of suffering ("The experiment should be so conducted as to avoid all unnecessary physical and mental suffering"); and continued consent ("The human subject should be at liberty to bring the experiment to an end"). Similar international declarations—Geneva (1949) and Helsinki (1964)—followed.

Later revelation of experiments in the United States without the knowing and informed consent of the human subjects eventually led to the Belmont Report[10] and then the Common Rule, the bedrock of academic research ethics. Among the most noteworthy (and infamous) of these experiments was the U.S. Public Health Service's Tuskegee Syphilis Study, which, in the words of the Belmont Report, "studied" the untreated course of the disease using "disadvantaged, rural black men." The six hundred "participants" were told they would receive free medical care, among other benefits. However, the participants were not, in fact, treated for syphilis. This included approximately four hundred participants who were known to have syphilis even after penicillin was determined in 1947 to be an effective treatment. The "experiment" ran from 1942 until 1972, when it was disclosed by a whistleblower and stopped.

The Stanford Prison Experiment (1971) was a social psychology experiment conducted for the Office of Naval Research to provide insight on the interaction between guards and prisoners in military prisons. Student volunteers were wittingly cast in the roles of guards and prisoners in a mock confinement facility. However, the students were not told how long they would be required to participate. When the "guards" exceeded their briefs and descended into cruelty, the "prisoners" were not permitted to leave the experiment.

Finally, the MKultra program was one of several classified programs in which military and CIA personnel were given psychotropic drugs to evaluate the use of drugs as interrogation tools and for other "national security" purposes. Some of the subjects "volunteered" to participate in experiments but were not told the true purpose of the experiment and were secretly administered LSD. One service member, the named plaintiff in *United States et al v. Stanley* (483 U.S. 669, 1987) volunteered for "a chemical warfare testing program" in 1958. Other persons were not aware they were part of a program of experimentation at all and therefore also not aware they were receiving LSD and other drugs to test the drugs' impact on unwitting subjects. One subject, an army chemist named Frank Olson, fell from a building to his death while unwittingly under the influence of LSD. In response to these disclosures, President Ford issued Executive Order 11905 (1976) providing in section 5(d) restrictions on experimentation:

> Foreign intelligence agencies shall not engage in experimentation with drugs on human subjects, except with informed consent, in writing and witnessed by a disinterested third party, of each such human subject and in accordance with the guidelines issued by the National Commission for the Protection of Human Subjects of Biomedical and Behavioral Research.

In 1979, the National Commission for the Protection of Human Subjects of Biomedical and Behavioral Research issued its report, known as the Belmont Report after the Smithsonian Institution facility where the commission met. The report distinguishes between medical practice and research. It then enunciates three basic ethical principles:

1. *Respect for persons.* Individuals should be treated as autonomous agents, and persons with diminished autonomy are entitled to protection. This requires adequate information and voluntary consent.

2. *Beneficence.* Research should do no harm and maximize possible benefits and minimize possible harms.

3. *Justice.* The benefits and burdens of research should be distributed in a just manner. Equals ought to be treated equally. "An injustice occurs when some benefit to which a person is entitled is denied without good reason or when some burden is imposed unduly."

The report concludes that application of the general principles results in the following three requirements:

1. *Informed consent.* Subjects should have adequate information and opportunity to understand what will happen to them and why. The information should be presented in a manner that is comprehensible to the subjects and consent should be free from coercion or undue influence.

2. *Assessment of risks and benefits.* The research must be justified based on a careful and positive assessment of the risks and benefits of the research, using data as well as assessment of the probabilities and magnitude of potential harms.

3. *Selection of subjects.* The selection of research subjects should involve fair procedures and outcomes consistent with the principle of justice. Less burdened and vulnerable classes of persons should be called upon first, except where the research is directly related to the specific conditions of the class involved.

The Belmont Report was subsequently incorporated into the Common Rule and is implemented at universities through internal review boards. As of January 2019, all research universities comply with the Common Rule as a matter of law (attached to federal funding) or policy (as a matter of discretion applied to privately funded research). Once invoked, the IRB mechanism is primarily procedural rather than prohibitory. As called for by the Belmont Report, the IRB process requires consideration of the costs and benefits of research; a determination that alternative mechanisms to accomplish the same research objective do not exist; review of the design of any research experimentation; and the inclusion of knowing and voluntary consent from any subjects.

The Common Rule is not the only federal rule or mechanism addressing research ethics, nor the only academic rule. Government restrictions and regulations also apply to federally funded research involving embryonic stem cells. The dual use research of concern (DURC) policy covers life-science (pertaining to living organisms and their products) research that could be utilized for both benevolent and harmful purposes and thus characterized by the United States government as "dual use research" (DUR). Dual use research of concern is defined as:

> Life sciences research that, based on current understanding, can be reasonably anticipated to provide knowledge, information, products, or technologies that could be directly misapplied to pose a significant threat with broad potential consequences to public health and safety, agricultural crops and other plants, animals, the environment, material, or national security.[11]

The DURC policy is intended to encourage "a culture of responsibility" and "to ensure that dual use research of concern is identified at the institutional level and risk mitigation measures are implemented as necessary." These measures include steps to provide for biosafety, physical security, and personnel reliability. The DURC covers research involving fifteen high-consequence agents and toxins, such as anthrax. In addition, it covers seven categories of experiments, such as "enhances the harmful consequences of the agent or toxin." Specific compliance responsibilities are assigned to funding agencies, recipient institutions, and principal investigators (the academic term of art for responsible grant official).

In addition, the government regulates certain biotechnology applications pursuant to the coordinated framework for regulation of biotechnology.[12] Established in 1986 under the auspices of the Office of Science and Technology Policy (OSTP), within the executive office of the president, this framework addresses biotechnology regulation in academia and industry. The framework links policy to a patchwork of enabling laws assigning responsibilities and authorities to different agencies, such as the FDA, USDA, and EPA, over certain food, drugs, plants, and animals. Although not immediately applicable to AI, the framework is an example of a federal response to emerging technologies and warrants review for lessons applicable to AI. On the positive side, it illustrates what a comprehensive and lasting policy approach might look like in terms of government process. On the negative side, the regulation is static, relying as it does on a listed approach. An emerging technology such as AI requires a more fluid response.

As a matter of policy, many universities subject other forms of research to IRB review as well. Some universities, for example, have institutional animal care and use committees, or their equivalent, to address the ethical treatment of animals in research. Some universities subject embryonic cell research to limitations and oversight beyond that subject to federal funding restrictions. Princeton University has a small unmanned aircraft systems policy (SUAS).[13] The policy: (1) imposes restrictions on the operation of SUAS on university property; (2) prohibits certain persons and certain types of UAS from being flown on university property; and (3) includes an enforcement mechanism referencing federal, state, and local law.

Finally, many universities, or components of universities, require online training through the Collaborative Institutional Training Initiative (CITI). This is a consortium of schools that contribute to the production of online education in "research ethics, compliance, and professional development." The CITI website notes that its training is "used worldwide by over 2,200 organizations and more than 1 million users."[14] The program could serve as an AI ethics platform as well.

Conclusions

1. There already exists a framework and a process within academia and within the federal government for regulating sensitive research and development, which can serve as models for AI regulation.

2. Universities are not limited by federal law in whether and how they shape IRB policy review of AI research and experimentation. They are limited by imagination, will, and bureaucratic inertia. While it is easy to conclude that certain types of research should be precluded, it is also easy to see why blanket prohibitions are problematic. What is noteworthy is that most IRB processes do not include additional review mechanisms beyond those addressed to human experimentation research. For example, one might expect to find more requirements to review all or certain uses of animals for research and experimentation, or the use of certain infectious diseases to conduct research in synthetic biology.

3. The policy question for academics and the government is what types of AI research or experimentation should be subject to IRB review, if any? Such an IRB might review and validate the following illustrative project components or indicate why they are not applicable to the research or experiment in question:

   A counterintelligence plan. A statement regarding the security implications, if any, of the research, including procedures for ensuring the reliability of participants and their foreign connections, if any.

   A data management plan. Such a plan might articulate the legal authority for the collection and use of machine learning data sets; incorporate minimization and retention procedures regarding the data; and provide a security plan for the ongoing cyber security of the data.

   Proof of algorithmic design. A statement of algorithmic design indicating how it will be used, what it will search for, how it will control for bias, and how it will provide for transparent and accountable results.

   Research parameters and limitations. Indication as to whether AI applications will be linked to the university's IT systems or the internet, and if so, subject to what controls and safeguards.

   Declaration of responsibility. The designation of official(s) responsible for specific aspects of research or its safeguards beyond the designation of a principal investigator responsible for overall performance of the research.

FROM CORPORATE SOCIAL RESPONSIBILITY TO CORPORATE SECURITY RESPONSIBILITY

As noted throughout, AI research, development, and deployment is driven by the private sector. This is true of national security as well as commercial applications. That makes purposeful choices about the regulation of private industry a national security necessity. It also makes corporate social responsibility, especially to national security, a compelling subject for policy consideration. Moreover, where self-regulation in the form of CSR proves inadequate, the government is more likely to affirmatively seek to influence behavior and outcomes through law. Thus, industry actors, and not just academics, should take an active interest in how CSR is defined and applied. This section explores the concept of CSR and then reviews additional sources of leverage the government may use where CSR falls short.

Corporate Social Responsibility

Where the law is silent or inadequate, or government policy uncertain, CSR may be the primary source of policy influence to guide corporate behavior. With AI, this might be known as corporate ethics or corporate *security* responsibility. CSR may derive from patriotism, as was the case with AT&T and electronic surveillance before FISA established a system of court review and orders requiring carrier compliance. It is also true of the traditional defense companies associated with the defense industrial base, where business and patriotism often align.[15] CSR can also derive from a sense of market self-interest, client pressure, altruism, employee pressure, or all four at once.

This was the apparent case with Google's participation in the Maven Project. In an open letter to Google CEO Sundar Pichai in August 2018, over three thousand employees implored the company to "cancel the Maven Project," which the letter described as "a customized AI surveillance engine that uses 'Wide Area Motion Imagery' data captured by U.S. government drones to detect vehicles and other objects, track their motions, and provide results to the Department of Defense."[16] The letter invoked the company's then-motto—"Don't Be Evil"—and stated, among other things, "This plan will irreparably damage Google's brand and its ability to compete for talent" and "We cannot outsource the moral responsibility of our technologies to third parties." Google subsequently canceled its participation in the project.

Amazon employees have also engaged in grassroots protests of the company's involvement in AI security applications, most notably Amazon's involvement in the next generation of DOD's cloud computing enterprise. However, Amazon CEO, Jeff Bezos, responded differently than Google's Pichai. Amazon's efforts to win the contract continued with Bezos widely quoted saying,

> We are going to continue to support the DOD and I think we should. It does not make any sense to me—one of the jobs of a senior leadership team is to make the right decision even when it's unpopular. . . . And if big tech companies are going to turn their back on the U.S. Department of Defense, this country is going to be in trouble. This is a great country and it needs to be defended.[17]

Whether this reflects a difference in philosophy about AI and CSR between two of the AI giants, or just a different assessment of the importance of defense contracts to the company's business model, is not clear. What is clear is that CSR will continue to be influenced by consumer views, employee views, corporate and brand reputation, and the ability to attract human capital.

CSR is not a new concept. It has been a field of academic study since the 1950s; however, as the scholars S. N. Bhaduri and E. Selarka recount, the impetus for corporations to act out of a sense of social responsibility as well as business interest has changed over time.[18] In the 1950s and 1960s, CSR was driven from the C-Suite, if it was there at all, based on the interests of the leadership team. It was defined by philanthropic giving, especially to the arts, but also included such things as efforts to update company towns.[19] The 1970s and 1980s saw the advent of grassroots campaigns by shareholders and the public for corporate divestment in support of the anti-apartheid movement in South Africa. There was no regulatory requirement to do so; indeed, in the case of the United States and United Kingdom, government policy at times disfavored divestment. Nonetheless, many companies divested based on real and perceived market pressure from consumers, or potential consumers, expressing their own sense of social responsibility. The 1990s, in turn, saw the ascendency of environmental stewardship as a CSR value.

What is CSR? One study cites over twenty-five different definitions.[20] One definition describes CSR as a range of corporate obligations—economic, legal, ethical, and discretionary. In this sense, CSR is what guides the policy choices corporations make addressing competing pressures and values—for example, whether to privilege safety over speed or security over profit, or whether to adopt what the Europeans refer to as a precautionary approach, purposefully erring on the side of safety or security in risk management. Adaeze Okoye of the University of Brighton looks at CSR from a procedural perspective using a "stakeholder model."[21] In this model, the responsibility is to a process of communication and collaboration between stakeholders—government, corporations, and society—and not to a particular outcome or value. No doubt, CSR derives from as many inputs as there are corporations. Adherence to best cybersecurity practices, for example, is an exercise in social responsibility but also good business. For this reason, Darren Tromblay, former intelligence analyst and commentator, refers to CSR as "triple bottom line accounting," measuring social, environmental, and financial outcomes, each intended to appeal to consumers, attract human capital, and enhance a company's bottom line.[22]

However, there is a school of thought, associated with the economist Milton Friedman, that the responsibility of a corporation, social or otherwise, is to its shareholders, and that means a responsibility to maximize profit. Friedman wrote: "There is one and only one social responsibility of business—to use its resources and engage in activities designed to increase its profits, so long as it stays within the rules of the game, which is to say, engages in open and free competition without fraud."[23] Businesses are in the business of business. For-profit businesses exist to make a profit. A CEO that does not do so is not likely to remain the CEO. At the same time, it is worth noting that as a matter of law, corporate officers and boards of directors do not have a fiduciary duty to the corporation or its shareholders to maximize profit, but rather to exercise sound business judgment.

For directors and officers, corporate fiduciary duty is generally defined with respect to the "interests of the corporation." The qualifier "generally" is used because corporate law is governed by state rather than federal law, which is, in part, why so many corporations are incorporated in Delaware, where state law is favorable to corporate interests. That means that corporate duties may vary from state to state. However, the Model Business Corporation Act sets a baseline: "Each member of the board of directors . . . shall act: (1) in good faith, and (2) in a manner the director reasonably believes to be in the best interests of the corporation." Corporate officers generally have three fiduciary duties. First, a duty of care, which is an obligation to exercise their authority in good faith and with the ordinary judgment of a prudent person in a similar position. This is sometimes referred to as the business judgment rule. Second, a duty of loyalty, which generally means with the interest of the corporation in mind—not, for example, an officer's own conflicting interests (although sometimes conflicts might be disclosed and authorized, in which case the process is as important as the substance). The requirement to act in good faith may be viewed as a separate third duty or as an integral component of the duty of care and of loyalty.

In August 2019, the Business Roundtable issued a "Statement on the Purpose of a Corporation," declaring "a fundamental commitment to *all* our stakeholders," including "delivering value to our customers"; "investing in our employees"; "delivering fairly and ethically to our suppliers"; "supporting the communities in which we work"; and "generating long-term value for our shareholders." The statement is noteworthy for three reasons. First, the Business Roundtable is an "association of chief executive officers of America's leading companies" (and lobbying organization) representing more than 15 million employees and US$7 trillion in revenues. Over 180 CEOs have signed the statement. Second, the statement appears to adopt a stakeholder model of CSR, with emphasis on long-term value to shareholders, as opposed to short-term profits. Third, the statement represents a notable shift from the Roundtable's 1997 statement, which adopted the Friedman perspective, declaring, in bold letters: "In the Business Roundtable's view, the paramount duty of management and of boards of directors is to the corporation's stockholders." The 2019 statement is surely an exercise in corporate communications and marketing, not a statement of individual corporate policy. Skeptics have adopted a wait-and-see attitude, pointing to, among other things, the disconnect between individual corporate policies and the long-term consequences of climate change on customers, employees, and communities.[24] The statement, however, may reflect an awareness of consumer values. It can also serve as a vehicle to invigorate debate about AI and CSR as well as greater consensus about the security responsibilities of American corporations.

Why does CSR matter? Corporations, and those who lead corporations, have more policy discretion in how they define their social and security responsibilities with respect to AI than policymakers and lawyers may assume. Moreover, the CEOs of over 180 of America's largest and most profitable corporations agree. Profit is a motive, but it is not an exclusive or singular requirement.

Assessment

CSR is a critical component of AI regulation because so little of AI practice is delimited by law. Restated, the law's boundaries are wide, leaving ample room for corporate policy discretion. However, as Richard Danzig notes, "There is no American consensus about the American responsibilities of American corporations."[25] Corporations, like governments, act for multiple reasons at once, including reasons of public perception and profit. Thus, when Apple's Tim Cook expresses a responsibility to protect the privacy of iPhone users, he is certainly also expressing a business judgment that more consumers will buy a secure phone than one that has a trapdoor. CSR is public relations as well as altruism.

There is no obligation for corporations to apply CSR principles; however, to the extent they do not do so, they may encounter increased government pressure in the form of unwanted publicity, litigation, and the prospect of legislative or regulatory compulsion. Four issues, in particular, may determine how much pressure.

1. ***The need for a uniform security approach.*** National security policy only works if it is *national* in scope and actually provides for the security of the United States. CSR is an uncertain foundation on which to rest national security. It lacks uniformity and is unpredictable in result. Corporations are not required to hold or share security values, and even when they do, they rightly remain free to emphasize one value in one context and a different value in another. There is also a security-business dilemma. One corporation's act of security responsibility may be another corporation's business opportunity as it fills the vacuum of demand for a product or application, perhaps from an authoritarian regime. A global economy with multilateral corporations adds to the challenge of uniformity.

2. ***The security-business trade-off of business with China.*** A central challenge to defining CSR for American corporations with global markets is when, how, and subject to what conditions to engage in business in China and with China. Here, conditions can mean Chinese conditions, such as access to technology, as well as U.S. conditions, such as CFIUS-based restrictions on partnering with certain companies or in certain sectors. The nature of AI data and the hardware supply chain make it inevitable that American corporations will face values choices in conducting business in China or with Chinese companies. The COVID-19 pandemic will surely change America's economic as well as diplomatic relationship with China. One lesson learned already is that the United States should not rely on single source, and in some cases foreign source, supply chains. But COVID-19 will not change the financial incentives for accessing the Chinese market, nor China's interest in AI technology and data. Just as the encryption debate ultimately requires corporations to break one way or the other,

so, too, corporations will have to make affirmative choices when security and market interests conflict in China and elsewhere; "neutrality" is not a neutral option when U.S. and Chinese interests or requirements conflict. Where these choices fall, and whether they fall with consistency, will go a long way in determining whether the U.S. government responds with exhortation or new sanctions laws or IEEPA and CFIUS trade restrictions. Corporations would be wise to make purposeful choices based on careful and proactive considerations of long-term policy rather than the immediate interests in a given security or business moment.

3. *Encryption.* Perhaps the most visible and serial debate about CSR in the area of national security involves encryption and the going-dark debate. This debate has been ongoing at least since Clipper Chip in the 1990s. It continues today, manifest in arguments over whether Apple should be compelled to create a means for government to access iPhone data, when ordered to do so by a court. The issue remains open, in part, because the government has interests on both sides. However, this may change. It may change in the direction of encryption as the public becomes consciously aware of the potential of AI to unmask data and connections within that data. Or it may change in the other direction, were the government unable to prevent the occurrence of a catastrophic event on account of its lack of access to encrypted communications or devices.

4. *Public perceptions of privacy.* U.S. views of privacy are different than European views. In general, the U.S. constitutional and statutory privacy regime is designed to protect private information from government search and seizure without lawful cause, and to prevent its misuse once obtained. European views, reflected in the EU General Data Privacy Regulation, lean toward the protection of individual privacy from external actors generally and place greater emphasis on voluntary and actual consent to disclosure and use versus constructive consent in the form of the Third Party and other doctrines. But this may change.

Public views may change with greater awareness and understanding of AI and the IoT. The public may awaken, as the Supreme Court did in *Carpenter*, to the realization that AI algorithms allow the aggregation of data in ways that emasculate privacy whether data is in public or private hands. The affirmative conduct of social media companies or their inability to respond effectively to real world events, like the Christchurch attacks, may also generate change. If so, corporations may first seek to head off binding regulatory requirements with discretionary expressions of CSR. Whether they do so effectively and sincerely will drive the debate. Perceptions and the law may also change in response to the COVID-19 pandemic and the real and perceived need for AI-driven contact tracing in order to return to "normal." One senses that, like a giant tanker splitting ocean waves, the pandemic will further harden and divide the public into privacy and security camps as it has divided some Americans into "open the economy" and public health camps.

These issues, alone or collectively, are likely to determine the extent to which AI is regulated by law or discretionary corporate policy. Rather than wait for events to determine public sentiment and compel policy, policymakers and corporate leaders would be wise to fully engage in a public-private dialogue about corporate security responsibility before turning to the additional levers of influence described below.

Levers for Influencing Corporate Behavior

Law and government policy can influence corporate conduct in multiple ways. Where the government is a consumer, as with military hardware, it can set standards and impose contractual requirements. However, this type of influence is limited to those companies working in this space. The government can also shape corporate practice using the bully pulpit, as illustrated by the 2019 campaign to discredit Huawei as a 5G security risk.

Federal or state law can impose or compel behavior through direct regulation as in the case of environmental standards like the California fuel efficiency standards or the federal prohibition on the use of DDT. The government can also condition market access through the licensing and permit process. The CFIUS process is a case in point, where the government can require foreign-owned or -directed corporations to mitigate national security concerns or bar their market participation.

Federal and state law can also incentivize behavior, a form of indirect regulation. This can be done with tax credits, favorable grant and loan terms, or antitrust exemptions, all of which are authorized in the DPA. The government can also influence behavior through the threat of criminal sanctions, such as those found in export control laws and those regulating financial transactions with governments, entities, and individuals designated by the president under IEEPA and specific sanctions legislation.

Federal and state law can also incentivize corporate risk taking and investment by limiting or eliminating liability. The Public Readiness and Emergency Preparedness Act of 2005, for example, provides immunity from tort liability (in the absence of willful misconduct) for the development, manufacture, testing, distribution, and administration of countermeasures for public health emergencies. The act covers vaccines, drugs, and other products, and requires a predicate declaration of public health emergency from the secretary of health and human services. Likewise, the Cybersecurity Information Sharing Act provides liability protection to entities that share threat information and defensive measures with the government and certain designated private information-sharing centers and organizations.

Most notably for AI, section 230 of the Communications Decency Act of 1996,[26] with limited exception, exempts social media platforms from liability for what is posted on their platforms. The law states: "No provider or user of an interactive computer service shall be treated as the publisher or speaker of any information provided by another information content provider." The exemption was intended to negate a 1995 New York state case[27] applying the New York libel standard for a publisher to an internet service provider (ISP) on the theory that the ISP was playing an editorial role as host. Congress responded with section 230. The law was intended to protect ISPs to encourage development of the internet. It worked. One policy question now is whether the law has worked too well, allowing ISPs and social media platforms a free pass when it comes to third party conduct on their platforms. A second question is whether the role and responsibility of platforms is best addressed through law, regulation, or self-regulation in the form of CSR policy.

Leverage can also be asserted through regulation of the insurance industry, insurance costs, and limitations on coverage. Litigation may have the same effect, because it may influence the cost of insurance or affect reputation and thus market share.

International regulation and practice can also shape domestic corporate behavior where foreign regulatory compliance may be a requirement for market entry or presence, or where compliance makes it too costly to maintain multiple standards of conduct. The former circumstance is evident in the way companies respond to Chinese requirements to transfer technology or limit access to the internet. It is also evident in the manner that social media companies have addressed the General Data Protection Regulation (GDPR) and country-specific content laws. Because of the First Amendment, for example, U.S. law is less permissive than the GDPR in regulating hate speech. Germany, on the other hand, because of its experience with Nazi fascism, goes beyond the GDPR in criminalizing hate speech. Social media platforms, therefore, must decide whether it is more cost- and result-effective to apply a uniform standard, adopt distinct country-specific standards, or opt out of a market altogether.

Finally, the government can influence corporate behavior by establishing best practice standards and certifying those practices. Corporations may have a market and marketing incentive to adopt those standards to validate their products and service quality.

TAKEAWAYS

1. Where AI is concerned, ethics codes should include indicative actions illustrating compliance with the code's requirements. Otherwise, individual actors will independently define terms like "public safety" and "reasonable" subject to their own competing values. This will result in inconsistent and lowest common denominator ethics.

2. Most AI R & D is academic and corporate; therefore, IRB and CSR practice are critical in filling the gaps between law and professional ethics. They are also essential in identifying regulatory gaps. Policymakers, take note.

3. Policymakers should consider the "Universal Guidelines for Artificial Intelligence," which build upon the Asilomar principles, among other existing ethical frameworks, laws, and conventions, as a legislative checklist. That is not to say they should adopt the guidelines. Rather they should use them to make purposeful and deliberate choices about what to include or not include in an AI regulatory regime comprised of law, ethics, and CSR.

4. Academic leaders and government officials should actively consider whether to subject AI R & D to IRB review. They should further consider whether to apply a burden of proof, persuasion, or a precautionary principle to high-risk AI activities, such as those that link AI to the internet, pose CI risks, link to kinetic and cyber-weapons, or remove humans from an active control loop.

5. Corporations have discretion in whether and how to adopt CSR national security policies. They should consciously do so, defining what it means to be an "American corporation," to use Richard Danzig's term. That also means

they should create a governance process with which to do so. As with government, it is easier to set corporate policy outside the context of crisis and litigation. Like the national security lawyer who articulates why following the law also improves security, the CSR advocate should articulate why an action is good for business and not just the right thing to do.

6. The government often enunciates policy in terms of public-private partnerships. Corporations should consider doing so as well, by adopting a stakeholder model of CSR. A stakeholder model shares the burden and the responsibility between industry and government to find common ground, mitigate risks, and identify long-term shared interests, including national interests in AI security.

7. Policymakers, lawyers, and corporate leaders should actively engage in ongoing dialogue regarding the four issues that may define the tone, tenor, and content of government-industry relations: uniformity in response, business with and in China, encryption, and privacy.

8. Sometimes the security problem is not with CSR, but with the inability of the government to enunciate a clear policy or adopt a single position. Some corporations may well align with one government value over another. In such cases, the problem is not necessarily with corporate governance, but with the government itself. The government should check the mirror before critiquing corporate conduct.

9. In all regards, policymakers should consider whether we, as a nation, are effectively wielding the instruments available to maximize the security benefits of AI while minimizing the risks. This requires consideration of policy and law, but also ethics, academic regulation, and CSR.

ELEVEN

The Centaur's Choice

CONCLUSION

Law and ethics seek to guide, influence, and in some cases control human behavior. The challenge with AI, the centaur's dilemma, is how best to regulate machine behavior as well as human behavior and the interface between the two. To do so in a wise and comprehensive manner, policymakers must, at minimum, accomplish four tasks.

First, *policymakers must act*. They must make purposeful decisions—decisions of law, policy, and process. And they should do so in as transparent, responsible, and accountable a manner as security permits. That is the manner most likely to lead or compel like-minded response from other states and thus avoid the asymmetric dilemma of regulating one's own conduct while other states do nothing. Transparency also permits policymakers to better see problems and adjust ineffective policy. Clear lines of responsibility, authority, and accountability allow policymakers to better determine whether problems, and thus solutions, are technical, procedural, or rooted in policy or personality shortcomings. The complexity of regulating AI, its fields and subfields, along with AI's disparate stakeholders, can make this space feel ungovernable. However, if the U.S. government does not take a position or act to fill the vacuum on what laws do or should apply to AI, the answers will arrive by default anyway. Legal policy will be determined in a decentralized manner by individual actors, reflecting the specific interests of those actors.

Second, *policymakers must shape and wield the power of all three purposes of national security law.*

The authority to act, and the left and right boundaries of action. Law and policy guidance is needed to define the government's authority to collect, retain, search, and use data from the IoT, from existing databases, from overseas, and from the internet to fuel AI and against which to run AI applications. Law and policy are also needed to regulate the collection, storage, use, and transfer of data held in private or foreign hands. We know this. Likewise, law and policy are necessary to define supply chain and counterintelligence responsibilities and requirements for government, as well as industry and academic actors. We know this, too. In the absence of statutory boundaries, the boundaries of governmental action will necessarily fall upon the First, Fourth, and Fifth Amendments, with all the uncertainty, inconsistency, and tension of constitutional law and litigation. It also means that corporate and academic boundaries will depend as much on policy—ethics, IRBs, and CSR—as they do on national policy set in law.

Another thing the government can do immediately is determine how it might use existing law to answer AI governance and authorization questions. In doing so, it might also identify issues most likely to lead to litigation or legislative dispute and either reach accord on those issues with key parties or find opportunities to test and adjudicate the reach and limits of existing law rather than delay until a later moment of crisis.

This might be done by using existing authority and seeing who objects, why, and how. This might also be done using legislative vehicles, such as the periodic reauthorization of the DPA. "Adjudication" might also occur within the executive branch at the policy table, or by putting key legal questions before the office of legal counsel or the lawyers' group. By litigating and adjudicating questions now, the government and commentators will have a better understanding of what elements are needed (or need amendment) within an AI legal regime.

Essential process set for machine speed. Law and policy rarely keep pace with technology. Where technology is emerging—which is to say, arriving in unexpected and exponential manner—substantive law and policy will not keep pace. We know this. That places a premium on getting the process right—timely, contextual, and meaningful—by having the right people involved in the design of AI, developing doctrine for AI, and in the room when AI is used. It also means having a process that can operate at machine speed through pre-delegation—to machines and to the human decisional chains—

but that is also nimble enough and human enough to take control or retain control of AI applications when it is wise or necessary to do so. That is the Turing test of process.

In government, commentators refer to "whole of government" problems and solutions. These involve challenges that reach across departments and disciplines and require the resources and skills of multiple agencies. Most national security problems do. AI does. AI also requires a whole of nation response—or, to use an apt phrase coined by Lyad Rahwan (director of the Max Planck Institute for Human Development and associate professor at MIT), "society-in-the-loop."[1] Such a process will offer industry, academia, and the public opportunity to voice the pros and cons of options as well as condition expectations going forward. Moreover, the viability of most AI policy goals, like supply chain security or accountable design, inexorably link constituencies. Likewise, the most important national security applications for the government may depend on private data and academic know-how. Therefore, an effective as well as enduring framework must include all three constituencies and operate with their acceptance, or at least acquiescence. This requires law.

Legal values and national security values. What is lawful is not necessarily what is wise. Policy should be guided by core constitutional values, especially those embedded in the First, Fourth, and Fifth Amendments. Many of these values are also security values or bring with them security virtues. These values will also generate the most controversy in shaping policy or in the public's response to policy that addresses the sometime tension between security and liberty. Questions about authority are often proxies for underlying disputes over values. Should the law favor privacy or security, or is it possible to favor both at once? This tension is not new. The constitution is intended to provide for the common defense *and* preserve liberty. Over time, there have been new contexts and opportunities to debate and address these tensions. The Cold War presented one context, 9/11 another. An AI technology race will present a third. And it will come with new dimensions, new actors, new threats, and new perceptions about how the First, Fourth, and Fifth Amendments should apply to the interaction between government and the public, as well as government and private industry.

The two questions policymakers need to urgently address today are: Does the government have the authority it needs to wield the power and potential of AI for national security purposes? And does U.S. law and policy addressed to AI data, bias, and use reflect our constitutional values and our considered ethical principles? Corporate and academic actors need to ask, as Richard

Danzig has, what does it mean to be an American corporation? Or an American university?

Third, *policymakers must meet and purposefully address the centaur's dilemma.* How to harness the power and promise of AI without losing control over the implications of its use. It is the centaur's dilemma, rather than centaur dilemma, because the human part of the centaur has a choice. Dire predictions aside, humans are not passive actors in an inexorable march forward. As this book demonstrates, we have choices, lots of them. This is our destiny. We own AI and we can shape it. One of the challenges of AI regulation is also a virtue. There is ample opportunity to shape the field, because there are so many possibilities to do so with the ways AI applications are researched, designed, and deployed; with software, hardware, and design; and with each individual application.

Law is a search for metaphor. That is part of the common law. And it is what lawyers do when they do not find law on point. They fill the void by analogy. Policymakers do, too. They seek to influence the future by looking to the past for historical parallels and lessons—policy metaphors. Generals are sometimes said to prepare to fight the last war rather than the next. The challenge is drawing the right lesson from the past while appreciating that the future will be different from the past.

With AI, there are useful legal and policy analogies from which to adopt, adapt, and apply lessons, principles, and law. From the law of armed conflict, we draw six immediate principles that apply directly to the use of AI as a military enabler for logistics, intelligence, and command, as well as potentially as a lethal weapon. These principles also serve as analogy for AI generally through adoption and adaption. They are:

Weapons testing. If states are required to test weapons for compliance with the law of armed conflict, why not AI applications as well?

Duty to instruct. States are required to provide appropriate instruction to military members on the law of armed conflict. Why not require instruction on the law and ethical use of AI?

Command responsibility. AI philosophers bemoan the advent of autonomous and automatic systems. But autonomy need not eliminate responsibility. The doctrine of command responsibility illustrates. It remains in effect in armed conflict whether the commander fully appreciates what is going on or not. The commander must exercise command and control or put in place processes that allow him to do so. Further, the doctrine can be adapted and adopted to apply to civilian uses of AI.

Perfidy and ruse. The law of armed conflict distinguishes between lawful and unlawful efforts to deceive the enemy. The distinction reflects real law, black letter law that is enforceable. Why not do the same with certain deep fakes, AI applications that could affect critical infrastructures, and nuclear command and control.

Targeting principles and prohibitions. AI raises the prospect of autonomous weapons. It may also change the meaning of military objective—in practice, if not in law. If law seeks to guide the use of AI, now is the time to shape the principles and prohibitory lines that might apply, for example, to the targeting of AI labs in industry and academia.

Like-minded initiatives. The Ottawa Treaty and process demonstrates that where consequences are diffuse, power may be diffuse as well. Individual states and actors need not wait for the dominant powers to act to regulate AI.

Fourth, *policymakers should study and apply past lessons.* Joseph Nye has observed, "Large groups and organizations often learn by crises and major events that serve as metaphors for organizing and dramatizing diverse sets of experiences. The Berlin crises and particularly the Cuban missile crisis of the early 1960s played such a role."[2] Hurricane Katrina and 9/11 played a similar role with respect to homeland security. The COVID-19 pandemic will play a similar role. What will we learn and what should we already have known that applies to AI? The following are five such lessons:

1. We should prepare for challenges we know will come. AI is such a challenge. COVID-19 was too. The United States and the world had strategic notice that a pandemic would come; epidemiologists and security specialists have been saying so for years. What they did not know until December 2019 and January 2020 was when and in what form. Likewise, we know now that AI is coming and coming hard with known risks and potential benefits. What we do not know is when the breakout moments will occur and what they will look like. But we had better be prepared. AI specialists should ask: Is my message getting through? If not, is that a failure in communication, or is it a lack of policy priority and will? With pandemic planning the message was received, but it did not translate into sufficient policy priority. It is not clear in which category AI falls. Do policymakers understand what is coming?

2. COVID-19 also reminds us that expertise matters. Health policy requires science. AI requires engineers. Supply chains require logisticians. Vaccines require biologists. Policy generalists and politicians can no more address AI by themselves as they can COVID-19. AI will require a team effort to

include technologists, statisticians, lawyers, and ethicists. When you are the one in need of care, you do not care how old your EMT, doctor, nurse, or physician assistant is; you care that they know what they are doing. You want the right people in the room at all levels of government and in industry too. Time now to identify those people for AI.

3. Government process can be good or bad. Good process leads to better results; bad process leads to bad results. With COVID-19 we have seen both. Time now to identify process that works and works well for AI. Everything is harder when it is not planned, practiced, or prepared.

4. National security policy works best when it is national in scope, clearly communicated, and consistently applied. Like COVID-19, AI is not someone else's challenge or problem; it will affect all aspects of society as well as national security. It will involve industry, academia, and the government working together, which requires leadership that can unite diffuse constituencies around shared goals and values. And, like public health, AI is not a quick-fix challenge; it will require sustained effort across administrations and across political, regional, and functional divides. That requires leaders who can see over the horizon, have vision, can set goals, and know how to provide experts the time, resources, and space they need to create, set, and implement sound policy and programs.

5. Finally, law matters. Law allows systemic challenges to be met with systemic rather than episodic responses, but only if we use the law wisely and well. In moments of panic and crisis law can help us hold to good process and keep to our values, by defining those values in advance, setting the right and left boundaries of action, and requiring mechanisms for meaningful legal oversight and policy appraisal. Why does law matter? Because without it, we will not wield the power and potential of AI as wisely and beneficially, nor manage its risks as well.

However, there is risk in drawing too many lessons from too few crises. Governments and bureaucracies often behave differently in crisis than in periods of calm permitting deeper reflection.

With AI, one might hope we do not learn solely from crises. Rather, as Nye suggests with respect to cybersecurity, why not apply the lessons learned from the nuclear arms race *now* rather than wait for a crisis to do so tomorrow. Here are some of the lessons.

- Arms races have an inexorable momentum, especially when harnessed to the energy and virtue of national security—the national security imperative. For this reason, regulation will not emerge spontaneously from the critical protagonists in industry, government, and academia. Policy actors must make it happen.

- Policymakers must make conscious choices to regulate AI and control the AI arms race. That requires driven leadership. In the Cold War nuclear arms race, that leadership came from the top, as well as from within the bureaucracy. Think of how closely President Eisenhower is associated with the IAEA, President Kennedy with the Limited Test Ban Treaty and the hotline, President Nixon with the BWC, President Reagan with Reykjavik and the INF, and Presidents Reagan, Bush, and Clinton with the CWC.

- One arms control lesson is that it is a lot easier to delimit the development and deployment of weapons before they are conceived, developed, and deployed than after. It is also easier to do so in times of relative stability and détente than during times of overt or cold war. Moreover, once a state achieves a real or perceived tactical advantage—for example, in bombers, missiles, or submarines—it is less likely to negotiate away that advantage in exchange for an overall strategic gain in stability. *But*, if necessary, control is possible in times of crisis and hostility. We have seen it done during the Cold War.

- From the nuclear arms race we also learn of the importance of doctrine as well as how doctrine shapes concepts like first use, assured destruction, and deterrence. These concepts did not emerge from whole cloth. They emerged over time. These Cold War concepts return today with new resonance without an accompanying doctrine or concept of deterrence and control. One lesson from the Cold War is that we are unlikely to get doctrine right at the outset. Nuclear doctrine was tested and debated in universities and war colleges, think tanks and situation rooms; this is not yet the case with AI. In the absence of an agreed-upon doctrine, individual entities and actors will define their own left and right policy and doctrinal boundaries, program by program and project by project. Remember, "You get what you inspect, not what you expect."

- The nuclear arms race also illustrates the importance of consciously defining a culture of security, safety, and control, where the risks are great and the timelines small. Further, even where the culture is professional and practiced, mistakes happen. During the Cold War nuclear arms race, redundancy proved critical, as did having humans in the loop.

- Human decision and chance also played a role. Even where command and control was designed and consciously exercised at the highest levels to prevent accidental or unintentional war, critical decisions were made—by Fidel Castro and his air defense forces to shoot down an American U-2 —and not made—by Lieutenant Colonel Petrov and Commander Arkhipov—that could have resulted in nuclear calamity. AI command and control must ensure that low-level actors, allied actors, or indeed software does not dictate or determine outcomes that are not intended at the national level of policy decision and command.

- Finally, the CWC, in text and in practice, demonstrates that the international regulation of a dual-use technology and industry is possible. While verification is not perfect, the CWC offers a viable model of verification to include an international organization, on-site inspections, and trade secrets protection. The Outer Space Treaty, in turn, offers one template for addressing liability from AI in the global commons.

Armed with such knowledge, one might ask six critical questions:

1. Should the United States and/or the international community— unilaterally, bilaterally, or multilaterally—forgo or renounce an AI competency? And in any case, what is the most effective vehicle by which to do so—for example, international law, domestic law, executive directive, or policy statement? And should such efforts be pursued on a unilateral, bilateral, and/or multilateral basis?

2. Should the United States or international community establish an agency—domestic, international, or both—to regulate the development of AI and/or ensure its use for specific or delimited governmental purposes?

3. Should the United States develop a doctrine for AI in national security context, to include principles of command and control and delegation?

4. Should the United States, and/or select actors, and/or the international community, develop rules of the road and other confidence building measures in the AI field?

5. If so, what form should these endeavor(s) take? And, if not now, when?

6. Should the United States develop a purposeful legal and ethical regime to regulate the use of AI for national security and do so cognizant of all three

purposes of law? Conversely, what are the risks and consequences of not doing so?

AI is not a runaway train. It is a train with human conductors who can either step up and conduct or sit back and hope the train arrives on schedule at the right station and does not jump the rails en route. The governance question is who should or will decide to conduct this journey and in what manner. That requires purposeful and informed decisions about technology, policy, and law.

NOTES

Chapter 1

1. See Jeffrey Ding, "Deciphering China's AI Dream, Governance of AI Program," Future of Humanity Institute, Oxford University, March 2018; Elsa Kania, "China's Artificial Intelligence Revolution," *Diplomat*, July 27, 2017; "A Next Generation Artificial Intelligence Development Plan," China State Council (July 2017), https://flia.org/notice-state-council-issuing-new-generation-artificial-intelligence-development-plan/.

2. See Remco Zwetsloot, "Strengthening the U.S. AI Workforce: A Policy and Research Agenda," Center for Security and Emerging Technology, September 2019; Bruce Anderson, "These Are the Fastest-Growing Jobs around the World," https://business.linkedin.com/talent-solutions/blog/trends-and-research/2019/fastest-growing-jobs-2019.

3. McKinsey Global Institute, Artificial Intelligence: The Next Digital Frontier (June 2017).

4. CTBTO Preparatory Commission, "Manhattan Project" (2019), www.ctbto.org/nuclear-testing/history-of-nuclear-testing/manhattan-project/.

5. National Security Commission on Artificial Intelligence (NSCAI), Interim Report, November 2019, 7.

6. Ibid., 8.

Chapter 2

1. Nick Bostrum, *Superintelligence: Paths, Dangers, Strategies* (Oxford University Press, 2014), 6.

2. *Artificial Intelligence and Life in 2030: One Hundred Year Study on Artificial Intelligence*, Stanford University, Report of the 2015 Study Panel, September 2016, 4.

3. Processing Power Compared, https://pages.experts-exchange.com/processing-power-compared.

4. Here is an example of a "simple" algorithm used to search a sorted array. A sorted array is data sorted in a particular order. A binary search compares the value at hand to the middle of the array. This example is taken from https://www .codementor.io/learn-programming/3-essential-algorithm-examples-you-should -know):

```
def binary_search(arr, value, offset=0)
mid = (arr.length) / 2

if value < arr[mid] binary_search(arr[0...mid], value, offset) elsif value > arr[mid]
binary_search(arr[(mid + 1)..-1], value, offset + mid + 1)

else
return offset + mid
end

end
```

5. "The Return of the Machinery Question," *Economist*, Special Report, Artificial Intelligence, June 25, 2016, 6.

6. United Nations Institute for Disarmament Research (UNIDIR), "The Weaponization of Increasingly Autonomous Technologies: Artificial Intelligence," 2018, 5.

7. Ben Buchanan and Taylor Miller, *Machine Learning for Policymakers: What It Is and Why It Matters*, Harvard Kennedy School, Belfer Center for Science and International Affairs, June 2017, 6. The discussion of machine learning is drawn from this report; the EOP Report *Preparing for the Future of Artificial Intelligence*; Kevin Hartnett, "Neural Networks Need a Cookbook: Here Are the Ingredients," *Science*, February 3, 2019; and the UNIDIR Report, which are four of the most accessible explanations I have found.

8. Buchanan and Miller, 9.

9. UNIDIR, 3.

10. Ibid.

11. Cade Metz, "DeepMind Can Now Beat Us at Multiplayer Games, Too," *New York Times*, May 30, 2019.

12. Buchanan and Miller, 15.

13. Bostrum, 12.

14. Kevin Hartnett, "Neural Networks Need a Cookbook," *Wired*, February 3, 2019.

15. Ryan Calo, "Artificial Intelligence Policy: A Primer and Roadmap," *U.C. Davis Law Review*, vol. 51 (2017), p. 421.

16. Richard Danzig, "An Irresistible Force Meets a Moveable Object: The Technology Tsunami and the Liberal World Order," *Lawfare Research Paper Series*, August 28, 2017, 5.

17. M. L. Cummings, "Artificial Intelligence and the Future of Warfare," Chatham House, Research Paper, January 2017, 4.

18. Mihir Zaveri, "Prosecutors Don't Plan to Charge Uber in Self-Driving Car's Fatal Accident," *New York Times*, March 5, 2019.

19. Cade Metz, "India Fights Diabetic Blindness with Help from AI," *New York Times*, March 10, 2019.

20. *United States v. Scheffer*, 523 U.S. 303, 309, 312 (1998).

21. Executive Office of the President, "Preparing for the Future of Artificial Intelligence," cover letter, 2016.

22. Cummings, 6.

23. Alfred Whitney Griswold, Address at Yale University, June 9, 1957.

24. *The National Artificial Intelligence Research and Development Strategic Plan*, National Science and Technology Council, Networking and Information Technology Research and Development Subcommittee (October 2016),14.

25. Katja Grace and others, "When Will AI Exceed Human Performance? Evidence from AI Experts," *Journal of Artificial Intelligence Research*, vol. 62 (July 31, 2018).

26. The Google Lab DeepMind announced in October 2019 that its AlphaStar software was capable of defeating 99.8 percent of all human players in the *StarCraft II* video game. The milestone is noteworthy, since "The game's complexity is much greater than chess, because players control hundreds of units; more complex than Go, because there are ten to twenty-six possible choices for every move; and players have less information about their opponents than in poker." Nick Statt, "DeepMind's *StarCraft II* Is Now Better than 99.8 Percent of All Human Players," Verge, October 30, 2019.

27. "Perspectives on Research in Artificial Intelligence and Artificial General Intelligence Relevant to DOD," The Mitre Corporation, *Jason Report* (2017), 2.

28. Chris Meserole, "What Is Machine Learning?" Brookings, October 4, 2018.

29. "Autonomous Weapons Open Letter from AI & Robotics Researchers," IJCAI Conference, July 28, 2015, https://futureoflife.org/open-letter-autonomous-weapons/.

Chapter 3

1. National Commission on AI, 12.

2. Drew Harwell, "FBI, ICE Find State Driver's License Photos Area a Gold Mine for Facial-Recognition Searches," *Washington Post*, July 7, 2019. See, GAO, Face Recognition Technology: The FBI Should Better Ensure Privacy and Accuracy, May 2016; Face Recognition: DOJ and FBI Have Taken Some Actions in Response to GAO Recommendations to Ensure Privacy and Accuracy, but Additional Work Remains, June 4, 2019.

3. *Carpenter v. United States*, 585 U.S. __ (2017) (slip op. 12–14).

4. San Bruno, "Now Playing, Everywhere: Can the World's Biggest Video-Sharing Site Police Itself?" *Economist* (May 4, 2019), 17–19.

5. *Nuclear Monitoring and Verification in the Digital Age*, Nuclear Verification Capabilities Independent Task Force of the Federation of American Scientists, Third Report, September 2017, 10.

6. See, "Biotechnology: The U.S.-China Dispute Over Genetic Data," *Financial Times*, July 31, 2017; prepared statement of Edward H. You, supervisory special agent, FBI, "Safeguarding the Bioeconomy: U.S. Opportunities and Challenges," March 16, 2017, www.uscc.gov/sites/default/files/Ed_You_Testimony.pdf.

7. Scott Shane, "CIA Role in Visit of Sudan Intelligence Chief Causes Dispute within Administration," *New York Times*, June 18, 2005.

8. See, John Prados, The Record on Curveball, *The National Security Archive*, November 5, 2007, https://nsarchive2.gwu.edu/NSAEBB/NSAEBB234/.

9. An earlier version of this section, along with portions of Chapters 8 and 10 were originally published as Chapters 11 and 23 in *Law of Artificial Intelligence* (American Bar Association, 2019).

10. See, *Unmanned Systems Integrated Roadmap: 2017–2042,* Statement A, OSD (Aug. 2018), http://cdn.defensedaily.com/wp-content/uploads/post_attachment/206 477.pdf.

11. NSCAI at 31.

12. "Autonomous Weapons: An Open Letter from AI and Robotics Researchers," July 28, 2015, International Joint Conference on Artificial Intelligence.

13. See, "Non-State Actors with Drone Capabilities, New America," www. newamerica.org/international-security/reports/world-drones/non-state-actors-with-drone-capabilities/; T. X. Hammes, "Technology Converges Non-State Actors Benefit," Hoover Institute, February 25, 2019, www.hoover.org/research/technology-converges-non-state-actors-benefit; "Remote Warfare Increasingly Strategy Choice for Non-State Actors," *UK Defence Journal,* https://ukdefencejournal.org.uk/remote -warfare-increasingly-strategy-of-choice-for-non-state-actors/.

14. Department of Defense, *Law of War Manual,* June 2015 (updated December 2016), 353, https://dod.defense.gov/Portals/1/Documents/pubs/DoD%20Law%20 of%20War%20Manual%20-%20June%202015%20Updated%20Dec%202016. pdf?ver=2016-12-13-172036-190.

15. Giles Edwards, "How the Dreadnought Sparked the Twentieth Century's First Arms Race," BBC News, June 2, 2014.

16. *Unmanned Systems Integrated Roadmap,* 23.

17. Ibid., 17.

18. See, *Unmanned Systems Integrated Roadmap* and Department of Defense Directive, 3000.09, Autonomy in Weapons Systems, November 21, 2012.

19. United Nations Institute for Disarmament Research, *The Weaponization of Increasingly Autonomous Technologies: Artificial Intelligence,* no. 8, March 28, 2018, 5, www.unidir.org/publication/weaponization-increasingly-autonomous-technologies -artificial-intelligence.

20. Remarks by Secretary of Defense Carter at a Force of the Future Event at the City College of New York, November 1, 2016, https://dod.defense.gov/News/Tran scripts/Transcript-View/Article/993211/remarks-by-secretary-carter-at-a-force-of -the-future-event-at-new-york-city-col/.

21. *Unmanned Systems Integrated Roadmap,* 22.

22. Scott Crino and Andy Dreby, "Drone Technology Proliferation in Small Wars," *Small Wars Journal,* https://smallwarsjournal.com/jrnl/art/drone-technology-proliferation-small-wars; Oriana Pawlyk, "Air Force Wants to Decrease Manning for Its UAVs," Military.com, February 24, www.military.com/daily-news/2018/02/24/ air-force-wants-decrease-manning-its-unmanned-vehicles.html.

23. Craig Whitlock, "Drone Combat Missions May be Scaled Back Eventually, Air Force Chief Says," *Washington Post,* November 13, 2013.

24. *Unmanned Systems Integrated Roadmap,* p. 22.

25. Cheryl Pellerin, "Project Maven to Deploy Computer Algorithms to War Zone by Year's End," *DOD News,* July 21, 2017.

Chapter 4

1. M. L. Cummings, "Artificial Intelligence and the Future of Warfare," Chatham House (research paper), January 2017, 12.

2. Sydney Freedberg Jr., "Artificial Stupidity: Fumbling the Handoff from AI to Human Control," *Breaking Defense*, June 5, 2017.

3. See, David Evans, "Vincennes: A Case Study," *Proceedings Magazine*, U.S. Naval Institute, August 1993; Luke Swartz, "Overwhelmed by Technology: How Did User Interface Failures on Board the USS *Vincennes* Lead to 290 Dead?" http://xenon.stanford.edu/~lswartz/vincennes.pdf.

4. See, Hiroko Tabuchi and David Gelles, "Doomed Boeing Jets Lacked Two Safety Features that Company Sold Only as Extras," *New York Times*, March 21, 2019; David Gelles and others, "Boeing Was 'Go, Go, Go' to Beat Airbus with the 737 Max," *New York Times*, March 23, 2019.

5. See, Craig Timberg and others, "How Social Media's Business Model Helped the New Zealand Massacre Go Viral," *Washington Post*, March 18, 2019; Hamza Shaban, "Facebook to Reexamine How Livestream Videos Are Flagged after Christchurch Shooting," *Washington Post*, March 21, 2019; Damien Cave, "Australia Passes Law to Punish Social Media Companies for Violent Posts," *New York Times*, April 3, 2019.

6. William Burr, "The 3 A.M. Phone Call," National Security Archive Electronic Briefing Book No. 371, March 1, 2012, https://narchive2.gwu.edu/nukevault/ebb371/.

7. Robert Gates, *From the Shadows* (New York: Simon & Schuster, 1996).

8. Sewell Chan, "Stanislav Petrov, Soviet Officer Who Helped Avert Nuclear War, Is Dead at 77," *New York Times*, September 18, 2017. See also, Harrison Smith, "Stanislav Petrov, Soviet Officer Credited with Averting Nuclear War, Dies at 77," *Washington Post*, September 18, 2017.

9. Burr, "The 3 A.M. Phone Call."

10. *Unmanned Systems Integrated Roadmap: 2017–2042*, Office of the Secretary of Defense, Statement A (August 2018), 24.

11. Jack Goldsmith, "Reflections on U.S. Economic Espionage, Post-Snowden," *Lawfare* (blog), December 10, 2013; Jack Goldsmith, "The Precise (and Narrow) Limits on U.S. Economic Espionage," *Lawfare* (blog), March 23, 2015.

12. Greg Allen and Taniel Chan, *Artificial Intelligence and National Security*, Belfer Center for Science and International Affairs, July 2017, 2, 37.

13. See, David Kushner, "The Real Story of Stuxnet," *IEEE Spectrum*, February 26, 2013; Council on Foreign Relations, Cyber-Operations Tracker, www.cfr.org/interactive/cyber-operations/stuxnet; Paul Kerr and others, "The Stuxnet Computer Worm: Harbinger of an Emerging Warfare Capability," *Congressional Research Service*, December 9, 2010.

14. Gregory Allen, *China's Artificial Intelligence Strategy Poses a Credible Threat to U.S. Tech Leadership*, Council on Foreign Relations, December 4, 2017.

15. Open letter, July 28, 2015, www3.nd.edu/~dhoward1/FLI%20-%20Future%20of%20Life%20Institute.pdf.

16. See, Sarah P. White, "Understanding Cyberwarfare: Lessons from the Russia-Georgia War," Modern War Institute, West Point, March 20, 2018; Laurens Cerulus, "How Ukraine Became a Test Bed for Cyberweaponry," *Politico*, February 20, 2019;

Intelligence Community Assessment, "Assessing Russian Activities and Intentions in the Recent U.S. Elections," January 6, 2017 (https://mwi.usma.edu/wp-content/uploads/2018/03/Understanding-Cyberwarfare.pdf; www.politico.eu/article/ukraine-cyber-war-frontline-russia-malware-attacks/; www.dni.gov/files/documents/ICA_2017_01.pdf).

17. "Next Generation Artificial Intelligence Development Plan," State Council, July 20, 2017, as quoted in Elsa Kania, "China's Artificial Intelligence Revolution," *Diplomat*, July 27, 2017.

18. Ryan Calo, "Artificial Intelligence: A Primer and Roadmap," *U.C. Davis Law Rev.* 51 (2017), 5.

19. Remarks of Fran Townsend before the ABA Standing Committee on Law and National Security, January 12, 2018, www.c-span.org/video/?439644-1/frances-townsend-speaks-forum-national-security.

20. James Lacey, "How Does the Next Great Power Conflict Play Out? Lessons from a Wargame," *War on the Rocks*, April 22, 2019.

21. Humans are involved in the decision chain—in writing the codes that inform algorithms that drive the trades—but the codes are opaque to public inspection and regulation, even if the economic and potential national security consequences are not.

22. Iain Burns, "Putin Reveals Fears that Robots with Artificial Intelligence Will One Day 'Eat Us' and Asks Head of Russia's Largest Tech Firm How Soon It Will Happen," DailyMail.com, September 22, 2017, www.dailymail.co.uk/news/article-4909172/Putin-reveals-fears-robots-one-day-eat-us.html.

23. Stephen Hawking, Speech, Opening of the Leverhulme Centre for the Future of Intelligence at Cambridge University, 2016.

24. Camila Domonoske, "Elon Musk Warns Governors: Artificial Intelligence Poses 'Existential Risk,'" NPR, *The Two-Way*, July 17, 2017.

25. Nick Bostrum, *Superintelligence: Paths, Dangers, Strategies* (Oxford University Press, 2014), chapter 8.

26. Ibid., 25.

27. Murray Campbell, Interview with Lisa Eadicicco, "Artificial Intelligence: The Future of Humankind," *Time*, May 12, 2016, 41.

28. *Artificial Intelligence and Life in 2030, One Hundred Year Study on Artificial Intelligence, Report of the 2015 Study Panel,* Stanford University, September 2016, 10.

29. Ibid., 4.

30. Calo, 431.

31. Campbell, Interview with Lisa Eadicicco, 41.

Chapter 5

1. Matt Mittelsteadt, e-mail to the author, November 6, 2019.

2. See, Government Accountability Office, "Face Recognition Technology: FBI Should Better Ensure Privacy and Accuracy," May 2016.

3. The reference here is to Daniel Webster's famous statement regarding anticipatory self-defense: "It will be for that government to show a necessity of self-defense instant, overwhelming, and leaving no choice of means, and no moment for deliberation." See, James E. Baker, *In the Common Defense* (Cambridge University Press, 2007), 196–200.

4. See, Walter Pincus, "Military Got Authority to Use Nuclear Weapons in 1957," *Washington Post*, March 21, 1998; "Cyber Analogies," edited by Emily Goldman and John Arquilla, Calhoun Institutional Archive of the Naval Postgraduate School, February 28, 2014.

5. Thank you to my teacher and friend Bob Kimball for the first two examples.

6. See, "Background to 'Assessing Russian Activities and Intentions in Recent U.S. Elections': The Analytic Process and Cyber Incident Attribution," Office of the Director of National Intelligence, January 6, 2017, www.dni.gov/files/documents/ICA_2017_01.pdf.

7. See, Daniel Kahneman, *Thinking Fast and Slow* (New York: Farrar, Straus and Giroux, 2011).

8. *Youngstown Sheet & Tube Co. et al. v. Sawyer*, 343 U.S. 579, at 634 (1952) (Justice Jackson, concurring).

9. 5 U.S.C. §3331.

Chapter 6

1. *National Federation of Business, et. al. v. Sebelius*, 567 U.S. 519 (slip op. 20) (2012).

2. Ibid., 36–37.

3. Order Compelling Apple, Inc. to Assist Agents in Search, February 16, 2016, Central District of California, Sheri Pym, United States Magistrate Judge.

4. Tim Cook, "A Message to Our Customers," February 16, 2016, www.apple.com/customer-letter/.

5. Office of Inspector General, "A Special Inquiry Regarding the Accuracy of FBI Statements Concerning Its Capabilities to Exploit an iPhone Seized During the San Bernardino Terror Attack Investigation," Department of Justice (March 2018), 4.

6. In re Order Requiring Apple, Inc. to Assist in the Execution of a Search Warrant Issued by This Court, February 29, 2016, Eastern District of New York, James Orenstein, United States Magistrate Judge.

7. Office of the Inspector General, Department of Justice, "A Special Inquiry Regarding the Accuracy of FBI Statements Concerning Its Capabilities to Exploit an iPhone Seized During the San Bernardino Attack Investigation," March 2018, 7.

8. *Citizens United v. Federal Election Commission*, 558 U.S. 310 (2010).

9. See, *Universal City Studios v. Corley*, 273 F. 3d 429 (2nd Cir. 2001); *Bernstein v. Department of Justice*, 922 F. Supp. 1426 (1996) and 176 F. 3d 1132 (9th Cir. 1999).

10. David Golumbia, "Code Is Not Speech," *Uncomputing*, April 13, 2016.

11. "The question in every case," Holmes wrote, "is whether the words used are used in such circumstances and are of such a nature as to create a clear and present danger that they will bring about the substantive evils that the United States Congress has a right to prevent. It is a question of proximity and degree. When a nation is at war, many things that might be said in time of peace are such a hindrance to its effort that their utterance will not be endured so long as men fight, and that no court could regard them as protected by any constitutional right." Schenck and others were convicted of violating the Espionage Act for handing out pamphlets encouraging resistance to the draft during World War I. *Schenck v. United States*, 249 U.S. 47 (1919).

12. *United States v. Progressive, Inc.*, 467 F. Supp. 990 (W.D. Wis. 1979).

13. *Brandenburg v. Ohio*, 395 U.S. 444 (1969). Brandenburg, a member of the KKK, was convicted of violating an Ohio law prohibiting advocating criminal syndicalism. The court reversed on the ground that Ohio could not prohibit speech unless it "is directed to inciting or producing imminent lawless action and is likely to incite or produce such action." The Ohio law, and the trial judge's instructions, did not distinguish between mere advocacy and incitement.

14. Jed Rubenfeld, "Are Facebook and Google State Actors?" *Lawfare* (blog), November 4, 2019.

15. *New York Times Co. v. United States*, 403 U.S. 713 (1971).

16. *Holder v. Humanitarian Law Project*, 561 U.S. 1 (2010).

17. *Daubert v. Merrell Dow Pharmaceuticals, Inc.*, 509 U.S. 579 (1993).

18. *Crawford v. Washington*, 541 U.S. 36 (2004).

19. *United States v. Katz*, 389 U.S. 347 (1967).

20. *In Re Terrorist Bombings, U.S. Embassies, East Africa*, 552 F.3d 157 (2nd Cir. 2008).

21. *United States v. Verdugo-Urquidez*, 494 U.S. 259 (1990).

22. *United States v. Miller*, 425 U.S. 435 (1976).

23. *Smith v. Maryland*, 442 U.S. 735 (1979).

24. *Riley v. California*, 573 U.S. 373 (2014).

25. *United States v. Wicks*, 73 M.J. 93 (2014).

26. *United States v. Jones*, 565 U.S. 400 (2012).

27. Although the court did not say so, the government (meaning the joint FBI and Metropolitan Police Department task force) did not help its case by obtaining a warrant "authorizing installation of the device in the District of Columbia . . . within ten days," and then proceeding outside the terms of the warrant by installing the GPS device on the eleventh day, replacing the device's battery once during the twenty-eight days while the vehicle was parked in Maryland, beyond the warrant's jurisdiction.

28. See 18 U.S.C. Section 2703(d).

29. *United States v. Carpenter*, 819 F.3d 880 (slip op. 9) (6th Cir., 2016).

30. *Carpenter v. United States*, 585 U.S. __ (2018).

31. *Carpenter*, at 585 U.S. ___ (Justice Kennedy, Dissenting) (slip op. 2).

32. *Carpenter* (slip op. 13–14).

33. *Klayman v. Obama*, 957 F. Supp. 2nd 1 (D.C., 2013).

34. *ACLU v. Clapper*, 959 F. Supp. 2nd 724 (S.D. New York, 2013).

35. *Matthews v. Eldridge*, 424 U.S. 319 (1976).

36. *Latif v. Holder*, 969 F. Supp. 2nd 1293 (Dist. Ct., D Ore., 2013).

37. "Memorandum for the Attorney General, Re Applicability of Federal Criminal Laws and the Constitution to Contemplated Lethal Operations Against Shaykh Anwar al-Aulaqi," July 16, 2010, Office of Legal Counsel, Department of Justice, 38–39.

38. See, *Loomis v. Wisconsin*, 881 N.W. 2nd 749 (Wisc. 2016), cert. denied 137 S. Ct. 2290 (2017).

39. Richard A. Posner, *Preventing Surprise Attacks: Intelligence Reform in the Wake of 9/11* (Lanham, Md.: Rowman & Littlefield, 2005), 88. Posner's analysis of 9/11 and the 9/11 Commission Report, in my view, is compelling; however, I believe his cost/benefit terrorism risk analysis is off the mark.

40. See, Brief of Petitioner, the United States, in the Supreme Court of the United States, October Term, 1951.

41. Selective Service Act, § 18.

42. Harry S. Truman, Radio and Television Address to the American People on the Need for Government Operation of the Steel Mills, excerpted at www.trumanlibrary.gov/public/SteelStrike_DocumentSet.pdf.

43. See Chong-do Hah and Robert M. Lindquist, "The 1952 Steel Seizure Revisited: A Systematic Study in Presidential Decision Making," *Administrative Quarterly*, vol. 20, no. 4 (December 1975).

44. *Youngstown v. Sawyer*, 343 U.S. 579, 585-86, 587 (1952).

45. Ibid., 680 (Justices Minton, Vinson, and Reed, dissenting).

46. Ibid, 635–36 (Justice Jackson, concurring).

47. Ibid., 654 (Justice Jackson, concurring).

48. Ibid., 603 (Justice Frankfurter, concurring).

49. Brief of Petitioner, United States, in the Supreme Court of the United States, October Term, 1951.

50. *Hamdan v. Rumsfeld*, 548 U.S. __(2006) (slip op., 29–30).

Chapter 7

1. See, the Office of Foreign Assets Control Sanctions website, www.treasury.gov/resource-center/sanctions/pages/default.aspx; see also, "The U.S. Export Control System and the Export Control Reform Initiative," Congressional Research Service, April 5, 2019.

2. P. L. 100-707 (1988); 42 U.S.C. 5121 et. seq., §202(c).

3. 16 U.S.C. §§791–828c (the emergency authority is found at §824a(c) of the code and §202(c) of the act.

4. P. L. 102-555 (1992); 15 U.S.C. 4201 et. seq.

5. 50 U.S.C. §1701.

6. For a comprehensive review of IEEPA (and sanctions regimes generally) see, Adam Smith and others, *U.S., E.U., and U.N. Sanctions: Navigating the Divide for International Business* (Bloomberg Law, 2019).

7. 35 U.S.C. chapter 17, §§181–88; Steve Aftergood, "Invention Secrecy Increased in 2016," *Secrecy News,* Federation of American Scientists, December 14, 2018, https://fas.org/blogs/secrecy/2016/invention-secrecy-2016/; G. W. Schulz, "Government Secrecy Orders on Patents Have Stifled More Than 5,000 Inventions," *Wired*, April 16, 2013.

8. *Report to Congress, Fiscal Year 2016, Annual Industrial Capabilities,* 11.

9. Ibid.

10. See, Cheryl Pellerin, "Deputy Secretary: Third Offset Strategy Bolsters America's Military Deterrence," *DOD News,* October 31, 2016.

11. Ibid.

12. The December 2017 tax bill, for example, pulled in opposite directions. On the one hand, the bill included a provision to tax the tuition-waiver benefits that graduate students receive at most U.S. universities, which could have undercut a distinctive U.S. strength. The provision remained in the bill until the eleventh hour. On the other hand, corporate tax incentives and waivers directed at high tech companies and

global social media companies to encourage them to retain corporate headquarters within the United States remained in the bill and were enacted.

13. 10 U.S.C. 2500(1).

14. P. L. 111-67, §2, September 30, 2009.

15. §1791 of the National Defense Authorization Act for FY 2019, P. L. 115-232, which reauthorizes the relevant sections of the DPA from September 30, 2019 until September 30, 2025.

16. §702 of the DPA at 50 U.S.C. App. §2152(2)(14).

17. §705(c)(d) of the DPA at 50 U.S.C. App. §2155.

18. §706(b) of the DPA at 50 U.S.C. App. §2156.

19. Legal Authorities Available to the President to Respond to a Severe Energy Supply Interruption or Other Substantial Reduction in Available Petroleum Products, Memorandum for the President for Transmission to Congress, Theodore B. Olson, Assistant Attorney General, Office of Legal Counsel, November 15, 1982, quoting H. R. Rep. No. 2759, 81st Cong., 2nd Sess. 4 (1950).

20. Donald S. Frey, "Maintaining Economic Freedom under the Defense Act of 1950," 18 *Univ. of Chicago Law Review*, 218 (1950).

21. E.O. 13917, "Delegating Authority under the Defense Production Act with Respect to Food Supply Chain Resources during the National Emergency Caused by the Outbreak of COVID-19," April 28, 2020.

22. Ibid., and E.O. 13909, "Prioritizing and Allocating Health and Medical Resources to Respond to the Spread of COVID-19, March 18, 2020; E.O. 13910, "Preventing Hoarding of Health and Medical Resources to Respond to the Spread of COVID-19," March 23, 2020; and, E.O. 13911, "Delegating Additional Authority under the Defense Production Act with Respect to Health and Medical Resources to Respond to the Spread of COVID-19," March 27, 2020.

23. See "Statement from National Security Professionals on the Urgent Need to Utilize the Defense Production Act Fully," March 25, 2020, https://s.wsj.net/public/resources/images/DPA-Statement.pdf; James E. Baker, "It Is High Time We Fought this Virus the American Way," Op-ed, *New York Times,* April 3, 2020.

24. FEMA, "Federal Priorities and Allocations System," www.fema.gov/federal-priorities-and-allocations-system.

25. As cited in note 21.

26. Department of Defense, Regulation 4400.1-M, *Department of Defense Priorities and Allocations Manual.*

27. The Defense Priorities and Allocations System Training Course, Department of Commerce, Bureau of Industry and Security, April 26, 2017, www.bis.doc.gov/index.php/documents/other-areas/strategic-industries-and-economic-security/1615-dpas-training-slides/file.

28. Bureau of Industry and Security, Department of Commerce, www.bis.doc.gov/index.php/documents/sies/500-list-of-programs-authorized-by-the-department-of-defense-to-use-the-dx-dpas-priority-rating-highe/file.

29. *Defense Production Act Committee Report to Congress, 2011,* ii.

30. *Defense Production Act Committee Report to Congress, 2015,* iii.

31. §722(b)(2) of the DPA at 50 U.S.C. §2171.

32. Department of Defense Industrial Policy website, www.businessdefense.gov/Programs/DPA-Title-III/.

33. DPA, Title III.

34. As cited in note 23; see Baker, "From Shortages to Stockpiles: How the Defense Production Act Can Be Used to Save Lives, Make America the Global Arsenal of Public Health, and Address the Security Challenges Ahead," *Journal of National Security Law and Policy*, vol. 11, no. 1 (2020).

35. By one count, that of research assistant Tom Clifford, there are 396 cases that mention the DPA, but most do so in passing. Of these cases, five address section 705, upholding the government's industry assessment authority but with minimal statutory analysis. See, for example, *Westside Ford, Inc. v. United States*, 206 F.2d 627 (9th Cir. 1953); *Wockner v. United States*, 211 F.2d 490 (9th Cir. 1954); *United States v. IBM*, 461 F. Supp. 732 (SDNY 1978).

36. "The Committee on Foreign Investment in the United States (CFIUS)," Congressional Research Service, updated May 15, 2019, 18.

37. Cade Metz, "Tech Giants Are Paying Huge Salaries for Scarce AI Talent," *New York Times*, October 22, 2017.

38. Title IV, Public Law 91-648, January 5, 1971. The Office of Personnel Management uses the authority to issue regulations found at 5 U.S.C. §3301 to implement the IPA authority.

39. President Dwight D. Eisenhower, "Remarks at the National Defense Executive Reserve Conference," November 14, 1957.

40. See, Department of Commerce website, www.bis.doc.gov/index.php/other-areas/office-of-technology-evaluation-ote/industrial-base-assessments.

41. DPA §104(a), 50 U.S.C. App. §2074.

Chapter 8

1. Robert K. Massie, *Dreadnought: Britain, Germany, and the Coming of the Great War* (New York: Penguin Random House, 1991).

2. Giles Edwards, "How the Dreadnought Sparked the Twentieth Century's First Arms Race," BBC News, June 2, 2014.

3. Ibid.

4. This section draws heavily on Fred Kaplan's outstanding book, *The Wizards of Armageddon* (Stanford University Press, 1983). The Center for Arms Control and Non-Proliferation offers fact sheets on arms control subjects and treaties, including accessible history and background; so do the Department of State web pages for particular instruments and topics.

5. William Broad, "Scientist at Work: Joseph Rotblat; Still Battling Nuclear Weapons Fifty Years after Manhattan Project," *New York Times*, May 21, 1996; "Atomic Scientist Turned Peace Activist Dies," NBCNews.com, September 1, 2005.

6. *A Report on the International Control of Atomic Energy*, Prepared for the Secretary of State's Committee on Atomic Energy, March 16, 1946.

7. *Wizards of Armageddon*, 289.

8. Thomas Powers, "The Nuclear Worrier," *New York Review of Books*, January 18, 2018.

9. *Wizards of Armageddon*, 191.

10. Ibid., 183.

11. Ibid., 270.

12. Fred Kaplan, "Rethinking Nuclear Policy: Taking Stock of the Stockpile," *Foreign Affairs*, August 1, 2016.

13. Eric Heginbotham and others, "China's Evolving Nuclear Deterrent: Major Drivers and Issues for the United States," RAND Corporation, 2017.

14. Ibid., xi, 16.

15. Ibid.; see also, "China's Nuclear Arsenal Was Strikingly Modest, but That Is Changing," *Economist*, November 21, 2019.

16. "Appendix B, Unrecovered Nuclear Weapons and Classified Components," https://fas.org/sgp/othergov/doe/cg-hr-3/appb.pdf; "Broken Arrows: Nuclear Weapons Accidents," www.atomicarchive.com/Almanac/Brokenarrows_static. shtml.

17. Bruce Riedel, "Remembering Sandy Berger and the Day He Saved the World," Brookings, December 2, 2015.

18. William J. Perry Project, "Nuclear Accidents," www.wjperryproject.org/new-page-1. Patricia Lewis and others, *Too Close for Comfort: Cases of Near Nuclear Use and Options for Policy* (London: Chatham House, 2014).

19. Richard Rhodes, "Quantifying the World: In an Age of Great Scientists, Enrico Fermi Was One of the Greatest," *New York Times Book Review*, January 28, 2018, 12.

20. Daniel Voll, "Edward Teller: What I've Learned," *Esquire*, January 29, 2017.

21. See, Emily Goldman and others, *Cyber-Analogies*, Calhoun Institutional Archive of the Naval Postgraduate School, February 28, 2014, including "Introduction" by Emily Goldman and John Arquilla and "The Offense-Defense Balance and Cyber Warfare," by Keir Lieber.

22. "Summary, Department of Defense Cyber Strategy, September 2018," https://media.defense.gov/2018/Sep/18/2002041658/-1/-1/1/CYBER_STRATEGY_SUM MARY_FINAL.PDF.

23. See, William Burr and Thomas Blanton, "The Submarines of October—U.S. and Soviet Naval Encounters during the Cuban Missile Crisis," National Security Archive, October 31, 2002, https://nsarchive2.gwu.edu/NSAEBB/NSAEBB75/. The events are recounted by others as well, including Nick Bostrum, who named a room at the Future of Humanity Institute after Arkhipov. Raffi Khatchadourian, "The Doomsday Invention: Will Artificial Intelligence Bring Us Utopia or Destruction?" *New Yorker*, November 23, 2015.

24. Jeremi Suri, "What's a Nuclear Hotline Good for Anyway?" *Foreign Policy*, January 9, 2018.

25. Ibid.

26. The idea of an Open Skies Treaty dates to President Eisenhower, but was implemented by President George H. W. Bush. Since its inception, the United States has conducted approximately two hundred flights over Russia and Russia seventy flights over the United States. Parties are required to accept a certain number of overflights, which require seventy-two-hour prior notice and the filing of a flight plan twenty-four hours prior to overflight. Data collected by one party may be shared with

any of the treaty's thirty-two parties. Proponents of the treaty note that the overflight mechanism can serve as a CBM for smaller states without national technical means to otherwise conduct the same overhead reconnaissance, like the Baltic states. It also serves as a CBM with respect to military exercises and troops' movements, as well as arms development. The treaty, they note, has been particularly important as a mechanism to collect data to rebut Russian disinformation regarding its activities in Ukraine. The treaty can also be used as a signaling mechanism in the event of military exercises and build-ups. Critics argue that the United States has other mechanisms to collect the same data, that Russia benefits more from its overflights, and that Russia has cheated by denying overflight access to Kaliningrad and the Russian-Georgian border around Abkhazia and South Ossetia. Press reports indicate that the Trump administration has considered withdrawing from the treaty. See Alex Ward, "Trump May Soon Ban Russian Observation Flights over U.S. Military Bases. That's a Bad Thing," *Vox*, October 10, 2019.

27. IAEA fact sheet.

28. "IAEA Safeguards: Stemming the Spread of Nuclear Weapons," International Atomic Energy Agency, www.iaea.org/topics/safeguards-in-practice.

29. Frank Leith Jones, "Dismantling the Soviet Threat: Senator Sam Nunn and the Problem of 'Loose Nukes,'" http://shfg.org/resources/Documents/3-Jones.pdf.

30. A DTRA scorecard can be found at the DTRA website, https://www.dtra.mil/DTRA-Mission/Partnering/Nunn-Lugar-scorecard/.

31. See, Department of State website entries for the text of each instrument and relevant background from the perspective of the USG. See also the websites of the Arms Control Association and Center for Arms Control and Non-Proliferation for relevant fact sheets and background.

32. Frans G. von der Dunk, "The Origins of Authorization: Article VI of the Outer Space Treaty and International Space Law," in Frans G. von der Dunk (ed.), *National Space Legislation for India: Proposal for a Draft Framework* (Leiden: Brill, 2011), 3–28; E. R. Finch, "Space Liability and World Peace," *University of Miami Inter-American Law Review* vol. 2, no. 28 (1970).

33. Loren Grush, "How an International Treaty Signed Fifty Years Ago Became the Backbone for Space Law," *Verge*, January 27, 2017.

34. In this regard, policymakers should consider the work of scholars like David Arceneaux, who conduct comparative studies of nuclear command and control. Arceneaux identifies alternative models of command, including: (1) delegated control; (2) conditional delegation, in times of crisis; and (3) assertive control, centralized retention of decisional authority. Each results in different methods of weapons storage, technical specifications, and command structure.

35. *Nuclear Monitoring and Verification in the Digital Age*, Nuclear Verification Capabilities Independent Task Force of the Federation of American Scientists, Third Report, September 2017, 10.

36. "The Crossbow—A Medieval Doomsday Device?" *Military History Now*, May 23, 2012.

37. Francois Bugnion, "From Solferino to the Birth of Contemporary International Humanitarian Law," www.icrc.org/en/doc/resources/documents/article/other/solferino-article-bugnion-240409.htm.

38. Hays Parks, "Part IX of the ICRC 'Direct Participation in Hostilities' Study: No Mandate, No Expertise, and Legally Incorrect," *NYU Journal of International Law and Politics*, vol. 42, no. 769 (2010), 771.

39. R. Roffey, A. Tegnell, and F. Elgh, "Biological Warfare in a Historical Perspective," European Society of Clinical Microbiology and Infectious Diseases, *CMI*, vol. 8 (2002), 450–54.

40. The history behind the U.S. position with respect to the BWC is principally drawn from Jonathan Tucker and Erin R. Mahan, "President Nixon's Decision to Renounce the U.S. Offensive Biological Weapons Program," Center for the Study of Weapons of Mass Destruction, National Defense University, October 2009. See also, Jonathan B. Tucker, "A Farewell to Germs: The U.S. Renunciation of Biological and Toxin Warfare, 1969–70," *International Security*, vol. 27, no. 1 (Summer 2002).

41. NTI is a nonprofit formed in 2001 by Senator Sam Nunn and CNN founder Ted Turner to inform the public about, and to reduce the threat of, nuclear weapons and later biological, chemical, and cyber-weapons.

42. The Biological Weapons Convention, Nuclear Threat Initiative, 13–14.

43. OPCW, fact sheet 5, www.opcw.org/sites/default/files/documents/publications/fact_sheets/05.pdf.

44. OPCW, fact sheets 1–10, www.opcw.org/sites/default/files/documents/publications/fact_sheets/01.pdf; Daniel Feakes, "Evaluating the CWC Verification System," *Disarmament Forum*, vol. 4 (2002).

45. Jonathan B. Tucker, "U.S. Ratification of the Chemical Weapons Convention," Center for the Study of Weapons of Mass Destruction, National Defense University (December 2011), 3.

46. Senate Resolution 75, 105th Congress, 1st session, April 24, 1997, U.S. Senate's Conditions to Ratification of the CWC, 16.

47. Tucker, "U.S. Ratification of the Chemical Weapons Convention," 16.

48. See, the Australia Group website maintained by the Australia Group secretariat at https://australiagroup.net/en/.

49. Ibid.

50. Jonathan B. Tucker, "Verifying the Chemical Weapons Ban: Missing Elements," Arms Control Association, January 1, 2007, 6.

51. OPCW fact sheet 5.

Chapter 9

1. At least twenty-four states had fallen behind their obligations as of 2008. "U.N. Mine Action Team Still in Business," Global Policy Forum, April 2008, www.globalpolicy.org/component/content/article/175/31352.html.

2. This is the view of many commentators, for example, Veronica Kitchen, "From Rhetoric to Reality: Canada, the United States and the Ottawa Process to Ban Land Mines," *International Journal*, vol. 57, no. 1 (Winter 2001/2002). It is also the opinion of the author based on observations at the time.

3. The Trump administration announced a change in policy on January 31, 2020, that it would permit the use of APLs elsewhere.

4. *Department of Defense Law of War Manual,* June 2015 (updated December

2016), 302, citing the *Field Manual 27-10, Department of the Army Field Manual, Law of Land Warfare,* July 1956.

5. Hague Convention IV of October 1907, Respecting the Laws and Customs of War on Land, article 23(b), cited in the *FM 27-10, Department of Army Field Manual, Law of Land Warfare,* July 1956, §31,17.

6. *Law of War Manual,* §5.22.1, 320.

7. Rule 63, "Use of Flags or Military Emblems, Insignia or Uniforms of Neutral or Other States Not Party to the Conflict," IHL database, International Committee of the Red Cross, https://ihl-databases.icrc.org/customary-ihl/eng/docs/v1_rul_rule63.

8. *Law of War Manual,* §5.23.1.4, 323.

9. Ibid., §2.6, 65–69.

10. *Law of Land Warfare,* 22.

11. "A Guide to the Legal Review of New Weapons, Means, and Methods of Warfare: Measures to Implement Article 36 of Additional Protocol I of 1977," *International Review of the Red Cross,* vol. 88, no. 864 (January 2006), 933.

12. International Committee of the Red Cross, Commentaries to Additional Protocol I to the Geneva Conventions, Commentary of 1987, Article 36 New Weapons, §1476.

13. DOD Directive 5000.1, The Defense Acquisition System, 2003, section E.1.1.15.

14. *Law of War Manual,* §6.2.2, 338.

15. ICRC Commentaries, note 13, Article 35 Basic Rules, §1402.

16. "A Guide to the Legal Review of New Weapons, Means, and Methods of Warfare," *International Review of the Red Cross,* vol. 88, no. 864 (December 2006), 937, quoting the Australian instruction on new weapons. However, not many states publish their Article 36 procedures.

17. Ibid., 935.

18. Remarks, Deputy Secretary of Defense Bob Work to the CNAS Defense Forum, Washington, D.C., December 14, 2015.

19. Department of Defense Directive, 2311.01E, "DOD Law of War Program" (certified current as of February 22, 2011), §5.7.3.

20. Department of Defense Directive 2311.01E, §5.11.8.

21. See, Memorandum of Understanding on the Application of IHL between Croatia and the Socialist Federal Republic of Yugoslavia; and Agreement on the Application of IHL between the Parties to the Conflict in Bosnia and Herzegovina, cited in ICRC, CIL, rule 142.

22. *Law of War Manual,* §18.23.2, 1140; Law of Armed Conflict, lesson 6, Command Responsibility, ICRC, June 2002, www.icrc.org/en/doc/assets/files/other/law6_final.pdf. Note the agreement between DOD and the ICRC on this point.

23. *In re: Yamashita,* 327 U.S. 1 (1946).

24. There are a number of internet sources recounting the *Queenfish* incident. I have relied on Roger Dingman, *Ghost War: The Sinking of the* Awa Maru *and Japanese-American Relations, 1945–1995* (Naval Institute Press, 1997), which appears to be the most reliable account I could find. I was not able to locate a record from the court-martial. See also, Law of Armed Conflict, lesson 6.

25. There are some reports that Admiral Nimitz, apparently finding the punish-

ment too lenient, subsequently gave the members of the court-martial a letter of reprimand, an act which in today's military justice system would be viewed as unlawful command influence. However, Dingman dismisses this story as rumor.

26. *Law of War Manual*, §18.23.3.

27. ICRC, lesson 6, Law of Armed Conflict, Command Responsibility (June 2002),16.

28. ICRC, Customary IHL, rule 153, Command Responsibility for Failure to Prevent, Repress, or Report War Crimes, https://ihl-databases.icrc.org/customary-ihl/eng/docs/v1_rul_rule153.

29. The 2018 Cyber-Security Strategy (at least the unclassified Summary of the Strategy) moves the dialogue forward, acknowledging that much of the persistent engagement between adversaries in cyberspace occurs below the level of armed conflict and thus entails legal principles and doctrine drawn from outside the law of armed conflict.

30. *Law of War Manual*, §2.4, 60.

31. Ibid., §5.6, 208.

32. The drivers were given warning before the vehicles were attacked and destroyed. Michael Gordon, "U.S. Warplanes Strike ISIS Oil Trucks in Syria," *New York Times*, November 16, 2015; Butch Bracknell, "Warnings to Civilians Directly Participating in Hostilities: Legal Imperative or Ethics-based Policy?" *Lawfare* (blog), November 29, 2015; Aurel Sari, "Trucker's Hitch: Targeting ISIL Oil Transport Trucks and the Need for Advanced Warnings," *Lawfare* (blog), December 2, 2015.

33. *Unmanned Systems Integrated Roadmap: 2017–2042*, Department of Defense, Statement A, August 2018, 22.

Chapter 10

1. *American Bar Association Model Rules of Professional Conduct*, model rule 1.1 and 1.3.

2. Ibid., model rule 2.1.

3. For definitions and discussion, see *Department of Defense Law of War Manual* and Defense Innovation Board, "AI Principles: Recommendations on the Ethical Use of Artificial Intelligence by the Department of Defense," 55, November 2017.

4. NSPE has approximately 26,000 members, www.nspe.org/membership/about-nspe.

5. See the IEEE website at www.ieee.org/about/today/at-a-glance.html.

6. "Stanford Statement on Fact-Finding Review Related to Dr. Jiankui He," April 16, 2019, https://news.stanford.edu/2019/04/16/stanford-statement-fact-finding-review-related-dr-jiankui/. For background, see, Pam Belluck, "Stanford Clears Professor of Helping with Gene-Edited Babies Experiment," *New York Times*, April 16, 2019; Pam Belluck, "Gene-Edited Babies: What a Chinese Scientist Told an American Mentor," *New York Times*, April 14, 2019.

7. Sui-Lee Wei, "Chinese Scientist Who Genetically Edited Babies Gets 3 Years in Prison," *New York Times*, December 30, 2019 (citing Xinhua, China's official news agency).

8. See, U.S. Department of Health and Human Services, "Federal Policy for the Protection of Human Subjects ('Common Rule')," www.hhs.gov/ohrp/regulations-and-policy/regulations/common-rule/index.html.

9. Howard Brody and others, "United States Responses to Japanese Wartime Inhuman Experimentation after World War II: National Security and Wartime Exigency," *Camb. Q. Health Ethics*, vol. 23, no. 2 (April 2014), 220–30; Stefan Riedel, "Biological Warfare and Bioterrorism: A Historical Review," *Proceedings Baylor University Medical Center*, vol. 17, no. 4 (October 2004), 400–06; www.ncbi.nlm.nih.gov/pmc/articles/PMC1200679/.

10. *Belmont Report: Ethical Principles and Guidelines for the Protection of Human Subjects of Research; National Commission for the Protection of Human Subjects of Biomedical and Behavioral Research*, April 18, 1979.

11. U.S. Government Policy for Institutional Oversight of Life Sciences Dual Use Research of Concern, September 24, 2014 (release date), September 24, 2015 (effective date), 7, www.phe.gov/s3/dualuse.

12. "Coordinated Framework for Regulation of Biotechnology," Executive Office of the President, Office of Science and Technology Policy, June 26, 1986, 51 FR 23302, www.aphis.usda.gov/brs/fedregister/coordinated_framework.pdf.

13. Princeton University, "Unmanned Aircraft Systems, Use of Small Unmanned Aircraft Systems (sUAS) on University Property Policy," January 16, 2017, https://drones.princeton.edu/learn-more/policies-and-procedures/princeton-suas-policy.

14. See, Citi Program (Collaborative Institutional Training Initiative) website, https://about.citiprogram.org/en/homepage/.

15. See, Arthur Herman, *Freedom's Forge: How American Business Produced Victory in World War II* (New York: Random House, 2012).

16. See, https://static01.nyt.com/files/2018/technology/googleletter.pdf. The undated open letter became public in April 2018.

17. "Bezos: If Big Tech Turns Its Back on the Pentagon, 'This Country Is Going to Be in Trouble,'" *Washington Business Journal*, October 17, 2018.

18. S. N. Bhaduri and E. Selarka, *Corporate Governance and Corporate Social Responsibility of Indian Companies* (Singapore: Springer Science + Business Media, 2016), chapter 2, "Corporate Social Responsibility Around the World—An Overview of Theoretical Framework and Evolution."

19. Nikil Saval, "Utopia Abandoned," *New York Times*, August 28, 2019.

20. Gail Ridley, "National Security as a Corporate Social Responsibility: Critical Infrastructure Resilience," *Journal of Business Ethics* vol. 103 (2011), 112.

21. Ibid.

22. Darren E. Tromblay, "Tech Pressure on Privacy: National Security Requires a Fuller View of Corporate Social Responsibility," *Just Security*, July 19, 2018.

23. Quoted in *Corporate Governance and Corporate Social Responsibility of Indian Companies*, 15.

24. See, for example, Andrew Winston, "Is the Business Roundtable Statement Just Empty Rhetoric?" *Harvard Business Review*, August 30, 2019.

25. Richard Danzig, "An Irresistible Force Meets a Moveable Object: The Technology Tsunami and the Liberal World Order," *Lawfare Research Paper Series*, vol. 5, no. 1 (August 28, 2017), 11.

26. 47 U.S.C. §230.

27. *Stratton Oakmont, Inc. v. Prodigy Services Co.*, Supreme Court, Nassau County, New York, Trial IAS Part 34, May 24, 1995.

Chapter 11

1. Iyad Rahwan, "Society-in-the-Loop: Programming the Algorithmic Social Contract," *MIT Media Lab*, August 12, 2016.

2. Joseph S. Nye, "Nuclear Lessons for Cyber Security?" *Strategic Studies Quarterly* (Winter 2011), 30.

INDEX

ABA (American Bar Association), 259, 263

ABMs. *See* Anti-Ballistic Missile

Academic ethics, 265–72

Accountability: and algorithms, 88; and arms control, 203; and black box decisionmaking, 84; ethical standards for, 256–57, 259; importance in DOD application, 28; legal framework for decisionmaking, 76; in national security applications of AI, 45; in national security law, 74; in new weapons reviews, 237; in nuclear weapons regime, 189; and Ottawa Treaty, 225; in statutory regulation of national technology industrial base, 174–75; and training, 242

Accuracy: and algorithms, 88, 107; and bias, 126, 129, 131, 133; and black box decisionmaking, 84–85; ethical issues, 257; and machine learning, 17; and machine speed, 79; in narrow AI, 21; and national security applications of AI, 45; in national security law, 72, 76; threshold for, 29; Turing test for, 76

ACDA (Arms Control and Disarmament Agency), 217

Acheson, Dean, 181

ACLU v. Clapper (2013), 119

Administrative Procedures Act of 1946, 145

Affordable Care Act of 2010, 95–96

Afghanistan: and Convention on Cluster Munitions, 229; local attire worn by military units in, 231; non-state actors using IEDs in, 227; shutter control on commercial satellites during military operations in, 144

Agency, ethical issues related to, 256

AGI. *See* Artificial general intelligence

AI Impacts, 26

AI Singapore Effect, 53

Alexa, 12, 105

Algorithms: AI relying on, 3, 13–15; for arms control, 188, 205, 222; for augmentation, 88; censorship via, 53, 104; and constitutional law, 104–07, 112, 114, 121, 123–30, 132–33; data dependence of, 29, 72; for decision-making, 59–60, 83–89; and deep learning, 17; design of, 126, 129; and ethical issues, 257, 261–62, 265, 278; facial recognition, 29, 31, 257; for intelligence operations, 32–33, 37; legal framework for, 72; for military

www.ingramcontent.com/pod-product-compliance
Lightning Source LLC
Chambersburg PA
CBHW030639270326
41929CB00007B/127